Cybercrime and Jurisdiction

A Global Survey

Series Editors

For other titles in the Series see p. 355

Information Technology & Law Series 11

Cybercrime and Jurisdiction

A Global Survey

edited by

Bert-Jaap Koops and Susan W. Brenner

contributions by

Susan W. Brenner
Roberto Chacon de Albuquerque
Noel Cox
Pavan Duggal
Peter Grabosky
Jessica R. Herrera-Flanigan
Paul de Hert
Gus Hosein
Henrik W.K. Kaspersen
Bert-Jaap Koops
Jeong-Hoon Lee
Fernando Londoño
Pauline C. Reich
Ulrich Sieber
Henrik Spang-Hanssen
Gregor Urbas
Ian Walden
Giovanni Ziccardi
Rodrigo Zúñiga

T·M·C·Asser Press
The Hague

The *Information Technology & Law Series* is published
by T·M·C·ASSER PRESS
P.O. Box 16163, 2500 BD The Hague, The Netherlands
<www.asserpress.nl>

T·M·C·ASSER PRESS English language books are distributed exclusively by:

Cambridge University Press, The Edinburgh Building, Shaftesbury Road,
Cambridge CB2 2RU, UK,
or
for customers in the USA, Canada and Mexico:
Cambridge University Press, 100 Brook Hill Drive, West Nyack, NY 10994-2133, USA

<www.cambridge.org>

The *Information Technology & Law Series* is an initiative of IT*e*R, the National Programme for Information Technology and Law, which is a research programme set up by the Dutch government and the Netherlands Organisation for Scientific Research (NWO) in The Hague. Since 1995 IT*e*R has published all of its research results in its own book series. In 2002 IT*e*R launched the present internationally orientated and English language *Information Technology & Law Series*. This series deals with the implications of information technology for legal systems and institutions. It is not restricted to publishing IT*e*R's research results. Hence, authors are invited and encouraged to submit their manuscripts for inclusion. Manuscripts and related correspondence can be sent to the Series' Editorial Office, which will also gladly provide more information concerning editorial standards and procedures.

Editorial Office
eLaw@Leiden, Centre for Law in the Information Society
Leiden University
P.O. Box 9520
2300 RA Leiden, The Netherlands
Tel. +31(0)715277846
E-mail: <ital@law.leidenuniv.nl>
Web site: <www.nwo.nl/iter>

Single copies or Standing Order
The books in the *Information Technology & Law Series* can either be purchased as single copies or through a standing order. For ordering information see the information on top of this page or visit the publisher's web site at <www.asserpress.nl/cata/itlaw11/fra.htm>.

ISBN 10: 90-6704-221-8
ISBN 13: 978-90-6704-221-5
ISSN 1570-2782

Cover and lay-out: Oasis Productions, Nieuwerkerk a/d IJssel, The Netherlands
Printing and binding: Koninklijke Wöhrmann BV, Zutphen, The Netherlands

SUMMARY OF CONTENTS

TABLE OF CONTENTS

ABBREVIATIONS

AC	Appeal Cases, Law Reports (3rd series) (UK)
AFP	Australian Federal Police
All ER	All England Law Reports (England & Wales)
ALR	Australian Law Reports
Am. Bus. L.J.	American Business Law Journal
AP	Associated Press
BBS	Bulletin Boards System
BGBl.	*Bundesgesetzblatt* [German Federal Law Gazette]
BGH	(German) Bundesgerichtshof [German Federal Supreme Court]
BGHSt	*Entscheidungen des Bundesgerichtshofes in Strafsachen* [Decisions of the German Federal Supreme Court in Criminal Cases]
BT-Dr.	*Bundestagsdrucksache* [German Parliament Printed Papers]
CA	Court of Appeal
CC	Criminal Code
CCC	Convention on Cybercrime
CCP	Code of Criminal Procedure
CETS	Council of Europe Treaty Series
CFAA	Computer Fraud and Abuse Act
Ch	Chancery Division, Law Reports (3rd series) (England & Wales)
CIA	Confidentiality, integrity, and availability
Cm	Command Paper
CoE	Council of Europe
COT	Código Orgánico de Tribunales [General Courts Code]
CPC	Criminal Procedure Code
CPS	Crown Prosecution Service
CRNZ	Criminal Reports of New Zealand
C.S.M.C.	Critical Studies in Mass Communication
CSIS	Canadian Security Intelligence Services
Cth	Commonwealth
DCR	District Court Reports (New Zealand)
DDoS	Distributed denial-of-service
DoS	Denial-of-Service
DRC	Democratic Republic of the Congo
DRM	Digital Rights Management
DSP	Deputy Superintendent of Police
East	E.H. East King's Bench Reports
EAW	European arrest warrant
EC	European Community
ECHR	European Court of Human Rights
ECPA	Electronic Communications Privacy Act
EFF	Electronic Frontier Foundation
EPIC	Electronic Privacy Information Center

ER	English Reports (England & Wales)
ETS	European Treaty Series
EU	European Union
F	Federal Reporter (US)
F Supp	Federal Reporter Supplement (US)
FATF	Financial Action Task Force on Money Laundering
FBI	Federal Bureau of Investigation
F.T.	Official Journal of the Danish Parliament [Folketings Tidende]
FTC	Federal Trade Commission
G7	Group of Seven
G8	Group of Eight
GA	General Assembly
GCSB	Government Communications Security Bureau
HCA	High Court of Australia
ICANN	Internet Corporation for Assigned Names and Numbers
ICJ	International Court of Justice
ICT	Information and communications technology
IMC	Indymedia
INS	Immigration and Naturalization Services
INTERPOL	International Criminal Police Organisation
ISP	Internet Service Provider
IT	Information technology
J	Judge
JFBA	Japan Federation of Bar Associations
MLA	Mutual legal assistance
MLAT	Mutual Legal Assistance Treaty
MP	Member of Parliament; *in chapter on Chile:* Public Prosecutor [Ministerio Público]
NATO	North Atlantic Treaty Organisation
NCPP	Code of Criminal Procedure (Código Procesal Penal)
NGO	Non-Governmental Organisation
NJCM-Bulletin	Nederlands Juristen Comité voor de Mensenrechten Bulletin
NStZ	*Neue Zeitschrift für Strafrecht* [New Journal for Criminal Law]
NZ	New Zealand
NZAR	New Zealand Administrative Reports
NZLR	New Zealand Law Reports
OAS	Organization of American States
OECD	Organisation for Economic Co-operation and Development
OJ	Official Journal of the European Union
PC	Judicial Committee of the Privy Council
PCIJ	Permanent Court of International Justice
QB	Queen's Bench Division, Law Reports (3rd series) (England & Wales)

RCMP	Royal Canadian Mounted Police
RDJ	Revista de Derecho y Jurisprudencia [Review of Law and Jurisprudence]
ReichsStGB	*Reichsstrafgesetzbuch* [German Reich Criminal Code]
RGBl.	*Reichsgesetzblatt* [German Reich Law Gazette]
RGSt	*Reichsgerichtsentscheidungen in Strafsachen* [German Reich Decisions in Criminal Cases]
RIPA	Regulation of Investigator Powers Act
RPT	Reconciliation Project Team
s. (ss.)	Section (Sections)
SCR	Supreme Court Reports (Canada)
SIS	Security Intelligence Service
StGB	*Strafgesetzbuch* [German Criminal Code]
StPO	*Strafprozessordnung* [German Code of Criminal Procedure]
UfR	Danish Case Reporter (Part A) or Journal of Law (Part B) [Ugeskrift for Retsvæsen]
UK	United Kingdom
UN	United Nations
UNGA	United Nations General Assembly
URL	Uniform Resource Locator
U.S.	United States of America
USPQ	United States Patents Quarterly
Vic	Victoria

Chapter 1
CYBERCRIME JURISDICTION – AN INTRODUCTION

Bert-Jaap Koops and Susan Brenner*

Cybercrime is a primary example of cross-border crime. Computer networks connect all countries of the world, and evil-doers can cause significant harm anywhere in the world without leaving their home desk – or, if they have a wireless laptop, their lazy couch. The potential harm is remarkably varied, ranging from individuals not being able to access their personal computer for a few hours or stumbling across racist or obscene material on the Internet, to a company's internal network being inaccessible for 24 hours or trade secrets being stolen, and to a government's public web sites being blocked or seeing state secrets appear on the web. Financial losses range from a few hundred dollars being extorted to multi-million dollar losses caused by cyberfraud or cybersabotage. Increasingly, as the Internet penetrates ever more into the world's core activities, cybercrime also involves the risk of terrorist attacks bringing down a major part of the Internet, and therewith causing an economic and social disaster on a global scale. A small group of hackers, spread across four continents and invisible in third-floor attic rooms with simple computer equipment, can basically attain the same disastrous results that in the past were only reserved for groups with money to spare and arms to buy and were willing to take the risk of being physically noticed in their crime or terrorism preparations. This is a disturbing thought.

It is vital that cybercrime is combated. This requires law-enforcement expertise, manpower, legislation, and policy priorities within the ambit of crime-fighting. Sure enough, many countries are making considerable efforts in this area, and results are visible in hackers being convicted and virus spreaders being traced to their third-floor attic room. However, the utterly transnational character of cybercrime makes many of the current initiatives to fight cybercrime look weak. All too often, it is the local whiz-kid who is being caught, simply because he makes beginner's mistakes and is easy to catch, while the organized groups, perhaps working from countries

* Prof. Dr Bert-Jaap Koops is Professor of Regulation & Technology at the Tilburg Institute for Law, Technology, and Society (TILT), of Tilburg University, the Netherlands. Prof. Susan W. Brenner is NCR Distinguished Professor of Law & Technology, University of Dayton School of Law, Dayton, Ohio, United States.

B-J. Koops and S.W. Brenner (Eds), Cybercrime and Jurisdiction

where the rule of law is not always taken too seriously, are left unheeded. This creates major risks for the global community.

If we are to break out of this narrow, national focus of cybercrime-fighting, countries must shift emphasis and focus on international investigation and prosecution of cybercrimes. Since criminal law is, however, still very much a national matter, this is easier said than done. International co-operation is vital but cannot be sufficient: often, other countries simply do not have the will, the resources, or the right legislation to find evidence or to arrest a perpetrator. This means that countries will have to consider searching for digital evidence themselves, for instance, through computer networks, and to start prosecutions in their own country against foreign cybercriminals. Here, however, the problem of sovereignty emerges: to what extent can countries claim a say over foreign evidence, foreign nationals, foreign territory? It is this problem of the need for cross-border action clashing with sovereignty claims that is the focus of this book.

1.1 Substantive and Procedural Cybercrime Jurisdiction

A major issue in cross-border crimes is substantive jurisdiction: which country has the legal basis to prosecute suspects and convict the perpetrator? And if more than one country has jurisdiction: which of them will have priority? It is not only a matter of the right formal legal basis to prosecute, but also a practical matter of having the necessary ingredients available: evidence and witnesses, the suspect, and a desire to handle the case – all of which must be present for a prosecution to make sense.

Mirroring the question of which country has jurisdiction to prosecute, the tricky issue of cross-border criminal investigation also commands attention. Computer networks enable searches across the world, and police officers can infiltrate on-line child-porn groups regardless of where the pedophiles are located. To what extent can a country claim extraterritorial procedural jurisdiction, that is, the power to investigate on the territory of other countries? And how do countries interpret the location of a network search – is the search done in a-territorial cyberspace, on the territory where physical computers are located of which the contents are examined, or on the territory of switches that transfer the bits and bytes of the search queries?

Cybercrime jurisdiction is far from straightforward. Many countries do not have specific legislation for this: they simply rely on traditional jurisdiction provisions to decide whether they have jurisdiction or not. However, these traditional provisions typically claim territorial jurisdiction, that is, if the crime was committed within their territory, or investigation powers executed on their territory. But when exactly can a cybercrime or cyber-investigation be considered to take 'place' on a 'territory' when it essentially consists of immaterial bits and bytes that may take any route – and usually different routes – across those of the world's Internet cables that happen to be determined for them by local Internet switches?

At an extreme end of jurisdiction claims, some countries that do have cybercrime jurisdiction provisions, such as Malaysia, have such sweeping provisions that they can theoretically claim jurisdiction for any cybercrime committed anywhere. 'This Act shall apply if, for the offence in question, the computer, program or data was in Malaysia *or capable of being connected to or sent to* or used by or with a computer in Malaysia at the material time' [emphasis added].[1] Similarly, some countries would like to have as wide a jurisdictional scope for their cyber-investigation powers as possible. The United States, for instance, enticed two Russian hackers to visit a bogus company in the United States, wormed out their passwords, and therewith copied the contents of their computers located in Russia, all the while claiming that they did not infringe Russian sovereignty because the FBI agents never left U.S. soil. The Russian authorities thought differently, and – ineffectively, but symbolically – charged the FBI agents with hacking in Russia.[2]

1.2 Traditional Bases for Jurisdiction

In order to appreciate the intricate questions of cybercrime jurisdiction that are triggered by the examples of Malaysia and the United States, and that will be tackled further on in this book, it is important to have some knowledge of traditional views of jurisdiction. When can a state normally, that is, traditionally, claim jurisdiction? We give a brief outline here.[3]

'Jurisdiction' encompasses several discrete concepts, including jurisdiction to prescribe, jurisdiction to adjudicate, and jurisdiction to enforce. Jurisdiction to prescribe is a sovereign entity's authority 'to make its law applicable to the activities, relations, or status of persons, or the interests of persons in things (...) by legislation, by executive act or order, by administrative rule (...) or by determination of a court.' Jurisdiction to adjudicate is a sovereign entity's authority 'to subject persons or entities to the process of its courts or administrative tribunals' for the purpose of determining whether prescriptive law has been violated. Jurisdiction to enforce is a sovereign entity's authority 'to induce or compel compliance or to punish noncompliance with its laws or regulations, whether through the courts or by use of executive, administrative, police, or other nonjudicial action.'[4]

---

[1] Art. 9 Malaysia Computer Crimes Act.1997, available at <http://www.ktkm.gov.my/template01.asp?Content_ID=379&Cat_ID=4&CatType_ID=85> (under 'Cyberlaws').

[2] See S.W. Brenner and B.J. Koops, 'Approaches to Cybercrime Jurisdiction', 4 *Journal of High-Technology Law* (2004), pp. 1-46, at p. 21-23, and chapter 16 of this book.

[3] This section is based on Brenner and Koops, loc. cit. n. 2, to which we refer for a more elaborate description.

[4] See *Restatement (Third) of Foreign Relations Law of the United States* (1987) (hereafter: Restatement), § 401. The Restatement is a 'treatise or commentary' on jurisdictional and other principles of international law; it is 'not a primary source of authority upon which, standing alone, courts may rely for propositions of customary international law. *United States* v. *Yousef*, 327 F.3d 56, 99 (2d Cir. 2003).

Traditionally, all three types of jurisdiction have been based primarily upon the concept of territory. A nation (or a state) had jurisdiction to prescribe what was and was not proper conduct within its physical territory and had jurisdiction to enforce those prescriptions against actors whose unlawful conduct had occurred within its territory. This concept of jurisdiction followed from the basic principle that a sovereign entity had the lawful authority to exert control within 'its territory generally to the exclusion of other states, authority to govern in that territory, and authority to apply law there.'[5] From this, it would follow that no nation could apply its criminal laws to conduct occurring within the physical territory of another nation.[6]

The twentieth and twenty-first centuries' increased geographical mobility and use of telecommunications technology undermined certain of the assumptions that gave rise to the traditional model of jurisdiction.[7] It became much easier for someone to commit a criminal act in one country and quickly flee the country, thereby frustrating its ability to apply its criminal laws to the perpetrator; it also became possible for someone in Alisonia[8] to commit a criminal act against a victim physically situated within the territory of Bobland without the Alisonian ever leaving her own country.

Reflecting the concern with national sovereignty noted above, extradition treaties require 'double criminality,' i.e., require that the conduct at issue constitutes a crime in both countries for extradition to be permissible.[9] Absent such a requirement, an Alisonian citizen could be prosecuted by Bobland for conduct that occurred entirely within Alisonia, and that was quite legal under Alisonian laws, but that violated the laws of Bobland. To allow such an eventuality would be to undermine Alisonia's sovereign authority – its jurisdiction – over its citizens and others within its borders.

The concept of requiring double criminality for extradition and the proposition that nations have sovereign authority over those within their territorial boundaries still retain their validity, but the past few decades have seen an expansion in the premises that can support the exercise of criminal jurisdiction. Jurisdiction is no longer predicated solely upon one's having been physically present within a nation at the time the offense was committed. Under the modern conception of jurisdic-

---

[5] Restatement, op. cit. n. 4, § 206 comment b.

[6] See, e.g., The Apollon, 22 U.S. (9 Wheat) 362, 371 (1824). Cf., United Nations Convention Against Transnational Organized Crime, Art. 4 ('Protection of Sovereignty') (2000), available at <http://www.uncjin.org/Documents/Conventions/dcatoc/final_documents_2/convention_eng.pdf>. See generally Restatement, op. cit. n. 4, § 206 comment b.

[7] See, e.g., Marc D. Goodman and Susan W. Brenner, 'The Emerging Consensus on Criminal Conduct in Cyberspace', *U.C.L.A. Journal of Law & Technology* (2002), p. 3, available at <http://www.lawtechjournal.com/articles/2002/03_020625_goodmanbrenner.php>.

[8] Rather than talk about the vague countries A and B, we here extend the customary characters of cryptographic literature, Alice and Bob, to fictitious countries Alisonia and Bobland.

[9] See, e.g., Goodman and Brenner, loc. cit. n. 7, at pp. 18-24.

tion, a nation can be thought to have jurisdiction to prescribe law with regard to any of the following:

1. (a) conduct that, wholly or in substantial part, takes place within its territory; (b) the status of persons, or interests in things, present within its territory; (c) conduct outside its territory that has or is intended to have substantial effect within its territory;
2. the activities, interests, status, or relations of its nationals outside as well as within its territory; and
3. certain conduct outside its territory by persons not its nationals that is directed against the security of the state or against a limited class of other state interests.[10]

A somewhat different and expanded list of bases for jurisdiction claims is:[11]

1. territoriality
   a) location of acts
   b) location of tools (such as computers)
   c) location of persons
   d) location of the result
   e) location of anything that has some connection to the crime
2. personality
   a) nationality of the perpetrator
   b) nationality of the victim
3. other interests
   a) protection of the country's interest
   b) universality

Notwithstanding this expansion of the predicates for exercising jurisdiction, it is still the case that '[t]erritoriality is considered the normal, and nationality an exceptional, basis for the exercise of jurisdiction.'[12]

Even under an expanded view of jurisdiction, however, a nation can only exercise jurisdiction to prescribe when the exercise of such jurisdiction is reasonable.[13] Whether the exercise of jurisdiction to prescribe is reasonable or not should be determined by considering various factors, such as the strength of the link of the activity to the territory of the regulating state, the importance of regulation to the

---

[10] Restatement, op. cit. n. 4, § 402. See also Ray August, 'International Cyber-jurisdiction: A Comparative Analysis', 39 *American Business Law Journal* (2002), p. 531, who distinguishes four different bases to justify the exercise of jurisdiction in criminal cases: '(1) the territorial nexus, i.e., where the offense was committed; (2) the nationality of the person committing the offense; (3) a protective nexus that allows the exercise of jurisdiction when a national interest of the forum state is at stake; and (4) the universality nexus which gives courts jurisdiction over 'certain offenses that are recognized by the community of nations as being of universal concern.'

[11] Brenner and Koops, loc. cit. n. 2.

[12] Restatement, op. cit. n. 4, § 402 comment b.

[13] Restatement, op. cit. n. 4, § 403(1).

regulating state and the extent to which other states regulate such activities, and the importance of the regulation to the international political, legal, or economic system.[14] Reasonableness is also required for jurisdiction to adjudicate: nations only have authority to exercise adjudicative authority through their courts if the relationship between that nation and the person or thing that is the object of the adjudicative effort is sufficiently close. Factors to take into account include whether the suspect is present or domiciled in the territory of the state, and whether the person has carried on outside the state an activity having a substantial, direct, and foreseeable effect within the state.[15]

1.3 Diverging Views

On the basis of a sample survey we have made earlier of jurisdiction provisions across the globe, we found that the bases for jurisdiction outlined above can well be and in fact are applied to cybercrime. Perhaps surprisingly, territoriality still turns out to be a prime factor, despite the non-physical nature of the bits and bytes that usually constitute a cybercrime; apparently, cyberspace is not considered so a-territorial after all. Occasionally, personality claims and protection claims occur as well in relation to cybercrime. The major conclusion we drew, however, is that countries and states turn out to have quite varying scopes and bases in their cybercrime jurisdictional provisions. We have noted divergence rather than approximation, particularly in the interpretation of territorial connections and the use of the principle that countries can protect themselves.[16]

This will lead to problems when jurisdiction conflicts emerge whenever a serious cross-border cybercrime occurs that multiple states have an interest in prosecuting. At the same time, negative jurisdiction conflicts are a risk with offenses like a virus that has wreaked havoc around the world; perhaps no particular country will claim jurisdiction, since it has only suffered a fraction of the harm caused by the virus, and since the country of residence of the perpetrator may not have the means or the will to prosecute.

As we concluded from our earlier survey,[17] it is vital that more effort be put into fine-tuning and possibly approximating countries' and states' creation and exercise of jurisdiction in relation to cybercrime. This should preferably be undertaken at a global level, or at least at the level of the Council of Europe's Cybercrime Convention, which has also been signed – but not yet ratified – by the United States, Canada, South Africa, and Japan.[18] This Convention already contains some provisions on

[14] See ibid., § 403(2) for an extensive list of factors.
[15] Ibid., § 421(2).
[16] Brenner and Koops, loc. cit. n. 2, at pp. 44-46.
[17] Ibid.
[18] Convention on Cybercrime, Budapest 23 November 2001 (CETS 185), available at <http://conventions.coe.int/Treaty/EN/WhatYouWant.asp?NT=185>.

cybercrime jurisdiction,[19] but much more should be done if cybercrime jurisdiction is really to be resolved in an effective, internationally concerted way.

1.4 Aim and Structure of This Book

Since cultural and legal traditions play a major part in countries' views on the exercise of criminal law and sovereignty, approximation of countries' diverging cybercrime and jurisdiction legislation requires serious reflection. This book intends to facilitate this process by offering such reflection. We have asked experts from a broad sample of countries across the world to describe and analyze their country's legislation and stance on cybercrime jurisdiction. After chapters on the Council of Europe's Cybercrime Convention and on international co-operation in criminal matters, which together set some form of international frame of reference, thirteen country reports are included in alphabetical order. Rather than drily replicating the conclusions of all previous chapters in a summary, the book concludes with one of the most urgent 'next steps' that need to be taken: an attempt at resolving positive jurisdictional conflicts when several jurisdictions seek to prosecute a cybercriminal at the same time.

Reflecting the stages in which cybercrime law is developing across the world, some countries have quite developed legislation and doctrines on cybercrimes, and the country reports as a result can offer in-depth discussions of the jurisdiction intricacies that cybercrime gives rise to. Other countries have less developed legislation and literature on cybercrime, and their reports as a result pay relatively more attention to cybercrime itself, with only a first step towards addressing jurisdiction issues. We feel that, taken together, the thematic chapters and the country reports thus offer a wonderful view of the wide gamut of cybercrime legislation and jurisdiction positions across the world.

With this in-depth survey of views and practices of cybercrime jurisdiction, we hope to contribute to a more concerted international effort towards effectively fighting cybercrime.

Bibliography

Ray August, 'International Cyber-Jurisdiction: A Comparative Analysis', 39 *Am. Bus. L. J.* (2002) p. 531.

S.W. Brenner & B.J. Koops, 'Approaches to Cybercrime Jurisdiction', 4 *Journal of High-Technology Law* (2004), pp. 1-46, available at <http://www.jhtl.org/V4N1/JHTL_Brenner_Koops_Article1.pdf>.

---

[19] See chapter 2 of this book.

MARC D. GOODMAN & SUSAN W. BRENNER, 'The Emerging Consensus on Criminal Conduct in Cyberspace', *U.C.L.A. Journal of Law & Technology* (2002), pp. 3-24, available at <http://www.lawtechjournal.com/articles/2002/03_020625_goodmanbrenner.php>.

AMERICAN LAW INSTITUTE, *Restatement (Third) of Foreign Relations Law of the United States* (1987), <http://www.ali.org/ali/foreign.htm>.

Chapter 2
JURISDICTION IN THE CYBERCRIME CONVENTION

Henrik W.K. Kaspersen*

2.1 Introductory Remarks

In this essay, I will make a *tour d'horizon* about the issues related to jurisdictional competence, in particular with regard to cybercrimes. Since I do not have the ambition here to propose a final solution for jurisdiction in cyber space, I prefer to restrict myself to a number of observations. In particular, I will consider and analyse jurisdiction issues related to the text of the Council of Europe's Cybercrime Convention (hereafter: CCC).[1] I will give some background information on the present text of the Convention and consider the choices made in the Convention against the background of present jurisdiction principles as applied in public international law.

Cybercrime is a term of 'hype' and not a legal definition. The term may include any crime that has been committed by means of electronic equipment or in an electronic environment. When I follow the categorization of the substantive-law chapter of the Cybercrime Convention (Arts. 2-9),[2] cybercrime is any crime directed against computer systems and networks and their information content (cybercrime in a narrow sense); it also includes computer-related crimes like fraud and forgery in the broadest sense committed by electronic means, offences concerning a violation of intellectual-property rights on protected works in an electronic form, and content-related offences, in particular criminal content. The procedural part of the Cybercrime Convention brings under the heading of cybercrime also those crimes for the investigation of which electronic evidence has to be collected and safeguarded from computer systems or networks. One of the common elements of these

* Prof. Dr Henrik W.K. Kaspersen is director of the Computer/Law Institute of the Vrije Universiteit of Amsterdam. He chaired the Council of Europe drafting committees that developed the Recommendation of 1995, the Cybercrime Convention of 2001, and the First Additional Protocol to the Convention on Racism and Xenophobia of 2003.

1 Council of Europe, Convention on Cybercrime, Budapest, 23 November 2001 (CETS 185), <http://conventions.coe.int/Treaty/en/Treaties/Html/185.htm>.

2 See also First Additional Protocol to the Convention on Cybercrime, concerning the criminalization of acts of a racist and xenophobic nature committed through computer systems, 23 January 2003 (CETS 189), <http://conventions.coe.int/Treaty/en/Treaties/Html/189.htm>.

B-J. Koops and S.W. Brenner (Eds), Cybercrime and Jurisdiction

crimes is that they may be committed wholly or partially on the territory of different states because of the perpetrator's use of international global communication networks.

Under public international law, it is self-evident that a sovereign state is entitled to establish jurisdiction over offences that occur on its territory. In this respect, however, a much more interesting question is how to deal with the sometimes extraterritorial nature of cybercrime and the relation of the states involved in view of the investigation and prosecution of such crimes.

2.2 Jurisdiction Rules in the Cybercrime Convention

Article 22 CCC contains certain jurisdiction rules that refer to the substantive law provisions in Articles 2-11 of the Convention. These rules reflect the application of a number of different jurisdiction principles. The aim of Article 22 is to ensure that Parties to the Convention establish the required level of extraterritorial jurisdiction. The article also deals with situations where two or more Parties claim jurisdiction over a cybercrime (concurrent jurisdiction). This aim is clearly included in the terms of reference for the drafting committee of the Cybercrime Convention, i.e., to 'examine (…) the question of jurisdiction in relation to information technology offences,[3] e.g., to determine the place where the offence was committed (*locus delicti*) and which law should accordingly apply, including the problem of *ne bis in idem* in the case of multiple jurisdictions and the question how to solve positive and how to avoid negative jurisdictions conflicts.'[4]

2.2.1 **Territoriality principle**

In an electronic environment, the main basis for establishing jurisdiction over criminal acts is still the territoriality principle. The Explanatory Report to the Convention does not pay much attention to this.[5] As long as the crime takes place within the national territory, it is self-evident that national law-enforcement authorities, acting within the scope of domestic law, are entitled to investigate and to prosecute those crimes. This also seems perfectly reasonable at the beginning of a chain of action by a user of an electronic communication network or communication service. A physical location can be identified where a natural person applies electronic equipment in order to obtain access to or to initiate and maintain electronic communications. At such a location, the user is subject to applicable domestic law as fol-

[3] The broad notion of cybercrime as used in the Council of Europe Recommendation R(95) 13 concerning problems of criminal procedure law connected with information technology.

[4] See Council of Europe, Convention on Cybercrime (CETS 185), *Explanatory Report* (8 November 2001), <http://conventions.coe.int/Treaty/en/Reports/Html/185.htm>, para. 11.

[5] Ibid.

lows from the territoriality principle. It should be noted that whether or not a perpetrator is acting at a certain location depends in the first place on the legal definition of the crime. For instance, obtaining unauthorized access to a computer system or network can be considered to be undertaken at the physical location where the perpetrator applies the instruments for the crime. Those instruments can be his computer system, including technical tools to break security measures of the computer system to which he seeks to obtain access. At the same time, one can argue that the perpetrator is also acting at the physical location where the target system is located, making use of the instruments under his control, i.e., the computer software and the communication facilities of the Internet that bring him to the ports of the victim's system. In case of a content-related offence, the elements of 'dissemination', 'offering', or 'making available' of criminal information refer rather to an action from the physical location where the perpetrator is present. The effects of these types of offences, however, may be experienced on the territory of another state and therefore may be considered as having been committed on the territory of the latter state.

2.2.2 **Ubiquitous nature of cybercrimes**

De Schutter was one of first to argue that determining the *locus delicti* of cybercrimes in accordance with the principles outlined in the previous section could lead to multiple and possible conflicting jurisdiction claims, because the distinction between the traditional criteria are blurring in the electronic environment.[6] It is difficult, if not impossible, to clearly distinguish between the location (i) where the perpetrator acts, (ii) where he applies his instruments, and (iii) where the damaging effects of the crime are felt. Theoretically, this could bring numerous jurisdiction conflicts between states, which would require the development of specific mechanisms to resolve the conflicts.

Despite the order in the terms of reference, the Cybercrime Convention does not provide rules or criteria on how to determine the *locus delicti* with regard to cybercrimes. The Convention is silent on this point and thus leaves the matter to national law and relating case law. Providing for rules here would mean that a special regime were to be created for cybercrimes that may or may not be applicable to other crimes. Moreover, there will be little difference between the decisions of national courts assuming so-called subjective territorial jurisdiction, i.e., related to the question whether or not the perpetrator acted on the territory of the state concerned. These may be difficult to establish, because all aspects of the conduct involved in the commission of the crime are taken into account, such as the preparation of a crime (conspiracy), attempt, and aiding and abetting. It is also necessary to consider the liability of legal persons or any combination thereof.

---

[6] B. de Schutter, 'Grensoverschrijdende computercriminaliteit' [Cross-Border Computer Crime], in H.W.K. Kaspersen (ed.), *Computermisdaad en Strafrecht* [Computer Crime and Criminal Law] (Antwerp-Deventer 1986), pp. 143-160 at pp. 148-151.

2.2.3 **Substantial link**

More divergence can be expected in the determination of subjective territorial jurisdiction, i.e., concerning the relation of the act with the territory of the state. How substantive must the link of the criminal act or the alleged perpetrator be to a sovereign state for its national courts to assume jurisdiction? The notorious Yahoo case,[7] brought before a French court in 2000, clearly demonstrated that the decisions of the French courts did not have overall support, in particular not in the United States. Conduct that was perfectly lawful under the U.S. First Amendment was also a violation of French criminal law.[8] The French court based its decision to assume (objective) jurisdiction upon the fact that the damage resulting from the conduct had been experienced in France. It is a long debate to sort out whether or not the damage had indeed occurred in France, but if it did, the court was right in its reasoning. Does this mean that the French decision threatens freedom of speech on the Internet? I do not think so. This would only be the case if the French verdict could have been executed in the United States, which was not the case. Where criminal information is made available over the Internet, national courts will rather assume that no damage is caused in the national territory if the information is in a foreign language or obviously directed to other nationals. Anyway, the drafters of the Cybercrime Convention at the time did not see a need to regulate. It may nevertheless be useful to research to what extent nationally applied criteria and principles could be brought together.

2.3 Other Jurisdiction Principles

States can establish extraterritorial jurisdiction on the basis of several other jurisdiction principles. The application of such principles is usually not cybercrime-specific, but it may add to the concurrence of jurisdictions as described by De Schutter.[9] Therefore, let us consider what Article 22 of the Convention has brought us in this respect. The article obliges, in paragraph 1 *littera* a, the territoriality principle to be applied to the offences as defined in Articles 2-11 CCC. As commonly accepted under public international law, a state may establish territorial jurisdiction on board ships flying its flag or on board aircraft registered under the law of that state. The Cybercrime Convention turns this competence into an obligation for its Parties under *litterae* b and c: Parties should establish jurisdiction over offences committed on board such ships and aircraft – of course within the limits and conditions of international law.

---

7 Tribunal de grande Instance, Paris, 20 November 2000 (verdict available in English at <http://www.juriscom.net>).

8 Art. R-645-1 of the French Penal Code prohibits the exhibition of Nazi symbols in public.

9 De Schutter, loc. cit. n. 6, at pp. 148-151.

2.3.1 High seas and outer space

The text of the Convention in Article 22 does not deal with satellites.[10] It was realized that those features are important chains in international and global communication networks. Satellites are moving in a predetermined orbit at the moment of launching. For the functioning of a satellite network, ground stations take care of sending and receiving information flows to and from a satellite. Being located within the territory of a particular state, the communications involving criminal offences by and through that particular ground station are subject to territorial jurisdiction of the state involved. This would be different if one was dealing with a manned space shuttle and the crew of that shuttle committed crimes in outer space, as occurs in any self-respecting space movie. Space law does not seem to take such situations into account and does not provide a basis for rules of public international law in order to deal with such questions. The Convention does not go into the issue of jurisdiction in outer space, because it is a complicated matter and does not seem to be relevant here, at least not for the very near future.[11] Surprisingly, others seem to assume that the Party that registers a satellite may assume (territorial) jurisdiction thereover in a similar manner as over ships and aircraft.[12] Where the satellite is being used for communications between legal subjects on earth, the universality principle as applied in *littera* d of the same article should provide for a solution (see section 2.3.3).

2.3.2 Nationality principle

Article 22 paragraph 1 *littera* d CCC contains two obligations. Firstly, Parties are obliged to establish jurisdiction over the offences defined in the Convention when committed by one of their nationals on the territory of another Party, provided that the conduct is criminal under the law of that Party. The mechanism is known under the name of the nationality principle. The rationale of the principle is that nationals should obey the law, even if they are not on the territory of the home state. A logical restriction is that the conduct must also be criminal under the law of the country where the act was committed (dual criminality). Secondly, Parties are also obliged to establish jurisdiction over offences committed by their nationals at a location that falls outside the scope of the territorial jurisdiction of any state, i.e., not necessarily a Party to the Convention.

---

[10] See *Explanatory Report*, op. cit. n. 4, para. 234: 'The drafters decided that such a provision was unnecessary since unlawful communications involving satellites will invariably originate from and/or be received on earth. As such, one of the bases for a Party's jurisdiction set forth in para. 1(a) – (c) will be available if the transmission originates or terminates in one of the locations specified therein.'

[11] The existing U.N. Treaties, like the Outer Space Treaty of 1967, the Astronaut Return Treaty 1975, the Registration Treaty of 1975, the Liability Treaty of 1972 and the Moon Treaty of 1979 are not directed towards dealing with jurisdictional issues over space vehicles. The regulation of jurisdiction over space vehicles might interfere with the principles and content of these treaties.

[12] Jordan J. Paust, et. al., *International Criminal Law* (Durham 1996), p. 123.

2.3.3 Universality principle

The latter obligation is obviously inspired by the most far-reaching extraterritorial jurisdiction principle: the universality principle. The validity of this principle is not uncontested. At present, it is generally recognized that universal jurisdiction can only be established in as far as public international law empowers states to do so.[13] It should be avoided that the application of the principle can justly be considered as interference in a country's internal affairs. States – or most likely, the courts of a state – may therefore limit the scope of the universality principle, e.g., by requiring that there is a relation between the crime involved and the domestic legal order – the nexus requirement.[14] Treaties that apply universal jurisdiction – mostly in cases of very serious crimes – contain other limitations in order to prevent overly broad application.[15]

The limitations set out in Article 22 paragraph 1 *littera* d CCC are twofold. It concerns only nationals of the Party involved, and the location and situations to which this principle can be applied are rather of an exceptional nature, i.e., it may apply to criminal conduct committed on non-registered ships on the high seas and on board of space shuttles in outer space. For example, a perpetrator commits a cybercrime sitting in a stateless vessel or in a rowing boat on the high seas by communication through a communication satellite, or an astronaut commits a cybercrime from the space shuttle by wireless means. These examples show that it is clear that the second obligation does not refer to frequently occurring situations.

Since it may not be expected that all the jurisdiction principles referred to above – the extended territoriality principle, the passive nationality principle, and the restricted universality principle – can be applied within the framework of domestic legal principles and traditions, Article 22 paragraph 2 CCC provides for a reservation possibility. Parties may reserve the right not to implement the whole or a part of the content of *litterae* a-d of Article 22 paragraph 1. The minimum common level therefore comes down to the traditional territoriality principle. Most Parties to the Cybercrime Convention are used to applying *littera* b and c. In my expectation, the first part of *litterae* d will be applied by a substantial number of Parties, whereas

[13] See, e.g., Peter Malanczuk, *Akehurst's Modern Introduction to International Law* (London/New York 1997), p. 199.

[14] Several U.S. Supreme Court decisions use this requirement; in Europe, see, e.g., German BGH, 13 February 1994, *NStZ* 1994, 232, BGH April 30, 1999, *NStZ* 1999, 396.

[15] See, e.g., the U.N. Convention against Torture and Other Cruel, Inhuman or Degrading Treatment or Punishment (New York, 10 December 1984). Parties are obliged to prosecute an alleged offender, irrespective of the state in which those crimes were committed, but only if the offender is found on the territory of the Party concerned. Similar limitations were known from older international instruments like the International Convention for the Suppression of Counterfeiting Currency of 20 April 1929, and the European Convention on the Suppression of Terrorism, 21 January 1977. The latest addition, the European Convention on the Prevention of Terrorism of 16 May 2005, contains an obligation to investigate if a Party is informed about the facts and the alleged offender may be present in its territory.

most Parties will probably not implement the second part of *littera* d. It is therefore difficult to tell in which cases multiple jurisdiction will occur, apart from the question whether this will lead to jurisdiction conflicts.

2.4 Rights of the Defendant

Asserting extraterritorial jurisdiction, of course, may affect the interests of the alleged perpetrator. Protection of these interests is not envisaged by public international law, because it only regulates the relations between sovereign states. In order to protect these interests, states are entitled to make arrangements or to enact specific legislation individually. In the terms of reference of the drafting committee that prepared the text of the Cybercrime Convention, this issue is clearly put on the agenda.[16] In the case of the existence of multiple jurisdictions, the alleged offender may run the risk of multiple national prosecutions, whether or not he is physically present in the prosecuting state. When visiting that state and passing through customs, verdicts of which he is not aware may unexpectedly be served upon him and lead to his arrest and detention. Yet Article 22 does not demonstrate any such guarantees for the alleged offender. The article only regulates inter-Party relations. The Explanatory Report does not provide any further indication as to why this issue was omitted. I will try to explain this below.

2.5 International Law: A Matter of Pragmatism?

There seems to be a great deal of pragmatism in international practice. Conflicts very seldom lead to legal procedures. Serious jurisdiction conflicts are rare. However, if we look at the expectations as given above, should not more be done than is agreed in Article 22 paragraph 5 CCC: a mandatory consultation of Parties, without the establishment of further criteria or procedural regulation?

2.5.1 **Extradition**

Effective exercising of jurisdiction requires the availability of the alleged offender in the hands of the prosecuting state. The international agreements to achieve that goal are primarily the extradition instruments. In Europe, the multilateral Council of Europe Convention on Extradition of 1957 includes a *ne bis in idem* protection (double jeopardy) for the alleged offender in its Article 9,[17] and so does the EU

[16] See Terms of Reference, para. 11, under v, Explanatory Memorandum: 'the problem of *ne bis in idem* in the case of multiple jurisdictions (…).'

[17] *ETS* 24. Note the reservations to the article made by several Member States.

European arrest warrant of 2002 in its Article 3 paragraph 2.[18] Modern bilateral instruments between other Parties will usually include double-jeopardy protection, but it cannot be said that it is included in all treaties, in particular not in older ones. After all, it was the conviction of the drafting committee that double jeopardy should be regulated at the level of extradition and not at the level of jurisdiction. This was feasible, because the Cybercrime Convention obliges the Parties to make the offences as defined in Articles 2-11 CCC extraditable, provided that they are sanctioned under national law with deprivation of liberty for a maximum period of at least one year (see Art. 1 under a) or the minimum penalty as defined in an applicable extradition treaty between the parties (see Art. 1 under b).

2.5.2 International co-ordination

Prior to decisions to prosecute, criminal investigations take place. In the case of multiple jurisdictions, an alleged offender could become the object of several investigations by different national law enforcement authorities, resulting in a multiple infringement of his privacy and privacy-related interests, and possibly putting a burden on other persons involved like witnesses. Public international law cannot prevent national law-enforcement authorities from undertaking measures which are necessary to protect the domestic legal order – as defined by national criminal law, as long as they do not interfere with the internal affairs of another state. The Cybercrime Convention does not – and should not – contain provisions dealing with the co-ordination of national criminal investigations concerning the same crime or perpetrator. Nevertheless, Article 26 CCC[19] contributes to a better co-ordination of criminal investigations, in order to improve the efficacy of such investigations, but also to reduce the burden for the suspect and other persons involved.[20] The article enables law-enforcement authorities to spontaneously provide 'criminal' information to the authorities of other Parties without a prior request for mutual assistance. According to paragraph 2, confidential information may be provided subject to conditions that the receiving Party has to respect. If it cannot respect these conditions because of its domestic (procedural) law, it should notify the other Party, which may then consider whether or not to provide the information. The application of Article 26, however, does not influence the competence of the information-providing Party to further investigate and prosecute a case, if it wishes to do so. If a criminal case has international ramifications, it is very unlikely that law-enforcement authorities will not seek contact through Interpol with authorities in other

---

[18] *OJ* L190, 18/07/2002, pp. 0001-0020. No reservations could be made to this article.

[19] The article was copied from earlier Council of Europe Conventions, like the Convention on the Laundering, Search, Seizure and Confiscation of the Proceeds of Crime (CETS 141) and Art. 28 of the Criminal Law Convention on Corruption (CETS 173).

[20] See, e.g., *Explanatory Report*, op. cit. n. 4, para. 239, on Art. 22 para. 5, which expresses a similar interest.

countries, which may lead to the co-ordination and concentration of investigations at an early stage.

Article 22 paragraph 3 contains a very traditional provision, well-known from all time international criminal praxis. It contains the rule *dedere aut judicare*. If a Party does not extradite its nationals at the request of another Party to the Convention, it should prosecute the alleged offender itself. If – apart from the nationality status of the alleged offender – other grounds for refusal are invoked, the obligation to prosecute is void. Because of the harmonization of cybercrime provisions as envisioned by the Convention, the Party that is not able to extradite because of the nationality of the alleged offender will be able to prosecute, because the conduct is criminal in the requesting state as well as in the home state of the alleged offender. However, as a consequence of the possible declarations and reservations with regard to the criminal offences defined in the Convention, there is a possibility that the conduct of the alleged offender amounts to a crime in all its details, while the crime itself cannot be proven according to the law of the requested Party. This does not mean that extradition could be refused on the basis of a lack of dual criminality, because extradition practice encompasses the conduct rather than the detailed elements of the criminal provision. Modern instruments give even less meaning to the condition of dual criminality, through the establishment of categories of crime rather than referring to definitions of the crimes involved.[21] It is self-evident that the requesting Party will provide all the information and evidentiary material necessary to be able to prosecute.

Article 22 paragraph 4 leaves unaffected the choice of jurisdiction principles that a Party wants to apply under its domestic law, as long as at least the principles referred to in paragraphs 1-3 are applied as regulated. Also, at this point, the Cybercrime Convention allows Parties to go beyond the level of obligations which it defines – here is one of the places in the Explanatory Memorandum where this is explicitly stated. This flexibility is necessary because, otherwise, conflicts and uncertainties could occur in determining extraterritorial jurisdiction, e.g., when cyber-offences contained in the Convention would be criminalized under domestic law in the form of a technology-independent provision, such as could happen in the case of the implementation of Articles 7, 8, 9, and 10. A Party may wish not to apply all the principles of Article 22 to traditional crimes and their variants.

2.6 Positive Jurisdiction Conflicts and the Need for Flexibility

Article 22 paragraph 5 recognizes that multiple jurisdiction may lead to positive jurisdiction conflicts. The drafting committee chose a flexible but not very formalized procedure. The obligation is that Parties should consult each other, i.e., exchange their views on the most appropriate Party to prosecute the crime in a particular

[21] EU Arrest Warrant, *supra* n. 18.

case. The provision contains the element of 'where appropriate'. This does not refer to a situation where a Party estimates that the expected outcome of the consultation is apparent. The element rather refers to situations where one of the Parties involved has already announced its will not take further action, or where a Party fears that prosecution in the other Party state would jeopardize its own investigation or prosecution. In such a case, consultation may be postponed.

The provision does not contain criteria to determine the most appropriate jurisdiction. Nevertheless, one could think of a number of arguments, such as where the alleged offender is arrested and whether or not he can be extradited, where the victims of the crime are, and where the evidence of the crime has been collected. Also, other elements can be taken into account, such as the general level of penalties under domestic criminal law, the way verdicts are executed, the relationship with other criminal investigations, the relationship with other perpetrators or persons who were aiding and abetting, etc. It would be going much too far, in particular within the framework of a Convention, to give specific weight to all these different and divergent factors. Note that the provision does not force the consulting Parties to choose one jurisdiction for prosecution. They may, for example, agree that one Party prosecutes the main suspect while the other Party will deal with other participants in the crime.

2.7 Obligation to Prosecute?

The fact that a state has established jurisdiction over a particular crime does not mean that the state is obliged to investigate and prosecute it. Whether or not a crime is to be investigated or prosecuted follows from domestic criminal policy and from domestic criminal law. Exceptionally, states may by international instrument agree that certain crimes have to be prosecuted by one of them, e.g., in the case of international crimes like war crimes, genocide, and crimes against humanity. Is there a need to impose a duty on states to prosecute cybercrimes, and if so, which principle should be applied to establish jurisdiction over such facts? The first question to be dealt with is the seriousness of the cybercrimes, i.e., could they form a serious menace to the security of a state and the enforcement of its legal order? The substantive provisions of the Convention form a broad range of more or less obnoxious and dangerous forms of conduct. Because of the general and wide scope of the definition of a computer system, which includes objects from very powerful systems to microprocessors (see Art. 1 CCC), the CIA offences[22] in Articles 2-6 of the Convention may concern petty offences as well as serious crimes. Human life may be at stake in the case of vital systems, but this element is lacking in the definitions of the Convention. Moreover, if human life is put at risk, those cases will be pros-

[22] CIA offences are offences against the confidentiality, integrity, or availability of computers or computer networks.

ecuted as such and may be abstracted from their electronic environment. Of course, CIA crimes may cause considerable damage, e.g., in the case of massive DDoS (distributed denial-of-service) attacks on the military, or terrorist conduct that could be described as information warfare on vital communication networks.

Therefore, it should be studied whether particular cybercrimes involve such a risk to human life and legal order that states should be obliged to prosecute alleged offenders found on their territory. Such an obligation could be the object of another additional Protocol to the Convention. It should be noted that precise definitions of the offences are needed in order to delineate them from the present definitions. If such crimes can be established, the second question is how and to what extent the Parties to the Convention should be obliged to establish jurisdiction over these offences.

2.8 Jurisdiction Principles and Extraterritorial Criminal Investigations

Under the working title 'transborder network search', discussions already started in the Council of Europe as part of the preparation for Recommendation R(95) 13 of 1995 on criminal-procedure issues. In the absence of any concrete national or international court decision, it was left aside whether a state whose law enforcement officers would access on-line a computer system on the territory of another state and would subsequently copy data from such a system, would interfere with the internal affairs of the latter state. Under public international law, there is no rule that law enforcement officers of one state can lawfully execute their duties as imposed by national law, nor can they invoke legal competences or coercive measures in that state as provided by their national law. For these reasons, obtaining on-line access to a computer system in another state could fall under the hacking provision or other criminal provisions of that state.[23] This would not only mean that there is interference with the internal affairs of that state, but also that the prosecution of that particular law enforcement officer would be possible. In 1995, it was therefore recommended that states should conclude agreements as to what extent law enforcement authorities would be authorized to carry out on-line criminal investigations in each other's computer systems.[24] Again, one of the main topics in the negotiations on the Cybercrime Convention was the transborder network search as comprised in the terms of reference of the Drafting Committee.[25]

[23] Note that Art. 2 CCC – illegal access – allows Parties to implement the provision without any restricting elements, like the infringement of security measures.

[24] I was informed that two states involved in the negotiations on the Recommendation tried to conclude a bilateral agreement on the matter. Negotiations, however, were abandoned because of the sensitivity and the complexity of the matter.

[25] *Explanatory Report*, op. cit. n. 4, para. 11, under iv: 'the use, including the possibility of transborder use, and the applicability of coercive powers in a technological environment (...).'

The question of transborder search was debated in several bodies outside the Council of Europe, such as the United Nations and the G8, within the framework of the 1998 Action Plan.[26] No international consensus was achieved on the question whether under public international law a transborder investigation in a foreign computer system or network as such would constitute a violation of the sovereignty of the state hosting the computer system and data on its territory. Two extreme standpoints can be found. On the one hand, it was said that the computer system and its data content were physically located in the territory of the state and therefore would fall exclusively under that state's sovereignty. Accessing the computer system and the data would therefore not be possible without the consent of that particular state. Others argue that where a computer system in a state is part of an international communications network, it implies permission for use, not only to the citizens of other states but also, to the same extent, to its law enforcement authorities. Between these extreme positions, one finds all kinds of nuances leading to conclusions that transborder searches should be allowed or should only be allowed under specific conditions.

The issue was debated again during the Cybercrime Convention negotiations, but soon, a pragmatic position was taken. Countervailing opinions about the question whether transborder searches had to be considered a violation of public international law could only be reconciled by drafting a specific regulation about this in the Convention. Having said that was one thing, drafting the procedures and conditions for it was another. For a long time, no progress was made at all. Amongst other things, one particular issue was vehemently debated without final agreement: the question of notification to the other Party if a transborder search had taken place and electronic evidence had been collected.[27] Debates were also strongly influenced by parallel discussions by the G8 at the same time. Finally, it had to be concluded that public international law did not provide much lenience for transborder searches, which meant that Parties to the Convention would have to come to a specific arrangement. However, no agreement could be reached about such an arrangement. Parties could not oversee the implications of such a regulation and, as was argued further, the time was not ripe for such a far-reaching instrument. For this reason, the Convention in the end leant strongly on mutual assistance as an instrument for international co-operation, defining a number of measures in order to enable expedited assistance and the application of freezing orders in order to preserve volatile electronic data.

Nevertheless, a provision was included that reflects the vision of the negotiators concerning public international law with regard to transborder searches. Article 32 of the Convention is only a small step, but it is at least a step forward. It addresses

---

[26] See Lyon Group, *Action Plan on Fighting High Tech Crime* (1997), and follow-ups, available on the G8 web site <http://www.g8.utoronto.ca>.

[27] The principle was retained in the European Mutual Convention with regard to the interception of electronic communications, *OJ* C197 12.07.2000.

two situations. Accessing and downloading by a law enforcement officer is possible if the data is 'open source'. 'Open source' means accessible to the public without the need to follow specific procedures. It does not require that the computer system is a public system. This situation, therefore, cannot refer to cases where access is obtained by hacking into the foreign computer system. The second case refers to a situation where a citizen of Party A has lawful access to a computer system and data located in Party B and has the right to disclose such data. According to Article 32 *littera* b, the law enforcement authorities of Party A may search that data if they have obtained the lawful and voluntary consent of that person. In this case, it does not matter whether the data are secured by access codes or security measures, as long as the person referred to has the right of lawful access, irrespective of the fact that other persons may also have access rights. Further, the person in question must have the right to disclose the data, which means that the operation cannot be undertaken if the person is bound by a duty of secrecy. This duty of secrecy may be imposed by law or by contract, under the law of Party A or any other state.

A third situation was discussed but not included in the final text of the Convention. Self-help in the form of a transborder search should be possible in emergency cases, i.e., in matters of life and death concerning law enforcement officers, undercover agents, and witnesses. Negotiations failed to establish a common understanding of emergency cases. Furthermore, the Convention was going to provide for more flexible and expedited mutual assistance, which could also be used in emergency cases. The provision was therefore withdrawn.

2.9 Concluding Observations

Jurisdiction rules in the Cybercrime Convention combine traditionally known and well-recognized jurisdiction concepts. It contributes to customary international law by obliging its Parties to establish jurisdiction over the offences defined in the Convention. Since Parties may always go beyond the obligations of the Convention, the obligation in Article 22 may have a wider impact than only cybercrimes.

Apart from the principle of territorial jurisdiction, no jurisdiction principle other than the nationality principle is applied. Article 22 does not contain an obligation for the Party to investigate or to prosecute, in contrast to international instruments that deal with very serious crimes like genocide and crimes against humanity.

Judicial interpretation of the *locus delicti* may lead to different results, in particular concerning the assumption of objective territorial jurisdiction. It could be questioned whether the development of common criteria within the framework of cybercrimes is desirable, in particular because of possible implications for other types of (traditional) crimes. Decisions of national courts determining *locus delicti* are indeed very divergent. However, it seems useful to analyze national court decisions in order to establish a common set of principles for cyberspace.

Article 22 of the Convention – as a rule of international law – does not contain safeguards for individual alleged offenders, like *ne bis in idem.* Such guarantees can usually be found in extradition treaties and laws, as well as in other mutual assistance arrangements to which the Cybercrime Convention is connected.

Investigative measures cannot be executed on the territory of another country without that country's permission. On-line searches in foreign computer systems are only allowed to the extent as formulated in Article 32 CCC – concerning publicly available data, or with lawful authorized consent. Other measures may be considered a violation of the territorial sovereignty of the Party on whose territory the searched system is located.

Transborder searches therefore require an international agreement. Where in the real world joint police teams improve the possibilities for a co-ordinated and more effective investigation of transborder crime,[28] such a solution would not work in the virtual world. The evaluation of the Cybercrime Convention that is to take place before 1 July 2006 will show whether the instrument of transborder searches can still be dispensed with next to the means for flexible and expedited mutual assistance.

Bibliography

Peter Malanczuk, *Akehurst's Modern Introduction to International Law* (London/New York 1997).

Jordan J. Paust, et. al., *International Criminal Law* (Durham 1996).

B. de Schutter, 'Grensoverschrijdende computercriminaliteit' [Cross-Border Computer Crime], in H.W.K. Kaspersen (ed.), *Computermisdaad en Strafrecht* [Computer Crime and Criminal Law] (Antwerp-Deventer 1986), pp. 143-160.

[28] See *OJ* C121, 23.03.2003, pp. 1-6.

Chapter 3
INTERNATIONAL CO-OPERATION AS A PROMISE AND A THREAT

Gus Hosein*

Despite everything else that is discussed in this chapter, this chapter is really about the meaning of jurisdiction. Jurisdiction is not always a clear concept. For the most part 'jurisdiction' is considered a legal concept, usually about the reach of a court's ability to preside over a given case. In the world of political science and government, it is often associated with the reach of the rule of law as established within a geographic and political area. Importantly, the history of jurisdiction is linked with other concepts such as power and sovereignty.

The concept of jurisdiction is steadily being replaced by the notion of global governance. The distinctions between differing jurisdictions are being blurred by new transportation and communication capacities, regulatory and economic realities, amongst many other dynamics. This transformation in itself is not a new concept, so for the purpose of this chapter I will take it as a given.

Now that we no longer have kings, queens, and emperors, we have allowed jurisdiction to become only a legal issue. In time, we have forgotten that jurisdiction is also a highly political concept. We need to recall that power and sovereignty are integral ingredients to our understandings of jurisdiction. That is, it is increasingly common to have a 'laissez-faire' attitude to jurisdiction. We see international co-operation as a natural progression due to our new realities and capacities. Yet it is premature to ignore power dynamics and sovereignty concerns, as they will rear their ugly heads.

This chapter will question this benign view of international co-operation as an inevitability and as progress. Of course international co-operation is deemed a positive force in most areas involving spillover effects and globalization, such as environmental and trade policies. In the area of criminal law enforcement we see a particular prevalence of positive connotations regarding international co-operation.

* Dr Gus Hosein is a Visiting Fellow at the Department of Information Systems at the London School of Economics. He is also a Senior Fellow at Privacy International, a London-based non-governmental organization. The research for this chapter was funded by the Open Society Institute and the Social Science Research Council.

B-J. Koops and S.W. Brenner (Eds), Cybercrime and Jurisdiction

Therefore this chapter will also look into some cases of international co-operation in criminal matters to identify the more problematic dynamics of 'co-operation'. So long as we continue to see co-operation as a natural progress and benign process, at best we merely ignore issues such as sovereignty and forget the lessons of democracy; or we could be blind to those who wield power without accountability.

3.1 Questioning International Co-operation

On 17 May 2005, something entirely non-unique happened. The Council of Europe summit outlined an action plan for the coming years. The action plan was relatively uncontroversial, containing many progressive statements such as adherence to international human rights standards, combating racism and discrimination, respecting cultural diversity, and strengthening democracy. The section of the action plan dealing with security contained calls for co-operation in combating terrorism, co-ordination with international organizations, strengthening ties with international agencies to combat crime and money laundering, ratification of conventions. A large portion of the section on crime dealt with the topic of this very book.

> 'We condemn all forms of ICT use in furthering criminal activity. We therefore urge all member states to sign and ratify the Convention on Cybercrime and to consider signature of its Additional Protocol concerning the criminalisation of acts of a racist and xenophobic nature committed through computer systems, the first binding international instruments on the subject.'[1]

The CoE action plan sees co-operation as part and parcel of the modern progressive agenda to defend against terror and to support democracy. The CoE action plan very much sums up the dynamics of 'co-operation': for a given country, co-operating involves interacting with other countries' governments and agencies and adhering to requests for action, but it also involves transforming domestic law through ratification, harmonizing domestic law with international standards and foreign equivalents.

The CoE is not an exceptional case. Every political intergovernmental organization has said similar things.

The logic is thus.

Fact 1: There are increases in transnational trade; transborder flows of people, products and data.

Fact 2: Enforcing current laws in this environment is challenged because it involves the stretching of jurisdiction.

---

[1] Ministers' Deputies, Action Plan, Cm Documents, Cm (2005)80 final 17 May 2005, <http://www.coe.int/t/dcr/summit/20050517_plan_action_en.asp>.

Fact 3: There are increased threats such as crime and terrorism, environmental change, and the lack of global standards.

RESULT: International co-operation and new governance structures are necessary and necessarily good.

It is in the last step that we are making a dangerous leap of reason. From the same strain of logic that sees 'international co-operation' as a good in itself, we also find those who contend that 'adhering international obligations' and 'harmonization' are equally positive forces of policy change. If international agreements are political tools, sustaining some purposes, values, and goals; and if some international agreements are selected for adoption nationally, we need to ask why these agreements were chosen, and what their essence really is. No to Kyoto but yes to trade agreements? Yes to the International Criminal Court but no to extradition agreements with Jordan? Why do countries adhere to some requirements but not to others?

Even in the most essential components and activities of our world, even in the critical area of the war on terrorism, we must interrogate claims and arguments that international co-operation and governance is a necessity, an inevitability, and a good thing in itself. This is not to say that global solutions are not required. But it may be important for us to interrogate the assumptions and ask who is proposing co-operation, what are the political values being sustained and goals beings sought, and what are we changing and which risks are we introducing?

3.2 Traversing a History of Jurisdiction

Many of these changes and transformations have arisen due to the changing conception of jurisdiction. Approaching it through the legal conceptualization, we can easily say that there appears to be a conflict between domestic regulation in an international environment. That is, governments are usually entitled to enact and enforce laws within their jurisdiction; it is, after all, their sovereign right to do so. This 'principle of sovereignty' can be explained as government's exclusive power within its own borders and virtually nowhere else.[2]

Governments may encounter opposition to their sovereignty even whilst operating within their own borders. Two of these significant challenges to sovereignty are overflow activities from beyond a jurisdiction and unenforceability of existing laws because of foreign influences. A number of examples may be offered of each challenge. Consider a country that decides to enact a law banning the development of a specific drug. The effectiveness of the regulation is questionable if another country does not have this same regulation. Unless the first country can prevent the drug from entering at all entry points, the drug will be available in contravention of the

[2] Jonathan W. Leeds, 'United States International Law Enforcement Cooperation: A Case Study in Thailand', 7 *Journal of International Law and Practice* (1998) pp. 1-14.

spirit of the law. Similarly for air pollution: strict controls on air pollution creation in one state may make no difference if a bordering state has no similar controls thus allowing an overflow. In each case, the regulation continues to incur costs and burdens without regard to its effectiveness.

The above-stated examples are decades old. With transborder data flows within digital networks and the associated products and services, these challenges are indeed exacerbated. Action may be conducted from a distance, where the overflow of activity can occur without an individual having to physically enter the jurisdiction. Creating border controls in such a situation becomes even more challenging, on a technological level, generating concerns amongst actors such as bordering countries, non-governmental organizations, and industries. Such concerns may include costs to industry for operating under a regulatory regime, impacts of the considered action upon civil liberties, threats of jurisdictional arbitrage if burdens are too high for the regulated institutions or the regulated activity, and risks to a changing and volatile technological environment.

While somewhat outdated, there was an interesting debate in the 1990s on how to solve the problem of jurisdiction. A number of scholars at the time studied what is considered to be the regulation of 'cyberspace' or 'the Net'. If the debate had to be described as two-sided, then we could separate them along the lines of 'new bottles' and 'old wine'. That is, one side argued that we were dealing with new infrastructure and thus changes needed to be made to our lives and ways; the other side argued that our lives and ways were unchanging and that the wine was in fact not all that new nor remarkable.

3.2.1 'New bottles': Everything is different

On the one side of the debate, the 'new bottles' scholars warned that traditional rules and mechanisms would damage the infrastructure on our horizons and would thus harm our potential. Under traditional notions of sovereignty and jurisdiction, governments relied on borders to enable their power, give effect to their rules, create legitimacy, and notice to those who were regulated. Jurisdiction was therefore essential to regulation; but over computer networks, this was challenged. David Johnson and David Post famously stated:

> 'The rise of the global computer network is destroying the link between geographical location and: (1) the power of local governments to assert control over online behavior; (2) the effects of online behavior on individuals or things; (3) the legitimacy of the efforts of a local sovereign to enforce rules applicable to global phenomena; and (4) the ability of physical location to give notice of which sets of rules apply.'[3]

[3] David R. Johnson and David G. Post, 'Law And Borders – The Rise of Law in Cyberspace', 48 *Stanford Law Review* (1996) p. 1367, <http://www.cli.org/X0025_LBFIN.html#I.%20%20Breaking%20Down%20Territorial%20Borders>.

In effect, 'cyberspace' challenged the sovereignty of governments. Going back to the two challenges identified above, 'cyberspace' created overflow effects because of the idea of action at a distance, but also, because of its architecture, it created an environment that resisted government action. At a time when governments were trying to regulate through domestic initiatives, Johnson and Post advised:

> 'Many of the jurisdictional and substantive quandaries raised by border-crossing electronic communications could be resolved by one simple principle: conceiving of Cyberspace as a distinct "place" for purposes of legal analysis by recognizing a legally significant border between Cyberspace and the "real world."'

Johnson and Post were making both descriptive and normative arguments. First their claim is that applying regulation limited by geographic borders to an a-geographic-border environment would be senseless. Their second claim, which always went less noticed, was that regulation by one jurisdiction will have spillovers immediately upon another because of the a-geographic-border nature of cyberspace.

There is certainly some evidence of this 'spillover'. Some countries consider a source of information to be within their jurisdiction if it can be accessed by nationals, regardless of the physical location of the server. Court decisions in Australia,[4] for example, have considered U.S. web sites to be under the jurisdiction of their courts, and thus subject to Australian law. This places Internet service providers around the world under problematic legal situations where they have to comply with laws from a number of jurisdictions on top of their own national laws.

Put another way, if the United States were to regulate a specific form of speech, and since much of the Internet exists within the United States, then this would have the effect of regulating that speech elsewhere. Consider the case of the French court case implicating Yahoo! for enabling the auctioning of Nazi memorabilia.[5] Yahoo! was ordered to prevent French nationals from accessing the sections of its web site that traded in Nazi artifacts. The challenges of identifying 'French nationals' whilst on-line are significant, however. Eventually Yahoo! prevented all users from accessing the auction site. In the first case, an American rule would have *de facto* effects upon the rest of the world; in the second, a French rule would spill over and affect all other jurisdictions.

3.2.2 **'Old wine': Nothing new**

As opposed to this 'new bottles' approach, the other side of the debate saw the issue as 'old wine'. In this approach, it was argued that we must treat conduct in

---

[4] I.e., *Gutnick* v. *Dow Jones & Co Inc* [2001] VSC 305 (28 August 2001).

[5] See Yaman Akdeniz, 'Case Analysis of League against Racism and Antisemitism (Licra), French Union of Jewish Students v. Yahoo! Inc. (USA), Yahoo France, Tribunale De Grande Instance De Paris, Interim Court Order, 20 November 2000', 1 *Electronic Business Law Reports* (2001) No. 3.

'cyberspace' and the Internet just as we have treated all other forms of transnational activity. That is, cyberspace transactions do not inherently warrant any more deference by national regulators. A policy established by one country will always affect another.

Much of the 'old wine' approach depends on the notion that there is nothing new concerning the Internet. Multi-jurisdictional activity has become increasingly common since the changes in transportation and communication technologies in the first half of the 20th century. This coincided with the rise of the regulatory state, and despite the concerns of jurisdictional arbitrage, conflicts of jurisdictions became well understood. Even in legal cases dealing with multiple jurisdiction, courts applied universal customary laws tied to no particular sovereign authority, such as law merchant, the law maritime, or the law of nations. None of this is new. According to a leading legal expert on this approach, Jack Goldsmith:

> 'In modern times a transaction can legitimately be regulated by the jurisdiction where the transaction occurs, the jurisdictions where significant effects of the transaction are felt, and the jurisdictions where the parties burdened by the regulation are from.'[6]

In the case of data flows, this should be no different. Regarding the proponents of the 'new bottles' approach as 'regulation skeptics', Goldsmith argues:

> 'the skeptics underestimate the potential of traditional legal tools and technology to resolve the multi-jurisdictional regulatory problems implicated by cyberspace. Cyberspace transactions do not inherently warrant any more deference by national regulators, and are not significantly less resistant to the tools of conflict of laws, than other transnational transactions.'[7]

In truth, countries have been successfully regulating data flows. The European Union finalized a harmonizing directive on data protection in 1995 that included two articles regulating transborder data flows, preventing the transfer of data to countries without adequate data-protection laws. Countless countries have implemented some form of regulations on freedom of expression to regulate against harmful content.

Transnational conflicts have often been resolved through the harmonization of laws. With regards to the Internet, we have seen initiatives emerging from the United Nations, the Council of Europe, the Organizations for Security and Cooperation in Europe, and the G8 to deal with these conflicts and the differences in legal systems.

To sum up, there are those who use the 'new bottles' claim to argue that there are spillovers if one country regulates; and those who argue that the problem is merely 'old wine' in that it is possible to regulate multi-jurisdictional activity in the same way as we have always addressed conflicts. A solution to the whole debate about

---

[6] Jack L. Goldsmith, 'Against Cyberanarchy', University of Chicago Law School, *Occasional Papers* No. 40, <http://www.law.uchicago.edu/academics/againstcyberanarchy.html>.

[7] Ibid.

jurisdiction would be the generation of international standards for co-operation, and the harmonization of rules and practices. This is, after all, how we have always done things.

3.3 Reaching for Harmonization: International Co-operation in Criminal Matters

3.3.1 Co-operation as a response to terrorism

With data flows within transnational digital networks and the associated products and services, the transborder problems have become relatively clear. Action may occur from a distance, where the overflow of activity can occur without an individual having to physically enter the jurisdiction. Whether it is the penetration of computers or the downloading of pornography, this conduct can occur across borders preventing law-enforcement agencies, with their traditionally bordered jurisdictions, from conducting investigations and generating evidence. Therefore, the argument goes, we need to harmonize our practices.

When governments realized the challenges and new threats of terrorism involving sub-state actors and action at a distance involving high-tech crime, international solutions were immediately sought. Although such mechanisms were all used in other times, their frequency is increasing, leading to policies being adopted and laws being transformed. Governments are warned that failing to comply with international covenants and pressures may result in their countries becoming safe havens for criminality, being outed and shamed by the international community, their own law-enforcement agencies being unable to co-operate in international investigations, being unable to conduct national investigations due to insufficient capacity, or their own industries being unable to conduct commerce due to resultant trade and border restrictions.

One sign of the rise of international covenants to today's challenges is the response to the terrorist attacks of 11 September 2001.[8] The United Nations responded with Resolution 1368 calling on increased co-operation between countries to prevent and suppress terrorism. NATO invoked Article 5, claiming an attack on any NATO member country is an attack on all of NATO. The Council of Europe condemned the attacks, called for solidarity, and also called for increased co-operation in criminal matters. Later the Council of Europe Parliamentary Assembly called on countries to ratify conventions combating terrorism, lift any reservations in these agreements, and extend the mandate of police working groups. The European Union responded similarly, pushing for a European arrest warrant, common legislative frameworks for terrorism, increasing intelligence and police co-operation, freezing

[8] As I have written in the EPIC and Privacy International yearly report on Privacy and Human Rights, and Index on Censorship, September 2005.

assets and ensuring the passage of the Money Laundering Directive. The OECD furthered its support for the Financial Action Task Force on Money Laundering and, along with the G7/8 and the European Commission, called for the extension of its mandate to combat terrorist financing. Indeed, these responses seem rational and logical; terrorism is an international problem after all.

Since then, international organizations continue to be very busy. The Asia-Pacific Economic Community may have tense trade negotiations, but year in and year out declarations emerge calling for enhanced identity documents and travel surveillance. The Association of Southeast Asian Nations may disagree on how to deal with Burma, but they are willing to share intelligence information within the region. 'G5' nations, being Britain, France, Germany, Italy, and Spain, may disagree on trade barriers, tariffs, and foreign policy, but they meet frequently to agree on deportation, asylum, and communications surveillance policies. Whenever the G8 meets, one wonders whether tensions will flare between the United States and France or Russia on issues dealing with Iraq or Iran, but each summit ends with another declaration on the surveillance of travel and communications, or the standardization of identity documents. The Gulf Cooperation Council (GCC) meets yearly to call for the eradication of the 'filth' of terrorism, and calls for measures to regulate money laundering. In the Organization of American States, Brazil and Mexico may complain to the United States concerning new immigration practices that include fingerprinting all visitors; but peace reigns when the U.S. Department of State announces grants to fund the OAS for 'the training of customs and border officials, to study ways to improve border management practices, and to support a comprehensive aviation security program.'[9]

All these agreements mask vast differences between countries below the surface. It is almost easier to agree on counter-terrorism strategies than it is to wage war on a country, to settle trade disputes, or to establish environmental protocols. International co-operation is now part of the lingo of foreign relations. And the language seems intent on removing 'obstacles' to co-operation.

3.3.2 **Case: Maher Arar and the international co-operation in intelligence**

Increased calls for international co-operation may seem uncontroversial. In reality international co-operation can raise highly controversial situations, often creating more problems than it solves. What is more interesting is to note the differences, the strains, when co-operation goes awry, or when it goes all too well.

Consider the case of Maher Arar. Arar is Syrian-born but was carrying a Canadian passport when he was stopped and detained while changing planes on a trip from Tunisia and Switzerland through New York JFK airport on his way back to Canada on 26 September 2002. He was questioned by U.S. authorities using docu-

[9] U.S. Department of State press statement, 'State Department Support for Organization of American States Anti-terrorism Project', 4 August 2004.

ments attained from the Canadian police and intelligence services, and they searched through his computer for his contacts and any other information of value. After two weeks of continued detention and interrogation, he was informed by the Immigration and Naturalization Services that he would be sent to Syria; when he complained that he was likely to be tortured in Syria, he was informed that the INS was not the body that deals with the Geneva Convention regarding torture.[10] He was then flown on a U.S. Government plane to Jordan on condition that he would be sent to Syria. The Syrians claim to have imprisoned Arar as a gesture of goodwill toward the United States.[11]

While in Syria he claims he was tortured.[12] Ten months later the Syrians, looking to co-operate with someone after the United States had cut ties with Damascus, sent him back to Canada; though other reports claim that the Prime Minister of Canada had to write an appeal directly to Syria's President. When the U.S. Department of Justice was questioned on the deportation of Arar to a country known for its torturing of prisoners, the department spokesman stated: 'We acted fully within our laws and within the applicable international treaties and conventions.'[13] The then-Attorney General John Ashcroft claimed that he had received assurances from the Syrians that there would be no torture involved.[14] This was all at a time when the Bush Administration was staring down the Syrians over their support for terrorism in the run-up to the war in Iraq.

Even after repeated queries into the role that the Canadian authorities had played in his arrest and deportation, the Canadian Government continually refused to comment. The Canadian Prime Minister at the time, Jean Chrétien, later called Arar's treatment as 'unacceptable and deplorable', though not his responsibility. According to Chrétien, 'the people who are responsible for the deportation of this gentleman to Syria are in the government of the United States, not the government of Canada.'[15]

The next Prime Minister of Canada announced a judicial inquiry into what went wrong, as he said, 'to get to the bottom' of the case.[16] Even with this level of support for the inquiry, opposition to it was still mounted by the Canadian Government. The Government tried to prevent the disclosure of information and ensured

---

[10] Maher Arar's Statement, 4 November 2003.

[11] DeNeen L. Brown and Dana Priest, 'Chrétien Protests Deportation of Canadian: Prime Minister Calls U.S. Treatment of Terror Suspect "Completely Unacceptable"', *Washington Post* (6 November 2003), p. A24.

[12] Maher Arar's Statement, 4 November 2003.

[13] Curt Anderson, 'Ashcroft: No Laws Broken in Canada Case', *AP* (19 November 2003).

[14] Jeff Sallot, 'U.S. trusted Syria's assurances on Arar: Ashcroft', *Globe and Mail* (21 November 2003).

[15] Brown and Priest, loc. cit. n. 11.

[16] Jeff Sallot, 'Fighting release of Arar data normal, PM says', *Globe and Mail* (17 December 2004).

that the Government can secretly appeal any decisions made by the presiding judge that would divulge sensitive information.[17]

The information that eventually emerged from the inquiry shed some light on the dynamics between the various Government agencies on intelligence matters. Nine months into his detention in Syria, the Canadian Security Intelligence Services (CSIS) was concerned that the return of Arar would only cause problems. According to a draft note from the Department of Foreign Affairs,

> 'There is not sufficient evidence against Arar for him to be charged with anything in Canada. CSIS has made it clear to the department that they would prefer to have him remain in Syria, rather than return to Canada.'[18]

CSIS also admitted that the treatment that Arar received worried them because it would make it difficult to deport other people to Syria.[19] Similarly, the Royal Canadian Mounted Police (RCMP) admitted that though they had limited faith in the idea that he was a terrorist, the agency was concerned that his release could cause future embarrassment to Canada, particularly if it was eventually discovered that he was indeed a terrorist.[20] Finally the CSIS admitted that they have many agreements to share intelligence with countries that are suspected of engaging in torture, though they claim that such exchanges are done 'very carefully'.[21]

More information emerged from an internal inquiry by the RCMP. In this investigation it was found that

- the RCMP knew of the U.S. plans to deport Arar to Syria, but failed to notify others within the Canadian Government;
- the police did not obtain a search warrant when they seized documents relating to Arar's real estate, that was later used by the U.S. authorities as justification of his links with Al-Qaeda since a suspected terrorist had acted as a witness to a 1997 lease;
- the Government knew that Arar was on the U.S. terrorist watchlist and was even informed by U.S. officials that Arar was on his way to New York;
- the Canadian authorities had previously arranged to interview Arar but decided against this when he insisted that a lawyer be present;
- the Canadian Government faxed to the Americans a list of questions to ask Arar;
- Canadian authorities assured U.S. Government that their intelligence was reli-

[17] Colin Freeze, 'New secrecy laws delay Arar hearings', *Globe and Mail* (30 July 2004).

[18] Michael Den Tandt and Brian Laghi, 'CSIS wanted Arar kept in Syria, memo shows', *Globe and Mail* (4 June 2005).

[19] Oliver Morre, 'CSIS was worried Arar case could end deportations to Syria', *Globe and Mail* (20 December 2004).

[20] Colin Freeze, 'Mounties warned against release of Arar', *Globe and Mail* (27 November 2004).

[21] Colin Freeze, 'Torture ties may exist in Arar case, ex-spy chief says', *Globe and Mail* (22 June 2004).

able, though the internal investigation found 'the reliability assessment of that information was inaccurate.'[22]

The RCMP's internal inquiry predicted that even more information could be discovered but RCMP officers decided against speaking to the internal investigation because they felt that they should only testify to the forthcoming inquiry.

Months later the Government's lawyers at the judicial inquiry argued that RCMP officers should not be called to testify because it would jeopardize national security.[23] Syria also refused to co-operate with the judicial inquiry.[24] Despite previous statements to the media regarding Arar's certain guilt, the U.S. ambassador to Canada declined to participate in the inquiry, with officials from the U.S. Government stating that 'Our view is that it's not appropriate for foreign ambassadors to testify before committees of inquiry of nations other than their own.'[25]

Arar is also filing a civil suit in the United States against the U.S. authorities involved in his deportation. However, U.S. officials maintain that 'clear and unequivocal' but classified evidence shows that he is an Al-Qaeda member. They are seeking the dismissal of his lawsuit, partly by claiming privilege due to 'state secrets', arguing that the courts have no jurisdiction over national security and foreign relations.[26]

At the time these facts were being uncovered, the Solicitor General of Canada stressed that the Arar case should not prevent further co-operation and sharing of intelligence and other information with the United States. He argued: 'We need to keep our focus, and not lose our focus in terms of national security issues, over this incident or any other. We need to look forward.' Shortly thereafter, the Canadian Solicitor General and the U.S. Attorney General announced the creation of two more joint U.S.-Canada teams of law-enforcement, immigration and customs officials.[27]

I am being careful not to say anything regarding Arar's possible guilt. Technically it is not our job to assess that: clear procedures and courts of law establish guilt. Not immigration officers, Attorneys General, and Syrian authorities, Prime Ministers, Solicitors General, and others under the guise of 'international co-operation'. In a system as the one that we are developing, the great challenge will be how to trace accountability. One wonders where Arar's legal representatives could look to for jurisdiction over this case. The judicial inquiry has jurisdiction in Canada, though despite it being established by the Prime Minister, it could not call on those who are responsible for the activities in question. The inquiry could not establish

[22] Jeff Sallot, 'Mounties bungled Arar file', *Globe and Mail* (25 September 2004).

[23] Michael Den Tandt, 'RCMP shouldn't testify before Arar inquiry: Ottawa', *Globe and Mail* (3 May 2005).

[24] Colin Freeze, 'Syrians give Arar inquiry the cold shoulder', *Globe and Mail* (6 July 2004).

[25] Colin Freeze, 'U.S. envoy is latest to shun the Arar inquiry', *Globe and Mail* (9 July 2004).

[26] Nina Bernstein, 'U.S. Defends Detentions at Airports', *New York Times* (10 August 2005).

[27] Curt Anderson, 'Ashcroft: No Laws Broken in Canada Case', *AP* (19 November 2003).

jurisdiction over Syrian and U.S. authorities. The RCMP's internal investigation was a closed affair and yet could still not call the necessary witnesses. And Arar's standing in the United States is limited by the fact that he is a foreigner, and the courts have little jurisdiction over national security and foreign relations.

The Arar case personifies some of the pitfalls of international co-operation. We need to approach the topic with care and not presume that the sharing of intelligence, evidence, and individuals can be done freely without some form of restraint. And the outcomes are not always good.

3.4 Harmonization and International Co-operation involving Information Technology

3.4.1 Co-operation as a necessity for cybercrime

The extradition of individuals, the transfer of investigative data, and co-operation in the surveillance and the collection of evidence is increasingly a common component of most international agreements on criminal matters. Multilateral and international organizations are working to ease this co-operation through the creation of agreements, conventions, protocols, and standards. The Council of Europe was amongst the first to apply these principles to 'cybercrime'.

The substance of the Council of Europe Convention on Cybercrime is covered with authority elsewhere in this book.[28] Quickly put, the CoE convention consists of three sections. The first and second sections ensure that all countries have on their statute books the same substantive crimes (e.g., hacking) and similar powers of investigation (e.g., interception of communications, search and seizure).

The third section of the Convention enables international co-operation. This is arguably the most controversial component of the convention since it creates what can be considered as the largest and broadest mutual legal-assistance treaty to date. Surprisingly, though, most of the public attention for the convention focused on the investigative powers and substantive crimes. The Convention calls on all parties to co-operate

> 'to the widest extent possible for the purpose of investigations or proceedings concerning criminal offences related to computer systems and data, or for the collection of evidence in electronic form of a criminal offence.'[29]

The convention thus does not restrict this co-operation to cybercrime investigations; it involves co-operation in all investigations of criminal offences involving

[28] See chapter 2 of this book.

[29] Art. 23 Convention on Cybercrime (hereafter: CCC) on 'General principles relating to international co-operation.'

computer systems and data. It is fair to say that this is likely to incorporate most modern investigations.

The convention requires international co-operation in all forms of investigative powers. In accordance with the second section of the Convention, all countries must ensure that their national law-enforcement agencies may compel the preservation, disclosure and production of data, the search and seizure of computer systems, and real-time collection of data.[30] The international co-operation section ensures that all foreign law-enforcement agencies can compel a country to use domestic investigative powers upon request. If country B may assist country A in investigating a crime that occurred in country A, country B is practically obliged to respond to a request from A.

There are grounds for refusing to comply with a request from another country. Parties may refuse to assist in an investigation if it is believed that the suspected crime is deemed to be a political offence, prejudices its sovereignty, security, *ordre public*, or other essential interests.[31] The Explanatory Report of the Convention tries to disregard these grounds:

> 'In order to promote the overriding principle of providing the widest measure of co-operation (see Articles 23, 25), grounds for refusal established by a requested Party should be narrow and exercised with restraint. They may not be so expansive as to create the potential for assistance to be categorically denied, or subjected to onerous conditions, with respect to broad categories of evidence or information.'[32]

Similarly, refusal of assistance on privacy and data protection grounds may be invoked 'only in exceptional cases'.[33]

In a few limited circumstances, Governments may refuse assistance on grounds that the investigation fails the test of dual criminality. The principle of dual criminality is that country B can only co-operate with country A's investigation if the offence under investigation in country A is also a crime under the laws of country B. Without dual-criminality requirements, country B could be required to collect evidence on a citizen without that citizen having contravened any domestic law.

Although Governments may require dual criminality as a precondition for assistance, the convention does not support it. In fact, the convention obliges them to abandon or disregard dual criminality in the case of preservation of traffic data, i.e., logs and other data regarding communications made on-line. The convention's Explanatory Report argues that dual criminality is 'counterproductive' on a number of grounds. First, the 'modern trend' is to eliminate dual criminality for all but the most intrusive powers, and the preservation of traffic data is not considered by the

---

30 Chapter II section 2 CCC.

31 Art. 27(4) CCC.

32 Council of Europe, Convention on Cybercrime, *Explanatory Report*, available at <http://conventions.coe.int/Treaty/EN/Reports/Html/185.htm>.

33 Ibid., para. 269.

drafters as being intrusive as there is no disclosure of communication contents involved. Second, establishing dual criminality may take too long, and in that time data may be deleted, removed or altered.

Remarkably little is said on grounds for refusing assistance in real-time surveillance across borders. In the specific case of preservation and access to traffic data, the Convention acknowledges that domestic law may minimize co-operation because of the difficulty in providing access to this form of data. A requirement is established that 'each party shall provide such assistance at least with respect to criminal offences for which real-time collection of traffic data would be available in a similar domestic case.'[34] The use of 'at least', according to the CoE, is designed to encourage permission for as broad assistance as possible, 'even in the absence of dual criminality.' This is a remarkably lax assessment of the situation, particularly as the interception of communications and access to 'metering' data is a widely-acknowledged interference with the right to privacy under Article 8 of the European Convention on Human Rights.

Human-rights groups vocally opposed this lack of dual criminality and other basic protection in international co-operation. A number of entreaties were made by coalitions of NGOs but there was practically no response from the CoE. A coalition of data-protection regulators and officials in Europe also appealed to the CoE to change the policy arguing that while

> '[t]his is a desirable objective in terms of effective law enforcement and fight against crime. However, it may not pass the test of necessity, appropriateness and proportionality as required by Human Rights instruments implemented into constitutional and specific national law.'[35]

Industry was also concerned because of how this creates legal uncertainty. The European Telecommunications Networks Operators (ETNO) appealed to the CoE to change this component of the convention.

> 'Therefore, ETNO considers it essential that any proposed measures meet the following requirements: (...)
> Application of a dual criminality test in cases of cross-border cooperation
> Cross-border co-operation should not lead to operators or ISPs receiving directly orders from a foreign law enforcement body.'[36]

All of these articulated concerns did not lead to substantial changes in the convention, however.

---

[34] Art. 33(2) CCC.

[35] Art. 29 Working Party, 'Opinion 4/2001 On the Council of Europe's Draft Convention on Cybercrime' (22 March 2001), Brussels, 5001/01/EN/Final WP41.

[36] European Telecommunications Network Operators, 'ETNO Reflection Document on Data Protection and Privacy Aspects of the Draft Council of Europe Convention on Cyber-Crime (Version 25)', *ETNO Reflection Document* RD148 (2001/02).

Industry is indeed in the most precarious situation. According to David Goldstone and Betty-Ellen Shave, with Betty Shave being the head of cybercrime policy for the U.S. Department of Justice, harmonization of law would be ideal because otherwise uncertainty will prevail.

> 'The variation among procedural laws can be exacerbated by direct conflicts among the procedural laws of different countries. This problem is best exemplified by the scenario presented in In re Grand Jury Proceedings (United States v. Bank of Nova Scotia), where a Canadian bank was held in civil contempt for failing to comply with an order enforcing a grand jury subpoena duces tecum notwithstanding the fact that compliance with the subpoena would have required the bank to violate a Bahamian bank secrecy rule. As more companies take advantage of computer networks to operate internationally, those companies increasingly become subject to the laws of multiple nations. As more investigations of crime committed over those networks are conducted – and as the laws regulating privacy of electronic data evolve – more conflicts are sure to arise.'[37]

Interestingly, these differences in legal systems were acknowledged by the CoE, but instead of arguing for greater constraint in the prescribed powers, the differences were used to highlight the problems in requiring dual criminality for mutual legal assistance.

This leaves many actors within an investigation in precarious situations. Service providers may not know what investigation they are aiding, and whether the investigation is in fact legal; governments may not even know if the investigation they are ordering involves a breach of a domestic law; and individuals who are the subject of these investigations may have few rights of recourse. In the next section I will present a practical situation of how international co-operation in investigations can create unique, and troubling, situations.

3.4.2 **Case: Investigating Indymedia**

'Indymedia' (IMC) describes itself as 'a network of individuals, independent and alternative media activists and organizations, offering grassroots, non-corporate, non-commercial coverage of important social and political issues.'[38] According to Indymedia, its content is widely read, with the transfer of over 3.2 terabytes of information a month, serving over 18 million page views a month.

On 7 October 2004, over 20 websites administered by the Independent Media Center were taken off-line. This was a result of the seizing of two servers, named 'Ahimsa1' and 'Ahimsa2', that served the content of a number of media 'collectives' around the world.

---

[37] David Goldstone and Betty-Ellen Shave, 'International Dimensions of Crimes in Cyberspace', 22 *Fordham International Law Journal* (1999) p. 1924.

[38] See <http://www.indymedia.org.uk/en/static/about_us.html>.

While there is no central hub to this organization, a volunteer for IMC established a contractual relationship with Rackspace Managed Hosting, a San Antonio-based Internet hosting company. The servers were physically located in London, England. The contract was between Rackspace UK and the said individual.

On 7 October 2004, Rackspace informed the individual that Rackspace had received a U.S. commissioner's subpoena from a 'requesting agency'. Though Rackspace refused to provide a copy of the subpoena on the advice of counsel, on 8 October Rackspace released a statement.

> 'In the present matter regarding Indymedia, Rackspace Managed Hosting, a U.S. based company with offices in London, is acting in compliance with a court order pursuant to a Mutual Legal Assistance Treaty (MLAT), which establishes procedures for countries to assist each other in investigations such as international terrorism, kidnapping and money laundering. Rackspace responded to a Commissioner's subpoena, duly issued under Title 28, United States Code, Section 1782 in an investigation that did not arise in the United States. Rackspace is acting as a good corporate citizen and is cooperating with international law enforcement authorities. The court prohibits Rackspace from commenting further on this matter.'[39]

A 'commissioner's subpoena' under Title 28 section 1782 U.S.C. enables a Court to authorize an individual, usually an assistant U.S. attorney, to issue subpoenas in order to assist foreign and international tribunals.

According to reports from AFP, an FBI spokesperson stated that the subpoena was 'on behalf of a third country', but the FBI spokesperson later said that the FBI was not involved. Indymedia and the associated news coverage spent the next few days trying to find out who that 'third country' was. The facts seemed to point to Switzerland, Italy, or the United Kingdom. The Swiss were suspected because Swiss authorities had previously placed pressure on Indymedia for information on posters and demanded the removal of content. On 12 October a Swiss federal prosecutor admitted that while he was investigating a case involving Indymedia, he had not asked for a seizure. There were some reports that the Italians were seeking the servers but there was no explanation as to why.

The greatest confusion arose when it became a political issue in the United Kingdom. On a number of occasions MPs asked the UK Government in Parliament as to what happened. When asked which UK law-enforcement agency was involved in the seizure that had after all taken place in London, the Home Office Minister responded on 18 October: 'I can confirm that no UK law-enforcement agencies were involved in the matter referred to in the question posed by the Hon. Member for Sheffield, Hallam.'[40]

On 27 October the Government was asked which foreign governments had requested the seizure of the servers. The Government responded that no one had

---

39 9 October 2004, audio available at <http://houston.indymedia.org/news/2004/10/33604.php>.

40 Hansard (20 October 2004).

asked for anything, and on 2 November it was confirmed that not even the Americans had made representations in the case. Though in a letter response to a question from one MP, a Home Office Minister stated that

> 'Unfortunately, I am not in a position to comment on this particular matter, but I can provide general information. It is standard Home Office policy neither to confirm nor deny the existence or receipt of a mutual legal assistance request. However, where the UK has received a valid request, we will seek to execute it within the framework of our domestic law. This will include being provided with sufficient evidence to justify the actions sought.'[41]

The Home Secretary himself admitted on the 28th of October that the Home Office had not even received a prior notification of the seizure. In a letter in response to a query from an MP, the Home Secretary stated that:[42]

> 'While I cannot comment in detail on the reasons behind the US action I hope that I can clarify the situation for him. Rackspace, which is based in the USA, sought to comply with a US court order simply by ordering their United Kingdom subsidiary to access the servers, which they duly did. There was no UK involvement in this process. I am confident that any action taken by the US authorities in this case would be in accordance with US law.'[43]

The fact that the British authorities were not involved in a seizure on British territory was quite surprising to everyone involved.

There was a public response to this specific case, particularly over the lack of certainty as to who actually seized the server and for what purposes. As Mark Thomas said in the New Statesman, this case 'was the equivalent of the FBI storming the Guardian's offices and demanding that the paper hand over all its computers, including those that hold details of its writers and photographers.'[44] Jeremy Dear, General Secretary of the British NUJ, put it similarly: 'To take away a server is like taking away a broadcaster's transmitter. It is simply incredible that American security agents can just walk into a London office and remove equipment.'[45]

Civil society also entered the fray. Anriette Estherhuysen of the Association for Progressive Communication stated that: 'We are disturbed by the apparently arbi-

---

[41] Letter from Caroline Flint to Glenda Jackson MP, available at <http://www.indymedia.org.uk/en/2004/11/300405.html>.

[42] It may be relevant to note that the recipient of the letter was a former Home Secretary now on the opposition benches.

[43] Letter from David Blunkett to Michael Howard (8 November 2004), available at <http://www.indymedia.org.uk/en/2004/11/301362.html>.

[44] 'Mark Thomas finds that Voltaire has been rewritten' (8 November 2004), <http://www.newstatesman.com/200411080014>.

[45] National Union of Journalists, 'Protest at Indymedia seizure' (13 October 2004), <http://www.nuj.org.uk/inner.php?docid=824>.

trary and extreme measures taken to silence an independent internet-based source of information. This is a violation of freedom of expression across international frontiers.'[46] The editor of the International Press Institute, David Dadge, was quoted as saying: 'The fact that the authorities' actions are shrouded in mystery leaves Indymedia in the Kafkaesque position of not knowing the identity of its accusers or the nature of their claim.'[47]

Rackspace reported that the servers were returned on 12 October and were operational by 14 October. It was only at about that time that it was discovered why these actions may have taken place. An Italian prosecutor in Bologna was quoted in an article as saying that she had requested IP log information through an MLAT to the United States, but did not seek the seizure.

Indymedia then decided that lawyers in the United Kingdom, Italy, and the United States must be able to communicate with each other to start unraveling what had happened. A UK law firm advised Indymedia that it could do little to pursue a case against Rackspace without access to the actual subpoena.

The Electronic Frontier Foundation (EFF), a U.S.-based non-governmental organization, came to Indymedia's aid by filing a motion on 25 October 2004 to unseal the subpoena and other information relating to the case in the U.S. EFF sought to uncover which agencies and governments were responsible for the seizure. In its motion, the EFF argued that Indymedia and the general public were left with no knowledge of the reasons or nature of the seizure.

> 'Citing a gag order, Rackspace has not revealed the contents of the seizure order, the requesting agency, or even confirmed the identity of the court that issued it. Apparently requested by an unidentified foreign government, the secret order was served to San Antonio-based Rackspace Managed Hosting, which hosts IndyMedia's servers.'[48]

The motion was filed on the grounds that in U.S. law one has the right of access to know the reasons for direct injuries under First and Fourth amendment rights (freedom of speech and protection from unlawful search and seizure), and even under common law by stating that 'the public and the press have a clear and compelling interest in discovering under what authority the government was able to unilaterally prevent Internet publishers from exercising their First Amendment rights.'[49]

The Assistant U.S. Attorney Don J. Calvert argued the Government's case for keeping the files sealed. First, the Government argued that neither EFF nor Indymedia

---

[46] 'APC condemns 'arbitrary' seizure of IndyMedia web servers by US and European law enforcers' (12 October 2004), <http://www.apc.org/english/news/index.shtml?x=26809>.

[47] Quoted in IMC Press Release No. 4 (14 October 2004), 'Indymedia's hardware is returned, but many questions remain', <http://docs.indymedia.org/view/Global/AhimsaPressrelease>.

[48] EFF, 'Press Release: EFF Challenges Secret Court Order: Motion Demands Information About the Seizure of Indymedia's Servers', <http://www.eff.org/news/archives/2004_10.php#002029>.

[49] EFF to the United States District Court of Western District of Texas, San Antonio Division, In re Commissioner's Subpoena to Rackspace managed hosting, Motion to unseal and for expedited hearing, <http://www.eff.org/Censorship/20041022_Indymedia_Motion_to_Unseal.pdf>.

have standing to make the request: 'The parties to the instant action are the requesting foreign country, the United States government, and the party on whom the subpoena was served, Rackspace'.[50]

The Government also argued that Article 8 of the treaty between the United States and the 'requesting country' entitled 'protecting confidentiality and restricting use of evidence and information' and states:

> '2. If deemed necessary, the Requesting State may *request* that the application for assistance, the contents of the request and its supporting documents, and the granting of such assistance be kept confidential'. [emphasis added]

The Government stated that since such a request had been made to the United States, the unsealing of the documents would violate the treaty, and under Article VI of the Constitution, treaties shall be the supreme law of the land to which judges of every state shall be bound. Finally, the Government argued that the documents 'pertained to an ongoing criminal terrorism investigation' and the unsealing would 'seriously jeopardize the investigation'. 'The non-disclosure is necessitated by a compelling government interest.'

The EFF had its opportunity to respond in turn. On the issue of jurisdiction and standing, the EFF responded that parties who are not part of the litigation still have standing to challenge the closure of judicial proceedings or confidentiality orders. On the issue of confidentiality and the said 'treaty', the EFF was able to find the treaty that was being quoted and discovered that it was in fact the treaty on mutual legal assistance between the United States and Italy from 1985. The EFF went to that treaty and saw that the Government was quoting from Article 8(2); but EFF pointed that Article 8(1) states that:

> '1. When necessary, the Requested State may *require* that evidence and information provided, and information derived therefrom, be kept confidential in accordance with stated conditions.' [emphasis added]

The EFF argued that this language meant that the U.S. may *require* confidentiality but Italy may only *request* it. The EFF went on to say: 'The provision cited by the Government is permissive rather than compulsory, and as this Court had the discretion to decline Italy's confidentiality request, it has the power to unseal the documents after the fact.' The EFF also reminded the court that no treaty obligation to a foreign government can trump the Bill of Rights.

On the issue as to whether there is a compelling need due to the 'ongoing criminal terrorist' investigation, the EFF argued that despite the reference to terrorism,

[50] Don J. Calvert the Assistant United States Attorney to the United States District Court of Western District of Texas, San Antonio Division, In re: Commissioner's Subpoena to Rackspace managed hosting, Government's Response to Motion to Unseal, <http://www.eff.org/Censorship/Indymedia/20041109_indymedia_govt_response.pdf>.

the Government failed to assert a national security interest in non-disclosure. And anyway, the EFF noted, it is well established that 'important First Amendment values' cannot be overcome by 'a mere assertion of "national security".' The EFF also pointed out that as it became clearer that the request was for assistance in an Italian criminal matter, and that the order was unrelated to any federal investigation, and that even Italy has spoken about the case to AP where the prosecutor was quoted as saying that she sought the logs investigating a specific case involving Romano Prodi, the then-President of the European Commission, the EFF concluded that the Government's argument was falling apart. Confidentiality was therefore unnecessary.

On 20 July 2005, the court granted the EFF's motion and ordered most of the documents to be unsealed but with redaction.[51] The documentation was released on 1 August 2005. What it disclosed was just as alarming as the circumstances of the case known to date. The case details became more colored. On 30 July 2004, the request was received from Italy and filed in the U.S. District Court and was sealed. It requested the production of logs from the necessary servers.[52] U.S. assistant attorney Calvert requested the job of commissioner on the case to collect evidence on behalf of the court. This authorizes the commissioner to submit the evidence collected to the requesting foreign court or authority. In arguing for this, the Government stated that

> '[i]n executing Italian requests, the Treaty obligates United States courts to compel a person to produce a document, record or article or to appear and testify "to the same extent as would be required for criminal investigations or proceedings" in the United States.'

The request came from Minister of Grace and Justice of the Italian Government in connection with an investigation by the Bologna Public Prosecutor's office (BPP) asking for assistance in obtaining records of log files in relation to the creation and updating of the web spaces of specific URLs during the period of the events of the case. The case involved a number of attacks on European officials using explosives in delivery packages. The delivery packages included letters explaining the attacks. The BPP launched an investigation under Section 280 of the Italian Penal Code, i.e., 'Attacks for terrorist or subversive purposes', punishable by a term of not less than six years' imprisonment.

[51] United States District Court for the Western District of Texas, San Antonio Division, In re: Request from Requesting State Pursuant to the Treaty Between the United States of America and the Requesting State on Mutual Assistance in Criminal Matters in the Matter of Romano Prodi, Order Granting in part Motion to Unseal, Orlando L. Garcia, U.S. District Judge (20 July 2005), <http://www.eff.org/Censorship/Indymedia/order_unsealing.pdf>.

[52] In re: Mutual Assistance in Criminal Matters in the Matter of Romano Prodi (Received 30 July 2004), <http://www.eff.org/Censorship/Indymedia/unsealed/01.pdf>.

Copies of the letters in the explosive packages were found on the Indymedia site, though the URLs were redacted from the unsealed documents. The Italian request named Indymedia as being at a Seattle address, and named Rackspace in San Antonio as the hosting company. Judge Orlando Garcia of the San Antonio Division Court approved the appointment of Calvert as a Commissioner of the court to: collect evidence through Commissioner's subpoenas, provide notice to those who are identified in the request as parties to whom notice should be given ('and no notice to any other party shall be required'), and adopt procedures to collect the evidence requested, consistent with its use in the investigation or proceeding for which Italy has requested assistance.[53]

One outstanding issue is that on 21 December 2004, U.S. Assistant Attorney Calvert certified that he authorized a subpoena to Rackspace compelling the production of a copy of the server in order to get the logs.[54] However, the original Commissioner's subpoena to Rackspace from Calvert demanded only 'log files in relation to the creation and updating of the web spaces corresponding to' particular URLs.[55] Rackspace reported that it had received a federal order to provide hardware, but the court documents are conflicting on this matter.

Another outstanding issue from the Indymedia case is how could the United States seize hardware from the United Kingdom without the support of the UK authorities? The UK government was surprisingly open concerning its lack of participation in the seizure. There may be a case to make that Rackspace UK overreacted to the request from the U.S. authorities. UK legal advisors to Indymedia did not feel as though they could take Rackspace UK to task for handing over the server, they were not in a position to do so until the subpoena had been unsealed. Whether Rackspace UK is at fault is a matter that can now be decided by the courts.

It can be argued, however, that Rackspace was fully complying with U.S. law. Goldstone and Shave above pointed to the likely conflict of laws that would arise particularly due to the case of *United States* v. *Bank of Nova Scotia*.[56] In that case, the Bank of Nova Scotia refused to respond to a request from the U.S. authorities for banking information because the information was kept in the Bahamas; granting access to this information would break Bahamian banking secrecy laws. In this case the courts decided against the Bank of Nova Scotia. According to the court,

> 'In a world where commercial transactions are international in scope, conflicts are inevitable. Courts and legislatures should take every reasonable precaution to avoid

[53] In re: Mutual Assistance in Criminal Matters in the Matter of Romano Prodi, Order (31 July 2004), <http://www.eff.org/Censorship/Indymedia/unsealed/05.pdf>.

[54] In re: Mutual Assistance in Criminal Matters, Certification (21December 2004), <http://www.eff.org/Censorship/Indymedia/unsealed/18.pdf>.

[55] Commissioners Subpoena, United States District Court Western District of Texas, to Rackspace Managed Hosting (13 August 2004), <http://www.eff.org/Censorship/Indymedia/commissioners_subpoena.pdf>.

[56] In re: Grand Jury Proceedings (*United States* v. *Bank of Nova Scotia*), 691 F.2d 1384 (11th Cir. 1982), cert. denied, 462 US 1119 (1983).

> placing individuals in the situation [the Bank] finds itself. Yet, this court simply cannot acquiesce in the proposition that United States criminal investigations must be thwarted whenever there is conflict with the interest of other states. (…) The foreign origin of the subpoenaed documents should not be a decisive factor. The nationality of the Bank is Canadian, but its presence is pervasive in the United States. The Bank has voluntarily elected to do business in numerous foreign host countries and has accepted the incidental risk of occasional inconsistent governmental actions. It cannot expect to avail itself of the benefits of doing business here without accepting the concomitant obligations.'

Rackspace is left in the situation where it is complying with U.S. law and yet possibly breaking UK law, and this is entirely legal because Rackspace elected to do business in the United Kingdom.

This is a very surprising rationale that goes against everything we were once promised when we heard of such things as globalization and the Internet. What is most surprising is that this has always been the law of the land, it is not the creation of the Cybercrime Convention that enabled this multi-jurisdictional quagmire. Rather, the convention may result in making the matter worse. It is indeed old wine – one that has only matured.

3.5 Can International Co-operation be Regulated?

In each of the cases described above, every actor was placed in a number of precarious positions.

- Canadian authorities shared data with U.S. authorities to conduct investigations in a manner that failed in Canada. The U.S. authorities conducted action on a connecting-flight passenger as though he was attempting to get access to the United States. Syria acted as an arm of the United States in taking Arar but was also very much in trouble with the U.S. administration at the time. And Arar was sent to the country of his birth instead of the country of his citizenship and even final destination.
- Indymedia communities in Brazil had their information taken off-line because Italian investigators asked the U.S. authorities to grant them access to information on visitors to a site hosted in the United Kingdom by a company that is originally based in Texas. We could ask why the Italians did not go directly to the British authorities, but this was possibly because they did not know that the servers were hosted in the United Kingdom. In fact we will never know, because as the UK Home Secretary stated, the government of the United Kingdom does not comment on mutual legal-assistance matters.

Something is indeed happening to jurisdiction. During the times of kings and queens and emperors, jurisdiction was a matter of sovereignty, the freedom of the sovereign to decide what is good and what is right. After this period it can be said that it became a matter of legitimacy: laws applied to the reach of the courts, and these laws were made by the hand of legislators. Even the executive was to be tied down by the courts and the law.

With the advent of globalization and increased concerns of sub-state actors operating at the global scale, we have also created regimes of international co-operation that are increasingly informal. Before, when two countries wished to co-operate, judges had to sign agreements, letters were sent by diplomats, and the process could take years. We have replaced that system with a more stealthy set of procedures. But these procedures lack accountability and can create more problems than they solve.

Small organizations like Indymedia end up having to try to establish legal links in three countries. Individuals like Maher Arar find it challenging to get their own country to claim jurisdiction over their welfare. In both cases, traditional structures have stepped in to try to resolve what had gone wrong; I worry that these are the exception to the rule. Due to media attention, both the Indymedia and Arar cases managed to be raised at the highest levels in respective governments. Inquiries and appeals were launched. This cannot have been the first time or the last time that such powers will be used, but this is among the only cases that have garnered such attention.

Yet we continue to develop this new system of co-operation, just presuming that it is good and necessary. Countries are claiming that we must all ratify the Convention on Cybercrime that enables exactly this form of co-operation across borders, ranging from extradition to seizure. We do not question this momentum towards international agreements and conventions and instead we shame countries who act unilaterally. The Solicitor General of Canada argued that we should not stop the Arar case from letting us create more agreements with the United States on such matters; and Canadian authorities worried that Arar's story may prevent further deportations to Syria. And so the ball rolls on and we continue to generate more of these agreements and conventions. And they continue to be seen as positive steps forward and inevitable.

The accountability in these new systems is appalling. Every actor involved in each of these cases tried to avoid answering questions. The most common answer was that the askers of these questions were beyond their jurisdiction. The United States is refusing to answer for Arar's treatment by saying that he is without standing in the courts and the courts have no standing on matters of national security; likewise, the U.S. authorities argued that Indymedia had no standing because only Rackspace was implicated by the subpoena. Getting information out of the Italians and the Canadians was no easier, even while the British claimed that they do not discuss such matters. It is probably fair to say that if the British had been approached instead of the U.S. authorities, we would never have heard about the case at all. This is an opaque system that we are building.

Few are monitoring these developments. Our accountability structures of courts, the media, and even civil society are mostly focused on national developments, even all these years after the dawn of globalization. This seems to render the old debate over whether this involves old wine or new bottles almost silly. Both sides of the debate were correct: national laws will hamper our international development, and yet conflicts of laws have always occurred so there is nothing really new. More of these types of developments are to come, and old problems will hamper our new bottles.

The purpose of this chapter was not to try to solve the debate. Rather it was to point out that jurisdiction is still a contentious issue. We must not see international co-operation as some inevitable or benign event. We must look closely at what happens and ask the question whether, after all these years of removing the divine rights of kings and transforming our political systems into democracies operating under the rule of law, now is really the right time to return to informal systems that create legal limbos that we worked so hard to avoid.

Bibliography

YAMAN AKDENIZ, 'Case Analysis of League against Racism and Antisemitism (Licra), French Union of Jewish Students, v. Yahoo! Inc. (USA), Yahoo France, Tribunale De Grande Instance De Paris, Interim Court Order, 20 November 2000', 1 *Electronic Business Law Reports* (2001) No. 3.

EPIC AND PRIVACY INTERNATIONAL, *Privacy and Human Rights 2004*, available at <http://www.privacyinternational.org/phr>.

JACK L. GOLDSMITH, 'Against Cyberanarchy', University of Chicago Law School, *Occasional Papers* No. 40, <http://www.law.uchicago.edu/academics/againstcyberanarchy.html>.

DAVID GOLDSTONE AND BETTY-ELLEN SHAVE, 'International Dimensions of Crimes in Cyberspace', 22 *Fordham International Law Journal* (1999) p. 1924.

INDEX ON CENSORSHIP, 'Globalising Big Brother' (September 2005).

DAVID R. JOHNSON AND DAVID G. POST, 'Law And Borders-The Rise of Law in Cyberspace', 48 *Stanford Law Review* (1996) p. 1367, <http://www.cli.org/X0025_LBFIN.html#I.%20%20Breaking%20Down%20Territorial%20Borders>.

JONATHAN W. LEEDS, 'United States International Law Enforcement Cooperation: A Case Study in Thailand', 7 *Journal of International Law and Practice* (1998) pp. 1-14.

Chapter 4
CYBERCRIME AND JURISDICTION IN AUSTRALIA

Gregor Urbas and Peter Grabosky*

4.1 INTRODUCTION[1]

The importance of jurisdiction in the investigation and prosecution of crimes that can easily be committed across borders is increasingly being highlighted by cybercrime.[2] Given the generally borderless nature of cyberspace, it is clear that crimes involving computers may involve offenders located in one jurisdiction (or several), victims located in another (or several others), facilitated using technology in yet others, and possibly having effects in still other jurisdictions.[3]

To take just one recent example, Romanian computer hackers sent an e-mail in May 2003 to the National Science Foundation's Amundsen-Scott South Pole Station science research facility, demanding money with the threat that they would otherwise send details of life-support systems and other data found on the station's server to 'another country' in order to expose its vulnerability. The e-mail contained data found only on the South Pole research facility's computer systems, demonstrating that it was not a hoax. The message also indicated that the network had

* Dr Gregor Urbas is Lecturer in Law at the Australian National University. Prof. Peter Grabosky is Professor in the Regulatory Institutions Network at the Australian National University.

[1] This chapter draws in part on material published in R.G. Smith, P. Grabosky and G. Urbas, *Cyber Criminals on Trial* (Cambridge, Cambridge University Press 2004). The authors would like to acknowledge the advice of Geoff Gray and Nigel Phair on earlier versions of this chapter. Opinions and interpretations herein are those of the authors and not necessarily those of the Australian Government.

[2] S.W. Brenner and B.J. Koops, 'Approaches to Cybercrime Jurisdiction', 4 *Journal of High Technology Law* (2004) p. 1. The term 'cybercrime' has increasingly replaced other expressions such as 'computer crime' or 'electronic crime' in recent literature; see Smith, et al., loc. cit. n. 1. It has also been adopted in some legal instruments, such as the Cybercrime Act 2001 (Cth) in Australia and the Council of Europe Convention on Cybercrime which came into force in July 2004.

[3] See D. Lanham, *Cross-Border Criminal Law* (FT Law and Tax Asia Pacific 1997); M. Hinton and C. Lind, 'The Territorial Application of the Criminal Law – When Crime is Not Local', 23 *Criminal Law Journal* (1999) p. 285; D.L. Speer, 'Redefining borders: The challenges of cybercrime', 34 *Crime, Law and Social Change* (2000) p. 259; S. Bronitt and M. Gani, 'Shifting Boundaries of Cybercrime: From Computer Hacking to Cyberterrorism', 27 *Criminal Law Journal* (2003) p. 303 at pp. 312-313; and P. Grabosky, 'Crime in a Shrinking World', *Trends and Issues in Crime and Criminal Justice* (March 1998) No. 83, available at <http://www.aic.gov.au/publications/tandi/tandi83.html>.

B-J. Koops and S.W. Brenner (Eds), Cybercrime and Jurisdiction

been penetrated, potentially with software that would cause harm if triggered by the hacker. With the involvement of the United States' Federal Bureau of Investigation (FBI) and Romanian police, the e-mail was traced to a Bucharest Internet cafe and two locals were arrested.[4]

As this example illustrates, the success of any investigation and prosecution involving such trans-jurisdictional cybercrimes depends heavily on international co-operation. Criminal justice authorities around the world have been co-operating for many decades in locating and arresting offenders, assisted greatly by formal agreements on extradition and mutual assistance in criminal matters. However, these mechanisms are themselves subject to international political relations, as Alldridge observes:[5]

> 'At the intersection of criminal law and international relations is the question of jurisdiction. Bad relations between states will lead to refusal to extradite, generous provision as to asylum and strict geographical limits upon jurisdiction. Good relations, or interdependence between states will lead to shared police information, shared policing, mutual cooperation and either reciprocal jurisdiction, or to granting "full faith and credit" to the laws of the other, with mechanistic extradition arrangements, including extradition without double criminality, or both.'

Thus, while the formal mechanisms governing jurisdiction and international co-operation can be described from the perspective of each country, it is important to bear in mind that less formal modes of communication between prosecutors and other government officials can be equally important in determining outcomes.

At a more formal level, it has been recognized for some time that differences between national laws and investigative procedures can be an impediment to transnational co-operation, so that international harmonization of important legal provisions is increasingly seen as desirable. In the cybercrime context, the most obvious response to this need for harmonization is the Council of Europe's Convention on Cybercrime, which came into force in July 2004.[6] Although Australia is not a signatory to this Convention, its provisions as incorporated into earlier drafts notably influenced the drafting of the Cybercrime Act 2001 (Cth), which is Australia's most important legislative advance in responding to the emerging threat of cybercrime, both nationally and internationally. This legislation is discussed in detail below.

Australian police and prosecutors also have to deal with the complexity that arises from a federal legal system with differences between laws within the country,

---

4 Federal Bureau of Investigation (FBI), 'The case of the Hacked South Pole' (18 July 2003), <http://www.fbi.gov/page2/july03/071803backsp.htm>.

5 P. Alldridge, *Relocating Criminal Law* (Aldershot, Ashgate 2000), p. 140, as cited in S. Bronitt and B. McSherry, *Principles of Criminal Law* (LBC 2001), p. 82.

6 See Council of Europe, 'Entry into force of the Council of Europe Convention on Cybercrime' (March 2004), <http://press.coe.int/cp/2004/135a(2004).htm>.

as well as those that exist internationally. Given that many criminal offences are governed by state and territory rather than by national law, there has been a parallel concern to harmonize laws and procedures within Australia. As pointed out in a recent governmental report:[7]

> 'The use of the same powers for intrastate and interstate investigations would avoid the complexities that could arise from the operation of two different sets of investigation powers. It would also eliminate the need for law-enforcement agencies to determine at an early stage in an investigation whether the criminal activities that are the subject of the investigation extend to other jurisdictions or are confined to one jurisdiction.'

Thus, the problem of jurisdictional divergence is especially relevant to the Australian response to cybercrime. Fortunately, considerable progress has been made towards a nationally agreed model, with several states and territories enacting laws based on the Cybercrime Act 2001 (Cth). It is expected that this process of harmonization will continue towards an increasingly national position.

With these considerations in mind, this chapter analyses cybercrime jurisdiction from an Australian perspective.

4.2 National Cybercrime Legislation

4.2.1 Jurisdictional overview

Australia has a federal legal system encompassing state, territory and Commonwealth laws. The six Australian states are New South Wales (NSW), Queensland (Qld), South Australia (SA), Tasmania (Tas), Victoria (Vic) and Western Australia (WA). As colonies, these united into a federation in 1901, forming the Commonwealth of Australia. The two main territories are the Australian Capital Territory (ACT) and the Northern Territory (NT), both established after federation and initially governed under the Commonwealth's legal jurisdiction but now self-governing. The complexity of Australian cybercrime legislation is largely due to the fact that each of these six states, the two territories, and the Commonwealth have their own criminal legislation and have enacted their own cybercrime laws.

The Australian Constitution provides that Commonwealth law is paramount in the sense that where an inconsistency arises between a valid Commonwealth law and a state law, the former prevails and the latter is invalid to the extent of the

[7] Leaders Summit on Terrorism and Multi-jurisdictional Crime, Cross-Border Investigative Powers for Law Enforcement, Report of the Standing Committee of Attorneys-General and Australasian Police Ministers Council Joint Working Group on National Investigation Powers, November 2003, available at <http://www.ag.gov.au>, page v; see also S. Cuthbertson, 'Mutual Assistance in Criminal Matters: Beyond 2000', 75 *Australian Law Journal* (2001) pp. 326-336.

inconsistency (s. 109). Given that the Commonwealth also has legislative power with respect to the territories (s. 122), Commonwealth laws also prevail over any inconsistent territory laws. In principle, therefore, it would be possible for the Commonwealth to assert legislative control over cybercrime by 'covering the field' in this area of law. However, there are important constitutional limits on the Commonwealth's legislative power.

Unlike the states and territories, which have general legislative power for the 'peace, order and good government' of their respective jurisdictions, the Commonwealth's legislative power is limited to prescribed topics (sections 51 and 52), such as international and inter-state trade and commerce, taxation, corporations, external affairs, currency and banking, intellectual property, etc. There is no general legislative power with respect to criminal laws, which are traditionally a state and territory matter. However, the Commonwealth can enact criminal offences in relation to its particular legislative competencies. Thus, Commonwealth offences exist in relation to corporate misconduct, some forms of fraud, telecommunications, crimes against internationally protected persons, terrorism, copyright piracy and trade mark infringement, to name a few. Clearly, some of these offences will be applicable to situations involving computers, but there is no single legislative competence with respect to cybercrime. Nonetheless, the Commonwealth's jurisdiction in this area has expanded dramatically.

4.2.2 **Historical overview of computer-crime laws**

During the 1980s, several Australian states and the Northern Territory enacted computer-specific offences relating to confidential information and unauthorized access to data. The states and territories also began to amend their existing criminal offences and laws relating to obscene publications, so that they applied where computers and computer-related technology were involved. These laws applied to all computers within their respective jurisdictions, but in 1989, the Commonwealth used its own legislative powers to enact criminal offences specifically protecting Commonwealth computers and data. The Commonwealth offences (former sections 76A–76F of the *Crimes Act 1914* (Cth)) criminalized unlawful access to or impairment of Commonwealth computers and data, carrying maximum penalties of up to ten years' imprisonment, as well as the use of Commonwealth facilities to commit other crimes. These offences were used through the 1990s, particularly in relation to computer fraud by employees of Commonwealth government departments.[8] Prosecutions under state and territory laws continued in parallel with these Commonwealth prosecutions. Where the offence involved Commonwealth computers, the Commonwealth Director of Public Prosecutions (CDPP) would normally have carriage of the matter, but otherwise state and territory authorities dealt with matters such as Internet fraud, on-line pornography and so on.

---

[8] See Smith, et al., loc. cit. n. 1, at p. 92 et seq.

At the beginning of the new millennium, however, the Commonwealth substantially expanded its jurisdictional reach by relying on its legislative power with respect to 'postal, telegraphic, telephonic, and other like services' under section 51(v) of the Constitution. This underpins Commonwealth laws on telecommunications, and with the enactment of the *Cybercrime Act 2001* (Cth), the *Criminal Code Act 1995* (Cth) was amended to include all Commonwealth computer-crime laws, including new offences relating to electronic communications. In particular, these laws criminalize any unauthorized access to or modification of computer data or impairment of electronic communications, where this is caused by means of a telecommunications service, with intent to commit a serious Commonwealth, state or territory offence (s. 477.1). This means that a good deal of computer hacking via the Internet, for example, in order to defraud or extort money, now falls within the scope of the *Cybercrime Act*. Of course, minor and non-Internet based unauthorized access or modification will still be prosecuted under state or territory computer-crime laws.[9]

The Commonwealth further expanded its regulatory control over the Internet with the enactment of the *Spam Act 2003* (Cth). This does not contain criminal offences as such, but allows for the imposition of large fines on persistent senders of unsolicited electronic messages.[10] The Commonwealth also has a leading role in setting standards for Internet content, through its classification system for films, video games, and publicly available web site content.

Finally, the Commonwealth has continued to expand its jurisdiction in relation to the Internet and electronic communications by enacting a suite of new telecommunications offences, including Internet child-pornography offences.[11] In addition, there have been new terrorism offences enacted over the past few years that may extend to forms of computer misuse approximating 'cyber-terrorism'.[12]

4.2.3 **Specific cybercrime provisions**

Hacking and related offences

All Australian jurisdictions have offences relating to unauthorized access and modification, with increasing harmonization towards the Commonwealth model.[13] As

---

[9] See G. Urbas and R. Smith, 'Computer Crime Legislation in Australia', 7 *Internet Law Bulletin* (2004) No. 2, pp. 53-56.

[10] See P. Argy, 'Will the new Code keep the lid on spam?', 8 *Internet Law Bulletin* (2005) No. 1, pp. 1-4.

[11] See E. Wong, 'Tough new laws for child pornography and other internet offences', 7 *Internet Law Bulletin* (2004) p. 89 at p. 104.

[12] See G. Urbas, 'Cyber-Terrorism and Australian Law', 8 *Internet Law Bulletin* (2005) No. 1, pp. 5-7. As these provisions remain largely untested in the courts, however, it is difficult to assess their effectiveness.

[13] See A. Steel, 'Vaguely Going Where No-one Has Gone: The Expansive New Computer Access Offences', 26 *Criminal Law Journal* (2002) p. 72.

noted above, the *Cybercrime Act 2001* (Cth) introduced a range of new offences into the *Criminal Code Act 1995* (Cth). The main offence relating to hacking is section 477.1, which prohibits unauthorized access, modification or impairment with intent to commit a serious offence.[14] In fact there are two distinct offences contained in this section. The first is in subsection (1) and requires that the unauthorized access, modification or impairment be by means of a carriage service.[15] Note that the serious offence involved can be an offence under Commonwealth, state or territory law, making the scope of section 477.1(1) quite broad. The second offence is contained in subsection 4 and does not require the use of a carriage service, but is limited to intent to commit a serious Commonwealth offence. A 'serious offence' is one punishable by five or more years' imprisonment, as provided in subsection 9. The maximum punishment for an offence under either limb of section 477.1 is the same as for the serious offence intended to be committed by means of the unauthorized act.

Supplementing section 477.1, there is a range of further serious offences relating to unauthorized modification or impairment of computers and data. Recklessly impairing data through unauthorized modification is prohibited under section 477.2, which carries a maximum penalty of ten years' imprisonment. Section 477.3 deals with impairment of electronic communications, which also carries ten years. In addition, there are less serious offences such as section 478.1, which deals with unauthorized access to and modification of restricted data. This is defined in subsection 3 as 'data to which access is restricted by an access control system associated with a function of the computer'. A further offence dealing with impairment of computer disk or credit-card data is found in section 478.2, punishable by two years' imprisonment. Finally, there are offences in sections 478.3 and 478.4 concerning data handling with intent to commit an offence, punishable by three years' imprisonment.

A new chapter in expanding Commonwealth jurisdiction has recently been opened with the enactment of the *Crimes Legislation Amendment (Telecommunications Offences and Other Measures) Act (No. 2) 2004* (Cth), which came into force on 1 March 2005. This added a new Part 10.6 to the *Criminal Code Act 1995* (Cth), containing a range of offences prohibiting the misuse of telecommunications networks:

- with the intention of committing a serious offence (s. 474.14);
- in order to make a threat (s. 474.15);

[14] The term 'unauthorized access, modification or impairment' is defined in s. 476.2, so that any of these acts is 'unauthorized if the person is not entitled to cause that access, modification or impairment'.

[15] The term 'carriage service' is defined as in s. 7 of the Telecommunications Act 1997 (Cth): carriage service means a service for carrying communications by means of guided and/or unguided electromagnetic energy.

- to make a hoax threat (s. 474.16);
- to menace, harass or cause offence (s. 474.17);
- to misuse an emergency call service (s. 474.18);
- to access or transmit child-pornography material (s. 474.19);
- to possess, control, produce, supply or obtain child-pornography material (s. 474.20);
- to access or transmit child-abuse material (s. 474.22);
- to possess, control, produce, supply or obtain child-abuse material (s. 474.23);
- to procure a person under 16 years of age for sexual purposes (s. 474.26); or
- to 'groom' a person under 16 years of age for sexual purposes (s. 474.27).

The first of these, section 474.14, is particularly broad. It criminalizes the use of a telecommunications network to commit a serious Commonwealth, state or territory offence. The maximum punishment is the same as that for the serious offence. However, unlike section 477.1 (discussed above), there is no requirement of unauthorized access, modification or impairment – thus, the use of the telecommunications network (including the Internet) may be authorized and quite legal, but it is still an offence if this use is accompanied by an intention through this connection to commit a serious offence.

The Explanatory Memorandum to the Bill introducing section 474.14 described its intended scope as follows:[16]

> 'Proposed subsection 474.14(1) will cover a broad range of preparatory activities that make use of telecommunications, undertaken with the intention to commit, or facilitate the commission of, a serious offence. "Connected", as defined in proposed section 473.1, includes connection otherwise than by means of physical contact, for example connection by radiocommunication. This means the proposed offence extends to, for example, the wireless connection of a mobile phone or other device to a telecommunications network with the requisite intention, as well the physical connection to a telecommunications network of, for example, network maintenance equipment, a telephone or a computer.'

And further:

> 'The proposed offence under subsection 474.14(2) will cover *any* use of equipment connected to a telecommunications network to commit, or facilitate the commission of, an offence. Examples of the type of conduct covered by the proposed offence range from the simple making of a telephone call to facilitate the commission of a bank robbery to the use of a computer connected to the Internet to electronically remove money from a financial institution's computer system.'

---

[16] *Crimes Legislation Amendment (Telecommunications Offences and Other Measures) Bill 2004* (Cth).

It can be expected that section 474.14 will largely displace the operation of the main Commonwealth hacking offence, section 477.1, discussed above. With these new telecommunications offences, it is also likely that Commonwealth authorities will assume a more dominant role in the investigation and prosecution of cybercrime offences.

Some state and territory jurisdictions retain their own distinctive hacking offences. For example, section 408D of the Queensland Criminal Code criminalizes use of a restricted computer without the consent of the computer's controller, punishable by two years' imprisonment. This provision is a rare example where the term 'hacking' is used in Australian legislation.[17]

Other Australian jurisdictions have adopted the terminology of 'unauthorized access and modification' used in Commonwealth offences, and several states (New South Wales, Victoria and South Australia) and territories (the Northern Territory and Australian Capital Territory) have substantially reproduced the Commonwealth 'model' offences in their criminal legislation.[18]

Illegal-content offences

Until very recently, illegal content such as child pornography has been dealt with exclusively under state and territory criminal laws (though the Commonwealth had a more limited role in relation to the general regulation of broadcasting and telecommunications). The age limit for the purposes of child-pornography offences varies across these jurisdictions, as does the definition of 'child pornography' itself and whether the use of computers to produce, receive or distribute such material is mentioned in the legislation.

However, the Commonwealth has recently enacted its own child-pornography offences, which target the use of a 'carriage service'[19] – essentially the Internet – to obtain access to or transmit such material. These have also been included in the new Part 10.6 of the *Criminal Code Act 1995* (Cth). Sections 474.19 to 474.22 contain these new offences, as well as some detailed defence provisions. Maximum penalties are ten years' imprisonment.

Other illegal-content offences, such as those relating to racial vilification, are less prominent in Australian law. The *Racial Discrimination Act 1975* (Cth), for example, contains provisions according to which Internet content can be declared 'unlawful' and ordered to be removed, but criminal penalties do not apply. An example of the application of these provisions to an Australian web site containing material questioning the historical occurrence of the Holocaust is the litigation surrounding the 'Adelaide Institute' web site.[20]

---

[17] The section heading for s. 408D is 'Computer hacking and misuse'.

[18] See Bronitt and Gani, loc. cit. n. 3, for an overview of Australian computer offences.

[19] See *supra* n. 15.

[20] See the case of *Jones* v. *Toben* [2002] FCA 1150 and the Full Federal Court appeal *Toben* v. *Jones* [2003] FCAFC 137. See also Y.F. Lim, 'Jones v Toben – Racial Discrimination of the Internet',

However, with the enactment of new telecommunications offences, Internet-based racial vilification may be captured under the new Commonwealth offence of using the Internet to cause offence, under section 474.17. The maximum penalty is three years' imprisonment. The Explanatory Memorandum introducing this offence states:

> 'Examples of the type of use of a carriage service the proposed offence may cover include use that would make a person apprehensive as to their safety or well-being or the safety of their property, use that encourages or incites violence, and use that vilifies persons on the basis of their race or religion.'

Thus, with the enactment of the new telecommunications offences, racial vilification using the Internet has become a Commonwealth criminal offence for the first time.

Other computer offences

A few jurisdictions have enacted offences relating to use of the Internet or e-mail to procure or 'groom' children for the purposes of sexual contact. For example, section 218A of the Queensland Criminal Code punishes by five years' imprisonment the use of electronic communication with intent to procure a person under 16 years of age to engage in a sexual act. It is notable that no real child need be involved in the commission of this offence. In a recent case, Queensland investigators posed as a 13 year-old girl ('becky_boo 13') in a chat and received e-mails from a man wanting to engage the girl in sexual activity. They arrested a 25 year-old man when he appeared at an agreed meeting point to meet the girl, only to find that he had been chatting to police all along.[21]

The Commonwealth has recently enacted similar offences relating to child procuring and 'grooming' as part of the recent telecommunications offences added to the *Criminal Code Act 1995* (Cth): sections 474.26 and 474.27. As with the Queensland offence, there is no requirement that a person under the age of 16 years actually be the target of procuring activity. These Commonwealth offences carry a maximum penalty of 15 years' imprisonment. Further machinery provisions relat-

---

5 *Internet Law Bulletin* (2002) p. 34; L. Seeto, 'Race hate and the Internet', 50 *Computers and Law* (2002) p. 21. Interestingly, the web site operator (Toben) was prosecuted in Germany in 2000 in relation to the same web site and was sentenced to a term of imprisonment; see <http://www.afs-rechtsanwaelte.de/urteil84.htm>. Cf., chapter 9, section 9.3.3, of this book.

[21] *R* v. *Kennings* [2004] QCA 162. In another recent Queensland case, however, in which police posed as a 14-year old ('Kathy_volleyball'), a conviction under s. 218A was overturned on appeal on the basis that the provision requires the defendant to believe that the person being contacted was under the age of 16 years. In this case, the defendant had given evidence that he had held no belief as to the age of Kathy_volleyball, and the Court of Appeal held that the jury have been misdirected on the application of s. 218A(8), which provides that evidence that a person (real or fictitious) was represented as being below a certain age is, in the absence of evidence to the contrary, proof that the adult believed the person was under that age. See *R* v. *Shetty* [2005] QCA 225 (24 June 2005).

ing to these offences are contained in section 474.28, and defences are contained in section 474.29. The Explanatory Memorandum to the Bill introducing these provisions stated:[22]

> 'Proposed sections 474.26–474.29 contain an offence regime targeting adult offenders who exploit the anonymity of telecommunications services (for example, the Internet) to win the trust of a child as a first step towards the future sexual abuse of that child. The practice is known as "online grooming".
> There are two steps routinely taken by adult offenders leading up to a real life meeting between adult and child victim that results in child sexual abuse:
> (i) The adult wins the trust of a child over a period of time. Adults often use "chat room" on the Internet to do this. They may pose as another child, or as a sympathetic "parent" figure. Paedophiles reportedly expose children to pornographic images as part of this "grooming" process. It is proposed to specifically criminalize this practice. Specific offences would remove any doubt about whether online "grooming" of a child before actual contact is 'mere preparation' (i.e. not a criminal offence) or an unlawful attempt to commit child sexual abuse.
> (ii) With the child's trust won, adults often use telecommunications services to set up a meeting with the child. Although this step is more likely to be characterised as an attempt to commit child sexual abuse than step (i), it is desirable to provide a firm justification for police action by enacting specific "procurement" or "solicitation" offences. This is consistent with the underlying rationale for the new offences: to allow law enforcement to intervene before a child is actually abused.'

With the enactment of provisions such as these, the Commonwealth has considerably expanded its jurisdictional reach into areas of criminal law that have been the responsibility of the states and territories.

4.2.4 **Relevant case law**

In some cases, the alleged offence may be insufficiently serious to serve as the basis for extradition. Such a case involved a resident of Melbourne who was accused of stalking a woman in Canada. The alleged offending communications included telephone calls and conventional letters; reference was also made to a web site and to e-mail messages sent to others in Canada. The Canadian woman, who had never set foot in Australia, complained to police in Toronto, who contacted Victoria Police with the allegation that the communications in question had caused fear on her part about the Melbourne man's intentions.

The likelihood that Canadian authorities would seek extradition for a relatively minor matter was small, and the facts of the case did not support a level of seriousness in Canadian law sufficient for extradition from Australia. Victoria police proceeded under section 21A of Victoria's *Crimes Act 1958* which came into operation

[22] *Crimes Legislation Amendment (Telecommunications Offences and Other Measures) Bill 2004* (Cth).

in January 1995. In July of 2000, the defendant denied that any harm was done to the Canadian woman, and argued further that if harm had been done, it was experienced in Canada and not in Victoria. The Magistrate observed that the relevant section of the *Crimes Act* contained no express provision relating to the extraterritorial application of the law, and that the fear or apprehension, an essential element of the offence, had to be experienced within the borders of Victoria. The Magistrate dismissed the charge, ruling that she did not have jurisdiction to hear the case.

The Director of Public Prosecutions appealed against dismissal of the charge, claiming that the Parliament of Victoria did have the power to create an offence with extraterritorial application, and that the Magistrate did indeed have jurisdiction. The Supreme Court set aside the Magistrate's ruling, holding that in this age of modern technology, Parliament could not have intended to confine the legislation to actions and effects occurring solely in Victoria:[23]

> 'Criminals are not respecters of borders. State and international boundaries do not concern them. They commit their evil acts anywhere and without thought to location. Movement between countries is much greater now than in the past and subject to less restrictions. Technology has reached the point where communications can be made around the world in less than a second. The Internet provides a speedy, relatively inexpensive means of communication between persons who have access to a computer and a telephone line. Access is not confined to ownership of a computer and businesses have sprung up offering access to the Internet for a small charge.
> The law must move with these changes.'

Notably, the Victorian legislature has since acted to clarify that the offence is to be understood as covering cyber-stalking and operating extraterritorially.[24]

In some instances, foreign authorities have been content to leave matters to Australian authorities, despite the potential for extradition. Such was the case in *R* v. *Steven George Hourmouzis*. Hourmouzis and an associate sent between six and seven million e-mails to addresses in Australia and the United States and posted numerous messages on the message boards of Yahoo!, Raging Bull, and Insidethe Web.com. The purpose of these communications was to encourage the purchase of shares in Rentech, Inc., a U.S. Corporation whose shares were traded on the NASDAQ exchange. The messages, which were sent over false names and relayed through third-party servers, heralded a price increase of up to 900 per cent in Rentech shares. Shortly thereafter, the volume of trading in Rentech increased tenfold, and its price doubled, before trading was halted and the company denied statements made in the various communications.

---

[23] *DPP (Victoria)* v. *Sutcliffe* [2001] VSC 43 (1 March 2001), per Gillard J., paras. 61-63. See further E. Ogilvie, 'Cyberstalking', *Trends and Issues in Crime and Criminal Justice* (2000), No. 166 (Australian Institute of Criminology), <http://www.aic.gov.au/publications/tandi/tandi166.html>.

[24] *Crimes (Stalking) Act 2003* (Vic), in effect from 10 December 2003.

Hourmouzis and his accomplice were engaged in a classic 'Pump and Dump' scheme: Hourmouzis, a Rentech shareholder, knew that he was communicating false information, and when Rentech's share price increased, Hourmouzis sold his shares in the company for a profit.

Hourmouzis had offended against the laws of both Australia and the United States. In addition to stock market manipulation, the volume of traffic generated by the spam e-mail was sufficient to constitute interference with the lawful operation of a computer. The offences were serious enough, but not so heinous as to move U.S. authorities to request extradition.

As was customary for offences of this nature, the U.S. Securities and Exchange Commission sought disgorgement and a temporary and permanent injunction to prohibit Hourmouzis and his associate from violating section 10(b) rule 10b-5 of the *Securities Exchange Act* of 1934. In essence, they were required to relinquish their ill-gotten gains, and to promise never to engage in such conduct again. U.S. authorities were confident in the capacity of the Australian Securities and Investments Commission (ASIC), the Australian counterpart of the SEC, to handle the prosecutions in Australia. ASIC filed 19 criminal charges against the two accused. Both pleaded guilty to disseminating information that was false or materially misleading and likely to induce the purchase of securities, and to interfering with, interrupting, or obstructing the lawful use of a computer. Both received two-year prison terms, which were suspended (Hourmouzis' after three months in custody).[25]

In other circumstances, however, foreign authorities may request extradition. This will be the case where the requesting country regards the offending conduct to be relatively serious, and the likelihood of a successful outcome (conviction and a severe sentence) greater in their own courts than in the courts of the requested country.

In December 2001, following a 14-month undercover operation, a co-ordinated international investigation called 'Operation Buccaneer' led to simultaneous raids and arrests in the United States, the United Kingdom, Australia, Finland, Sweden, and Norway. Led by the U.S. Customs Service and the U.S. Department of Justice, the operation was directed against an Internet software piracy organization called 'Drink or Die.' It was alleged that the group was responsible for the illegal reproduction and distribution of more than $50 million worth of pirated music, games, movies, and software.

In March 2003, a federal Grand Jury in Virginia returned an indictment against Hew Griffiths, a citizen and resident of Australia, charging him with one count of criminal copyright infringement and one count of conspiracy to commit criminal copyright infringement. Conviction on both counts could lead to a maximum sentence of ten years in federal prison and a US$500,000 fine.

---

[25] Victorian County Court, 30 October 2000, see <http://www.sec.gov/litigation/litreleases/lr16535.htm>.

Copyright infringement is an offence in Australia, but the protection of intellectual property enjoys a lower priority there than it does in the United States, where the formidable wealth and power of the software and entertainment industries are reflected in law and policy. It is by no means certain that, left to the mercy of the Australian judicial system, Griffiths would be convicted and receive a custodial sentence.

One can therefore understand the interest of U.S. authorities in prosecuting Griffiths on U.S. soil. They began extradition proceedings in June 2003 that Griffiths, for obvious reasons, resisted until the end. The basis of his challenge has been that the element of dual criminality was lacking; in other words, he maintained that what he was alleged to have done was not an offence under Australian federal or state law. In March 2004, a Magistrate determined that the alleged acts would not have constituted an extradition offence in the state of New South Wales, where proceedings were conducted. The Magistrate's order was quashed in the Federal Court of Australia in July 2004, and Griffiths appealed to the Full Federal Court. The appeal was dismissed in March 2005, with the Full Federal Court holding that it was sufficient that 'the type of work pirated was itself a type of work capable of attracting protection under the Australian Copyright Act.'[26] In September 2005, Griffiths unsuccessfully sought leave to appeal in the High Court of Australia.[27]

In a civil matter, the High Court of Australia embraced a more expansive conception of jurisdiction. Joseph Gutnick, a prominent businessman, was the subject of a comment in *Barron's Online* that he found offensive. In the courts of Victoria, he sued Dow Jones & Company, publishers of *Barron's Online*, for defamation. Dow Jones argued that the publication in question occurred in New Jersey in the United States, where the servers of *Barron's Online* were located. The High Court held that the harm to Gutnick's reputation would have occurred in Victoria:[28]

> 'It is only when the material is in comprehensible form that the damage to reputation is done and it is damage to reputation which is the principal focus of defamation, not any quality of the defendant's conduct. In the case of material on the World Wide Web, it is not available in comprehensible form until downloaded on to the computer of a person who has used a web browser to pull the material from the web server. It is where that person downloads the material that the damage to reputation may be done. Ordinarily then, that will be the place where the tort of defamation is committed.'

Thus, the High Court concluded, it was legitimate for Gutnick to pursue defamation proceedings according to Victorian laws which are arguably more protective of the reputations of public figures than might be the case in the United States.

---

[26] *United States of America* v. *Griffiths* [2004] FCA 879 (7 July 2004); *Griffiths* v. *United States of America,* [2005] FCAFC 34 (10 March 2005).

[27] *Griffiths* v. *United States of America & Anor* [2005] HCATrans 666 (2 September 2005).

[28] *Dow Jones and Company Inc* v. *Gutnick* [2002] HCA 56 (10 December 2002), para. 44.

4.3 Legal Provisions on Jurisdiction for Cybercrimes

Jurisdiction is governed somewhat differently for Commonwealth, state and territory offences. Until relatively recently, common-law principles regarding territorial jurisdictions were applied in the resolution of any jurisdictional disputes. These principles essentially analyzed jurisdiction along geographic lines, so that persons or events with sufficient geographical connection or 'nexus' with a particular locality were considered amenable to its jurisdiction. However, this meant that jurisdictional choices had to be made when more than one sufficient connection was present.[29]

For example, the case of *Ward* v. *The Queen*[30] concerned an appeal from a murder conviction in which the facts occurred across the Murray River, which marks the boundary between two states, Victoria and New South Wales. The accused had been standing on the Victorian bank of the Murray River when he fatally shot someone on the New South Wales side. The High Court was asked to decide whether jurisdiction was properly determined by where the act causing the death had occurred – the 'initiatory' theory of territorial jurisdiction – or by where the result of that act had occurred – the 'terminatory' theory. The Court decided that as the lethal result of the gunshot occurred in NSW, that state had jurisdiction, and it set aside the appellant's conviction under Victorian law.

Today, such jurisdictional questions have largely been clarified by legislation, which both defines the territorial boundaries of each jurisdiction and also specifies what connection is necessary for the law to apply.[31] The same is true for Commonwealth (i.e., national) jurisdiction, which also evolved on the basis of geographical nexus:[32]

> 'Traditionally, Australia had exercised criminal jurisdiction where the crime took place in its territory. But (like some other governments) it may take unilateral action against citizens or residents if they commit certain criminal offences on foreign soil. Two of the most familiar examples in Australia are prosecutions for paedophilia, and for war crimes. But in many cases, this may still require the cooperation of a foreign government in obtaining evidence and possibly in extraditing the offender.'

Thus, early extensions of criminal jurisdiction beyond Australia's national boundaries proceeded on the basis of nationality, with respect to particular categories of crime. Since then, a more systematic framework for Commonwealth jurisdiction has been established.

---

[29] See M. Goode, 'The tortured tale of Criminal Jurisdiction', 21 *Melbourne University Law Review* (1997) p. 411.

[30] [1980] 142 CLR 308.

[31] See Lanham, loc. cit. n. 3, and Hinton and Lind, loc. cit. n. 3.

[32] Grabosky, loc. cit. n. 3, p. 4.

4.3.1 Commonwealth legislation

The provisions in the *Criminal Code Act 1995* (Cth) relating to jurisdiction, which were added in 2000, are fairly complex.[33] Briefly, the Act distinguishes between 'standard geographical jurisdiction' and four kinds of 'extended geographical jurisdiction'. For each offence under Commonwealth law, the type of jurisdiction that applies is stated, otherwise standard geographical jurisdiction applies by default (s. 14.1).

Standard geographical jurisdiction
Subsection 14.1(2) defines standard geographical jurisdiction so that conduct by a person does not constitute an offence unless:

- the conduct constituting the alleged offence occurs wholly or partly in Australia or on board an Australian aircraft or ship; or
- the conduct occurs outside Australia but a result of the conduct occurs wholly or partly in Australia or on board an Australian aircraft or ship; or
- the offence is ancillary to conduct which occurs, or is intended to occur, wholly or partly in Australia or on board an Australian aircraft or ship.

The term 'ancillary offence' is defined to encompass derivative liability for primary offences by way of attempt (s. 11.1), complicity and common purpose (s. 11.2), innocent agency (s. 11.3), incitement (s. 11.4) and conspiracy (s. 11.5).[34]

Where standard jurisdiction applies, subsection 14.1(3) provides a defence if:

- the conduct constituting the alleged offence occurs wholly in a foreign country (and not on board an Australian aircraft or ship); and
- this conduct is not an offence under the law of the foreign country.

Subsection 14.1(5) provides a similar defence for ancillary offences. In both cases, the defendant bears an evidential burden in relation to the matters involved in the defence.[35]

Extended geographical jurisdiction
As noted, there are four kinds of extended geographical jurisdiction. In relation to cybercrime offences under the *Criminal Code Act 1995* (Cth), as introduced by the

[33] Part 2.7 (Geographical jurisdiction) was added by the *Criminal Code Amendment (Theft, Fraud, Bribery and Related Offences) Act 2000* (Cth), with full effect from 24 May 2001.

[34] See Dictionary to the *Criminal Code Act 1995* (Cth).

[35] An 'evidential burden' is defined in s. 13.3(6) as 'the burden of adducing or pointing to evidence that suggests a reasonable possibility that the matter exists or does not exist.' Under s. 142(1) of the *Evidence Act 1995* (Cth), this burden is discharged by proof on the balance of probabilities.

Cybercrime Act 2001 (Cth), section 476.3 states that extended geographical jurisdiction, category A, applies. For the more recent telecommunications offences added by the *Crimes Legislation Amendment (Telecommunications Offences and Other Measures) Act (No. 2) 2004* (Cth), section 475.2 similarly provides that extended geographical jurisdiction, category A, applies. Thus, this is the jurisdictional category of interest from the cybercrime perspective.

Extended geographical jurisdiction, category A, is defined in subsection 15.1(1) to mean that conduct by a person does not constitute an offence unless one of the standard geographical jurisdiction criteria applies, or:

- the conduct occurs outside Australia but, at the time of the alleged offence, the person is an Australian citizen or a body corporate incorporated under Australian law.

Thus, extended geographical jurisdiction, category A, adds to standard geographical jurisdiction the element that Australian citizens and corporations are also covered even where their conduct occurs wholly outside Australia. Where this form of jurisdiction applies, subsection 15.1(2) provides a defence similar to that outlined above for standard geographical jurisdiction and subsection 15.1(4) provides a defence for ancillary offences. In both cases, the defendant bears an evidential burden in relation to the matters involved in the defence.

In summary, for the main cybercrime offences under Commonwealth legislation jurisdiction will be asserted for primary offences where:

1. the conduct constituting the offence or a result of that conduct occurs wholly or partly in Australia or on board an Australian aircraft or ship; or
2. the alleged offender is an Australian citizen or an Australian company.

Finally, it should be noted that there are some offences, which may be committed through the use of computer-related technologies or which otherwise involve computers, to which different categories of extended geographical jurisdiction apply. An example is the main terrorism offence under Commonwealth law, found in section 101.1 (Terrorist acts) of the *Criminal Code Act 1995* (Cth). This provides that a person who commits a terrorist act is liable to imprisonment for life. A 'terrorist act' is defined in section 100.1 as an action or threat of action causing serious harm to persons or property, or endangering life or public safety, accompanied by the intention of advancing a political, religious or ideological cause, and done in order to intimidate an Australian or foreign government or the public.[36] Of particular interest is the fact that this definition explicitly covers any act or threat that 'seri-

[36] See M. Gani and G. Urbas, 'Alert or Alarmed? Recent Legislative Reforms Directed at Terrorist Organisations and Persons Supporting or Assisting Terrorist Acts', 8 *Newcastle Law Review* (2004) p. 19.

ously interferes with, seriously disrupts, or destroys, an electronic system including, but not limited to:

i) an information system; or
ii) a telecommunications system; or
iii) a financial system; or
iv) a system used for the delivery of essential government services; or
v) a system used for, or by, an essential public utility; or
vi) a system used for, or by, a transport system.

Thus, cyber-terrorism is covered by the terrorist offence provisions, at least insofar as sabotage of telecommunications and similar attacks are concerned. Such acts would fall within the definition of a 'terrorist act' if accompanied by the requisite political or similar intentions, and would be punishable by life imprisonment. In addition, there are provisions directed at the suppression of terrorist financing that may well apply predominantly to the on-line fund-raising activities of some groups.[37]

The jurisdictional category that applies to Commonwealth terrorism offences is *extended geographical jurisdiction, category D*, which is the widest of the categories. It is defined in section 15.4 of the *Criminal Code Act 1995* (Cth), so that a person commits an offence under the provision whether or not the conduct constituting the offence, or even a result of that conduct, occurs in Australia.[38]

Clearly, the extended geographical jurisdiction provisions under Commonwealth law, in their application to cybercrime, provide a powerful legal mechanism for responding to cross-jurisdictional threats. However, this mechanism should not be thought to displace, or to obviate the need for, international co-operation between law-enforcement agencies and harmonization of national laws and procedures. As stated by Bronitt and Gani:[39]

> 'The gaps that allow cybercriminals to hack and attack across borders with impunity are due more often to the lack of modern computer-specific offences, rather than want of jurisdiction – indeed, we believe that the better strategy would be to encourage a regional harmonisation of laws and effective extradition arrangements, rather than to extend the geographic reach of the criminal law. Promoting extraterritoriality as the solution – under the mantra "cybercrime knows no borders" – may prove to be an impotent symbolic gesture that will only enliven jurisdictional disputes between nations, and further discourage international collaboration in this field.'

---

[37] In particular, s. 101.5 (collecting or making documents likely to facilitate terrorist acts) and s. 102.6 (getting funds to or from a terrorist organization); see Urbas, loc. cit. n. 12.

[38] However, s. 16.1 provides that the Attorney-General's consent is required for prosecutions where the conduct occurs wholly outside Australia in certain circumstances.

[39] Bronitt and Gani, loc. cit. n. 3, at pp. 312-313.

4.3.2 State and territory legislation

The governing principle for state or territory jurisdiction is 'sufficient territorial nexus'. As noted above, this was interpreted using common-law principles, until legislation was enacted to make the concept more precise. An example is section 10C of the *Crimes Act 1900* (NSW), which provides in effect that there is sufficient geographical nexus if either the offence is committed wholly or partly in the state or the offence is committed wholly outside the state but it has an effect in the state. The effect of this provision is that New South Wales computer offences (based on the Commonwealth *Cybercrime Act* model, and contained in Part 6 of the *Crimes Act 1900* (NSW)) can apply to computer misuse that occurs outside the state or indeed outside Australia, so long as the offence has an effect in the state. This means, of course, that there is scope for considerable overlap between such state offences and other state or territory law, the Commonwealth offences discussed above, or indeed the computer crime laws of other countries.

4.4 Co-operation Arrangements

In Australia, as elsewhere, there are two basic forms of international co-operation relating to cybercrime. The first, which might be termed investigator-to-investigator assistance, occurs on an informal basis. Under these circumstances, investigators share information and provide assistance to each other, without reliance on legislation. Such means are appropriate where the information sought is publicly available.

Informal liaison between police of different nations long precedes the digital age. Australia is a member of Interpol, and the Australian Federal Police (AFP) has liaison offices in over thirty countries around the world. A number of nations have law-enforcement officers posted to Australia. Of specific relevance to cybercrime is the establishment of a 24/7 network of contacts, enabling nations to alert each other in real time to urgent matters. Australia's contact point is the Australian High Tech Crime Centre (AHTCC) at the headquarters of the Australian Federal Police. The 24/7 arrangements, which allow for a 'fast freeze, slow thaw' process for the preservation of volatile electronic evidence, have been established pursuant to the Council of Europe Cybercrime Convention. These arrangements are available not only to formal signatories to the Convention, but also to sympathetic non-signatory states. Although not a signatory to the convention, Australia has formally signed on to these arrangements.

Australia also has a formal regime for mutual assistance in criminal matters. Formal mutual assistance is invoked when the matter in question entails compulsory powers such as the execution of a search warrant in the requested country, or the extradition of a suspect to the requesting country.[40]

[40] See Cuthbertson, loc. cit. n. 7.

While formal mutual assistance can be requested of any country (even in the absence of diplomatic relations), it is usually easier when prior treaty arrangements are in place. Australia currently has bilateral mutual-assistance treaties with about twenty countries.

Even under the best of circumstances, however, the machinery of formal mutual assistance turns slowly. Requests must be processed through a central office in both requesting and requested countries, and usually requires approval at a ministerial or other high official level.

When an individual situated in Australia commits an offence against a person or institution located in a foreign country, a degree of co-operation between Australian and foreign authorities is required before an investigation and prosecution can proceed. Dual criminality may be required for formal, but not for informal legal assistance. First, in order to satisfy the criterion of dual criminality, the alleged misconduct must also constitute an offence under Australian law. A threshold of severity also applies, with offences where the maximum available penalty is less than one year's imprisonment.

The mobilization of compulsory powers, not to mention extradition, involves time-consuming and potentially costly processes. If authorities are confident that their foreign counterparts can do justice, they may well defer to them.

4.5 Cross-Border Investigation

Under Australian federal law, search powers related to computer evidence are no longer confined to specific locations. The *Cybercrime Act 2001* (Cth) envisaged that evidentiary data may be dispersed across a computer network, and allows searches for off-site data accessible through computers located on the search premises. The term 'data held in a computer' refers to 'any data held in a storage device on a computer network of which the computer forms a part'. There are no geographical limits specified, nor is there any requirement that consent be obtained from third parties. However, section 3LB of the *Crimes Act 1914* (Cth), inserted by the *Cybercrime Act*, requires the notification, where practicable, of the occupier of the remote premises. This can be more complicated than it sounds, because in the course of a search through a networked environment, one is not always certain 'where one is'. It is customary in Australia to advise foreign third parties after the fact that such a remote search has taken place. Section 3L(1) confers power on investigating officers to perform computer searches in order to access data (including data not held at the premises) based on a belief on reasonable grounds that the data might constitute evidentiary material and the equipment can be operated without any resulting damage.

Section 3LB then provides that, where data in premises other than the warrant premises has been accessed, the executing officer must inform the owner of those premises if this is 'practicable'.[41]

The interception of telecommunications is governed by the *Telecommunications (Interception) Act 1979* (Cth). The Act applies only to data in transit, not to stored data. For purposes of ordinary law enforcement, including cybercrime, the *Telecommunications Interception Act* does not authorize the interception by Australian authorities of telecommunications where the sender and the recipient are both overseas, even where the communications may take place within or between jurisdictions where such interceptions are not prohibited by law. Where one party is located in Australia, that party's communications to or from anywhere in the world may be intercepted pursuant to an appropriate warrant. The Act prohibits the interception of telecommunications within Australia by foreign governments. Subject to the mutual-assistance arrangements including the provision of dual criminality, interception could be undertaken on behalf of a foreign government by duly authorized Australian personnel.

It remains uncertain whether one can obtain a warrant for the interception of communications between two individuals both abroad, where the communications flows through the system of an Australian carrier, for example, if an offender in New York rings a co-conspirator in Angola, using an Australian telephone facility that allows her to dial back to Australia and call anywhere.

The *Telecommunications Interception Act* does provide for interception of telecommunications in order to obtain 'foreign intelligence', as opposed to conventional criminal investigations.[42] Section 11B allows the Attorney-General to issue to the Director-General of Security a 'named person warrant' for the collection of foreign intelligence. The Australian Security Intelligence Organisation (ASIO) may also obtain foreign intelligence within Australia.[43]

The *Surveillance Devices Act 2004* (Cth) covers a number of surveillance technologies, including aural, optical and tracking devices, in addition to data surveillance. It was enacted largely to overcome jurisdictional differences and to facilitate cross-jurisdictional investigations within Australia.[44] However, under Part 5, its surveillance warrant provisions may extend to extraterritorial investigations. Data surveillance provisions would appear to apply to transaction data, and not commu-

---

[41] There are related provisions governing search warrants in relation to computer-stored data under the *Australian Security Intelligence Organisation Act 1979* (Cth), in particular in s. 25(5) and (6).

[42] Defined as in the *Australian Security Intelligence Organisation Act 1979* (Cth): 'foreign intelligence' means intelligence relating to the capabilities, intentions or activities of a foreign power.

[43] See s. 17(1) of the *Australian Security Intelligence Organisation Act 1979* (Cth).

[44] This legislation was preceded by publication of the Leaders Summit on Terrorism and Multi-jurisdictional Crime, *Cross-Border Investigative Powers for Law Enforcement*, Report of the Standing Committee of Attorneys-General and Australasian Police Ministers Council Joint Working Group on National Investigation Powers (November 2003), available at <http://www.ag.gov.au>.

nications content in transit, which is covered by the Telecommunications Interception Act. Section 6(1) provides a definition:

> '*data surveillance device* means any device or program capable of being used to record or monitor the input of information into, or the output of information from, a computer but does not include an optical surveillance device.'

Part 5 contains section 42, which provides for extraterritorial operation of warrants where the 'surveillance has been agreed to by an appropriate consenting official of the foreign country'. Subsection (6) requires that, as soon as practical after commencement of surveillance under a warrant, the law-enforcement agency responsible for the surveillance must give the responsible Australian Minister evidence in writing that the surveillance has been agreed to by an appropriate foreign official. (It is uncertain whether this would bar the interception of communications in those jurisdictions where there are no legislative provisions, and therefore no appropriate consenting official. Perhaps one would simply seek consent from an ostensibly responsible minister such as the Minister of Justice, Minister for Telecommunications, or head of government.)

In addition to these requirements, section 43 of the Surveillance Devices Act provides that evidence obtained from surveillance undertaken in a foreign country cannot be tendered in evidence in Australian proceedings unless the court is satisfied that the surveillance was agreed to by an appropriate consenting official of the foreign country.

Beyond conventional law-enforcement powers, there are certain powers of remote search available in matters of national security. While the Australian Security Intelligence Organisation (ASIO) has powers to remotely access computers (under the authority of a warrant signed by the Attorney-General of Australia), the ASIO Act explicitly forbids deletion or alteration of data, or 'the doing of any thing, that interferes with, interrupts or obstructs the lawful use of the target computer by other persons, or that causes any loss or damage to other persons lawfully using the target computer.'[45]

Australian law nevertheless offers some protection to certain authorized investigators. The *Cybercrime Act 2001* (Cth) created a new section of the Criminal Code, section 476.5(1), under which a staff member of the Australian Secret Intelligence Service (ASIS) or the Defence Signals Directorate (DSD) is not subject to any civil or criminal liability for any computer-related act done outside Australia if the Act is done in the proper performance of a function of the agency.

---

[45] See s. 25A of the *Australian Security Intelligence Organisation Act 1979* (Cth).

4.6 Conclusion

The category of geographical jurisdiction that applies to the most important cybercrime offences under Australian law is 'extended geographical jurisdiction – category A' under the *Criminal Code Act 1995* (Cth). This means that Australia asserts jurisdiction where the conduct occurs wholly or partly in Australia, or a result of the conduct occurs wholly or partly in Australia, or the conduct occurs outside Australia but, at the time of the alleged offence, the person is an Australian citizen or a body corporate incorporated under Australian law. This gives Australia considerable jurisdictional reach for cybercrime offences. The scope of jurisdiction is even greater where such conduct falls within the terrorism offences under the Code, to which 'extended geographical jurisdiction – category D' applies, which is the widest of the categories (thus in principle covering cyber-terrorist acts committed anywhere, even by non-citizens). In practice, however, prosecution will only be undertaken by Australian authorities if there is a sufficient connection with the country and if, where necessary for obtaining evidence and bringing suspects before Australian courts, adequate mutual-assistance arrangements are available. The legislative framework does allow for cross-border searches to be conducted by Australian investigative and intelligence authorities, though with statutory requirements of notification to owners of warrant premises where practical. The legislation thus seeks to maintain a balance between effective law enforcement and reasonable restraints on the exercise of investigative powers both within and outside Australia's national borders.

Bibliography

S.W. Brenner and B.J. Koops, 'Approaches to Cybercrime Jurisdiction', 4 *Journal of High Technology Law* (2004) p. 1.

S. Bronitt and M. Gani, 'Shifting Boundaries of Cybercrime: From Computer Hacking to Cyberterrorism', 27 *Criminal Law Journal* (2003) p. 303.

S. Cuthbertson, 'Mutual Assistance in Criminal Matters: Beyond 2000', 75 *Australian Law Journal* (2001) pp. 326-336.

M. Goode, 'The tortured tale of Criminal Jurisdiction', 21 *Melbourne University Law Review* (1997) p. 411.

P. Grabosky, 'Crime in a Shrinking World', *Trends and Issues in Crime and Criminal Justice* (March 1998) No. 83, available at <http://www.aic.gov.au/publications/tandi/tandi83.html>.

M. Hinton and C. Lind, 'The Territorial Application of the Criminal Law – When Crime is Not Local', 23 *Criminal Law Journal* (1999) p. 285.

D. Lanham, *Cross-Border Criminal Law* (FT Law and Tax Asia Pacific 1997).

R.G. Smith, P. Grabosky and G. Urbas, *Cyber Criminals on Trial* (Cambridge, Cambridge University Press 2004).

D.L. Speer, 'Redefining borders: The challenges of cybercrime', 34 *Crime, Law and Social Change* (2000) p. 259.

A. STEEL, 'Vaguely Going Where No-one Has Gone: The Expansive New Computer Access Offences', 26 *Criminal Law Journal* (2002) p. 72.

G. URBAS AND R. SMITH, 'Computer Crime Legislation in Australia', 7 *Internet Law Bulletin* (2004) No. 2, pp. 53-56.

E. WONG, 'Tough new laws for child pornography and other internet offences', 7 *Internet Law Bulletin* (2004) p. 89.

Chapter 5
CYBERCRIME AND JURISDICTION IN BELGIUM AND THE NETHERLANDS. LOTUS IN CYBERSPACE – WHOSE SOVEREIGNTY IS AT STAKE?

Paul de Hert*

5.1 Introduction

Can one country punish Internet acts committed outside its geographical borders? Are its law-enforcement agents allowed to carry out extraterritorial investigations via computers? I look at these two questions, viz. the *locus commissi delicti* question and the procedural jurisdiction problem, from a broad public international law perspective. My answer will be illustrated with examples taken mainly from Belgium and the Netherlands.[1] These neighboring countries have formulated quasi-identical answers to the first question, but they differ with regard to the second question.

My analysis will show that there is no burning law-enforcement problem, but rather a justice problem for the extraterritorial suspect. The legal framework, although not conceived as a blueprint for extraterritorial law, recognizes some discretion for nation states to regulate extraterritorial matters. Even convinced internationalists are, because of their adherence to effective human-rights protection, inclined to accept an active, extraterritorial role for nation states.

In the past I have written in support of a pragmatic approach towards the phenomenon of crime on the Internet. In particular, I have applauded the then existing pragmatic approach of the European Union *not* to accelerate regulatory developments.[2] Doing *too* much overlooks the fact that principles of criminal law in gen-

* Prof.Dr Paul De Hert is Associate Professor of Law & Technology at the Tilburg Institute for Law, Technology, and Society (TILT), of Tilburg University, the Netherlands, and Professor of International Law at the Free University of Brussels, Belgium.

[1] A country report on Dutch and Belgian cybercrime legislation in general is not the aim of this chapter. For this, I refer to the Computer Crime Law Survey <http://rechten.uvt.nl/ccls/>, an electronic database on computer-crime legislation around the world, of which this author is co-founder.

[2] P. De Hert and K. Bodard, 'Internetmisdaad een uitdaging? Situering van de problematiek aan de hand van (kinder)pornografie', [Internet Crime: a Challenge?], *Algemeen Juridisch Tijdschrift* (1996-97), Dossier No. 7, pp. 97-124; K. Bodard, P. de Hert and B. de Schutter, 'Crime on Internet. A Chal-

B-J. Koops and S.W. Brenner (Eds), Cybercrime and Jurisdiction

eral apply to all media, that the threat from offensive Internet material is minimal, and that technology exists to protect children and sensitive individuals from the most questionable content. I still think that these arguments are valid, although recent initiatives such as the Council of Europe Cybercrime Convention and the 2005 EU Framework Decision on attacks against information systems are indicative of the change in attitude within policy circles.

One of the other arguments I used at the time to favor a mild 'hands-off' approach was based on the understanding of the many opportunities that ICT and the legal system offered to national law-enforcement authorities to combat crime, in particular cybercrime.[3] In this contribution, when focusing on the jurisdiction issue with regard to substantive criminal law and procedural criminal law, I (again) contend that, although there is a challenge for law enforcement, it is more or less rhetorical to hold that there is a major problem for law enforcement in the light of the problems that extra-jurisdictional activities by law-enforcement agencies create for suspected persons. Expanded jurisdiction with regard to cybercrimes and transborder law-enforcement powers, even those introduced on a unilateral basis, are today's reality. The best one can hope for, from a civil-liberty perspective, is a new principled decision by an international court to supplement the 1929 *Lotus* judgment by the International Permanent Court, which set some limits on jurisdictional powers as they were understood back then.

I will start with a brief discussion of central terms, such as 'sovereignty', 'jurisdiction' and 'territoriality'.

5.2 'Sovereignty', 'Jurisdiction', and 'Territoriality'

It looks so simple, when we believe Antonio Cassese – to name one of the most influential authors writing today on public international law. 'Territory' is the portion of land subject to the sovereign authority of a state. Between territory and sovereignty there exists at present an absolute nexus, since, with the exception of the Antarctic region and some other parts of the world, no territory exists that is not subject to sovereign power.[4] States are entitled to exercise over their territories all

lenge to Criminal Law in Europe', 5 *Maastricht Journal of European and Comparative Law* (1998) No. 3, pp. 222-261.

[3] This understanding was far from original. One of the arguments behind the 'hands-off' approach of the European Commission with regard to content control was convincingly practical: the Commission recognized that, in reality, the threat from illegal material is minimal. As a rule, 'it is virtually impossible to come across unwanted material by accident'. Also, controversial sites are clearly identifiable. See European Commission, *Illegal and Harmful Content on the Internet*, COM(96)0487final, p. 6, available at <http/www2.echo/lu/legal/en/Internet/content/communic.html>; European Commission, *Green Paper on the Protection of Minors and Human Dignity in Audiovisual and Information Services*, 16 October 1996, p. 12, available at <http/www.europa.eu.int/en/record/green/gp9610/protec.hml>.

[4] A. Cassese, *International Law*, 2nd edn. (Oxford, Oxford University Press 2005), pp. 82-83.

those powers inherent in their sovereignty. 'Sovereignty' includes several competences, or, as Cassese calls them, 'sweeping powers and rights'.[5] At the forefront stands the power to wield authority over all the individuals living in the territory. This power of the central authorities of a state to exercise public functions over individuals located in a territory is called 'jurisdiction'.

Other powers and rights included in the idea of sovereignty are:

- the power to freely use and dispose of the territory under the state's jurisdiction and perform all activities deemed necessary or beneficial to the population living there;
- the right that no other state may intrude in the state's territory (the right to exclude others or *jus excludendi alios*);
- the right to immunity from the jurisdiction of foreign courts for acts or actions performed by the state in its sovereign capacity;
- the right to immunity for state representatives acting in their official capacity;
- the right to respect for life and property of the state's national and state officials abroad.

'Jurisdiction' (the first power) manifests itself in various forms: *jurisdiction to prescribe* (that is, the power to enact legal commands or authorizations binding upon the individuals in the territory belonging to the state); *jurisdiction to adjudicate* (that is, the power to settle legal disputes through binding decisions, or to interpret the law with binding force for all persons and entities concerned) and *jurisdiction to enforce* (that is, the power to ensure through coercive means that legal commands and entitlements are complied with).[6]

The apparent logic and coherence of this presentation of terms and concepts is misleading. The relationship between the concepts is often more complex. *Prescriptive jurisdiction*, for instance, normally extends to the territory over which a state is sovereign, but, as will be discussed below, states may also enact legislation binding upon their nationals abroad, as well as laws applicable to other facts or forms of conduct engaged in abroad and considered prejudicial to the state. Also, there is an important role for 'consent'. States can consent to the extraterritorial activities of other states, even implicitly. A striking example of explicit consent can be found in the 1903 U.S.-Cuba Lease of Lands for Coaling and Naval Stations Treaty stating that '(t)he Republic of Cuba consents that during the period of occupation by the United States (...) the United States shall exercise complete jurisdiction and control over and within said areas.'[7] Moreover, the presentation of concepts

[5] Ibid., pp. 49-52.

[6] Ibid., pp. 49-50.

[7] This Guantanamo Bay Treaty can be found at <www.yale.edu/laweb/avalon/diplomacy/cuba/cyba002.htm>.

is hiding a reality which is unwilling to subordinate itself to the legal principles of international law. Cassese quotes American, Israeli, and British cases in which national judges have asserted jurisdiction over persons in custody, but who had been kidnapped by either American or British state officials abroad clearly contrary to international-law principles, such as the jurisdiction to enforce and the *jus excludendi alios*.[8]

The problem of simplicity has, however, a deeper dimension. Concepts and figures such as 'sovereignty' and 'states' lose significance when, for instance, the internal disorder in contemporary Africa is considered. The condition of postcolonial statehood in contemporary sub-Saharan Africa indeed appears to turn the 'Westphalian commonsense'[9] upside down.[10] African states are *quasi*-states, because, for the time being, they lack the features of empirical statehood: they possess '"judicial statehood" derived from a right of self-determination – negative sovereignty – without *yet* possessing much in the way of empirical statehood, disclosed by a capacity for *effective* and *civil* government – positive sovereignty.'[11] It can no longer be defended that Westphalian sovereignty is absolute or that there are no gradations in sovereignty. These are assumptions that are questioned both in theory and practice. States, also outside Africa, are confronted with numerous challenges and limitations. We already gave the example of kidnapping practices by secret services of persons in foreign countries without the permission of the country involved. Other illustrations are the use of force by regional organizations in the former Yugoslavia without a UN mandate; international pressure to intervene in the case of gross human-rights violations, and transnational crime challenging the capacity of national states to deal with security and law enforcement.

It is pure simplicity, also since principles of international law such as the concept of sovereignty are constructs based on sloppy historical analysis and neglect of state practices.[12] It is simplicity, finally, since political theorists have shown convincingly that there is an ideological use behind today's notions of 'sovereignty', 'states',

---

[8] Cassese, op. cit. n. 4, pp. 50-52, with reference to *US* v. *Alvarez-Macain*, *Dominguez* v. *State*, *Eichmann*, and *Regina* v. *Plymouth Justices, ex parte Driver*.

[9] The term is derived from S.N. Grovogui, 'Regimes of Sovereignty: International Morality and the African Condition', 8 *European Journal of International Relations* (2002) No. 3, pp. 315-338. The Peace Treaty of Westphalia (1648) is said to have laid the foundations for the sovereign state, a cornerstone of public international law.

[10] R.K. Ashley and R.B.J. Walker, 'Conclusion: Reading Dissidence/Writing the Discipline: Crisis and the Question of Sovereignty in International Studies', 34 *International Studies Quarterly* (1990) No. 3, pp. 367-416 at p. 381. See R.H. Jackson, *Quasi-States: Sovereignty, International Relations and the Third World* (Cambridge, Cambridge University Press 1990).

[11] R.H. Jackson, 'Quasi-states, Dual Regimes, and Neoclassical Theory: International Jurisprudence and the Third World', 41 *International Organization* (1987) pp. 519-549 at p. 529.

[12] R. Lesaffer, 'International Law and its History: the Story of an Unrequited Love', *The Tilburg Working Papers Series on Jurisprudence and Legal History* (2005), available through <http://www.uvt.nl/eer/papers>.

and 'jurisdiction'. We already touched upon the phenomenon of 'quasi-states'. Also, there is Foucault's well-known critique of the traditional perspective on power, as a governmental or state instrument. This philosopher argues that power should not always be seen in terms of its more obvious, institutional forms. Power needs to be understood 'as the multiplicity of force relations immanent in the sphere in which they operate and which constitute their own organization.'[13] Other theorists challenge the dominant territorial paradigm of sovereignty. Overlooking South African Apartheid strategy to lock up blacks in 'homelands' and contemporary Israeli strategy to create Palestinian 'enclaves', they question the absolute nexus between territory and sovereignty.[14] Blacks and Palestinians do have territory, but political sovereignty remains in the hands of those who have created the borders of the territories that Blacks and Palestinians have to or may not cross when they want to travel or go to work.

Pivotal to this understanding is Foucault *and* Hannah Arendt. *Eichmann in Jerusalem* challenges the geographical understanding of 'territory':

> '[Territory] relates not so much, and not primarily, to a piece of land as to the space between individuals in a group whose members are bound to, and at the same time separated and protected from, each other by all kinds of relationships, based on a common language, religion, a common history, customs and laws. Such relationships become spatially manifest insofar as they themselves constitute the space wherein the different members of a group relate to and have intercourse with each other.'[15]

This definition allows Arendt to defend the position that the Jewish community, before the creation of the State of Israel, lived in a symbolic territory. Eichmann's crimes could therefore be regarded as crimes against a legal-political community, viz. the Jewish ('crimes against Jews'), which, to believe Arendt, is to be preferred over the category of 'crimes against humanity'. This of course follows from Arendt's theory of human rights. World War II and the Holocaust, according to Arendt, are signs that 'human rights' have no sovereign status, without the existence of nation-states. 'Rights spring from within the nation,'[16] she observes. However, because nation-states can endanger human rights, an international community is needed to

[13] M. Foucault, *Histoire de la sexualité 1. La volonté de savoir* (Paris, Gallimard 1976), English translation: M. Foucault, *The History of Sexuality Vol. 1* (London, Penguin 1979); M. Foucault, *Résumé des cours. 1970-1982* (Paris, Julliard 1989), pp. 85-86.

[14] H. Dayan, 'Separatieregimes toen en nu: het anti-politieke opnieuw bezien' [Systems of Separation Now and Yesterday], 8 *Ethiek & Maatschappij* (2005) No. 1, pp. 7-26 (with English abstract).

[15] H. Arendt, *Eichmann in Jerusalem: a Report on the Banality of Evil* (New York, Viking Press 1963), p. 263. See also Y. Horsman, 'Misdaden tegen de mensheid: eerste bedrijf, scène twee: Eichmann in Jeruzalem' [Crimes against Humanity: First Act, Second Scene], 8 *Ethiek & Maatschappij* (2005) No. 1, pp. 58-66 (with English abstract).

[16] Arendt, ibid., p. 299. Notwithstanding developments towards interventions in cases of gross violations of human rights, Arendt's emphasis on the role of states remains accurate, as will be seen below.

see to human rights being respected by nation-states. In a subsequent work, *The Crisis of the Republic*, Arendt substantiates this vague notion of international community. Impressed by the institutional model of the United States, this community takes the form of a federal-council system based on the federal notion of subsidiarity, where power mechanisms are horizontal rather than vertical, and where, ultimately, the concept of sovereignty will disappear.[17]

Sovereignty may disappear one day and territory is more than a geographical space. These insights no doubt enrich the discussion about jurisdiction with regard to cybercrimes. Are the Belgian police protecting Belgian citizens against those selling child pornography through the Internet, or are they protecting the symbolic territory of all members of the Internet community? Another question that will be addressed below: is it wise or realistic to prohibit national extraterritorial initiatives in the fight against cybercrime, as long as there is no effective international alternative that is equally effective? As stated in the introduction, I will discuss the many possibilities of law enforcement on the Internet, possibilities that, for rhetorical reasons, are often downplayed. My tone will be often critical, but my answer to the said question will be nevertheless 'no'.

5.3 Cybercrime Legislation: Old and New

5.3.1 The strength of existing criminal-law instruments

Materials considered to be legal in one country may be illegal in another. Gambling is (still) prohibited in Belgium, but accepted in other countries. The same holds true for comparative advertising: although it is a common practice in the Netherlands, it was until recently prohibited in Belgium.

Gambling and advertising services can be provided on the Internet. If there is a legal vacuum, then it is a deliberate one. The Internet does not as such create new offenses, but enlarges existing differences in norms.[18] Studies in EU Member States, such as the Netherlands,[19] support this view. Punishable actions remain punishable

[17] H. Arendt, *The Crisis of the Republic* (San Diego, Harcourt Brace 1972), pp. 231-233. See more in detail T.L. Castelein, 'Mensenrechten en de organisatie van de politieke gemeenschap in het werk van Arendt, Ignatieff en Agamben' [Human Rights and the Organization of the Political Community in the Work of Arendt, Ignatieff en Agamben], 8 *Ethiek & Maatschappij* (2005) No. 1, pp. 67-83 (with English abstract).

[18] As the Commission rightly points out: 'All these activities fall under the existing legal framework. Therefore, the Internet does not exist in a legal vacuum, since all those involved (authors, content providers, host service providers who actually store the documents and make them available, network operators, access providers and end users) are subject to the respective laws of the Member States.' European Commission, op. cit. n. 3, p. 11.

[19] Th. De Roos and L. Wissink, 'Uitingsdelicten op het Internet en strafrechtelijke repressie' [First Amendment Crimes and the Use of Criminal Law], *Nederlands Juristenblad* (1996), p. 1729; A. Patijn, 'Grondrechten en nieuwe communicatietechnologieën: de rol van de wetgever' [Fundamental Rights

when committed through the Internet. Generally speaking, criminal laws are formulated in an abstract and technology-neutral way, allowing them to function in an Internet environment. Thus, most national judges find no difficulties in applying existing laws to Internet crimes. Although web sites are not listed in the Belgian *Strafwetboek* (Criminal Code, hereafter: CC) as possible instruments to disseminate wrongful content, revisionists are sent to jail by Belgian judges without much discussion.[20] A German court condemned a German student who compiled and sold child pornography through the Internet.[21] The facts came to public attention when journalists, surfing on the Internet, replied to his offer to sell images.[22] Similarly, in 1997, a French court had no difficulty in applying a century-old law on media crimes (*Loi du 29 juillet 1881*) to a case of hate speech, in which a singer-songwriter opened a web site with racist texts.[23]

An abundant jurisprudence shows the flexibility of intellectual property law, as can be illustrated by two Dutch cases. In the first case, it was held that a system operator offering computer programs through a Bulletin Board had violated the intellectual property rights of the author.[24] A similar violation arose when persons, using data from a computerized telephone directory (put on the market by the Dutch

---

and New Communication Technologies: the Role of the Legislator], *NJCM-Bulletin* (1996), pp. 797-806; A. Harteveld and J. Van Der Neut, 'Internet-providers in de strafrechtelijke gevarenzone' [Internet Providers and the Danger Zone of Criminal Law], *Delikt en Delinkwent* (1996), pp. 426-440.

[20] Defending revisionist or negationist theories is incriminated by the Law of 23 March 1995. These acts are punishable when they are 'made public' within the circumstances or publicity requirements described in Art. 444 Belgian CC: 'in public meetings or places, or in the presence of persons in non-public places, but accessible to persons with a right to meet in that place; or in whatever place whenever an insulted person and witnesses are present; or through writings (...) or images (…) presented in public; or through writings that are not made public but are sent or handed to different persons.' Siegfried Verbeke (see below, section 5.4.4) did not even question the use of Article 444 Belgian CC against his web site. The judge noted that 'the accused does not challenge the application of Article 444 when websites are used (...). Information and publications sold via a website (....) are accessible to the public.' Court of First Instance (criminal chamber) Antwerp, 9 September 2003, available through <http://www.antiracisme.be>. Cf., Court of First Instance (criminal chamber) Brussels, 15 January 2002, available through <http://www.antiracisme.be>.

[21] Arbeitsgericht [Court of Labor] Hamburg, 8 July 1997, *Computer und Recht* (1998) No. 1, pp. 33-36, annotated by I. Vassilaki.

[22] The case also clearly indicates that behind the rhetoric about technical means rendering Internet communications anonymous and giving too much leeway to criminals, there is an important human factor that prevents these criminals from succeeding: for their (illegal) services, a public is needed. In one way or another, there will often be a form of publicity, even when considering that, e.g., trafficking in human beings for sexual exploitation is often disguised as information about adoption, job offers, etc.

[23] Tribunal de Grande Instance de Paris, 10 July 1997, *Gazette du Palais* (18-20 January 1998), pp. 42-46, annotated by A. Cousin. The civil claim for compensation by the Jewish student organization that initiated the proceedings was rejected on technical grounds.

[24] Arrondissementsrechtbank Rotterdam, 24 August 1995, *Computerrecht* (1996), pp. 183-197, annotated by R. De Mulder.

PTT Telecom), offered those telephone numbers and names of telephone subscribers through the Internet.[25]

This last case could also haven been dealt with in terms of data protection, that is, the legal framework that grants privacy protection to all personal data. In a deliberation (*délibération*) of 8 July 1997, the French data-protection authority, the CNIL, underlined that French data-protection law is to be applied when telephone books are made available on the Internet.[26] Releasing such data on to the Internet creates the risk of interception, falsification, or misuse. In the light of these risks, inherent to the structure of the Internet, the CNIL recommends that telephone subscribers should always be informed about these risks and should be able to refuse without any cost that their details appear on the Internet.

Data protection in Europe and the Internet were designed for each other, and from the start, data-protection regulations contained extraterritorial provisions. The Belgium Data Protection Act (8 December 1992), for example, also applies to databases outside the country that can be consulted directly in Belgium (Art. 3 para. 1(2°)).

Civil law, finally, offers another example of an area of law which is fit to deal with extraterritorial problems. The European Communities Competences and Execution Treaty of 27 September 1968 was invoked by a British woman in London against a French magazine that had published her name and suggested that she was involved in drug trafficking. Following a preliminary question of the House of Lords, the Court of Justice interpreted the Treaty and, more specifically, the terms 'place where the facts that caused damage took place' (Art. 5(3)). The Court decided that in the case of an insult by means of an article in the press that was distributed in several countries, civil suits to obtain monetary compensation could be filed in the country of (the seat of) the publisher or in the countries where the publication has been spread *and* the reputation of a person has been damaged.[27] The way the criterion of the *locus delicti commissi* is formulated in the Treaty is not wholly beyond criticism, but there is no doubt that the Treaty does respond to the legal challenges of the Internet.[28]

---

[25] President Arrondissementsrechtbank Haarlem, 10 July 1996, *Computerrecht* (1996), pp. 198-201, annotated by P.B. Hugenholtz.

[26] CNIL, 'Délibération n° 97-060 du 8 juillet 1997 portant recommandation relative aux annuaires en matière de télécommunications', *Journal Officiel* (2 August 1997), p. 11571; *Gazette du Palais* (7-9December 1997), pp. 25-26.

[27] In this last case, however, monetary compensation could only be allowed for the damage undergone in this specific country. See Case C-68/93 *Fiona Shevill, Ixora Trading Inc., Chequepoint SARL, Chequepoint International* v. *Presse Alliance SA* of 7 March 1995, case reported in P. Vlas, 'Grensoverschrijdende belediging en artikel 5 sub 3 EEX', 44 *Ars Aequi* (1995) No. 11, pp. 880-887.

[28] See B. De Groote, 'Onrechtmatige daad en Internet' [Tort and the Internet], 4 *Nieuw Juridisch Weekblad* (2005) No. 120, pp. 902-915. This author defends the actual framework, compared with American court decisions where criteria are introduced to limit civil jurisdiction, for instance by demanding that not 'incidental harm' but 'the brunt of harm' can be located in a state. Nevertheless, De Groote regrets that the absolute formulation of the *locus delicti commissi* criterion in Art. 5 of the Treaty does not allow for exceptions in cases that *in concreto* demand for other criteria.

5.3.2 Deconstruction of the threat analysis at the national level

In my older publications, I contrasted the existence of case law showing the vitality of these older legal instruments with the striking observation that many national legislators did not wait for this case law, but chose to update their legislation immediately. This legislative activity of updating, in particular of pornography laws all over the world, should be understood not so much in terms of effectiveness but in terms of strengthening the symbolic function of criminal laws.[29] Through this updating, the message was spread that governments are taking care of the new media,[30] and that there is no threat coming out of the new virtual geographies, whatever popular press and social scientists may suggest.[31] New Internet laws want to bring comfort to all of us, also to Internet providers claiming immunities for their enterprises. Amending criminal-law principles will ensure they have a safe business. The idea that the normal application of criminal-law principles could imply their criminal responsibility (e.g., when they are aware of illegal web sites) suffocates these vital businessmen who (evidently) prefer a hands-off approach. Minor touches to legislation often hide political moves serving other purposes than effectiveness.

A similar deconstruction is possible with regard to rhetoric about justice being unable to combat cybercrime due to inadequate law-enforcement mechanisms or an unadjusted legal framework for effective law enforcement.[32] Evidence law in most European countries is surprisingly flexible. Civil-law countries in general do not regulate the presentation of evidence and have an open system of evidence, i.e., in principle, everything is admissible as evidence. In countries such as France, Portugal, Belgium, and Italy, this is indeed the case.[33] There seems to be, at least on

[29] M. Van De Kerckhove, 'Les lois pénales sont-elles faites pour êtres appliquées?', *Journal des Tribunaux* (22 May 1985), No. 5339, pp. 329-334.

[30] Cf., A. Klip, 'Uniestrafrecht is op hol geslagen' [Criminal Law in the Union in a Frenzy?], *Nederlands Juristenblad* (1997) No. 15, p. 667, heavily criticizing the Joint Action of the European Union on Human Trade and Sexual Abuse (adopted 24 February 1997, *OJ* 1997, L63/2): the document falsely suggests that lack of explicit and updated legislation and international co-ordination, rather than the lack of good management and professionalism, was the cause in Belgium of the Dutroux case, a sexual child-abuse scandal.

[31] D. Gunkel and A.H. Gunkel, 'Virtual geographies. The New Worlds of Cyberspace', 14 *C.S.M.C.* (1997) No. 2, pp. 123-137.

[32] See also Gallant, *International Legal Practitioner* (December 1997), p. 144. One of the crucial documents that contributed to the threat scenario is Recommendation R(95) 13 of the Committee of Ministers of the Council of Europe concerning problems of criminal procedural law connected with information technology, adopted on 11 September 1995, available at <http://www.coe.fr/cm/ta/rec/1995/95r13.htm>.

[33] See for a detailed discussion: Jean Pradel, 'Criminal Evidence', in J.F. Nijboer and W.J.J.M. Sprangers, eds., *Harmonisation in Forensic Expertise. An Inquiry into the Desirability of and Opportunies for International Standards* (Amsterdam, Thela Thesis 2000), pp. 411-429 at p. 416. See, for instance, Art. 427 French CCP, allowing any evidence for free evaluation, and Art. 125 Portuguese CCP, stating similarly that all evidence that has not been forbidden by law is admissible. The Belgian (cf., Art. 154 Belgian CCP) and Italian (Art. 189 Italian CCP) points of view are comparable.

paper, some complication with countries such as Germany and the Netherlands, which do not have an open system of evidence, but a system based on the notion of 'legality of the evidence', viz. the rule that accepted types of evidence are enumerated in the law. Since digital evidence is not mentioned in the Dutch *Wetboek van Strafvordering* (Code of Criminal Procedure, hereafter: CCP),[34] there might be reason to doubt whether this new type of evidence is acceptable. In practice, evidence law in the Netherlands and Germany is moving towards a system of freedom of evidence.[35] Usually, this is made possible through an extensive interpretation of the admitted categories of legal evidence. In this light, it is no surprise that the Dutch Computer Crime Act of 1993[36] did not contain any provision to alter or change the Dutch law of evidence in order to adapt it to digital or electronic evidence. There was simply no need for such an adaptation because of the flexibility in practice of the country's law of evidence.[37]

5.3.3 Cross-border investigation powers

A typical modern yardstick to measure the strength of national law-enforcement authorities is the issue of policing offensive materials originating from outside national boundaries. It looks like an impossible job for police officers stationed in Brussels or Amsterdam, and very often, they spread the message asking for new money or personnel. But is it impossible? Telecommunications entering the national boundaries can always be intercepted, and network operators, in particular those offering voice service, have in the past established working relations with law enforcement to facilitate lawful interception of communications.[38] Providers of web sites can always be localized, wherever they operate.[39] A simple phone call to foreign colleagues can do the rest, as is proven by the Birmingham University case, were British police initiated action after being contacted by net-surfing US Customs.[40] The *Levin* case[41] shows additional tricks for national law-enforcement agencies to catch cybercrime suspects abroad.

---

[34] Art. 339 Dutch CCP lists exhaustively all accepted types of evidence: the observations of the judge himself, statements by the suspect, witnesses, and experts, and written documents (*schriftelijke bescheiden*). German law includes statements by the accused, witnesses, and experts, and 'a view of something' (means of proof consisting of what can be perceived by the senses at the crime).

[35] See Pradel, loc. cit. n. 33, pp. 416-417; H. Nijboer, 'Criminal Justice System', in J.M.J. Chorus, et al., *Introduction to Dutch Law* , 3rd edn. (The Hague, Kluwer Law International 1999), pp. 383-434 at pp. 429-430.

[36] *Official Journal of the Netherlands* (*Staatsblad*) 1993, No. 33.

[37] For instance, computer evidence in the form of printouts of intercepted e-mails and of data gathered in computers can enter without difficulty in the category of written documents.

[38] About the possible role and the importance of prevention and non-governmental resources, see P.N. Grabosky, 'Crime in Cyberspace', in Ph. Williams and D. Vlassis, eds., *Combating Transnational Crime. Concepts, Activities and Responses* (London, Frank Cass 2001), pp. 195-208.

[39] About the impossibility to create anonymous web sites, see G. Wierda, 'Een slot op de deur. Randvoorwaarden voor rechtshandhaving op het Internet', *Computerrecht* (1996) No. 6, p. 234.

[40] Cf., chapter 3 of this book.

[41] See chapter 15, section 15.2, of this book.

In the past decade, we have witnessed several international regulations that have broadened law-enforcement powers or that have taken into account new ICT-based possibilities. Examples that come to mind are the 2001 Council of Europe Cybercrime Convention[42] and the 2005 EU Framework Decision on attacks against information systems.[43] The Cybercrime Convention, for instance, embodies basic rules that, once implemented by the Parties, make it easier for the police to investigate computer crimes, with the help of new forms of mutual assistance (preservation of computer-stored data, preservation and rapid disclosure of traffic data, system search and seizure, real-time collection of traffic data, and interception of content data). Also, the Convention enforces co-operation corresponding to the powers it defines, in addition to the traditional forms of international co-operation covered by older texts like the European conventions on extradition and on mutual assistance discussed below.

The 2005 EU Framework Decision does not add much to this, except for an interesting paragraph on jurisdiction (see *infra*). It is seemingly no more than an uninspired copy of the Cybercrime Convention, imposing on Member States a duty to adopt a common definition with regard to certain computer-related crimes and omitting a chapter on co-operation and law enforcement.[44] More relevant is the 2000 EU Convention on Mutual Assistance in Criminal Matters between the Member States of the European Union and its two protocols.[45] These documents supplement and build on the 1959 Council of Europe Convention on Mutual Assistance in Criminal Matters by developing and modernizing existing provisions governing mutual assistance in general.[46] Less known, but relevant for this chapter, are its provisions with regard to the interception of telecommunications.[47] This investigation technique was not dealt with in the 1959 CoE Convention. The 2000 EU Con-

---

[42] Council of Europe, Convention on Cybercrime, 23 November 2001 (CETS No. 185), available at <http://conventions.coe.int/Treaty/en/Treaties/Html/185.htm>. See chapter 2 of this book. Cf., P. de Hert and G. Lichtenstein, 'La signification de la Convention Européenne sur la cybercriminalité pour l'information et la coopération internationale', 10 *Vigiles* (2004) No. 5, pp. 149-165.

[43] Council Framework Decision 2005/222/JHA of 24 February 2005 on attacks against information systems, *OJ* L69/67, 16 March 2005.

[44] In EU policy circles, it is readily admitted that there is no other reason for the existence of the Framework Decision than the need to clarify what should be understood under the notion of 'computer-related crime' in the 2002 Framework Decision on the European arrest warrant (see n. 59).

[45] *OJ* C197, 12 July 2000. One protocol provides for mutual assistance in relation to bank accounts and banking transactions; the other improves and supplements the 1959 CoE Convention on Mutual Assistance in Criminal Matters and its additional Protocol. See also the Explanatory report, *OJ* C379, 29 December 2000.

[46] The content of the EU Convention with regard to the procedure very much resembles the procedure elaborated for the European arrest warrant (see n. 59).

[47] See Arts. 18-22 of the EU 2000 Convention. On the origins of and the background to these provisions, see Statewatch, *Memorandum to sub-committee "E" of the House of Lords Select Committee on the European Communities's inquiry into "Mutual assistance in criminal matters" (consideration of the draft Convention on Mutual Assistance in criminal matters)*, 25 November 1997, available at <http://www.statewatch.org/docbin/evidence/DrMLA.htm>.

vention allows interception at the request of a competent authority from another Member State – a judicial authority or an administrative authority designated for the purpose by the Member State concerned. Communications may either be intercepted and transmitted directly to the requesting Member State or recorded for subsequent transmission (Art. 18). Member States are to consider such requests in accordance with their own national law and procedures. Interception may also take place on the territory of a Member State in which earth satellite equipment is located, if the technical assistance of that Member State is not required by the service providers in the requesting Member State. Where interception takes place on the territory of a particular Member State because of the location of the subject, but no technical assistance is needed, the Member State carrying out the interception should inform the other Member State of its action.

The 2000 EU Convention is still not implemented in all EU Member States. In Belgium, it has been implemented by the Law of 9 December 2004 *concerning the international mutual assistance in penal cases and to change Article 90 of the Code of Criminal Procedure.*[48] The Act adds new paragraphs 6 and 7 to Article 90 CCP on the interception of telecommunications:

> '6. A proper foreign authority can, in the frame of a penal investigation, intercept temporarily private communications, take knowledge of them and record them during transmission, in case the person who is the subject of this measure is staying on Belgium territory and under the following terms:
> 1° No technical support is needed of any authority residing in Belgium.
> 2° The foreign government informs the Belgium judicial authority of the measure.
> 3° This possibility has been covered by an international judicial instrument between Belgium and the requesting state.
> 4° The decision of the investigating judge, as meant in para. 7, has not been notified to the foreign government.
> The data collected based on this paragraph can only be used if the Belgium judicial authorities approve the measure.
>
> 7. When the attorney receives the notification mentioned in para. 6(2°), he immediately brings the matter before an investigating judge. The investigating judge who has been requisitioned with this notification can decide that the measure is allowed corresponding to this article. He informs the proper foreign authority of his decision within 96 hours after receiving the notification by the Belgium judicial government.
> If he needs more time to come to a decision, he informs the requesting government, which allows him to have 8 more days to decide. The judge has to give the reasons why he will delay his decision.
> If the investigating judge does not allow the measures mentioned in para. 6, he informs the foreign authority of his decision and notifies them that the data which have been collected by the measure should be destroyed and may not be used before a court or during an investigation.

---

[48] *Belgisch Staatsblad/Moniteur Belge* [Official Journal of Belgium] 24 December 2004.

These provisions should be understood in the light of the difference between 'jurisdiction' and 'sovereignty'. A person, for instance a French citizen with a mobile telephone using a French provider, will, while entering Belgium, remain connected to the French provider whenever he remains close to the border. Technically speaking, a French investigating judge will be able to order an interception using his access to the French network, but legally speaking, the suspect is out of his reach, and the interception, when carried out, is taking place in Belgium.[49] The new legal framework resolves this conflict by recognizing 'sovereignty over Belgian territory' and sharing 'jurisdiction', while building in *a posteriori* safeguards for Belgian jurisdiction on its territory.

Neither the Cybercrime Convention nor the 1995 CoE Recommendation No. R(95) 13 Concerning Problems of Criminal Procedure Law Connected with Information Technology contain provisions regarding transborder interception, although the technical possibility already existed and there had been U.S. pressure to adopt the measure.[50] It may well be that the Council of Europe considered the issue not to be sufficiently mature. This attitude probably explains why other possibilities for national operating cyber-law-enforcement agencies are equally unexplored in the Cybercrime Convention.

Some Member States are more 'daring'. Their national bills explore new law-enforcement powers that are based on complete new understandings about the way criminal investigations and the roles of the respective parties should be organized. Later on, I will discuss new extraterritorial powers to search computers introduced in Belgian law by the 2000 Belgian Computer Crime Act.[51] Another example from this Act is the far-reaching duty to co-operate with law-enforcement authorities. The days are gone when suspects and witnesses had a passive position. The Act introduced a new Article 88quater CCP, allowing the investigating judge to impose the obligation on certain individuals to co-operate during an investigation. These individuals are described as persons whom the investigating judge thinks that they have special capacities concerning the computer that is the object of an investigation, or of services used to store, process, encrypt, or transfer data. The investigating judge can compel those individuals to provide information concerning how the system works or how one can get access to the stored data in an understandable format (the first duty). The investigating judge can even compel the individual to operate the system to deliver the data or to search it and to give access, to copy these data, or to make them inaccessible or delete them (the second duty). Refusal to co-operate can be punished. The first duty to grant access or to encrypt can also

49 L. Van Doren, W. De Schepper and W. Moonen, 'Nieuwe regels voor het afluisteren van telefoongesprekken' [New Rules for the Interception of Telecommunications], *Politiejournaal*, (2005) No. 3, pp. 19-22.

50 Statewatch, op. cit. n. 47, p. 4.

51 The Computer Crime Act [*Wet inzake informaticacriminaliteit/Loi sur la criminalité informatique*] of 28 November 2000, *Belgisch Staatsblad/Moniteur Belge* 3 February 2001, p. 2909, introduced new penal legislation concerning computer crimes in Belgium. It entered into force on 13 February 2001.

be imposed on suspects, which is of course not self-evident in the light of the *nemo tenetur* principle recognized in European human rights law.[52]

5.4 International Co-operation and the European Arrest Warrant

5.4.1 Today's possibilities

Of course, when national law enforcement does not work, there is always the possibility to make use of a helping hand from colleagues abroad. Literature on the Internet often stresses the weaknesses of international co-operation between law-enforcement authorities, but today's *possibilities* in this area are too easily forgotten. Indeed, technical evolutions do not only serve criminals, but also serve the judiciary. The Internet is in fact not the first phenomenon to cross borders; it is only a new variation on what has long been possible in telecommunications. For many years, police and judicial organs have been using the telephone, telegraph, and fax. The acquisition of information abroad is becoming possible without having to rely in every case on a cumbersome and delicate rogatory mission. The physical interstate co-operation can be initiated and prepared via telecommunications. Suspect databases even make it possible to spread requests for co-operation without requiring the requestor to give information concerning the suspect's specific place of abode.

International co-operation has also been strengthened in recent years. Supranational police bodies, such as Europol, Eurojust, Schengen, and Interpol, play a role in signaling, immediate action, education, and co-ordination.[53] Especially the signing of the 1990 Schengen Agreement has encouraged dynamism.[54] According to this agreement, extradition within Europe should from now on take place on the basis of the 1957 CoE Treaty on Extradition. However, Schengen goes further than

---

[52] See very critical on this, P. De Hert and G. Lichtenstein, 'De wet van 28 November 2000 inzake informaticacriminaliteit en het formeel strafrecht' [The Computer Crime Act of 28 November 2000 and Criminal Procedure Law], in Centrum voor Beroepsvervolmaking in de Rechten, *CBR Jaarboek 2002-2003* (Antwerp-Apeldoorn, Maklu 2003), pp. 345-420.

[53] See on Schengen, Europol, and Interpol: P. De Hert and J. Vanderborght, *Informatieve politiesamenwerking over de grenzen heen* [Cross-border Exchange of Police Data] (Brussels, Uitgeverij Politeia 1996). The Eurojust initiative is of a more recent date, designed to facilitate information exchange between authorities and cross-border co-operation in the investigation and prosecution of serious and organized crime. See Council Decision of 28 February 2002, *OJ* L63/1, 6 March 2002. Art. 10 of the 2005 EU Framework Decision on attacks against information systems foresees an important role for Eurojust in cases of multiple jurisdictions, viz. conflicts of positive jurisdiction (two or more states that declare themselves competent to prosecute a case).

[54] The Schengen Agreement is published in *International Legal Materials* (1991), p. 84. Later on, the Agreement was incorporated in EU law. See The Schengen acquis, *OJ* L239, 22 September 2000, pp. 19-62.

just repeating this older Treaty. It contains a provision that tempers the traditional requirement of double criminality, that is, the rule demanding that extradition is allowed only where acts stipulated in the request are categorized as criminal also by the domestic law of the requested state. This requirement, when linked to minimum penal thresholds, is often seen as an obstacle to effective co-operation.[55] Also, with regard to the procedures to be followed in extradition cases, Schengen creates more flexibility and also contains a regulation for cases in which there is a concurrence of requests for extradition.[56] Finally, the Schengen Agreement modifies the 1959 European Convention on Mutual Assistance in Criminal Matters.[57] One of the practical results of this is that, from now on, requests for domiciliary visits and seizures can be granted, even if the crime at issue does not form a very serious crime or when it forms only an administrative crime in the country where the help is requested.[58] One step further on this road towards optimization is the European arrest warrant. We will now discuss this legal instrument, followed by an illustration of its consequences in the area of cybercrime.

5.4.2 The 2002 framework decision on the European arrest warrant

Well aware of the fundamental changes to extradition law, the drafters of the Framework Decision on the European arrest warrant and the surrender procedures between Member States of the European Union, adopted on 13 June 2002,[59] have chosen to use new terms to denote the new mechanisms of 'extradition' (now: 'surrender') within the EU. This choice of terminology, although not uncontroversial, will become clear when the main features of the Framework Decision are discussed. A definition of the term 'European arrest warrant' (hereafter: EAW) is found in Article 1(1): 'The European arrest warrant is a judicial decision issued by a Member State with a view to the arrest and surrender by another Member State of a requested person, for the purposes of conducting a criminal prosecution or executing a custodial sentence or detention order.' This time, the traditional requirement of double criminality is not only tempered but removed to a large extent, although

[55] The requirement is not only tempered in the Schengen Agreement, but also put aside by creating the possibility for Member States to circumvent it by using of the possibility of accessory or additional extradition. See Art. 2(2) of the European Extradition Treaty and Art. 62(3) Schengen Agreement.

[56] Cf., Art. 17 European Treaty on Extradition.

[57] Council of Europe, European Convention on Mutual Assistance in Criminal Matters (*ETS* No. 30).

[58] P. De Hert, 'Internationale samenwerking inzake fiscale delicten en verbeurdverklaring voor en na Schengen' [International Co-operation with regard to Financial Crimes Before and After Schengen], in M. Rozie, ed., *Fiscaal straf-en strafprocesrecht* (Ghent, Mys en Breesch 1996), pp. 55-176 at pp. 116-117. Cf., Art. 51 Schengen Agreement.

[59] Council Framework Decision on the European arrest warrant and the surrender procedures between Member States of the European Union, 13 June 2002, *OJ* L190/1 (18 July 2002). See M. Plachta, 'European Arrest Warrant: Revolution in Extradition?', 11 *European Journal of Crime, Criminal Law and Criminal Justice* (2003) No. 2, pp. 178-194.

not completely abolished. Article 2(2) contains a list of 32 generic types of offenses for which it removes the possibility of examining double criminality.[60] This provision stipulates that these offenses, if they are punishable in the issuing Member State by a custodial sentence or a detention order for a maximum period of at least three years and as they are defined by the law of the issuing Member State, shall, under the terms of this Framework Decision and without verification of the double criminality of the act, give rise to surrender pursuant to a European arrest warrant.[61]

The most striking feature of the extradition system based on the Framework Decision is the removal of extradition outside the realm of the executive.[62] The sole responsibility for this procedure has been placed in the hands of the judiciary. Both the issuing and the executing authorities shall be such judicial authorities as are competent to issue or execute the EAW by virtue of the law of the issuing or executing state (Art. 6). Another striking feature is the removal of traditional grounds for refusing extradition. Both the elimination of the executive from the process and the removal of grounds for refusal are based on the idea that there should be *one* area of freedom, security, and justice within the EU and that within this area, Member States should strive to achieve mutual recognition of judicial decisions of the criminal-justice organs of the Member States.[63] Because extradition (or 'surrender') remains an intrusive measure for the suspect, the Framework Decision does not abolish altogether the traditional grounds of refusal. The system does not amount to 'automatic extradition' or surrender on demand,[64] and some grounds of refusal remain valid. Interesting for our purpose are some of the grounds for optional refusal provided for in Article 4, viz. the ground of non-prosecution and the two jurisdiction-related grounds.[65] The former prevents surrender in cases where the judicial authorities of the executing Member State have decided either not to prosecute the offense or to halt proceedings, or where a final judgment has been passed upon the requested person in a Member State, in respect of the same acts, which prevents further proceedings. The latter prevents surrender when an offense is regarded by the law of the executing Member State as having been committed in whole or in

[60] Outside the scope delimited by these 32 categories of offenses, the double-criminality requirement still prevails. For offenses other than those covered by para. 2, surrender may be subject to the condition that the acts for which the EAW has been issued constitute an offense under the law of the executing Member State, whatever the constituent elements or however it is described (Art. 2(4)).

[61] The offenses include, e.g., participation in a criminal organization, trafficking in human beings, sexual exploitation of children and child pornography, illicit trafficking in narcotic drugs and psychotropic substances, illicit trafficking in weapons, munitions and explosives, corruption, laundering of the proceeds of crime, counterfeiting currency, computer-related crime, facilitation of unauthorized entry and residence, murder, grievous bodily injury, illicit trade in human organs and tissue, kidnapping, illegal restraint and hostage-taking, racism, and xenophobia.

[62] Plachta, loc. cit. n. 59, p. 182.

[63] Ibid., p. 179.

[64] Ibid., p. 184.

[65] More in detail: ibid., pp. 186-187.

part in its territory or in a place treated as such; or when an offense has been committed outside the territory of the issuing Member State and the law of the executing Member State does not allow prosecution for the same offense when committed outside its territory.

5.4.3 **Implications of the EAW for cybercrime**

The first implication of the new extradition system in the EAW for the fight against cybercrime regards the requirement of double criminality. Among the offenses included in Article 2(2), which removes the possibility for examining double criminality, are sexual exploitation of children and child pornography, computer-related crime, and racism and xenophobia. Strictly speaking, this provision creates the possibility that Member States can be requested to surrender persons for acts that are not incriminated in their state. This possibility, firstly, raises the issue of differences between countries with regard to penalties and with regard to the minimum level of penalties. In extradition law, this might create a problem, since offenses penalized by only fines often do not give rise to extradition.[66] The problem is, again, not new; Internet only brings it to the surface in a different way. Some see in these differences a serious problem for the public order in the world at large and formulate pleas for a collective increase in the severity of sentencing of all Internet crimes until they become extraditionable.[67] A second issue that is raised regards situations in which some countries incriminate certain activities and other countries do not. I started my contribution with the examples of gambling and comparative advertising, which were prohibited in Belgium but accepted in other countries. Again, some see serious problems for the international public order. A criminal could relocate his activities to a criminal paradise and from this location misuse the Internet without fear of sanction. Initiatives such as the Cybercrime Convention and the EU Framework Decision on attacks against information systems thrive on these kinds of fears and therefore oblige all Member States to incriminate a series of Internet wrongdoings.[68]

---

[66] The traditional idea in extradition law is that extradition will only take place for very serious crimes. Most treaties therefore require minimum penalty thresholds for extradition for criminal offences. Both the 1957 European Extradition Treaty and the 1962 Benelux Extradition Treaty exclude extradition for offences without imprisonment or detention.

[67] See also B. Spruyt and B. de Schutter, *Grensoverschrijdende informaticacriminaliteit en de Europese strafrechtelijke samenwerking* [Transborder Computer Crime and the European Mutual Assistance in Criminal Matters] (Antwerp, Kluwer 1989), p. 63.

[68] Cf., 'Significant gaps and differences in Member States' laws in this area may hamper the fight against organised crime and terrorism, and may complicate effective police and judicial cooperation in the area of attacks against information systems. The transnational and borderless character of modern information systems means that attacks against such systems are often transborder in nature, thus underlining the urgent need for further action to approximate criminal laws in this area' (Preamble of the 2005 EU Framework Decision on attacks against information systems, fifth consideration). The Cybercrime Convention also provides that the offenses it details should be extraditable provided they

I am not convinced that this is the proper way to act. The classic idea of criminal law as a last resort should make us more sympathetic to differences with regard to incriminations and differences with regard to penalties. The starting point should remain that there will be extradition only for very serious crimes. When a country incriminates certain acts by fines only, this should, on the contrary, give a good indication that the condition of gravity is not fulfilled. In a certain way, it can be defended that the Framework Decision respects differences with regard to the use of criminal law, by no longer upholding the requirement of double criminality. There is no longer any need to force all Member States of a community to apply the criminal-law instrument in a uniform way. For the suspected individual, however, the new rules are a setback. As described above, Member States can be requested to surrender persons for acts not punishable in the executing Member State.

A second implication of the new European extradition framework for the fight against cybercrime regards the issue of jurisdiction. There is, properly speaking, no solid check on the legitimacy of the request. The judicial authorities in the requested Member States are not supposed to consider the amount of evidence and to answer the question whether this evidence is sufficient in the light of the presumption of innocence. Likewise, there is no obligatory check on the admissibility of the prosecution in the issuing Member State. In the name of mutual trust, these checks are not provided for on a standard basis. What remains is the possibility to make use of the grounds of optional refusal provided for in Article 4. Two of these grounds are the jurisdiction-related grounds mentioned above, which might be relevant for our purpose. However, especially with regard to the second ground (when the offense has been committed outside the territory of the issuing Member State and the law of the executing Member State does not allow prosecution for the offense when committed outside its territory), prudence is warranted. As I will explain later on, there is no such thing as a stringent set of rules with regard to determining territory. It may therefore be very difficult for a (local) judicial actor (for instance, a public prosecutor or an investigating judge) to assess the need to apply this ground of refusal. The practical implications of the Framework Decision are best made clear with the case of Holocaust denier Siegfried Verbeke.[69]

5.4.4 Illustration: the case of holocaust denier Siegfried Verbeke

In August 2005, the Belgian right-wing extremist Siegfried Verbeke was taken into custody at Schiphol Amsterdam airport. Verbeke, one of the leading European dis-

are punishable under the laws of both parties 'by deprivation of liberty for a maximum period of at least one year, or by a more severe penalty' (Art. 24(1)).

[69] P.R. Rodrigues, 'Belgian Holocaust Denier Siegfried Verbeke Caught', short comment published on the European Monitor Center against Racism and Xenophobia (2005). See for a description of the case in an earlier phase: P.R. Rodrigues, 'Crossborder Discrimination: Private International Law, the Denial of the Holocaust and the Internet', in T. Loenen and P.R. Rodrigues, eds., *Non-Discrimination Law: Comparative Perspectives* (The Hague/London/Boston, Martinus Nijhoff Publishers/Kluwer Law International 1999), pp. 397-410.

seminators of publications denying the Holocaust, publishes on his website theories that deny the Holocaust in four languages. Already in 1997, he was sentenced by the Dutch Supreme Court to a suspended term of six months' imprisonment and a penalty of 2,200 euro for violating Dutch anti-discrimination law by posting unsolicited leaflets to Dutch Jews.[70] However, the publicist kept on disseminating discriminatory content on his website Free Historical Research.[71] On April 14, 2005, the Belgian Court of Appeal of Antwerp sentenced Verbeke to one year imprisonment and ten years' deprivation of voting rights for violating the Act against Holocaust Denial and the Non-Discrimination Act.[72] The court took into account his activities in real life and on the Internet during the period 1996-2002.[73]

At this moment (September 2005), Verbeke is imprisoned in the Netherlands. The prosecutor's office in the Netherlands can prosecute Verbeke on the basis of a charge against him in 2003 for persistent publishing of right-wing extremist views on the Internet.[74] It can also choose to halt prosecution in the Netherlands and to extradite Verbeke to Germany, which has issued a European warrant for him. In December 2004, a Belgian court denied a similar German request because Verbeke is a Belgian citizen and his extradition would breach the principle of *ne bis in idem* (one cannot be prosecuted twice for the same criminal act). The basis of the German request to the Netherlands is a complaint by the same Dutch organizations that filed a complaint in the Netherlands. The Dutch court will hear the German request on September 27, 2005. The penalty in Germany for holocaust denial can be up to four years' imprisonment.

This case shows that one web site can be the source of jurisdictional claims by at least three countries. If, for the judges, the language used on the web site is the decisive criterion – this is only a guess since precise criteria for jurisdiction regarding web sites are nowhere spelled out – things can still become worse for Verbeke, who uses four popular European languages on his web site. Apparently, also, the earlier refusal of a Belgian court to extradite Verbeke to Germany did not refrain the Germans from issuing an arrest warrant. Perhaps – I do not know – this warrant is based on new or more recent facts.

It is also interesting to observe that transnational 'wrongs' like the exploitation of a revisionist web site can persuade victims or human rights organizations to go

[70] See for a brief discussion of the Dutch case law, including digital versions of the cases: C. de Fey, 'Veroordeling voor ontkenning van holocaust' [Conviction for Denying Holocaust], 4 May 2005, available at <http://www.lbr.nl/?node=3374>.

[71] 'Vrij historisch onderzoek' [Free Historical Research], <http://www.vho.org>.

[72] Court of Appeal, 14 April 2005, available through <http://www.antiracisme.be>. The Court confirmed an earlier judgment by the Court of First Instance (criminal chamber) of Antwerp, 9 September 2003 (see n. 20).

[73] See also 'Belgian Court Convicts Holocaust Denier', 9 September 2003, available at <http://www.icare.to/archiveaugustandseptember2003.html>.

[74] The Dutch antiracism organizations Magenta Foundation, Anne Frank House, the National Bureau against Racial Discrimination, and the Centre for Documentation and Information on Israel filed a criminal complaint against Verbeke in the summer of 2003.

'forum shopping'. Undoubtedly, a prosecution in Germany will benefit Verbeke less. He can only hope that the Dutch prosecutor will go on to prosecute in the Netherlands. As we saw earlier, the prosecutor can use one of the optional grounds of refusal, viz. 'when an offence is regarded by the law of the executing Member State as having been committed in whole or in part in the territory'. I recall a second optional ground of refusal, viz. refusing to surrender when an offense has been committed outside the territory of the issuing Member State and the law of the executing Member State does not allow prosecution for the same offense when committed outside its territory. The Dutch prosecutor could defend the position that the Belgian web site is outside German territory and that, since German is one of the three official Belgian languages, there is no reason for Germany to exercise jurisdiction.

However, as there is no such thing as a stringent set of rules with regard to determining territory (see *infra*), this outcome is very unlikely, especially in the light of Article 10 of the 2005 EU Framework Decision on attacks against information systems that, with regard to jurisdiction, supplements Article 22 of the Cybercrime Convention. In their urge to end all 'gaps in the legal framework', the EU drafters have created a regime in which all transborder crime creates positive conflicts of jurisdiction.[75] A similar regime, but to a lesser degree, was created in the Cybercrime Convention. A small paragraph in this Convention tries to remedy this conflict by imposing a guideline that 'the Parties involved shall, where appropriate, consult with a view to determining the most appropriate jurisdiction for prosecution.'[76] A bit more firm is Article 10 paragraph 4 of the 2005 EU Framework Decision:

> '4. Where an offence falls within the jurisdiction of more than one Member State and when any of the States concerned can validly prosecute on the basis of the same facts, the Member States concerned shall cooperate in order to decide which of them will prosecute the offenders with the aim, if possible, of centralizing proceedings in a single Member State. To this end, the Member States may have recourse to any body or mechanism established within the European Union in order to facilitate cooperation between their judicial authorities and the coordination of their action. Sequential account may be taken of the following factors:
> - the Member State shall be that in the territory of which the offences have been committed according to paragraph 1(a) and paragraph 2,
> - the Member State shall be that of which the perpetrator is a national,
> - the Member State shall be that in which the perpetrator has been found.'

Although these guidelines are not legally binding, there is some wisdom therein. The Dutch prosecutor can no longer decide for himself with regard to the prosecu-

[75] See especially Art. 10 para. 2 ('Jurisdiction') of the 2005 EU Framework Decision on attacks against information systems.

[76] See Art. 22 para. 5 Cybercrime Convention.

tion.[77] Some co-ordination with German colleagues, directly or via Eurojust, is needed. The last guideline suggests that in case of conflicting views, prosecution in the Netherlands is most evident. For Verbeke, this is a good thing. We do not expect revisionists to travel freely to Germany, since they know that German law is more severe than other systems of law.

The Verbeke case teaches us that there is no longer any legal gap within Europe. Both the EU Framework Decision on attacks against information systems and the EAW Framework Decision see to it that all computer-related crimes by persons in Europe (whether by nationals or non-citizens) are prosecuted – at least in principle.

Of course, this framework would be very much out of balance without a solid framework regulating the problem of *ne bis idem* in the case of multiple jurisdictions, in order to prevent that a person condemned in one state would be prosecuted for the same facts in another state. Unfortunately, this framework does not exist. Although most 'decent' countries in the world recognize the *ne bis in idem* principle in their legal system, there is no international principle of *ne bis in idem* to see to it that countries do not punish the same person for the same fact several times. There is only some self-restraint.[78] With transborder crime, such as cybercrime, this is hardly enough. Although the drafters of the Cybercrime Convention were assigned with the task to regulate the problem in the interest of the convicted person,[79] the Convention, in its final version, is silent on this matter.

All that Europe has is Article 54 of the 1990 Schengen Agreement.[80] This provision seems to remedy well for this striking gap in the human-rights protection of condemned persons,[81] but doubt remains. Article 55 of the Schengen Agreement contains exceptions to the principle of *ne bis in idem* that raise questions about the value of the principle with regard to 'real' transborder crime.[82] Also, there are legal

[77] See also Art. 57 Schengen Agreement.

[78] See Ch. Van Den Wyngaert, 'The Transformations of International Criminal Law as a Response to the Challenge of Organised Crime. General Report of the Fourth Section of the AIDP', *Revue Internationale de Droit Pénal* (1999), pp. 170-171; Ch. Van Den Wyngaert and G. Stessens, 'The international non bis in idem principle: resolving some of the unanswered questions', *International Comparative Law Quarterly* (1999), pp. 779-804.

[79] Cf., para. 11 of the Explanatory Report to the Cybercrime Convention, available at <http://conventions.coe.int/Treaty/en/Reports/Html/185.htm>.

[80] Art. 54 Schengen Agreement states: 'A person whose trial has been finally disposed of in one Contracting Party may not be prosecuted in another Contracting Party for the same acts provided that, if a penalty has been imposed, it has been enforced, is actually in the process of being enforced or can no longer be enforced under the laws of the sentencing Contracting Party.' Cf., Art. 56 Schengen Agreement. See on these provisions Klip, loc. cit. n. 30, p. 668.

[81] A Belgian judge made use of the Schengen provisions to cancel the prosecution of persons suspected of having committed several 'sex crimes', when it became clear that they had already been sentenced for the same facts in France. See Court of First Instance (criminal chamber) Ghent, 4 June 1977, *Tijdschrift Gentse Rechtspraak* (1997), pp. 244-246.

[82] See in particular Art. 55 para. 1 Schengen Agreement: 'A Contracting Party may, when ratifying, accepting or approving this Convention, declare that it is not bound by Article 54 in one or more of

practices in countries such as Belgium that raise even more questions. Facts can be prosecuted in Belgium when they can be qualified in a slightly different way compared to the first judgment rendered abroad. Thus, it was accepted by the Belgian Cour de Cassation in 1961 that the wrongful import of butter into Belgium should be considered a crime distinct from the crime of wrongful export from the Netherlands, with the practical result that a new prosecution and conviction, this time in Belgium, becomes possible.[83] Likewise, it is held that a person who buys drugs in the Netherlands and sells them in France and Belgium can be put on trial in Belgium for smuggling and selling drugs, even after a conviction for smuggling and selling drugs in France, 'because they are different offenses.'[84] These judgments, which are difficult to reconcile with the spirit of the Schengen Agreement,[85] are not isolated cases.[86] From the description of the Verbeke case above, we learn, however, that in this particular case, a Belgian court denied a German request to extradite Verbeke on the *ne bis in idem* ground.[87] Of course, this argument seems much more in line with the spirit of the principle as laid down in the Schengen Agreement.

5.5 Enlarged Jurisdiction

5.5.1 **Territoriality and Belgian and Dutch jurisdiction provisions**

I have already observed that there is no such thing as a stringent set of rules with regard to determining territory. To understand this, let us return to the *jurisdiction to prescribe*. This classical tenet of sovereignty denotes the power of states to enact

---

the following cases: (a) where the acts to which the foreign judgment relates took place in whole or in part in its own territory; in the latter case, however, this exception shall not apply if the acts took place in part in the territory of the Contracting Party where the judgment was delivered; (b) where the acts to which the foreign judgment relates constitute an offence against national security or other equally essential interests of that Contracting Party; (c) where the acts to which the foreign judgment relates were committed by officials of that Contracting Party in violation of the duties of their office (...).'

[83] Cassation 20 February 1961, *Passinomie* (1961), p. 664. See also T. Vander Beken, *Forumkeuze in het Internationaal Strafrecht* [Choice of Forum in International Criminal Law] (Antwerp, Maklu 1999), pp. 252-257; S. Brammertz, 'Traffic de stupéfiants et valeur internationale des jugements répressifs à la lumière de Schengen', *Revue de Droit Pénal* (1996), p. 1066.

[84] Court of First Instance (criminal chamber) Brussels, 9 March 1994, *Politeia* (1995) No. 6, p. 22, *Revue De droit Pénal* (1995), p. 295.

[85] See W.F. van Hattum, 'Grensoverschrijdende drugshandel in de Schengenstaten: geen "status aparte"' [Transborder Drugs Trafficking in the Schengen Area: No 'Status Aparte'], *Panopticon* (2001), pp. 248-249.

[86] Only very recently, the Cour de Cassation decided to bring the matter to the Court of Justice in Luxembourg to check whether this kind of case law is compatible with the Schengen Agreement. Cf., Cour de cassation 5 October 2004, 6 *Tijdschrift voor Strafrecht* (2005) No. 5, pp. 360-366.

[87] I have not been able to trace this judgment, which, to my understanding, has not been published in a legal journal.

legal commands or authorizations that bind the individuals in the territory belonging to the state. Prescriptive jurisdiction is not always limited to the territory. Under certain circumstances, it can be extended to individuals abroad. This amazing fact – territoriality of criminal law does not coincide with territorial sovereignty – explains why textbooks on international law recognize more than one ground upon which states can base their jurisdiction.[88] The starting point for jurisdiction is of course territorial jurisdiction. All the other grounds extend criminal jurisdiction outside state borders. States can, for instance, enact legislation binding upon their nationals abroad or can even go as far as to enact legislation which is applicable to acts performed abroad by foreigners against other foreigners. This extraterritorial legislation is for instance adopted for the purpose of exercising universal jurisdiction over terrorism.[89]

Normally, the territoriality principle is preferred, both for ideological reasons (the need to affirm territorial sovereignty) and because the territory where the alleged crime has been committed is the place where it is easier to collect evidence (it is therefore considered as the *forum conveniens*, or the convenient place of trial).[90] Hence, territoriality can be regarded as the default position of most criminal-law systems. This position explains, for instance, the provision in the Belgian Criminal Code stating that Belgian criminal law is only applicable to wrongs committed within the nation's territory, *except* when explicitly provided for by a statute (Arts. 3 and 4 Belgian CC).[91] A similar system exists in the Dutch *Wetboek van Strafrecht* (Criminal Code), where Articles 2-7 state the principles of applicability of Dutch criminal law. Under the principle of territoriality, Dutch criminal law is applicable to anybody who commits a criminal offense on Dutch territory or on board of a Dutch vessel or aircraft outside the Netherlands. Under the universality or protective principle, anyone who commits designated offenses against the interest of the Dutch state or Dutch financial interests outside Dutch territory falls under Dutch criminal-law jurisdiction. Under the active nationality principle, Dutch criminal

---

[88] Territorial jurisdiction stems from wrongs occurring within a nation's territory; nationality jurisdiction is based on an offender's being a national of the state taking jurisdiction; passive jurisdiction occurs when a victim is a national of the state; protective jurisdiction is based on the acts impinging upon important state interests of national security; and universal jurisdiction stems from the notion that some international prohibitions are so important that their violation by anyone, anywhere, warrants any nation's assuming jurisdiction. See I. Brownlie, *Principles of Public International Law*, 4th edn. (1990); Cassese, op. cit. n. 4, p. 49, and the references in H. Osofsky, 'Domesticating International Criminal Law: Bringing Human Rights Violators to Justice', 107 *The Yale Law Journal* (1997) p. 192.

[89] Cassese, op. cit. n. 4, p. 49, with reference to the 1986 US Omnibus Diplomatic Security and Antiterrorism Act, which asserted U.S. jurisdiction over attacks on U.S. citizens in foreign countries, and to the 2001 UK Anti-Terrorism, Crime and Security Act, which in s. 51 asserts jurisdiction over such offenses as causing a nuclear explosion without authorization, developing or transferring nuclear weapons, and assisting or inducing certain weapons-related actions overseas.

[90] Cassese, op. cit. n. 4, p. 451.

[91] These derogations are to be found in the Preliminary Title of the Belgian Code of Criminal Procedure.

law is applicable to anybody of Dutch nationality who commits, outside Dutch territory, either a designated crime or an offense when the requirement of double criminality is fulfilled. The designated crimes include, *inter alia*, offenses against the security of the Dutch state and royal dignity. Furthermore, Dutch criminal law applies to anybody whose prosecution by a foreign state has been transferred to the Netherlands pursuant to a treaty conferring jurisdiction to prosecute in the Netherlands. Finally, Dutch criminal law is applicable to a public official employed by a Dutch public service who commits, outside Dutch territory, serious offenses involving abuse of office.[92]

5.5.2 Two developments with regard to enlarged jurisdiction

Two developments stand out with regard to jurisdiction. First, there is a development towards increased use of provisions in national laws providing for enlarged or even universal jurisdiction in areas connected to human rights and international crimes, such as terrorism, hostage taking, child pornography, and human trafficking.[93] Cassese quotes a British Home Secretary stating in 2000 that the principle of jurisdiction in respect of very serious crimes such as torture is now established.[94] It is important to note in this respect that individual states (can) provide for enlarged jurisdiction without a treaty basis, either through statutory provisions or through jurisprudence. Thus, the Belgian 'sex' laws of 1995[95] created enlarged jurisdiction for the sex offenses defined in Articles 380quinquies through 383 CC. These crimes can be prosecuted by Belgian authorities, when committed abroad by Belgians or foreigners, 'even when the Belgium authorities did not receive a complaint or formal demand from the foreign authorities.'[96] An identical provision was introduced

---

[92] P.J.P. Tak, *The Dutch criminal justice system. Organization and operation*, 2nd edn. (Meppel, Boom 2003), p. 40.

[93] See Osofsky, loc. cit. n. 88, pp. 191-226. See for Europe: B. Huber. and G. Restle, 'Development of Criminal Law in Europe: An Overview', *European Journal of Crime, Criminal Law and Criminal Justice* (1994) No. 3, p. 297; De Hert, loc. cit. n. 58, pp. 164-168. See for Belgium: L. Dupont and R. Verstraeten, *Handboek Belgisch Strafrecht* [Textbook on Criminal Law] (Acco, 1989), p. 150; Ch. Van Den Wyngaert, *Strafrecht en strafprocesrecht in hoofdlijnen* [Criminal Law and Criminal Procedure Law: Main Elements] (Antwerp, Maklu 1994), Part I, pp. 119-122. See, e.g., the 1956 Supplementary Convention on the Abolition of Slavery, the Slave Trade, and Institutions and Practices Similar to Slavery and the 1984 Convention Against Torture and Other Cruel, Inhuman or Degrading Treatment or Punishment.

[94] Cassese, op. cit. n. 4, p. 49 with references.

[95] Act of 27 March 1995, introducing a new article 380quinqquies in the Penal Code and suppressing art. 380quater, °2 of this Code, *Moniteur Belge*, 25 April 1995; Act of 13 April 1995, aiming at combating human trade and child pornography, *Moniteur Belge*, 25 April 1995; Act of 13 April 1995, concerning sexual abuse against minors, *Moniteur Belge*, 25 April 1995. See J. Legreve and F. Tulkens, 'Aperçu critique de la législation belge en matière d'exploitation sexuelle des mineurs', 9 *Revue Trimesterielle des Droits de l'Homme* (1998) No. 3, pp. 3-26.

[96] See Art. 8 of the Act of 13 April 1995.

in German law.[97] Manufacturing child pornography abroad and/or putting it on the Internet can henceforth be prosecuted in these states.

Statutes that expand jurisdiction mark a growing assertiveness and recognition of the role that individual states can play in modern times. Practical limitations of the international legal system accounts for this development. The international legal system, even after the establishment of the International Criminal Court, lacks accessible, effective judicial forums and enforcement mechanisms. These limitations have reinforced the need to use national courts in individual states. Through the multiple use of provisions establishing enlarged jurisdiction, the role of national courts has been strengthened when it comes to enforcement of international human rights and international crimes.[98]

This changing role of national courts is, however, not taking shape with regard to cybercrime, with the exception of child-pornography crimes (*infra*). Neither the 2000 Belgian Computer Crime Act nor the 1993 Dutch Computer Crime Act contain special provisions with regard to jurisdiction. This situation is not self-evident, since computer crimes or cybercrimes qualify without any doubt as international crimes. Perhaps these crimes are not considered serious enough for the instrument of enlarged jurisdiction.[99] Maybe both laws are too old or were drafted in an older logic, ignoring the international dimensions of the crimes they consider. Some ground for this suggestion is given by the existence of jurisdictional provisions in the Cybercrime Convention and in the EU Framework Decision on attacks against information systems. These provisions oblige Member States to define extraterritorial jurisdiction on the basis of the 'active personality' principle.[100] Their inclusion in the texts has been defended with reference to the international character of

---

[97] Cf., P. Berger-Zehnpfund, 'Kinderpornographie im Internet', *Kriminalistik* (1996), No. 10, p. 636.

[98] Osofsky, loc. cit. n. 88, p. 204. Even self-declared 'internationalists' such as Michael Ignatieff, for whom state sovereignty is not a good in itself, remain faithful to the idea of strong states (controlled by an international body) needed to protect human rights. See M. Ignatieff, *Human Rights as Politics and Idolatry* (Princeton, Princeton University Press 2003), p. 35. Cf., H. Arendt, *supra*, n. 15 et seq.

[99] Some ground for this explanation is also given by Walden (see chapter 15 of this book) concerning the lack of extraterritorial provisions in British cybercrime law and the rejection of such provisions in a recent proposal to reform fraud law and to combat cyberfraud.

[100] Art. 22(d) Cybercrime Convention and Art. 10(1)(b) Framework Decision. The latter imposes upon Member States the obligation to prosecute and investigate cases involving offenses when (a) they have been committed in whole or in part on its territory (territoriality principle), (b) the offender is a national (active personality principle), or (c) it has been committed for the benefit of a legal person established in its territory. Para. 2 is intended to ensure that when establishing jurisdiction over offenses based on the territoriality principle, cases are included where (a) the offender commits the offense when physically present on its territory, or (b) the offense is against an information system on its territory. The third paragraph, in line with the provisions of the Cybercrime Convention, deals with cases where a Member State refuses to hand over or extradite a person suspected or convicted of such an offense to another third state; the refusing State will have to prosecute on its own initiative (*aut dedere aut judicare*).

cybercrime that requires procedural provisions on jurisdiction (and extradition) to ensure that offenders cannot escape prosecution.

Walden suggests that these provisions will oblige national governments to adopt appropriate provisions with regard to jurisdiction in national law (see chapter 15). Theoretically, this seems true, but in practice, the development towards an expanded principle of territoriality, extending the locus of the crime to include acts committed abroad, has important effects on jurisdiction that may limit the need for new legal provisions on jurisdiction.

This brings us to the *second development* with regard to jurisdiction: the expansion of the notion of territoriality through the work of national courts. There is indeed a widespread tendency in the case law of national judges to interpret the principle or ground of territorial jurisdiction extensively. As seen above, the Belgian courts are not, except for explicit statutory provisions, competent in extraterritorial cases. Legal practice shows that judges grant great leeway to the Belgian legal authorities when crimes are committed outside Belgian territory but impinge on Belgian interests.[101] The legal situation in Belgium and the Netherlands is very similar to the situation in Chile, as described elsewhere in this book (chapter 7).

In all these legal systems belonging to the civil-law tradition, there are several accepted theories, criteria, or answers to the *locus commissi delicti* question, viz. the question to what extent a wrongful act can be considered to fall within the territorial jurisdiction of a state. Within the Dutch and Belgian tradition, the following accepted criteria are applied:

- the *activity* criterion: the territory where the activity took place is the relevant one;
- the criterion of *the instrument* of the crime;
- the criterion of *the constitutive consequence*, and
- the *ubiquity criterion*: the *locus delicti* is every country where one of the constitutive elements of the crime can be located; it is therefore very well possible that an offense falls within the jurisdiction of more than one country.

Unlike in Germany and France , neither the Dutch nor the Belgian Criminal Code contains a real choice for one of these criteria; it is left to the courts to determine.[102] An analysis shows that whatever criterion is applied, it is almost always easily possible for a judge to declare himself competent and to hold that the events took place on 'his' or 'her' territory.[103] The ubiquity criterion in particular, by now the

[101] See De Hert, loc. cit. n. 58, pp. 109-111.

[102] Art. 9 of the German Criminal Code states that when assessing the relevant territory, the ubiquity criterion should be applied. In France, the same rule exists (Art. 113-2 French Criminal Code). See M. Masse, 'La compétence pénale française dans l'espace depuis l'entrée en vigueur du nouveau code pénal', *Revue de Science Criminelle* (1995) pp. 856-862.

[103] See also G.J.M. van Wijk, 'De lange hand van de personal computer. Locus delicti bij grensoverschrijdende computermisdaad' [The Long Hand of the Personal Computer. Locus Delicti in Cross-Border Computer Crime], 19 *Delikt en Delinkwent* (1989) No. 3, pp. 219-229.

most successful criterion within the civil-law tradition,[104] enables a flexible approach towards the *locus commissi delicti* question.[105] It allows countries to prosecute persons spreading computer viruses or racist information from computers abroad,[106] or persons who 'call' in by telephone from abroad when this conversation forms the starting point for a crime.[107] The flexibility of the ubiquity criterion explains without any doubt the total absence of jurisdiction provisions in the Belgian and Dutch Computer Crime Acts.

5.6 Jurisdiction and the Flexibility of International Law

5.6.1 The *Lotus* case

While discussing prescriptive jurisdiction, I observed that public international law is not restrictive with regard to jurisdiction. States have several grounds to extend criminal law outside their borders.[108] Much discretion is left to the national legislature; only practical limitations and some historically-inspired self-restraint seem to exist. It has rightly been said that the traditional limitation of criminal law to territorial jurisdiction is only of a pragmatic nature and that no principle of international law forbids enlargement of jurisdiction.[109] This situation goes back to the famous 1929 *Lotus* case, in which the Permanent Court of Justice – the predecessor of the present International Court of Justice[110] – took the view that states have a broad margin to decide upon jurisdiction.[111] There is only a question of violating sover-

[104] Ibid., p. 222 with references. See also chapter 7 of this book.

[105] Note that within the civil-law tradition, there is no willingness to accept the simple criterion of *result* or *effect*. To assert jurisdiction simply on the basis that an act has some result in a country is seen as an unacceptable way of expanding national jurisdiction. Therefore, the ubiquity criterion requires that it must be possible to localize one of the constitutive elements of the crime in a country, before it can assert jurisdiction. In practice, however, a broad application of the other criterion can lead to the same extensive result, and very often, judges apply a sloppy analysis and end up by applying the effects criterion. See Van Wijk, loc. cit. n. 103, p. 222; De Hert and Bodard, loc. cit. n. 2, p. 110; Th. Verbiest and E. Wéry, *Le droit de l'internet et de la société de l'information* (Brussels, Larcier 2001), p. 511.

[106] See for a critical analysis of Belgian and French case law accepting jurisdiction for racist web sites abroad: Verbiest and Wéry, op. cit. n. 105, pp. 511-512 with references.

[107] Cassation fr. crim., 10 October 1990, *Juris-Data*, No. 004039. See Verbiest and Wéry, op. cit. n. 105, p. 511.

[108] Cassese, op. cit. n. 4, p. 49.

[109] S. Manacorda, 'Le droit pénal international dans les réformes française et italienne', *Revue de Science Criminelle* (1995) No. 2, pp. 336-337; Ch. Van Den Wyngaert, 'De toepassing van de strafwet in de ruimte. Enkele beschouwingen', in *Liber Amicorum F. DUMON* (Antwerp, Kluwer 1980), pp. 501-525.

[110] The International Court of Justice is the principal judicial organ of the United Nations and is located in The Hague, the Netherlands.

[111] Permanent Court of International Justice (1927), *C.P.I.J. Rec. Publication Series A*, No. 10. The case is reprinted and discussed at length in E. Wise, E. Podgor and R. Clark, *International Criminal Law. Cases and Materials*, 2nd edn. (Newark, LexisNexis 2004), pp. 7-19; Ch. Van Den Wyngaert, *Kennismaking met het Internationaal en Europees strafrecht* (Antwerp, Maklu 2003), pp. 49-50.

eignty, the Court added, when prosecution officers of one country undertake actions on the territory of another country without permission.

Expanded jurisdiction is defended with two arguments. In the case of serious crimes, the argument goes that their gravity and magnitude simply warrant universal prosecution and repression. In all (other) cases, the second argument holds true that the exercise of enlarged prescriptive jurisdiction in itself does not amount to a breach of the principle of sovereign equality of states, nor does it lead to undue interference in the internal affairs of the state where the crime has been committed.[112]

The second argument seems to explain the position of the Permanent Court of Justice in *Lotus*, a case concerning two colliding vessels on the high seas. On 2 August 1926, a collision occurred between the French mail steamer Lotus, proceeding to Constantinople, and the Turkish collier Boz-Kourt, somewhere to the north of Cape Sigri. The Boz-Kourt sank and eight Turkish nationals perished. After having done everything possible to secure the shipwrecked persons, of whom ten were saved, the Lotus continued on its course to Constantinople, where it arrived on 3 August. Two days later, the French first officer of the Lotus was arrested by the Turkish police on a charge of manslaughter. He was subsequently put on trial and sentenced to imprisonment and a fine by a Turkish court. The French government contested the sanction, and the case was brought before the Permanent Court of Justice. The French government contended that the Turkish courts, in order to have jurisdiction, should be able to point to some title to jurisdiction recognized by international law in favor of Turkey. The Turkish government took the view that no rule of international law or customary law contained a prohibition for a state to expand jurisdiction to events committed outside state borders, viz. on the high seas. The Court was evenly divided 6-6; it was the president's vote that resulted in judgment for Turkey. The Court conceded that jurisdiction in principle was tied to territory and that states cannot exercise jurisdiction outside their territory without a legal basis in international law.

> 'It does not, however, follow that international law prohibits a State from exercising jurisdiction in its own territory, in respect of any case which relates to acts which have taken place abroad, and in which it cannot rely on some permissive rule of international law (...). Far from laying down a general prohibition to the effect that States may not extend the application of their laws and the jurisdiction of their courts to persons, property and acts outside their territory, it leaves them in this respect a wide measure of discretion which is only limited in certain cases by prohibitive rules; as regards other cases, every State remains free to adopt the principles which it regards as best and most suitable.'[113]

---

112 Cassese, op. cit. n. 4, p. 452, with references to courts that use these respective arguments.

113 Permanent Court of International Justice (1927), *C.P.I.J. Rec. Publication Series A*, No. 10, p. 19. This discretion left to the national states explains the recognition of the grounds of expanded jurisdiction that I discussed above.

5.6.2 *Yerodia* does not correct *Lotus* but proves my point

I believe it is time to ask whether the *Lotus* acquis is sufficiently solid to deal with today's problems and challenges. In fact, this question has been raised before and in a much wider context, viz. the context of the right of nuclear powers to use nuclear weapons.[114] In the more traditional context of criminal law, the question has also been raised.[115] Some authors regret the discretion that is left to national states with regard to criminal jurisdiction, both at the level of defining 'territory' (the ubiquity criterion and the criterion of effect) and at the level of opting for formal grounds for enlarged jurisdiction. Why prohibit things in other countries and prosecute cases that have no direct link with one legal system? Why police the world if no other country asks for this? Some specifically see in this context a danger of 'excessive jurisdiction' in cases of computer crime.[116]

We noted that states provide for enlarged jurisdiction without a treaty basis, either through statutory provisions or through jurisprudence. Manufacturing child pornography abroad or putting it on the Internet can now be prosecuted in states such as Belgium and Germany, even when neither the victim nor the offender originate from these countries (see *supra*). Asian criminals may laugh at this, but in a world characterized by mobility and plane-hopping, combined with alert systems such as the Schengen Information System, the Europol Information System, and the Interpol Information System,[117] the mobility of internationally-operating (Internet) criminals becomes seriously hindered, and their prosecution becomes only a question of patience. I contend therefore that technological developments give statutes that expand jurisdiction or principles that expand the notion of territory a great potential. States can more effectively punish and prosecute offenses committed outside national boundaries then was the case in 1926.

The turn towards ICT-based prosecution is the real trigger of the famous *Yerodia* case, which turned around the question whether Belgian 'genocide' law based on universal jurisdiction complied with international law.[118] This far-reaching Belgian

[114] 'Surely, speaking as we are today, about the alleged sovereign right to engage in actions that could destroy the planet, we might fairly ask whether it is "authorized" by international law. A moribund and controversial decision about two colliding vessels on the high seas is a very weak base on which to defend the raw power to destroy our Spaceship', R. Clark and M. Sann, quoted in Wise, et al., op. cit. n. 111, p. 19.

[115] Osofsky, loc. cit. n. 88, pp. 212-216. These pages contain an in-depth analysis of the many problems that might arise with enlarged jurisdiction.

[116] Verbiest and Wéry, op. cit. n. 105, p. 511. See also: M. Burnstein, 'Conflicts on the Net: Choice of Law in Transnational Cyberspace', 29 *Vanderbilt Journal of Transnational Law* (1996) No. 75, pp. 75-116. The more the Internet grows, the more the ubiquity criterion will lead to wider jurisdictional claims.

[117] See De Hert and Vanderborght, op. cit. n. 53.

[118] Act of 16 June 1993, modified by the Act of 10 February 1999, concerning the punishment of grave breaches of international humanitarian law, *Belgisch Staatsblad/Moniteur Belge*, 23 March 1999. See Stefaan Smis & Kim Van der Borght, 'Introductory Note on the Act Concerning the Punishment of

regulation was praised by human-rights organizations, but doubts were raised about its legality in international law. By rejecting all immunities, it led to tension with well-established rules of diplomatic law that accord functional immunity to Heads of State, Heads of Government, and Ministers of Foreign Affairs while they are in office, to allow them to perform their function unhindered. A dispute arose between Congo and Belgium when, on 11 April 2000, Judge Damien Vandermeersch of the Brussels Court of First Instance issued an international arrest warrant via Interpol for the detention of Mr. Abdulaye Yerodia Ndombasi (hereafter: Yerodia), who at that time was the Democratic Republic of the Congo Minister of Foreign Affairs.[119] On 17 October 2000, Congo started proceedings against Belgium before the International Court of Justice (ICJ) based on their declarations accepting the Court's compulsory jurisdiction, requesting the Court to declare that Belgium should annul the arrest warrant issued against Yerodia, because it violates the principle of sovereign equality among states.[120] On 14 February 2002, the ICJ ruled that Belgium had violated international law by allowing a Belgian judge to issue and circulate an arrest warrant *in absentia* against the then Foreign Minister of the Democratic Republic of the Congo. The Court held, by thirteen votes to three, that Belgium thereby failed to respect immunity from criminal jurisdiction and the inviolability that the incumbent Foreign Minister enjoyed under customary international law.[121]

Grave Breaches of International Humanitarian Law (10 February 1999)', 38 *International Legal Materials* (1999) pp. 918-920; Van Den Wyngaert, op. cit. n. 111, pp. 62-67. In 1993, Belgium enacted a law that placed it in the lead of a development in international and national law. The Belgian law of 1993, as amended in 1999, allowed Belgian courts to prosecute persons *in absentia* for genocide, war crimes, and crimes against humanity on the basis of universal jurisdiction. This meant that Belgian courts had jurisdiction to prosecute such crimes regardless of the crime's place of commission, the presence of the perpetrator on Belgian territory, the nationality of the perpetrator or the victim, or the time when the crime was committed. To bring a claim, a person did not have to be a Belgian national or reside in Belgium. The law, moreover, did not recognize immunities on the basis of the official position of the person.

[119] The warrant accused Yerodia of having committed grave breaches of the 1949 Geneva Conventions and crimes against humanity while serving in a non-ministerial post by making speeches in August 1998 that allegedly incited the massacre of Tutsi residents in Kinshasa.

[120] It was uncontested that (i) the arrest warrant referred to acts committed outside of Belgium; (ii) Yerodia was the DRC Foreign Minister at the time the warrant was issued; (iii) the accused was neither Belgian nor had he been present in Belgium when the warrant was issued; and (iv) no Belgian national was a direct victim of the alleged crimes.

[121] International Court of Justice, 14 February 2002, concerning the arrest warrant of 11 April 2000 (*Democratic Republic of Congo* v. *Belgium*), *ICJ Reports* (2002), pp. 3-87. The full text of the Court's decision, the opinions and declarations of the judges, and a press communiqué on this case is available at <http://www.icj-cij.org>. See also Wise, et al., op. cit. n. 111, pp. 45-51. By way of remedy, the Court found, by ten votes to six, that Belgium must, by means of its own choosing, cancel the arrest warrant and inform all the authorities to which that warrant was circulated. An amendment in 2003 brought the Belgian law into line with this ICJ judgment by setting aside immunities only as far as international law permits. This formulation allows the Belgian law to develop in line with international law rather than ahead of it. See Van Den Wyngaert, op. cit. n. 111, pp. 65-67; St. Smis and K. Van der Borght, *Belgian Law concerning The Punishment of Grave Breaches of International Humanitarian Law: A Contested Law with Uncontested Objectives* (July 2003), available at <http://www.asil.org/insights/insigh112.htm>.

Congo initially also challenged the legality of the Belgian Act itself, raising a broader question whether the disputed warrant, issued in an exercise of purported universal jurisdiction, complied with the rules and principles of international law governing the jurisdiction of national courts. This claim, however, was dropped. Given this fact, the Court assumed solely for the purpose of this case that Belgium had jurisdiction under international law to issue and circulate the warrant and left unanswered the principal question.

Yerodia is therefore a missed opportunity to question the validity of *Lotus*. In the opinions of the judges, the discussion is addressed. Judge Van Den Wyngaert, for instance, relying on the *Lotus* case, argues that universal jurisdiction, even to the extent that it is applied by the Belgian law, is compatible. On the other hand, the French Judge Guillaume asserts forcefully that universal jurisdiction *in absentia* as applied in Belgium is unknown to international law. More generally, he holds that times have changed since the *Lotus* case. International courts have been created, and more and more international conventions oblige states other than those on whose territory offenses are committed to confer jurisdiction on their courts to prosecute the authors of certain crimes when they are present on their territory. However, it would create total judicial chaos to accept that jurisdiction should be conferred upon the courts of every state in the world to prosecute such crimes in all circumstances.

Expanded jurisdiction, in particular universal jurisdiction, is controversial. It is not possible, based on a reading of the opinions of the judges in *Yerodia*, to judge whether there is sufficient ground to hold that *Lotus* should be revisited. Knowing the limits of the international system that is based on a logic of subsidiarity and that is limited to core crimes,[122] I tend to accept the *Lotus* acquis, also in cyberspace, granted that it is only used for serious transborder crimes. Together with Osofsky, I believe that most of the potential pitfalls of broader criminal jurisdiction should be addressed by statutory and litigative approaches,[123] but in the meanwhile, they can be avoided by a careful approach on the part of the responsible prosecution authorities, using their non-prosecutorial discretion.[124] What is absolutely needed are provisions on *ne bis in idem* such as those contained in the 1990 Schengen Agreement (see *supra*). It goes without saying that an international treaty imposing this principle forms a necessary counterbalancing element of tendencies towards broader criminal jurisdiction.

---

[122] See para. 10 of the Preamble and Arts. 1, 17, 18, and 19 of the Rome Statute on the International Criminal Court.

[123] Osofsky, loc. cit. n. 88, p. 193. Pp. 212-216 of Osofsky's article contain an analysis of the problems arising with enlarged jurisdiction. See also Burnstein, loc. cit. n. 116.

[124] Osofsky, loc. cit. n. 88, pp. 222-225 contain a useful set of guidelines to help to systematize the decision whether to prosecute. See also G. Vermeulen, 'Structuring Operational European Police Cooperation at a Pre-Judicial Stage: Future Trend in Criminal Investigation?', in J. Nijboer and J. Reijntjes, eds., *Proceedings of the First World Conference on New Trends in Criminal Investigation and Evidence* (Koninklijke Vermande 1997), pp. 447-452.

Contrary to the human-rights movement that favors expanded jurisdiction, I think that the problem with *Lotus* is not so much its attack on sovereignty (of states that have to tolerate expanded jurisdiction of others), but the attack on the freedom of the prosecuted persons.[125] It is easy to stay away from policing countries such as Belgium, but, especially with new instruments like the European arrest warrant, it is not easy to remain out of reach of internationally disseminated arrest warrants in a shrinking world. Only time can tell whether, under the conditions I set out above, *Lotus* is ready for revision.[126]

5.7 Extraterritorial Investigation

5.7.1 *Lotus* and the legality of extraterritorial law enforcement

Lotus is less well-disposed for internationally operating national states with regard to actual law enforcement. The Permanent Court of Justice took the view that states have a broad margin when deciding upon substantive jurisdiction, but that they violate sovereignty when their prosecution officers undertake actions on the territory of another country without permission. Hence the rule that the *jurisdiction to enforce* should normally be confined to acts committed on the state's territory. This type of jurisdiction 'cannot be exercised by a state outside its territory except by virtue of a permissive rule derived from international custom or from a convention.'[127]

Consent, either directly or given in a convention, is therefore crucial to understand the legality of actions undertaken by prosecution officers of one country on the territory of another without permission. A good example of a case in which this rule is applied is given by Cassese:

> 'On 8 May 2003 a delegation of the Italian Parliamentary Enquiry Committee charged with investigating the "Telekom Serbia" affair visited, unauthorized, the bankruptcy office of Lugano (Switzerland) to collect evidence on alleged embezzlement, corruption, and other offences in the purchase of "Telekom Serbia" by the Italian public telephone company Telecom. The Italians were briefly detained by the Swiss police at the request of the Swiss federal prosecutor, questioned, and charged with breach of Articles 271 and 273 of the Swiss Penal Code (punishing respectively unauthorized acts performed in Switzerland on behalf of a foreign State, and economic espionage). The

[125] P. De Hert, 'De soevereiniteit van de mensenrechten: aantasting door de uitlevering en het bewijsrecht' [Sovereignty of human rights: threats created by the law of extradition and by the law of evidence], 25 *Panopticon* (2004) No. 3, pp. 229-238.

[126] Cf., the opinion of the Japanese Judge Oda in *Yerodia*: 'the Court has shown wisdom in refraining from taking a definitive stance [on universal jurisdiction] as the law is not sufficiently developed and, in fact, the Court is not requested in the present case to take a decision on this point.'

[127] Permanent Court of International Justice (1927), *C.P.I.J. Rec. Public Series A*, No. 10.

> Federal Prosecutor contended that, instead of violating Swiss sovereignty, the Italian authorities should have requested the evidence through official channels, by means of a rogatory letter.'[128]

Other examples given by Cassese are 'kidnapping' cases such as *Eichmann*,[129] who was kidnapped in Argentina in 1960 by Israeli agents posing as private individuals, and taken to Israel; Argentina, not content with the apology offered by Israel, took the case to the UN Security Council, which called upon Israel to pay adequate compensation.[130]

When reading such examples, I wonder how sweeping the *Lotus* prohibition on consentless jurisdiction to enforce is in reality. The UN warning did not dissuade Israel from prosecuting Eichmann.[131] Also, in many examples furnished by Cassese, the reactions are often only of a political nature. Law does not seem to play a big role in these kinds of jurisdiction conflicts; it is not the first thing we come across when confronted with extraterritorial law enforcement. I know of no cases where the legal system has responded adequately against actions such as spying, kidnapping for criminal-law purposes, satellite spying of other countries, Echelon, etc. Moreover, I sense no willingness on the part of the international legal system to condemn violations of sovereignty by law-enforcement officials abroad. In this respect, the case law of the European Court of Human Rights does not seem to be wholly coherent.

On the one hand, there is the case of *Loizidou* v. *Turkey*,[132] in which the Court ruled that Turkey could be held responsible for violating the rights of Cypriots living in Turkey-occupied Northern Cyprus. The Court was of the view that '[t]he responsibility of a Contracting party may also arise when as a consequence of military action – whether lawful or unlawful – it exercises effective control of an area outside its national territory.'[133]

On the other hand, there is the case of *Öcalan* v. *Turkey*.[134] Öcalan was 'kidnapped' by Turkish agents in Kenya and brought to Turkey. Kenyan officials denied having played any part in the arrest or having been informed by the Turkish forces. Relying on the case law of various national courts,[135] the applicant maintained that

[128] Cassese, op. cit. n. 4, pp. 51-52 with reference to Italian newspapers.

[129] Cassese, op. cit. n. 4, pp. 50-52 with reference to *U.S.* v. *Alvarez-Macain*, *Dominguez* v. *State*, *Eichmann* and *Regina* v. *Plymouth Justices, ex parte Driver*.

[130] Cassese, op. cit. n. 4, p. 52 with references.

[131] District Court of Jerusalem, *The State of Israel* v. *Eichmann* (1961), 36 *International Law Reports* (1961-62), 18; Supreme Court of Israel, *Eichmann* v. *the State of Israel* (1962), 36 *International Law Reports* (1961-62), 277.

[132] European Court of Human Rights (ECHR) 23 March 1995, *Series A*, No. 310.

[133] Ibid., para. 62.

[134] ECHR 12 May 2005, *Öcalan* v. *Turkey*, available through <http://www.dhcour.coe.fr/eng/>.

[135] The applicant refered to the House of Lord's decision in the case of *R.* v. *Horseferry Road Magistrates' Court, ex parte Bennett*, [1994] 1 AC, p. 42; Court of Appeal of New Zealand, *Reg.* v. *Hartley*, New Zealand Law Reports 1978, Vol. 2, p. 199; United States Court of Appeals for the Second

the arrest procedures did not comply with Kenyan law or the rules established by international law, that his arrest amounted to an abduction, and that his detention and trial, which were based on that unlawful arrest, had to be regarded as null and void. The Court agreed that from the moment Öcalan was in Turkish hands, the Convention applied (para. 91).[136] Also, an arrest made by the authorities of one state on the territory of another state, without the consent of the latter, affects the arrested person's individual rights to security under Article 5 paragraph 1 (para. 85).[137] Co-operation between states, within the framework of extradition treaties or in matters of deportation, for the purpose of bringing fugitive offenders to justice, is perfectly possible within the framework of the European Convention on Human Rights, provided that it does not interfere with any specific rights recognized in the Convention (para. 86). This Convention is also the yardstick by which to measure extradition arrangements or, in the absence of a treaty, extradition practices between states when one is a party to the Convention and the other is not (para. 87). Then follows a crucial 'political' stand by the Court (para. 88):

> 'Inherent in the whole of the Convention is a search for a fair balance between the demands of the general interest of the community and the requirements of the protection of the individual's fundamental rights. As movement about the world becomes easier and crime takes on a larger international dimension, it is increasingly in the interest of all nations that suspected offenders who flee abroad should be brought to justice. Conversely, the establishment of safe havens for fugitives would not only result in danger for the State obliged to harbor the protected person but also tend to undermine the foundations of extradition.'

On this basis, the Court arrived at a hands-off approach: 'Subject to its being the result of cooperation between the states concerned and provided that the legal basis for the order for the fugitive's arrest is an arrest warrant issued by the authorities of the fugitive's state of origin, even an atypical extradition cannot as such be regarded as being contrary to the Convention' (para. 89). Irrespective of whether the arrest amounts to a violation of the law of the state in which the fugitive has taken refuge – a question that can only be examined by the Court if the host state is a party

Circuit, *United States* v. *Toscanino* (1974) 555 F. 2d. 267, 268; Constitutional Court of South Africa, 28 May 2001, *Mohammed and Dalvie* v. *The President of the Republic of South Africa and others* (CCT 17/01, 2001 (3) SA 893 CC).

[136] 'It is common ground that, directly after being handed over to the Turkish officials by the Kenyan officials, the applicant was under effective Turkish authority and therefore within the "jurisdiction" of that State for the purposes of Article 1 of the Convention, even though in this instance Turkey exercised its authority outside its territory.'

[137] Art. 5 para. 1 European Convention on Human Rights states: 'Everyone has the right to liberty and security of person. No one shall be deprived of his liberty save in the following cases and in accordance with a procedure prescribed by law: (...) (c) the lawful arrest or detention of a person effected for the purpose of bringing him before the competent legal authority on reasonable suspicion of having committed an offence or when it is reasonably considered necessary to prevent his committing an offence or fleeing after having done so.'

to the Convention – the Court requires proof in the form of concordant inferences that the authorities of the state to which the applicant has been transferred have acted extraterritorially in a manner inconsistent with the sovereignty of the host state and therefore contrary to international law (para. 90). To reach its conclusion, the Court ignored the official denial of Kenyan officials (see *above*). The existence of a Turkish arrest warrant disseminated through the Interpol machinery and the 'fact' that without some form of co-operation by the Kenyan police, the Turkish agents would never have succeeded, make the arrest lawful within the meaning of the Convention (para. 97).

> 'These aspects of the case lead the Court to accept the Government's version of events: it considers that at the material time the Kenyan authorities had decided either to hand the applicant over to the Turkish authorities or to facilitate such a handover. The applicant has not adduced evidence enabling concordant inferences (...) to be drawn that Turkey failed to respect Kenyan sovereignty or to comply with international law in the present case. (....) Consequently, the applicant's arrest on 15 February 1999 and his detention were in accordance with "a procedure prescribed by law" for the purposes of Article 5 § 1 of the Convention. There has, therefore, been no violation of that provision.'[138]

To the foregoing, one should add the deceptive case law of the European Court with regard to the exclusionary rule. Cases such as *Schenk* v. *Switzerland* show that the exclusionary rule does not form part of the European public order. Rather than focusing on the illegality of the means used to obtain evidence, the Court examines whether the procedure as a whole is handled fairly and whether the judges are not prejudiced.[139] This is primarily considered by the Court to be a matter of national law.[140] It is striking for our topic that the case of *Schenk* concerned the illegal gathering of evidence in another country: telephone calls involving a private person

---

[138] ECHR 12 May 2005, *Öcalan* v. *Turkey*, paras. 97-99.

[139] In the 1988 judgment *Schenk*, the person charged had been criminally convicted in his own country, partly on the grounds of the recording of a telephone call made by him. *Pierre Schenk* v. *Switzerland*, ECHR 12 July 1988, *Series A*, No. 140. See in the same sense *Lüdi* v. *Switzerland*, ECHR 15 June 1992, *Series A*, No. 238, para. 43; *Vidal* v. *Belgium*, ECHR 22 April 1992, *Series A*, No. 235-B, para. 33; *Dombo Beheer* v. *The Netherlands*, ECHR 27 October 1993, *Series A*, No. 274, para. 31; *Schuler-Zgraggen* v. *Switzerland*, ECHR 24 June 1993, *Series A*, No. 263, para. 66. Rather than dwelling on the lawfulness or unlawfulness of evidence, the Court looks to see whether the procedure as a whole has been carried out honestly and whether the judges have guarded themselves against prejudice. In Schenk's case, Art. 6 European Convention on Human Rights had not been violated (see paras. 47-48 and 51 of the judgment).

[140] In practice, this means that the exclusionary rule is not part of the European public order. In none of the systems studied by Tak and Lensing do procedural mistakes made during the preliminary investigation lead, in general, to illegally obtained evidence or to the inadmissibility of the Public Prosecutor. See P. Tak and J. Lensing, *Het vooronderzoek rechtsvergelijkend onderzocht* [Pre-Trial Investigation in a Comparative Perspective] (Arnhem, Gouda Quint 1990), p. 12.

were illegally recorded in France and subsequently handed over to Swiss judicial authorities.

This example shows that Europe is not wholly unaffected by the American dual-sovereignty theory,[141] viz. the theory that the exclusionary rule does not apply in cases where evidence is illegally obtained in another country.[142] The rule is not applied, in other words, to the domain of international judicial co-operation because it is assumed that the prosecuting country cannot blame the other country for negligence.[143] To this it should be added that judges in the prosecuting countries are often more reserved in their evaluation of alleged irregularities by civil servants and actions in foreign countries than they are in evaluating civil servants and actions within their own legal system.[144]

5.7.2 The legality of transborder access to stored computer data

I observed that the Cybercrime Convention has not exhausted all existing law-enforcement possibilities. I gave two examples, viz. duties for the suspect to co-operate by surrendering a computer password and intercepting foreign telecommunications. A third example is 'legal hacking' by law-enforcement officers in information systems located abroad. Article 32 of the Convention ('Transborder access to stored computer data with consent or where publicly available') only addresses two situations: first, where the data are publicly available, and second, where the Party has accessed or received data located outside of its territory through a computer system in its territory, and where it has obtained the lawful and voluntary consent of the person who has lawful authority to disclose the data to the Party through that system.[145]

---

[141] H. Hannum, R. Lillich and S. Saltzburg, *Materials on International Human Rights and U.S. Criminal Law and Procedure* (Washington, The Procedural Aspects of International Law Institute 1989), p. 115.

[142] U.S. Supreme Court, *United States* v. *Balsys*, 118 *United States Supreme Court Reports (U.S.)* (1998), 2218. The Supreme Court based itself on the following line of thought: the sovereign of one country can not let itself be bound by the rules of the sovereign of another country, even if basic rights are at stake. See also U.S. Supreme Court, *Heath* v. *Alabame*, 474 *United States Supreme Court Reports (U.S.)* (1995), 82. See, critically, St. Winger, 'Denying Fifth Amendment Protections to Witnesses Facing Foreign Prosecutions: Self-Incrimination Discrimination', 89 *The Journal of Criminal Law & Criminology* (1999) No. 3, pp. 1095-1140.

[143] J. Klifman, 'Het Akkoord van Schengen en internationale uitwisseling van gegevens ontleend aan afgeluisterde gesprekken' [The Schengen Agreement and the International Exchange of Intercepted Data], in G. Mols, ed., *Dissonanten bij het akkoord van Schengen* [Notes of Discord Regarding the Schengen Agreement] (Deventer, Kluwer 1990), pp. 143-145.

[144] J. Wöretshofer, 'Het Schengen-akkoord, dwangmiddelen en rechtsbescherming' [The Schengen Agreement, Coercive Powers and the Rule of Law], in Mols, op. cit. n. 143, pp. 116-117.

[145] 'Who is a person that is "lawfully authorised" to disclose data may vary depending on the circumstances, the nature of the person and the applicable law concerned. For example, a person's e-mail may be stored in another country by a service provider, or a person may intentionally store data in another country. These persons may retrieve the data and, provided that they have the lawful authority,

These two situations are, so I believe, not very controversial. I do not see what principle of international law will prohibit, for example, the Belgian police from consulting Internet foreign publicly-accessible files, newsgroups, or web pages. Even the second situation is not very spectacular.

One step further, however, is plain judicial hacking in foreign (secured) files. A 1995 Recommendation of the Council of Europe indicates that in emergency cases, this should be possible, and the Member States are summoned to conclude international contracts about this.[146]

This recommendation was inspired in particular by the rules on network searches that were inserted by the Computer Crime Act in the Dutch Code of Criminal Procedure. Article 125j Dutch CCP allows the person who conducts a search to also search in computer networks from computers located at the search premises, as far as the network is lawfully accessible to the people who regularly stay or work at those premises. By a decision of the legislator, based on his understanding of public international law, this network search cannot go beyond the Dutch borders.[147]

This kind of self-restraint also played a part at the level of the Council of Europe in preparing the Cybercrime Convention. The issue whether a country is permitted to access unilaterally computer data stored in another country without seeking mutual assistance was discussed at length by the drafters of the Convention.[148] The drafters ultimately determined that it was not yet possible to prepare a comprehensive, legally binding regime regulating this area. In part, this was due to a lack of concrete experience with such situations to date; and also, this was due to an understanding that the proper solution often hinged on the precise circumstances of the individual case, thereby making it difficult to formulate general rules. Ultimately, the drafters decided to only set forth in Article 32 of the Convention the two above-mentioned situations, in which all agreed that unilateral action is permissible. They agreed not to regulate other situations until such time as further experience has been gained and further discussions may be held in the light thereof.

With the 2000 Belgian Computer Crime Act, the Belgian legislator decided not to wait for an international solution with regard to network searches and consciously went one step further than the Cybercrime Convention. A new provision in the Code of Criminal Procedure allows the investigating judge to order a search of an information system. This search can be expanded to an interconnected system situated in another place:

---

they may voluntarily disclose the data to law enforcement officials or permit such officials to access the data, as provided in the Article', *Explanatory Report*, <http://conventions.coe.int/Treaty/en/Reports/Html/185.htm>, para. 294.

[146] Cf., Recommendation No. R(95) 13, op. cit. n. 32.

[147] See for a background analysis, P. De Hert, 'De strafprocesrechtelijke voorstellen inzake computercriminaliteit' [New Propositions with Regard to the Law of Criminal Procedure and Computer Crime], *Delikt en Delinkwent* (1993) No. 1, pp. 7-28.

[148] Cf., *Explanatory Report*, <http://conventions.coe.int/Treaty/en/Reports/Html/185.htm>, para. 293.

- if the expansion of the search is necessary to bring the truth concerning the investigated offense to the surface; and
- if other measures would be disproportional, or if there is a risk that without expanding the search, evidence would disappear or be lost (Art. 88ter para. 1 CCP).

The expansion of the search in an information system is limited to those systems, areas, or parts that the rightful operators are allowed to use or have specific access to (Art. 88ter para. 2 CCP). When the data are not situated on the territory, the order to search can still be given, but once the data are found, only copying is allowed. In that case, the investigating judge shall report the extraterritorial search immediately to the Minister of Justice, who will subsequently inform the competent authority of the other state (Art. 88ter para. 3 CCP).

Although this power to search in transborder systems is (still) not a license to 'hack' freely foreign systems, it may raise concerns about sovereignty. Belgium is clearly acting on a unilateral basis. In the preparatory works of the Computer Crime Act, the legislator acknowledged the sovereignty problem and recommended that the new power should not be used as a rule. When there is enough time, the traditional instrument of rogatory letters and mutual assistance should be followed.

The Belgian power to search a transborder system raises a number of questions. To begin with: are there any good arguments for such a power? The answer is 'yes'. We saw that the Cybercrime Convention allows for transborder network searches with consent. From a national perspective, it could be argued that even without consent, accessing certain files stored abroad should be possible. Indeed, I do not see what could stop a Belgian or Dutch investigative judge, within the framework of a legal search of a computer, from ordering a search through data files to which the resident of the house has access via Internet on a contractual basis, subject to the condition that the information has been accessed without technical or logical manipulation. A specific regulation for this is, in my opinion, not necessary, since a contractual limitation of access cannot be invoked against law-enforcement officers. The situation changes when a search through non-public files is taking place outside the framework of the domiciliary search or when access limitations (passwords) have to be breached.[149]

I stated above that the territoriality principle is preferred as a rule in criminal law, both for ideological reasons and because the territory where the alleged crime has been committed is the place where it is easier to collect evidence. The idea of *forum conveniens* in the case of network systems should be adapted, in the sense that the best place to collect evidence is not the territory of the person behind the

---

[149] B. de Schutter, et al., *Informaticagebeuren en strafvorderingsrecht* [Criminal Procedure in a Digital Environment] (Antwerp-Deventer, Kluwer Rechtswetenschappen 1992), pp. 32-39; H. Kaspersen, 'Aanbeveling Raad van Europa inzake de opsporing van strafbare feiten in een geautomatiseerde omgeving', *Computerrecht* (1995) p. 290.

computer, but the territory of the place, in cyberspace, where that person stores his information.

A second question has to do with the *Lotus* acquis. As we saw, this case was about colliding vessels on the high seas in 1926. The firm rejection by the court of physical intrusions by law-enforcement officials would still be upheld today, if a case was brought to the ICJ, but what about non-physical intrusions? As far as I can see, this is really hard to say. A plain prohibition of non-physical intrusions is difficult to imagine, in the light of existing spying devices (Echelon, satellites, etc.) that are in use today. Although network searches are by no means innocent, there is no physical trespassing of borders. Moreover, in the case of network searches, a plain prohibition of unilateral searches could too easily be used by persons to frustrate law enforcement, which would hamper the sovereignty rights of a state with regard to the individuals living in its territory.

In *Lotus*, the Court held that transborder law enforcement is possible on the basis of consent or of a permissive rule derived from international custom or convention (see above). One could argue that it is only a question of time before the world gets used to unilateral powers such as the Belgian one. A new *Lotus* decision today targeting the problems of the cyber-era would possibly result in the court's finding that the time is not yet ripe to decide on this issue. To be in line with the *Lotus* dictum, it is clear that a legal framework is needed similar to the one introduced by the 2000 EU Convention on Mutual Assistance in Criminal Matters between the Member States of the European Union, discussed above. We saw that this Convention allows interception by a Member State on the territory of another Member State in which earth satellite equipment is located, if the technical assistance of that the Member State is not required. The Convention allows such interceptions, but imposes upon the Member State in question the obligation to subsequently inform the other Member State of its action. A similar logic is incorporated in Article 88 Belgian CCP, but this still lacks 'a permissive rule derived from international custom or from a convention'.

I would like to suggest that not only states should be subsequently informed of the 'attack' on their sovereignty, but also the individuals abroad. 'Traditionally persons located on the territory of a certain state, fall under its jurisdiction. Their freedoms (…) are guaranteed under the law of that state. Likewise the infringements on this freedom should be allowed by the laws of that same state. The location of a target is therefore relevant. Exceptions of the principle of sovereignty can only be regulated by a Convention.'[150]

5.8 Conclusion

In this chapter, I have tried to show the many possibilities of today's legal framework for transborder law enforcement with regard to cybercrimes. Developments

[150] Quote taken from Statewatch, op. cit. n. 47.

with regard to ICT are recognized in law. The discretion that public international law leaves to national states with regard to jurisdiction is effectively used. A discussion about expanded jurisdiction in *Yerodia* has been avoided, leaving states with the large margin to act as defined in *Lotus*.

Some hold that the growing entanglement of the world community brings states to increasingly recognize and accept the enlargement of jurisdiction.[151] They assume that this will probably lead, in the long term, to more co-operation and harmonization.[152]

This 'meta' view of jurisdiction might be right from a state perspective, but it ignores the loss of freedom for the individual who can no longer escape the long arm of government by crossing borders.[153] Also, it underestimates the changed and, due to technology, strengthened nature of prosecution. I have, therefore, some doubts about a development towards growing recognition and acceptance. On the contrary, more conflicts between states may arise as the feeling grows that sovereignty is violated through more effective prosecution. There might be a need for a new *Lotus* case in the cyber-era.

Bibliography

K. Bodard, P. de Hert and B. de Schutter, 'Crime on Internet. A Challenge to Criminal Law in Europe', 5 *Maastricht Journal of European and Comparative Law* (1998) No. 3, pp. 222-261.

A. Cassese, *International Law*, 2nd edn. (Oxford, Oxford University Press 2005), pp. 82-83.

H. Osofsky, 'Domesticating International Criminal Law: Bringing Human Rights Violators to Justice', 107 *The Yale Law Journal* (1997) pp. 191-226.

M. Plachta, 'European Arrest Warrant: Revolution in Extradition?', 11 *European Journal of Crime, Criminal Law and Criminal Justice* (2003) No. 2, pp. 178-194.

Jean Pradel, 'Criminal Evidence', in J.F. Nijboer and W.J.J.M. Sprangers, eds., *Harmonisation in Forensic Expertise. An Inquiry into the Desirability of and Opportunies for International Standards* (Amsterdam, Thela Thesis 2000), pp. 411-429.

Ch. van den Wyngaert and G. Stessens, 'The international non bis in idem principle: resolving some of the unanswered questions', *International Comparative Law Quarterly* (1999), pp. 779-804.

Th. Verbiest and E. Wéry, *Le droit de l'internet et de la société de l'information* (Brussels, Larcier 2001).

---

[151] Osofsky, loc. cit. n. 88, p. 204.

[152] See chapter 7 of this book.

[153] On the liberty function of borders, see P. De Hert, 'Division of Competencies Between National and European Levels with Regard to Justice & Home Affairs', in J. Apap, ed., *Justice and Home Affairs in the EU. Liberty and Security Issues after Enlargement* (Cheltenham, Edward Elgar 2004), pp. 55-102.

Chapter 6
CYBERCRIME AND JURISDICTION IN BRAZIL. FROM EXTRATERRITORIAL TO ULTRATERRITORIAL JURISDICTION

Roberto Chacon de Albuquerque*

6.1 Introduction

Cybercrimes may affect several countries. Brazilian hackers can invade web sites located abroad and transfer money from foreign bank accounts to their own accounts. The opposite is also true. Foreign hackers can do the same against web sites located in Brazil. In both cases, action begins in the territory of one country and is completed in the territory of another. Jurisdiction, the power of a court to hear and decide a case before it, has traditionally been restricted by territorial limits. But cyberspace has no borders. Has cyberspace turned the concept of jurisdiction upside down? The exercise of extraterritorial jurisdiction can now become increasingly common.

Extraterritorial jurisdiction has not been traditionally defined by treaties. Domestic law has had a crucial role in defining its rules. Countries have adopted complicated long-arm statutory schemes to exercise extraterritorial jurisdiction. The exercise of extraterritorial jurisdiction can be traumatic. It invades the sovereignty of countries, creating insurmountable enforcement problems. Extraterritorial claims can be tricky at best. They have the potential to lead to conflicts and controversies. Divergent political, economic and legal conditions have led countries to restrict the exercise of extraterritorial jurisdiction and rely on international co-operation.

One of the fastest growing criminal activities on the planet, cybercrimes require the framing of a new concept of jurisdiction, based on consensus-building. Jurisdiction solely based on territorial limits is surely not able to deal with transborder cybercrimes. Neither is extraterritorial jurisdiction: it may conflict with sovereignty and prove inefficient. Every country has an interest in enforcing the rulings of its courts, as well as in providing legal protection and remedies to its citizens. Sovereignty favors the exercise of territorial jurisdiction. Countries that are involved in a

* Prof.Dr Roberto Chacon de Albuquerque is a lawyer and Professor of International Law at the Catholic University of Brasília.

B-J. Koops and S.W. Brenner (Eds), Cybercrime and Jurisdiction

supranational integration model, such as the European Union, which comprises the adoption of a supranational dispute-resolution system, may envisage extraterritorial jurisdiction in a different way. The European Union, following the path of the United States, has, pretty much like its transatlantic counterpart, a Supreme Court coming into being. The Court of Justice, the European Union's judicial supreme authority, located in Luxembourg, was originally designed to promote the national implementation of Community law. It may well develop into a court that increasingly limits or broadens, depending on the circumstances, extraterritorial jurisdiction claims among country members.

The international community, so far, has no Supreme Court. There is no transnational judicial body with coercive power. The International Court of Justice and the International Criminal Court may be considered as attempts to establish a transnational judicial body, but they have faced many obstacles.[1] Most of the international conflicts which occurred in the last fifty years, since the first session of the International Court of Justice was held, have been politically solved. Some never have, despite all the goodwill of the international community and the political will of world leaders. The decisions of the International Court of Justice have often been regarded only as indicative. It is surely too soon to predict what will happen with the International Criminal Court, but the opposition that has been faced by the Rome Statute, which created this court with unprecedented jurisdictional reach, is not auspicious. Key countries have not ratified the Rome Statute. Some have declared that they would not be bound by its signatory status.

Extraterritorial jurisdiction faces a challenge: how can it be enforced on a global scale, if there is no transnational judicial body at all to force a country to accept its exercise by another country? Extraterritorial jurisdiction, the power to enforce court rulings abroad, has usually been resented as an intrusion. It may be reminiscent of colonial powers stretching their authority territorially. History has many examples: Shanghai became a Western enclave during the 19th century. Each of the major Western countries had extraterritorial jurisdiction over their own citizens.[2] Cybercrimes surely have nothing to do with this, but what happened in the past may lead to the feeling that the exercise of extraterritorial jurisdiction is strictly connected to encroachments on sovereignty. So, what is the way out of this vicious circle?

In this article, we will analyze to what extent transborder cybercrimes should be subject to extraterritorial jurisdiction. Extraterritoriality in the past was often granted to foreigners residing in countries that were supposedly unable to render justice in a fair and balanced way. This kind of extraterritorial jurisdiction has been widely resented as an infringement of sovereignty. Transborder cybercrimes may lead to a

---

[1] See C. Perane-Moisés, 'O Princípio da Complementariedade no Estatuto do Tribunal Penal Internacional e a Soberania Contemporânea' [The Principle of Complementarity in the International Criminal Court Statute and the Current Sovereignty], 8 *Política Externa* (2000) No. 4, pp. 3-11.

[2] See G.W. Keeton, 'Extraterritoriality in International and Comparative Law', 72 *Recueil des Cours* (1948) No. 1, pp. 283-391 at pp. 299-306.

new surge in the application of extraterritorial jurisdiction. But should transborder cybercrimes not be perceived as an opportunity to foster co-operation among nations, to develop more co-ordinated law-enforcement efforts? We believe that extraterritorial jurisdiction, which extends the jurisdiction of a country over another country, should be superseded by what we call 'ultraterritorial jurisdiction'. The key goal of ultraterritorial jurisdiction, a concept that we will deal with further ahead, is co-operation, instead of intervention.

This article is divided into nine sections. Section 2 gives an indication of the current cybercrime provisions in Brazil, including – still rather scarce – case law. In section 3, we analyze cross-border cyber-investigation legislation, and, in section 4, substantive cybercrime jurisdiction. In sections 5 and 6, we give an overview of extraterritorial jurisdiction and its pitfalls.[3] Section 7 presents the provisions set forth by the Criminal Code on extraterritorial jurisdiction. Section 8 introduces the concept of ultraterritorial jurisdiction, and section 9 provides a conclusion.

6.2 Cybercrime Legislation

6.2.1 Substantive law

Brazil's Criminal Code dates back to the first half of the 20th century. More precisely, it was enacted in 1940. At that time, Brazil faced an intense period of modernization. The Second World War gave Brazil the chance to become industrialized. Trade with Europe and the United States had been virtually blocked. Industrialized goods could not be imported. The country's legislation was modernized. Not only the Criminal Code, but also the Code of Criminal Procedure were adopted in such circumstances. It goes without saying that both the Criminal Code and the Code of Criminal Procedure have been submitted to many changes since then.

One of these changes often passes unnoticed. The Criminal Code, contrary to common perception, has already been updated as regards cybercrimes. Law 9.983/00[4] has inserted several new provisions dealing with cybercrimes in the Criminal Code.[5] Most of these provisions, however, do not cover cybercrimes as a whole, but only cybercrimes targeted at the Public Administration.[6] It is desirable that the law should cover cybercrime as a whole, in view of the international harmonization

[3] For an overview of extraterritorial and universal jurisdiction, see ibid., and A. Concesi, 'A Jurisdição Universal' [Universal Jurisdiction], *Boletim Científico da Escola Superior do Ministério Público da União* (2003) No. 8, pp. 11-14.

[4] Law No. 9.983, of 14 July 2000 Changes Decree-Law No. 2.848, of 7 December 1940 – Criminal Code and adopts other measures.

[5] The new provisions of the Criminal Code are as follows: Art. 153, para. 1-A; Art. 313-A; Art. 313-B; and Art. 325, paras. 1 and 2.

[6] Lobbying from the public sector managed to speed up the approval of Law 9.983/00. Apart from that, there are no additional cybercrime provisions in the Criminal Code.

of cybercrime legislation. This is of the utmost importance, for instance, because extradition is often only available subject to the condition of double criminality.

In this section, we will analyze the relevant provisions: Article 153, paragraph 1-A, Article 313-A, Article 313-B, and Article 325, paragraphs 1 and 2.

Article 153, paragraph 1-A, is hacking-related.[7] It is the only provision that encompasses cybercrimes not specifically targeted at the Public Administration: it covers information whether or not 'contained in information systems or data banks of the Public Administration' [emphasis added]. It does not punish hacking proper, in other words unauthorized access to computer systems, but the unauthorized disclosure of information. This article does seem a little confusing, to say the least. It does not even make any reference to the expressions 'undue' or 'unauthorized', but rather to 'without just cause'. We may then assume that, although unauthorized, a person has the right to disclose information, if he has 'just cause' to do so. An employee may then have the right to disclose information, no matter how 'reserved or secret' it is, if this information is relevant to law-enforcement investigations. The margin of appreciation in the interpretation of the expression 'without just cause' can be considerable. It is up to the law to define what is 'reserved or secret information'. This issue has been subject to widespread debate. Some argue that the Federal Government may end up considering as 'reserved or secret information' everything that may be detrimental to its interests.

Article 313-A has introduced what we may call 'electronic peculation', that is, the electronic misappropriation of public funds.[8] Embezzlement of public funds has been a major concern in the last few years. Repeatedly divulged by the Press, it has considerably undermined the legitimacy of successive governments. But can we refer to 'electronic peculation'? Is there a specificity in any misappropriation of public funds through the Internet that necessitates the adoption of an 'electronic peculation' provision? We believe not. The fear of massive peculation, electronically carried out, has led to the insertion of Article 313-A in the Criminal Code. News about large embezzlements of public funds, targeted at the National Social Security Institute's data banks, has attracted public attention. Article 313-A punishes 'the authorized public officer' who inserts or facilitates the insertion of 'false

---

[7] Criminal Code, Art. 153 para. 1-A: 'To disclose, without just cause, reserved or secret information, as thus defined by the law, whether or not contained in information systems or data banks of the Public Administration: Penalty – detention, from 1 (one) to 4 (four) years, and a fine.' All translations from Brazilian legislation in this chapter are by the author.

[8] Criminal Code, Art. 313-A: 'The authorized public officer inserts false data, alters or unduly excludes correct data in information systems or data banks of the Public Administration with the intention of obtaining an undue advantage for himself or for another or to cause damage: Penalty – reclusion from 2 (two) to 12 (twelve) years, and a fine.' (In Brazilian criminal law, there are two kinds of confinement penalties. With reclusion ('reclusão'), the penalty must be served in a closed regime (high-security prison), a semi-open regime (work and farm camps), or an open regime (halfway house). With detention ('detenção'), the penalty must be served in a semi-open or an open regime. The difference between reclusion and detention is thus a difference between prison regimes according to the nature of the crime.)

data', alters or unduly excludes 'correct data in informatized systems or data banks of the Public Administration'. He must, as a result thereof, have the intention of obtaining an 'undue advantage' or 'to cause damage'. Article 313-B, on the other hand, punishes the unauthorized modification or alteration of information systems or computer programs.[9] Once again, the fear of massive embezzlement of public funds through the unauthorized modification or alteration of information systems or computer programs has surely played an important role in the adoption of Article 313-B. This offense, just like the one laid down by Article 313-A, must be committed by a public officer. Moreover, '[p]enalties are increased from one-third to one-half, if the modification or alteration results in damage to the Public Administration or to the administered citizen.'[10]

It is curious to note that another hacking-related provision has been inserted in the Criminal Code. Article 325 punishes the violation of official secrecy.[11] Once again, the objective is not to protect computer systems from unauthorized access. The goal is to protect the Public Administration from the disclosure of information, from the violation of official secrecy. The core of Article 325 is 'to reveal a fact of which one is aware as a result of the public office and which should remain secret, or to facilitate its disclosure'. Here, the Public Administration once more reveals its interest in keeping its records confidential. So far, Article 325 is not directly cybercrime-related. It does not yet mention any expression that refers to the cyberspace environment. Paragraph 1, nonetheless, states that the 'supplying and lending of a password or any other way' that permits or facilitates 'the access of an unauthorized person to information systems or data banks of the Public Administration' is subject to punishment. Whoever 'unduly utilizes restricted access' is also subject to punishment. Restricted access to what? 'To information systems or data banks of the Public Administration'. Paragraph 2 increases penalties 'if the action or omission results in damage to the Public Administration or to another'. Article 325 thus gets closer to Article 313-A. The ultimate goal is to protect the Public Administration from financial losses.

Hacking, the unauthorized access to computer systems, has not been criminalized as a specific offense. Notwithstanding this, if we consider the Internet as another

---

9 Criminal Code, Art. 313-B, *caput*: 'The public officer modifies an information system or computer program without authorization or requisition of the competent authority: Penalty – detention from 3 (three) months to 2 (two) years, and fine.' In Brazilian legislation, the *caput* is the heading of the article, which in the Criminal Code often generally describes the offense.

10 Criminal Code, Art. 313-B, sole paragraph.

11 Criminal Code, Art. 325: 'To reveal a fact of which one is aware as a result of the public office and which should remain in secrecy, or to facilitate its disclosure: Penalty – detention, from six months to two years, or a fine, if the fact does not constitute a more serious crime. *Paragraph 1.* The same penalties will be incurred by whoever: I – permits or facilitates, by means of attribution, supplying and the lending of a password or any other way, the access of an unauthorized person to information systems or data banks of the Public Administration; II – unduly utilizes the restricted access. *Paragraph 2.* If the action or omission results in damage to the Public Administration or to another: Penalty – reclusion from 2 (two) to 6 (six) years, and a fine.'

means to commit traditional crimes, hacking may be punished by the law. The Brazilian Constitution, Article 5(XII, last part), protects the secrecy of personal data. It states that 'the secrecy of correspondence and of telegraphic communications, of data and of telephonic communications is inviolable, except, in the last case, by judicial order, in the hypotheses and in the form that the law establishes for purposes of criminal investigation or criminal procedural instruction.' Not only stored data, but also transmitted data are subject to constitutional protection against unauthorized access. Law 9.296/96, Article 10, punishes, on the other hand, the interception of communications.[12] Article 5(XII, last part) of the Brazilian Constitution has indeed been amended by Law 9.296/96. Telematic, computer and telephonic communications are thereby protected. The interception of 'telematic, computer, or telephonic communications' requires 'judicial authorization'.[13] Hackers have actually been indicted for interception of communications, but we could argue that they should not have been. Does Article 10 not aim to protect citizens from the unauthorized interception of communications that is achieved primarily by law-enforcement authorities? Is it not protection against encroachments on civil liberties, rather than protection against hackers?

Given the lack of general provisions on cybercrimes, hackers have also faced charges on crimes that have been traditionally included in the Criminal Code, such as fraud, Article 171, and damage, Article 163. Article 171, *caput*, has a flexible wording: 'To obtain, for himself or for another, an illicit advantage, resulting in someone else, by inducing someone by means of an error, a trick, deceit or any other fraudulent means.' Trojan 'trick', 'deceit' or 'any other fraudulent means' that are used to obtain 'an illicit advantage'. The 'illicit advantage' that is obtained must be financially significant. Hackers who have spread viruses have been indicted for damage. Contrary to Article 171, Article 163 is not known for having such flexible wording.[14] It punishes damage to a 'thing' (*coisa*).[15] Legal experts are not unanimously in agreement as to whether computer software and computer data is a 'thing', given their intangible nature.

The Criminal Code has indeed no general provisions on cybercrimes.[16] An important opportunity has so far been missed: the opportunity to concentrate efforts

[12] Law 9.296, of 24 July 1996 Regulates Article 5(XII, last part) of the Federal Constitution.

[13] Law 9.296/96, Art. 10: 'It constitutes a crime to achieve the interception of telematic, computer, or telephonic communications, or to breach the secrecy of justice, without judicial authorization or with objectives unauthorized by the law: Penalty – reclusion from two to four years, and a fine.'

[14] Criminal Code, Art. 163, *caput*: 'To destroy, render useless or cause damage to someone else's thing: Penalty – detention from one to six months, or a fine.'

[15] A 'thing' (*coisa*) is everything that exists in nature – even if it has abstract characteristics – that can be object of a legal relationship, with the exclusive exception of the human being. It is related to the concept of a good (*bem*), but contrary to a good, a thing does not need to have any economic value.

[16] With 'general provisions', we mean articles that criminalize cybercrimes that target not only the Public Administration, but the public in general. It should be noted, however, that civil provisions may apply. Anyone who causes any kind of damage to another person, in the civil field, must repair it. If hackers destroy or render useless any hardware, software or computer-stored data, victims have the

on the approval of provisions that could, in line with the world trend, criminalize cyberfraud and hacking. The Public Administration's lobbying has, nonetheless, been stronger.

As regards on-line illegal content, Law 10.764/03[17] has recently amended the wording of Article 241 of the Children and Teenagers Statute. It has adapted Article 241 to the cyberspace environment: 'To present, produce, sell, supply, divulge or publish, by any means of communication, including the global network of computers or Internet, pictures or images with pornography or scenes of explicit sex involving a child or teenager: Penalty – reclusion from 2 (two) to 6 (six) years, and a fine.' It is interesting to note how quickly Article 241 has been updated, in contrast to the approval of general provisions on cybercrimes. This is surely, at least partially, due to the great impact that on-line child pornography has had on society. Brazil has become a large producer and exporter of this kind of on-line illegal content.[18] The public outcry against it has mobilized both catholic and evangelical segments of the National Congress to approve the new wording of Article 241. Other kinds of on-line illegal content, such as racist propaganda, have so far not attracted the same attention.[19]

Case law

There has so far been only one court ruling on cyberfraud. Two men were convicted of infecting computers with Trojan horse programs.[20] The personal data to which they had access, such as bank account numbers and passwords, were used to enter on-line financial transactions. They transferred money from the victims' bank accounts to their own bank accounts. The court ruling considered Trojan horse programs to be 'fraudulent means' in the sense of Article 171, *caput*, of the Criminal Code. The defendants were convicted of fraud,[21] gang formation,[22] and breach of secrecy.[23] Most cybercrime cases are still to come to trial.

---

right to file a claim for damages. According to the Civil Code, Art. 186: 'Those who, by an action or voluntary omission, neglect or imprudence, violate a right and cause a damage to another, even if exclusively a moral one, commit an illicit act.'

[17] Law 10.764, of 12 November 2003 amends Law No. 8.069, of 13 July 1990, which established the Children and Teenagers Statute and adopted other measures.

[18] Cybercafes and every Internet access service must register their clients in several Brazilian states. The goal is to combat the practice of cybercrimes. Clients must identify themselves and fill in a form with personal data.

[19] Some local Orkut communities have been subject to investigation on charges of racism against the black and Jewish communities. A black teenager's Orkut page has recently been targeted by dozens of racist messages. The attack took place in early 2005.

[20] See Justiça Federal, Seção Judiciária do Estado de Mato Grosso do Sul, Autos No. 2003.60.00.003970-6, Juíza Janete Lima Miguel Cabral, 31.12.2003.

[21] Criminal Code, Art. 171, *caput*.

[22] Criminal Code, Art. 288, *caput*: 'The association of more than three persons, in a group or band, with the purpose of committing crimes: Penalty – reclusion from one to three years.'

[23] Complementary Law No. 105, of 10 January 2001 establishes the secrecy of operations of financial institutions and adopts other measures, Art. 10: 'A breach of secrecy, outside the hypotheses

There are two interesting examples of court rulings in the civil-law field. A legal person requested reparation in the form of damages. Its computer system had been contaminated by an infected disk. The plaintiff did not adduce the disk for the court's examination. Rather, he produced his own examination of the evidence. The claim was only partially successful, given the plaintiff's refusal to adduce evidence in order to reduce legal fees.[24]

A case of reparation for moral damages is widely known by experts. The Credit Protection Service[25] has a nation-wide register of defaulting payers. Whoever is recorded on this register is hindered, for instance, from taking out a loan in the financial markets. Oddly enough, the defendant, the Credit Protection Service, argued that its computer system had been infected by a virus. The inclusion of the plaintiff's name in the register of defaulting payers should then be considered an act of God, the Credit Protection Service argued. The claim for damages should not therefore be accepted. The court was of a different opinion. It considered that computer infections by viruses, given the rapid development of technology and the widespread use of Internet, should not be considered an unlikely hypothesis. On the contrary, they should be considered a highly foreseeable and avoidable hypothesis. Computers, especially those with large public databases, should be protected with updated anti-virus software. The lack of such protection, which apparently led to the inclusion of the plaintiff's name in the register of defaulting payers, was considered to be negligent conduct. The computer system's infection was not considered to be an act of God. The compensation was thereby increased as the defendant's illicit conduct had lasted for more than two years.[26]

6.2.2 Procedural law

We are now going to give some remarks as regards data gathering and investigation powers. The Code of Criminal Procedure, Article 240,[27] lays down two categories of search possibilities: a search of ones domicile and a personal search.[28] There is no specific provision on computer network searches. A search of one's domicile must be preceded by judicial authorization. If a computer is seized and contains

---

authorized by this Complementary Law, constitutes a crime and subjects the persons responsible to the penalty of reclusion from one to four years, and a fine, by applying, when suitable, the Criminal Code, without prejudice to other pertinent sanctions.'

[24] See TJ/SP, 4ª C.D. Priv., AC 108.150-4/6-00, Relator Desembargador Narciso Orlandi, 15.02.2001, as mentioned in O. Kaminski, 'Brasil: Os Vírus de Computador e a Legislação Penal Brasileira' [Brazil: Computer Viruses and Brazilian Criminal Law] (9 February 2004), <http://www.cbeji.com.br/br/novidades/artigos/main.asp?id=2393>.

[25] Serviço de Proteção ao Crédito (SPC).

[26] See TJ/MG, 3ª C. Cív., AC 281.733-6, Relator Juiz Dorival Guimarães Pereira, 16.06.1999, as mentioned in Kaminski, loc. cit. n. 24.

[27] Code of Criminal Procedure, Art. 240, *caput*: 'A search of a domicile or a person'.

[28] A search of a domicile concerns the apprehension of evidence that is located, for instance, at an office. A personal search means a bodily search.

data of evidentiary value, the law-enforcement authorities must obtain a judicial authorization to access these data. As mentioned above, the Brazilian Constitution, Article 5(XII, last part) protects the secrecy of personal data. It may occur that law-enforcement authorities conclude that it is far more convenient not to conduct a search of a particular domicile, in order to seize a computer wherein the data of evidentiary value are stored. They may be easily deleted by the suspect. An on-line search may be necessary. To conduct this search, the law-enforcement authorities must also obtain a judicial authorization, except if the data they wish to have access to are not protected by any security mechanism, such as passwords. Not only stored data, but also data that are transmitted from one computer to another have constitutional protection. Telematic communications, data that are transmitted from one computer to another, can be intercepted by law-enforcement authorities. Once again, as we have pointed out above, a judicial authorization, according to Law 9.296/96, Article 10, is required.

Infiltration is governed by Law 9.034/95.[29] It must be connected to the repression of organized crime. Cyber-infiltration must be preceded by judicial authorization if, for instance, a mIRC group is password-protected from access by strangers.[30] If it is not protected from access by strangers, if it is a forum which is open to the public without restriction, then infiltration may occur without judicial authorization.

6.3 Cross-Border Cyber-Investigation

There is little doubt that cyber-investigation is a controversial issue. How can one bolster investigative technologies in law-enforcement units specializing in cybercrime? Transborder search and seizure of evidence may be inevitable. If country A has suffered a computer virus attack from an Internet user who is located in country B, should country A abstain from searching and seizing computer data located in country B? Should country A abstain from obtaining on-line evidence without the prior approval of country B? This is a core issue in transborder cyber-investigation. It is not easy to answer this question. At first, what kind of countries are we talking about? Is country A a high-tech country? Does it have all the necessary technological resources to conduct the transborder search and seizure of computer data? Is country B a low-tech country with few technological resources? If the answer is yes, we may be tempted to answer that country A should search and seize

[29] Law 9.034, of 3 May 1995 Establishes the utilization of operational means for the prevention and repression of actions practiced by criminal organizations.

[30] Law 9.034/95, Art. 2: 'The following proceedings of investigation and obtaining proof are allowed in any phase of the criminal prosecution, without prejudice to those already foreseen by the law: (...) V – infiltration by intelligence or police officers, in investigation tasks, constituted by the pertinent specialized bodies, by means of a detailed judicial authorization.'

computer data of evidentiary relevance to the cyber-investigation. But what about the principle of sovereignty? By doing this, country A will have to encroach on the supreme authority of country B within its own territory. Country A will indeed conduct a search and seizure within the territory of country B. All over the world, most law-enforcement authorities are not allowed to conduct a search without judicial authorization. Would then country A commit an illicit act? The answer, in the light of country B's legislation, is quite probably yes. The solution to this confused and complicated situation is unquestionably international co-operation. Countries should co-operate among themselves and work in unison in cyber-investigations.

Cyber-investigation faces increasing challenges due to the speed with which data are exchanged and deleted. How can one collect cyber-evidence in a speedy and timely fashion? If a crime has been committed abroad, is it reasonable to rely on letters rogatory to conduct a search and seizure of computer data, if they can be instantly deleted by the suspect? The answer is obviously no. If they are available on-line, law-enforcement authorities from country A will surely be tempted to conduct *ex situ* the search and seizure of these data. In other words, they may end up intercepting e-mails, invading computer systems and collecting data without the necessary judicial authorization from either country A or country B. A judicial authorization from country A, by the way, could be meaningless. Judicial authorities in country A cannot authorize this search and seizure in country B without the latter's consent. Waiting for law-enforcement authorities located in country B to conduct *in situ* the search and seizure may not be a plausible step to take. There are alternatives – to sign mutual legal-assistance agreements that create expeditious means to conduct the transborder search and seizure of these computer data is a good idea. Judicial mechanisms, such as letters rogatory, should be disregarded. Administrative mechanisms are a far better solution. Still better than signing mutual legal-assistance agreements can be participation forums such as the G8 Network of 24-Hour High-Tech Points of Contact.[31] Below we will verify the functioning of this network. Now, we are going to analyze how cyber-investigation works in Brazil.

At first, we must differentiate between 'stored data' and 'transmitted data'. Stored data are located, for instance, on the hard disk of computer systems or on transferable disks. Transmitted data are sent from one computer system to another computer system. They are in transit to somewhere. Stored data are the object of searches and seizures. Transmitted data, on the other hand, are the object of interception. They are tapped by law-enforcement authorities. Both the search and seizure of stored data and the interception of transmitted data require judicial authorization, but there are issues that should be taken into consideration. For example, a law-enforcement officer is authorized to conduct an overnight drug seizure at a given place. There, on a computer screen, he finds data that are pertinent to the investiga-

---

[31] I would like to thank Christopher Painter and Todd M. Hinnen for the information provided on the G8 Network of 24-Hour High-Tech Points of Contact.

tion. The suspect was just accessing an on-line database with clients' names and addresses. Does the law-enforcement officer have the right to seize these data? This means to copy and print them? We believe that he does, even if there is no judicial authorization. Judicial authorizations will be required, however, to conduct a search and seizure of computer data that are protected from access by means of security measures, such as passwords.

A law-enforcement officer also has the right to search and seize data available on-line, if these data are publicly available. This means he has the right to visit web sites, copy and print their content, if it is publicly available. The same holds true for publicly available databases. If they are protected from access by strangers, law-enforcement officers do not have the right to search and seize such computer data. It seems very strange that some hacker gangs actually have web sites that are publicly available and contain dates of planned attacks and other information that are crucial for cyber-investigation. Paedophiles have web sites with publicly available images of sex with children. In such cases any cyber-investigation, at a preliminary stage involving the gathering of data of evidentiary value in order to make feasible the suspects' prosecution, does not require judicial authorization. If the computer data are not publicly available (if, for instance, a password is required to access them) the law-enforcement officer needs judicial authorization. As regards transmitted data, law-enforcement officers always need judicial authorization to intercept them. The tapping of telephonic and telematic communications alike require judicial authorization.

As regards infiltrating on-line child-pornography networks, the same line of reasoning can be adopted. Judicial authorization is required if access to such networks is restricted, that is, if these networks are protected with security measures, such as passwords, from access by strangers. If, for instance, there is a child-pornography mIRC group, whose access is not protected by passwords, infiltration by law-enforcement officers does not need judicial authorization. In some mIRC groups, pedophiles gather to exchange images. In others, they plan trips to foreign countries for the sake of sexual tourism. They even organize auctions of children and teenagers. If such mIRC groups are not protected by any security measure at all, law-enforcement officers may infiltrate them without judicial authorization. We must highlight the fact that, in Brazil, infiltration must be connected to investigations associated with organized crime. On-line child-pornography networks are not the work of amateurs. They are usually highly organized groups.[32] If mIRC groups are not protected by security measures, law-enforcement officers then have the right to participate in the debates and to collect evidence, just as if they were on the

32 On how computer crime gangs operate nowadays in Brazil, headed by bosses who trade loyalty, see, e.g., M. Diniz, 'Polícia Prende Jovem Acusado de Chefiar Quadrilha de Hackers em MG' [Police Arrests Young Man Accused of Heading a Hacker Gang in MG] (1 December 2004), <http://www1.folha.uol.com.br/folha/cotidiano/ult95u102522.shtml>.

streets and talked to people there. If, on the other hand, they are protected by, for instance, a password, then infiltration requires a judicial authorization.

A final issue to consider is that computer data obtained in a foreign country may have an invalid evidentiary status in Brazil. The Federal Constitution, Article 5(LVI) does not recognize the value of illegal evidence: 'Evidence obtained through illicit means is inadmissible in the proceedings'. Evidence that has been illicitly obtained has no legal value. If, for instance, a foreign country has conducted a search and seizure of data located in Brazil and which are protected by security measures, this evidence is very likely to be considered invalid in Brazil. However, court rulings have interpreted Article 5(LVI) in a much more flexible way. If the evidence was collected under stringent conditions, it may be recognized as legal. For instance, if a telephone conversation was tapped by the family of someone who had been kidnapped, such evidence may be considered valid. If the victim of a crime, such as extortion, taps a telephone conversation with the perpetrator, this evidence may also be considered valid. Protection against the interception of telephonic and telematic conversation is indeed primarily directed at law-enforcement authorities. But even law-enforcement officers, under stringent conditions, may have to tap a telephone or telematic conversation without prior judicial authorization, if, for instance, a life-threatening situation is involved. Article 5(LVI) must be interpreted according to the circumstances, on a case-by-case basis. If the data have been obtained in a foreign country under stringent conditions, they may be considered valid. When, for example, they would surely have been deleted if law-enforcement officers would have had to wait for judicial authorization and, as a result thereof, someone would have been seriously injured, then this evidence will be valid.

Countries may have widely different evidential status rules. These rules, as we just have had the opportunity to verify, may be nuanced by court rulings. What is laid down in the law may often be applied in a much more subtle way. To avoid complications, they should inform each other about the legal requirements that must be observed in evidence collection. Once again, the solution is international co-operation. Countries should closely co-operate in the collection of computer data with evidentiary value that may be used abroad.

6.4 Substantive Cybercrime Jurisdiction

Cybercrimes belong to a category of offense that is known in Brazil as 'crime at a distance'. The Brazilian law has dealt with crimes at a distance for a long time. The result, in this kind of offense, does not occur at the place of the act which gave rise thereto. The result, as a matter of fact, can occur in different countries. There are many examples of crimes at a distance. The border between Brazil and Uruguay is not divided by large rivers. There are a number of twin towns along the frontier. A street or a square can separate the Brazilian and the Uruguayan side. It is called a 'dry frontier', undivided by natural barriers. There is no significant river or mountain to clearly separate the two countries. There is an interesting case of murder that occurred in this region and that is often cited in lectures. The offense was committed in no-man's land which divides Brazil from Uruguay. The perpetrator had begun to accomplish the crime on Uruguayan territory. The victim, mortally wounded, died on Brazilian territory. The result of the act in question, did not occur where the act had been carried out. The victim did not fall dead on the Uruguayan side of the border, but on Brazilian territory. In such cases, jurisdiction is determined by the place where the crime is completed, by the place where the result occurred, that is, in this particular case, in Brazil.

It may be easy to determine the place of the crime, when the action and the result occur in the same place. But it may be very difficult to determine the place of the crime when the initial act and its result occur in different places. The difficulties tend to increase if it is a transborder crime. For instance, a hacker can invade a computer system in country A and thereby have access to a financial institution's database in country B. Having access to bank account numbers and the passwords of high-ranking public officers, he may divert money from their bank accounts in country C. At first, we have to ponder where the act and the result actually occurred. This is not easy to determine. In country A, where the computer system was invaded? Country A can argue that it was the victim of a hacking offense. But the hacker had access to information which was not known to strangers, as well as bank account numbers and passwords in country B. This country may consider that a breach of secrecy had taken place within its territory. But the money was diverted from bank accounts located in country C. Can country C argue that it was the victim of cyberfraud? The situation becomes even more complicated when we consider that these countries probably have different legal systems with diverging jurisdiction rules. A fourth country, country D, may also appear in the scenario. Country D is home to the high-ranking public officers. If we considerer that there is no transnational judicial body with the ability to decide, based on a technical standpoint, which country has the right to prosecute and try the suspect, we have to assume that political and economic pressure can be decisive in solving this positive jurisdictional conflict. But can we indeed talk of one suspect, of 'he' or 'she'? Cybercrimes have been increasingly committed by international gangs. Members of these gangs may be located in distant countries. In country E those who created the software that enabled the invasion of the web site may reside. The gang's leader, who co-ordinated the actions of his subordinates, may live in country F. The financers, the fund providers, may live in country G. This example shows that international co-operation really is crucial in solving cybercrimes.[33]

---

[33] J.H. Jacottet Neto, 'Competência pelo Lugar da Infração dos Crimes Plurilocais e dos Crimes a Distância' [Competence According to the Place of the Offense in Multi-Locational Crimes and Crimes at a Distance], 1 *Revista do Ministério Público do Estado do Rio Grande do Sul* (1992) No. 26, pp. 65-75.

Jurisdiction claims can be fundamentally based on where the act was committed or where the result of that act took place. This panorama can become much more complicated if the act was partially committed in different places or the result also took place in different places. To solve these issues, legal doctrine has come up with the following widely known options:

a. the theory of action: the place of the crime is considered to be where the crime was initiated;
b. the theory of result: the place of the crime is considered to be where the result took place; and
c. the theory of ubiquity: the place of the crime is considered to be not only where the crime was initiated, but also where the result took place.[34]

None of these offer a final solution to determine the place of transborder cybercrimes and all have their pitfalls. If the theory of action is adopted, in the hacking case that we have mentioned above, the country where the hacker lives may claim jurisdiction, although the computer system has been invaded in country A. With the theory of result, country C may claim jurisdiction. The money was diverted from bank accounts located in country C. Country D, the home of the high-ranking public officers, may also claim jurisdiction on the same grounds. The ultimate victims, after all, are the citizens of country D. The theory of ubiquity, the most comprehensive of them all, is also the most prone to cause unimaginable problems. If the theory of ubiquity is adopted by the majority of the countries involved, each one is going to claim jurisdiction in the hacking case. Therefore, not only international co-operation, but also consensus-building is essential to decide which country is going to prosecute which suspects. Otherwise, suspects may benefit from the passing of time, by deleting data with evidentiary value and evading law-enforcement authorities.

Brazil clearly shows a preference for the theory of ubiquity. The Criminal Code, Article 6, sets forth that 'the crime is considered to have been perpetrated in the place where the action or omission occurred, wholly or partially, as well as where the result was produced or should have been produced.' What does this mean in practical terms? It means that Brazil can claim jurisdiction for cybercrimes that were committed on the national territory and for cybercrimes that produced or should have produced results on the national territory. No matter the *iter criminis*, the crime route, if any executory act has been committed on the national territory, in any phase of the crime's accomplishment, and even if any 'result was produced or should have been produced' in the national territory, Brazil can claim jurisdiction.

[34] Ubiquity comes from the Latin word 'ubique': everywhere. In Brazil, this term is used, as we have pointed out, to highlight that the country's criminal law may be applied regardless of where the crime was initiated and where the result occurred. As a matter of fact, Brazil's criminal law may then be enforced whatever the *iter criminis*, the route of the crime.

Brazil could have been country A, B, C, or D and still claim jurisdiction. In a hacking case, if the perpetrator is located in Brazil, Brazil can claim jurisdiction. The 'action or omission occurred, wholly or partially', on the national territory. If, on the other hand, the victim is located in Brazil, Brazil can also claim jurisdiction. The result, the computer-system invasion, 'was produced or should have been produced' in Brazil. The same holds true with the spreading of viruses. If computer viruses are spread from Brazil, Brazil can claim jurisdiction, and that is also the case if computer viruses destroy databases located in Brazil.

With on-line illegal content-related offenses, the panorama does not change. Brazil can claim jurisdiction for on-line illegal content, such as on-line child pornography, if this kind of cybercrime produces or should have produced results in the national territory. This means that if an on-line illegal content originating from abroad is available through the Internet in the national territory, Brazil can claim jurisdiction. To claim jurisdiction for on-line illegal content-related offenses, Brazil does not have to argue that a determinate person or a group of persons physically located on the national territory was affected by the perpetrator's behavior. On-line illegal content-related offenses in Brazil are considered to be what the doctrine identifies as 'mere conduct crimes' (*crimes de mera conduta*). Mere conduct crimes do not require evidence that a determinate person or group of persons was actually affected by the perpetrator's behavior. The perpetrator's mere conduct, e.g., divulging on-line illegal content by means of the Internet, is enough for the crime's completion. Rather than a determinate person or group of persons, the whole community is considered to be the target of the crime. But is this a plausible option? Is it not much more reasonable to contact foreign law-enforcement authorities of the country where the on-line illegal content originates, and to ask them to take the appropriate measures to prosecute and try those who are responsible for the on-line illegal content's propagation?

6.5 Extraterritorial Jurisdiction and Jurisdiction Conflicts

Jurisdiction for transborder cybercrimes can be increasingly claimed based on the territoriality principle: 'Brazilian law applies, without prejudice to conventions, treaties and rules of international law, to the crime committed on the national territory.'[35] Brazil can then claim jurisdiction for a transborder cybercrime, by considering that it was 'committed on the national territory', since 'the result was produced or should have been produced' on Brazilian territory.[36] By trying to safeguard one of the key aspects of national sovereignty, the ability of national courts to hear and decide cases, the territoriality principle can be given a worldwide reach, just like transborder cybercrimes.[37]

---

[35] Criminal Code, Art. 5, *caput*.

[36] Criminal Code, Art. 6.

[37] Brazil can also claim jurisdiction for attempted crimes, if the crime's completion was prevented within the national territory.

Conflicts in cybercrime jurisdiction raise two extreme theories, the theory of absolute territoriality and that of unlimited extraterritoriality. In the first theory, the law of a country applies to any and every person or thing situated within its national territory, without any exception and with total repudiation of any foreign law.[38] As we have seen, jurisdiction for cybercrimes can be claimed by Brazil based on the territoriality principle. The theory of unlimited extraterritoriality has to do with the law being applied extraterritorially. The scope of extraterritorial jurisdiction, as we have already had the opportunity to stress, is not defined by treaties. Each country chooses its set of extraterritorial jurisdiction rules. Customary international law and the principle of comity among nations also play their role.

There are five basic principles, recognized by customary international law, that frame extraterritorial jurisdiction. First, the territoriality principle. A country may prosecute and try those responsible for a crime, if it has a substantial effect within its national territory. Second, the principle of active nationality. A country has the right to prosecute its nationals for crimes committed abroad. Third, the principle of passive nationality. A country has the right to exercise jurisdiction because its nationals have been the victims of crimes committed abroad. Fourth, the principle of protection. It applies to serious crimes that affect the country's homeland security, such as espionage and treason. Fifth, the universal principle. A country has the right to prosecute crimes that are recognized by the international community as a whole as being of the utmost importance, such as war crimes, terrorism, genocide and the trafficking of human organs.[39]

Both the theory of absolute territoriality and the theory of unlimited extraterritoriality have their faults. The theory of absolute territoriality would result in total isolation from the international community.[40] It would indeed foster isolation among countries. The theory of unlimited extraterritoriality, on the other hand, endangers national sovereignty itself, if we consider the risk of constant extraterritorial jurisdiction claims by stronger countries over weaker ones. The application of the territoriality principle, in the context of extraterritorial jurisdiction claims for transborder cybercrimes, has the potential of provoking positive conflicts of law, if we bear in mind that one of the key characteristics of cybercrimes is the possibility of having several perpetrators and victims, spread throughout the world.

So many perpetrators and victims may be involved in a cybercrime that negative conflicts of jurisdiction can also become reality. Countries may simply become

---

[38] The Introduction Act to the Civil Code, Art. 7, *caput*, determines, for instance, that 'the law of the country where the person is domiciled determines the rules on the beginning and the end of personality, the name, capacity, and family rights.' A person may be physically situated within the national territory, but if he is domiciled abroad, that country's law has to be applied to solve, for instance, name-related issues. If the *lex non valet extra territorium* principle was strictly applied, it would produce unfair consequences for the parties involved.

[39] We could also mention the principle of representation that allows extraterritorial jurisdiction to be exercised, if the country where the perpetrator should be punished shows no sign of prosecuting him.

[40] *Lex non valet extra territorium.*

confused and end up not knowing what to do. To exercise jurisdiction over a person, the suspect must in most cases enter the national territory, except in the case of unconditional extraterritoriality. The suspect may then have to be extradited. Extradition, on the other hand, may not seem plausible in most cybercrime cases, such as hacking, the spreading of viruses, or on-line illegal content. The country where the suspect is physically located may quite probably believe that it has priority in prosecuting the perpetrator. The crime, after all, was committed within its national territory. It can be much simpler for the affected country, or for the affected countries, to co-operate in the investigation and prosecution of the cybercrime in the country where the suspect is physically located. This co-operation is even more crucial in the case of cybercrimes with multiple perpetrators and victims spread throughout different countries across the globe. In the case of the exercise of extraterritorial jurisdiction over property, international co-operation is also fundamental. To forfeit property abroad, the countries involved may often have to strike a deal amongst themselves. In the case of cyberfraud, it is quite unlikely that perpetrators have assets in the country of the victim's residence. They may, on the contrary, have assets in off-shore tax havens.

That is why the G8 Network of 24-Hour High-Tech Points of Contact is so important as a key instrument in the investigation and prosecution of transborder cybercrimes.[41] This Network was created at the instigation of the G8 Justice and Interior Ministers at their ministerial meeting in Washington, DC in 1997. Participating law-enforcement jurisdictions must have means of reaching a computer-crime law-enforcement expert on a 24/7 basis, and appropriate procedural tools must be in place to allow them to provide assistance to the requesting country or countries. The Network has grown since its inception from the original eight to a network of forty law-enforcement jurisdictions. It experienced a dramatic rate of growth in the aftermath of the 11 September 2001 attacks in the United States.[42] The G8 Network of 24-Hour High-Tech Points of Contact has been successfully used in the investigation of kidnapping, extortion and death-threat cases, terrorism cases, on-line fraud and identity theft cases, hacking cases, cases involving the propagation of computer worms, viruses and malicious codes, and many others. Administrative contacts, rather than judicial ones, are indeed a much more expeditious way to address the investigation and prosecution of cybercrimes. Evidence must be gathered on a timely basis. To avoid conflicts of law, law-enforcement authorities must contact each other, in the light of transborder cybercrimes, to formulate a strategy of investigation and prosecution.

---

[41] See Meeting of G8 Justice and Home Affairs Ministers (2004), *Communiqué* (11 May 2004), <http://www.cybercrime.gov/g82004/Communique_2004_G8_JHA_Ministerial_051204.pdf>.

[42] As of January 2005 the membership includes: Australia, Austria, Brazil, Canada, Croatia, Czech Republic, Denmark, Dominican Republic, Finland, France, Germany, Hong Kong, Hungary, India, Indonesia, Israel, Italy, Japan, Republic of Korea, Luxembourg, Malaysia, Malta, Mexico, Morocco, the Netherlands, New Zealand, Norway, Pakistan, the Philippines, Romania, Russia, Singapore, South Africa, Spain, Sweden, Taiwan, Thailand, Tunisia, the United Kingdom, and the United States.

6.6 Pitfalls of Extraterritorial Jurisdiction

Cyberspace, as we have already mentioned, knows no national borders. Offenders will surely benefit from this characteristic of the cyberspace environment. It may be much more appropriate to say that some of them have already benefited from this characteristic. The spreading of computer viruses is the most evident and visible side of the phenomenon. Computer viruses cross not only national borders, but continents. The case of Onel de Guzman, the Filipino who allegedly created the ILOVEYOU virus that struck computers around the world back in 2000, is paradigmatic. From the Philippines, he disseminated a computer virus that virtually led to a global computer breakdown. He, like many hackers, did not consider himself a hacker, but a programmer whose motivation was to learn. He did not believe that hackers should be held accountable for the damage caused by computer viruses. Software companies should be considered responsible for selling programs with security vulnerabilities. International co-operation was essential to locate the origin of the ILOVEYOU virus. Since then, cybercrimes have been increasingly committed by professionals. The tale of the lonely teenage hacker has been overtaken by a new reality. Organized-crime structures, with ramifications in several countries, have discovered that cyberspace is the ideal mechanism to internationalize their activities.

Extraterritorial jurisdiction has often been associated, as we have pointed out above, with encroachments on the sovereignty of countries. Extraterritorial claims still raise suspicions of unequal treatment under international law. The signing of the Nanjing Treaty in 1842 is considered as the first in a long series of concessions from China to Western countries. Shanghai indeed became a Western enclave during the 19th century. Each of the major Western countries had extraterritorial jurisdiction over their own citizens. Extraterritorial claims were used to restrict the authority of the Chinese legal system over Western citizens. Russia nowadays, on the other hand, has an extraterritorial claim in defense of Russians or Russian speakers abroad, namely in the territory of the former Soviet Union. How then should extraterritorial jurisdiction be conferred over cybercriminals, if there are two political factors which are detrimental to their prosecution and trial? First, it has traditionally been used to reduce or expand the territorial borders of countries all over the world. Second, it is invasive of another country's sovereignty and inevitably leads to conflicts. Conflicts that may arise from extraterritorial claims will only benefit cybercriminals. Computer evidence may disappear if it is not immediately preserved, witnesses may be overlooked, and memories may fade. To overcome these political factors and to avoid conflicts, countries should choose to co-operate in the formulation of a common strategy for evidence collection and the suspect's prosecution. It is absolutely crucial to start collecting evidence and statements as soon as possible. Extraterritorial claims may be waived if they are not brought in a timely manner.

Extraterritorial jurisdiction is closely connected to the principle of universal jurisdiction. The duty to either extradite or prosecute in international law, *aut dedere aut judicare*, has existed for a long time. It expresses the duty to extradite or prosecute a fugitive from justice and has been recognized and adopted by several international conventions worldwide. It exists with respect to all offenses in which another country is harmed. The country that has been harmed has the right to punish the accused, and the country where the accused is located should not hinder the exercise of this right. If this country refuses to extradite the accused, it has to prosecute him.

The principle of universal jurisdiction may also clash with the principle of sovereignty. Countries may try, for innumerable reasons, to keep their citizens from being prosecuted abroad. Some of the alleged reasons may be legitimate, others absolutely not. The principle of sovereignty can indeed be used to shield criminals and make the country a safe haven for illegal activities. Economic and political pressure from the international community may then be necessary to overcome the obstacles to prosecution. Common-law countries accept much more readily the principle of universal jurisdiction, contrary to civil-law jurisdictions.[43]

Most countries allow extradition on the basis of a treaty with the requesting country. Some allow extradition to be granted on reciprocity grounds. Many countries do not extradite their nationals at all; they prefer to prosecute them at home. Brazil is one of these countries. If a Brazilian citizen commits a crime abroad and thereafter enters the national territory, he shall benefit from the constitutional principle that no Brazilian citizen, as a general rule, can be extradited from Brazil.[44] He has the right to be prosecuted in accordance with Brazilian standards and norms. This may mean impunity: if the standards and norms of the place where the crime was committed are not compatible with those practiced in Brazil, he may be acquitted. If it is not possible to collect evidence in the same way as it would have been if the Brazilian citizen had been prosecuted abroad, he may also be acquitted. Offenders have already left the national territory and sought a safe haven abroad; some have succeeded. In Brasilia, Brazil's capital, a young man killed his girlfriend with unparalleled cruelty. He brutally beat her, stabbed her and burned her body. Soon thereafter, he fled to Denmark. Located by the Brazilian law-enforcement authorities, extradition was requested but not granted. Standards and norms in Brazil were supposedly not compatible with those in Denmark. He then fled to neighboring Germany. Germany has, so far, not granted his extradition either.

---

[43] There are basically two categories of countries with regard to how they apply extraterritorial jurisdiction. Countries that have widespread economic and/or political interests around the globe are prone to extend extraterritorial jurisdiction. Countries that do not have widespread economic and/or political interests around the globe, which are limited to their own national borders, tend to restrict extraterritorial jurisdiction. Globalization thus encompasses two kinds of countries: globalizing and globalized countries.

[44] Federal Constitution, Art. 5(LI): 'No Brazilian shall be extradited, except for naturalized Brazilians in the case of a common crime committed before naturalization, or proven involvement in the illicit traffic of narcotics and similar drugs, as laid down in the law.'

If a country wishes to exercise extraterritorial jurisdiction, it will often have to rely on the offender's extradition. Other alternatives, such as kidnapping the accused, are politically not recommended – ethical standards and principles are thereby disregarded. Extradition is based on the principle of collaboration between states. The offense on which a request for extradition is based must be an offense under Brazilian law. The principle of double criminality is strictly observed. The offense must be mutually recognized as being extraditable. It is in the interest of the international community that crimes do not go unpunished. Treaties have been implemented to allow extradition. They also usually foresee that a person can only be extradited for conduct that has been criminalized in the requesting and the requested country. Some treaties contain lists of extraditable offenses. This is why the harmonization of cybercrime legislation is so important. Diverging provisions on cybercrimes can lead to the denial of extradition, if double criminality is not recognized. Converging provisions on cybercrimes can, in contrast, simplify the granting of extradition. Brazil also adopts the principle of reciprocity. The accused can be surrendered to another country, if in a similar situation this country could surrender him to Brazil.[45]

Differences in language, culture, policing, and legal systems make the duty to extradite or prosecute in international law difficult to apply. Criminal evidence has to be obtained, preserved and translated. Several government departments must be involved during the whole extradition process. It may be easy to sign a treaty on extradition, but it may be very difficult to implement it. Indeed, there is often a huge divide between signing and implementation of treaties. This difficulty in implementation increases with the diversity of their members. Bilateral and regional treaties are much easier to implement than large-scale multilateral treaties. Implementation may take several years or decades. Conflicts on how the treaty must be interpreted and implemented can be considerable, depending on its subject-matter. Transborder cybercrimes, given their worldwide reach, have serious international consequences. But so does drug trafficking, which was maybe the first criminal activity with worldwide reach. Experience has proven that drug trafficking, no matter how serious it is, has been dealt with in a much better way by means of mutual legal-assistance agreements than with extradition treaties. Economic and political pressure have also proved to be important resources in the international struggle against drug trafficking.

Extraterritorial jurisdiction, which we will further analyze below, has two sides that are, at least seemingly, opposed to each other. Extraterritorial jurisdiction, as we have already had the opportunity to mention above, has not been traditionally

[45] Brazil may grant extradition only in cases of unconditional extraterritoriality, such as crimes against state security. In one specific case, an offense had been committed outside Belgian territory. Belgian criminal law could only be applied against the offender if he was in Belgium. Extradition was not granted. It was considered a case of conditional extraterritoriality. See STF, Ext. 423/BE-Bélgica, Relator: Ministro Aldir Passarinho, 29.05.1985, DJU 27.09.1985, p. 16607.

defined by treaties. Domestic law has indeed had a crucial role in defining its rules. No matter how strange it may sound, extraterritorial jurisdiction is territorially defined by national governments. If a country, according to its legal system, has extraterritorial jurisdiction over individuals and property located in foreign countries, it must have the ability to have these individuals extradited and to have their property forfeited. How will this be achieved? Extradition treaties and mutual legal-assistance agreements must be signed and implemented, if the country in question does not want to rely exclusively on the principle of reciprocity. But these treaties and agreements are not enforceable against rogue states. Rogue states are not even likely to sign such treaties and agreements. Extraterritorial jurisdiction may be of no use against hacker havens. If they sign such treaties and agreements, they will quite probably not implement them at all. Treaties and agreements, as we have already pointed out above, do not guarantee that extraterritorial jurisdiction will be exercised, that the accused will be extradited or prosecuted at home, or that the property will be forfeited. Extraterritorial claims can be extremely tricky. Divergent political, economic and legal conditions have led countries to restrict the exercise of extraterritorial jurisdiction and to rely on international co-operation. We are going to examine below how Brazilian law establishes its extraterritorial jurisdiction rules.

6.7 Extraterritorial Jurisdiction in Brazil

6.7.1 Unconditional extraterritorial jurisdiction

Article 7 of the Criminal Code lays down rules which are applicable to determine extraterritoriality. Extraterritorial jurisdiction under Brazilian law has two aspects: unconditional and conditional extraterritoriality. If it is unconditional, Brazilian law must be applied. Perpetrators in unconditional extraterritorial jurisdiction cases, according to Article 7, paragraph 1, are subject to Brazilian law, 'even if they have been acquitted or convicted abroad'. They may be prosecuted and tried *in absentia*. Perpetrators can indeed be tried in Brazil, even if they are absent from the national territory.

There are four kinds of crimes that are subject to unconditional extraterritoriality. The first one concerns crimes 'against the life or freedom of the President of the Republic' (Art. 7(I)(a)). Unconditional extraterritoriality rarely applies in reality. It is so serious, both politically and criminally, that it hardly occurs at all. Crimes 'against the life or freedom of the President of the Republic', committed abroad, have not been heard of since the beginning of Brazilian history. Article 7(I)(a) functions much more as a warning to the international community. If something happens to the President of the Republic, the highest authority in the country, Brazilian law must be applied. Cybercrimes do not fall under Article 7(I)(a). Hacking, the spreading of viruses and on-line illegal content, for instance, are not likely to pose any risk whatsoever to 'the life or freedom of the President of the Republic.'

Article 7(I)(b) subjects to unconditional extraterritoriality crimes 'against the patrimony or the public faith of the Union, Federal District, State, Territory, Municipality, public company, mixed-economy society, autarchy or foundation instituted by Public Power.' A foreigner could undertake a scheme to embezzle funds from a mixed-economy society.[46] As in most cases of fraud-related offenses, he would quite probably not be acting alone, but in co-operation with both national and foreign counterparts. Much more important than prosecuting and trying him in Brazil would be to confiscate the property that had come into his possession. A case of cyberfraud could fall under Article 7(I)(b). Located abroad, an offender could divert bank deposits to his own account. But cyberfraud is not primarily targeted at 'the patrimony or the public faith of the Union, Federal District, State, Territory, Municipality, public company, mixed-economy society, autarchy or foundation instituted by Public Power.' It is targeted at individuals who, unknowingly, pass on to third parties their bank account numbers and passwords. What about Article 153, paragraph 1-A, Article 313-A, Article 313-B, or Article 325, paragraphs 1 and 2, of the Criminal Code? Do the forms of conduct set out in these articles fall under Article 7(I)(b)? Article 153, paragraph 1-A, punishes the unauthorized disclosure of information 'whether or not contained in information systems or data banks of the Public Administration'. The conduct that is criminalized by Article 153, paragraph 1-A is not an offense 'against the patrimony or the public faith'. With Article 313-A, the answer could be different. Article 313-A has introduced what we have called 'electronic peculation'. Embezzlement of public funds may fall under Article 7(I)(b). The unauthorized modification or alteration of information systems or computer programs, foreseen by Article 313-B, could also fall under Article 7(I)(b). The violation of official secrecy, regulated by Article 325, paragraphs 1 and 2, could fall under Article 7(I)(b) as well. However, there is a problem here. Article 313-A, Article 313-B and Article 325, paragraphs 1 and 2, have limited reach. They must all be carried out by public officials. This limited scope is shared by the third kind of unconditional extraterritorial jurisdiction: crimes 'against the Public Administration, by those who are in its service' (Art. 7(I)(c)). Overall, unconditional extraterritorial jurisdiction can sometimes be applied to cybercrimes. Article 7(I)(b) and Article 7(I)(c) can be applied, for instance, in the case of embezzlement of public funds which is carried out electronically. Article 313-A, Article 313-B and Article 325, paragraphs 1 and 2, are all related to crimes 'against the Public Administration'.

The Criminal Code lays down a fourth and last kind of unconditional extraterritorial jurisdiction for crimes 'of genocide, when the perpetrator is a Brazilian or domiciled in Brazil' (Art. 7(I)(d)). We cannot envisage how Article 7(I)(d), concerning crimes 'of genocide', can have relevance as regards cybercrimes.

---

[46] Mixed-economy societies are stock-exchange companies. Both the public and the private sectors, in contrast to public companies, contribute financial resources to them.

6.7.2 Conditional extraterritorial jurisdiction

In all other cases foreseen by the Criminal Code, extraterritoriality is conditional. It is subordinated to a series of prerequisites that we are going to specify below. There are only four cases of conditional extraterritoriality.

Article 7(II)(a) determines the first kind of conditional extraterritorial jurisdiction. Crimes 'that, by treaty or convention, Brazil is obliged to repress'. There is a need to prosecute and try persons responsible for certain kinds of offenses that affect the international community as a whole. These are the *delicta juris gentium*, or international crimes, such as genocide. The preparation, execution and completion of such crimes can involve several countries. They are traditionally subject to treaties and conventions, allowing prosecution in any affected country. We cannot envisage how cybercrimes could be considered as serious offenses against the conscience and law of nations. Article 7(II)(b) foresees the second kind of extraterritorial jurisdiction: crimes 'carried out by a Brazilian'. Brazilian nationals, as a general rule, and as we have already stressed, are not subject to extradition. If Brazil does not surrender a national to another country, it has to punish him according to Brazilian law. Otherwise, impunity would prevail. The third kind of extraterritorial jurisdiction is determined by Article 7(II)(c): crimes 'committed on board Brazilian aircraft or vessels, merchant or private, when in a foreign territory, if they have not been tried there.' Brazilian law is applied in a subsidiary way in this case: only if, for any reason, such offenses have not been tried by the country that should have tried them.

For Brazil to exercise extraterritorial jurisdiction based on these three kinds of crimes, the following conditions must be met:

a. 'the perpetrator must enter the national territory' (Art. 7, para. 2, 'a');[47]
b. 'the conduct must also be punishable in the country where it was practiced' (Art. 7, para. 2, 'b');
c. 'the crime must be included among those for which Brazilian law authorizes extradition' (Art. 7, para. 2, 'c');
d. 'the perpetrator must not have been acquitted nor have served the sentence abroad' (Art. 7, para. 2, 'd'); and
e. 'the perpetrator must not have been pardoned abroad or, for other reasons, the punishability must not have been dispensed with, according to the most favorable law' (Art. 7, para. 2, 'e').

The fourth kind of conditional extraterritoriality is laid down in Article 7, paragraph 3: '[t]he Brazilian law also applies to the crime committed by a foreigner

---

[47] He cannot be prosecuted *in absentia*. It does not matter whether he entered the national territory voluntarily or not, for business or leisure reasons, or on brief or long stays. If he subsequently leaves the national territory, he shall continue to be liable to prosecution.

against a Brazilian outside Brazil'. Not only the conditions foreseen by Article 7, paragraph 2, 'a'-'e', must be met, but also the following requirements:

a. 'extradition was not required or was denied' (Art. 7, para. 3, 'a'); and
b. 'there was a request from the Ministry of Justice' (Art. 7, para. 3, 'b').

6.8 Ultraterritorial Jurisdiction

The cornerstone of extraterritorial jurisdiction that is applicable to transborder cybercrimes is the territoriality principle. A country may prosecute and try, as we have pointed out, those who have been responsible for a crime, if it has substantial effect within its national territory. Cyberspace surely knows no borders. The effects of transborder cybercrimes can be felt in different territories. Extraterritorial jurisdiction can then be claimed, based on the territoriality principle.

Other principles that determine extraterritorial jurisdiction can have a much less important meaning. For instance, the principle of active nationality: extraterritorial jurisdiction can be exercised over an individual because he possesses Brazilian nationality. Article 7(II)(b) determines that crimes 'committed by a Brazilian' are subject to Brazilian law. But it functions much more as a guarantee against impunity. Brazilian nationals, as a general rule, cannot be extradited, but have to be prosecuted and tried in Brazil. The principle of passive nationality is even less applicable. Extraterritorial jurisdiction is thereby exercised, according to Article 7, paragraph 3, concerning acts that cause harm to a Brazilian abroad. But the exercise of extraterritorial jurisdiction, as regards transborder cybercrimes, is meant to extend to foreigners who commit crimes abroad, the effects of which are felt in Brazilian territory. As for the principle of protection, which allows for extraterritorial jurisdiction when homeland security is at risk, we have seen that Article 7(I)(a) has limited scope. The universal principle means that extraterritorial jurisdiction can be exercised over individuals who commit crimes whose seriousness affects the international community as a whole, such as war crimes. Article 7(II)(a) does not apply to cybercrimes, which are not a category of *delicta juris gentium*. The principle of representation, whereby extraterritorial jurisdiction is exercised in a subsidiary way if the country where the perpetrator should be punished shows no sign of prosecuting him due to a lack of interest or of appropriate legislation, does not have much importance as regards transborder cybercrimes either. Article 7(II)(c) only applies to crimes 'committed on board Brazilian aircraft or vessels'.[48]

---

[48] For these crimes, the time of the crime – *tempus delicti* – may be relevant. This is defined by the theory of action. The Criminal Code has not adopted the theory of result or the theory of ubiquity. For the theory of action, a crime takes place in the very place of the act or omission, even if the moment of the result, the place where the damage is suffered, is different. This distinction has practical consequences. In the case where the result occurs later, the crime shall be considered to have been committed

We nevertheless do not believe that extraterritorial jurisdiction will play a major role in cyber-investigation and prosecution. Care should be taken when extending national jurisdiction to the international field. Given the difficulties in its application, extraterritorial jurisdiction should be regarded as a subsidiary tool, when other solutions are not at hand. International co-operation, economic and political pressure for the offender to be prosecuted where he is physically located are the best and most reasonable options. Extraterritorial jurisdiction may be exercised if a country approves a comprehensive law that allows it to take action in its national territory against foreign defendants. This could be especially convenient in the case of financial institutions that refuse to co-operate in handing over the assets of the convicted person. It may indeed be much more interesting for a country whose citizens have been harmed by a cyberfraud to force financial institutions in its national territory to compensate what has been lost. But there may be problems concerning this option. The defendants must have assets in financial institutions that have a branch or affiliated office within the national territory. If this is not the case, there will be no financial institutions to locally hand over the assets.

The competence of the International Criminal Court could be broadened to cover other kinds of crimes, such as cybercrimes. The International Criminal Court and cybercrimes actually have something in common. The International Criminal Court is an attempt to establish a transnational criminal judicial body, and cybercrimes are often a transnational criminal activity. Countries that are prone to invoking the principle of universal jurisdiction as regards certain kinds of crimes in which they are interested in combating, depending on the political circumstances that they face, could consider not only ratifying the Rome Statute, but also helping to strengthen the International Criminal Court. The International Criminal Court has potentially broken the backbone of sovereignty, at least as regards the crimes that are dealt with by the Rome Statute: war crimes, genocide, and crimes against humanity. But not every country has become a party to the Rome Statute. Some never will, at least in the near future. The International Criminal Court respects the principle of *aut dedere aut judicare*. If a country does not surrender a citizen to the International Criminal Court, it must prosecute and try him itself. It can no longer argue that the standards and norms where the crime has been committed are not compatible with its own standards and norms, nor can it acquit him based on the insufficient collection of evidence.

Cybercrimes do not fall under the competence of the International Criminal Court. And maybe, indeed, they should not. The International Criminal Court has the purpose of dealing with some extremely serious offenses against the conscience and law of nations. Economic and political pressure may be essential to put mutual legal-assistance agreements and treaties into practice, to enforce the duty to extra-

---

at the very moment of the act or omission. The Criminal Code, Art. 4, states: 'The crime is considered to have been committed at the moment of the act or omission, regardless of the moment of the result.'

dite or prosecute.[49] Libya, for instance, based on the principle of sovereignty, tried to keep their nationals who were responsible for the 1988 bombing of a Pan-Am jet over Lockerbie, Scotland, from being prosecuted abroad.[50]

Some countries have completely ignored mutual legal-assistance agreements and extradition treaties, but instead have kidnapped offenders abroad. There is a very recent case on this issue. In early January 2005, Venezuela started an investigation to determine whether agents from Colombia had kidnapped a rebel leader within its national territory. It was regarded as a violation of Venezuela's sovereignty. Colombia, on the other hand, considered that there had been no kidnapping, but rather the arrest of a criminal wanted on charges of drug trafficking and terrorism. Such kidnapping, or arrest, depending on the point of view, has affected diplomatic relations between Venezuela and Colombia.[51]

Differences in language, culture, policing, and legal systems do make extraterritorial jurisdiction difficult to apply. Training for lawyers, judges, prosecutors, and law-enforcement authorities in understanding and applying extraterritorial jurisdiction is extremely important. Embassy staff must have clear guidelines for dealing with extraterritorial jurisdiction. But should we not speak of 'ultraterritorial jurisdiction', instead of extraterritorial jurisdiction? As we have mentioned above, cyberspace has no borders. The effects of transborder cybercrimes can be felt in different national territories. Extraterritorial jurisdiction can then be claimed based on the territoriality principle. Transborder cybercrimes give a whole new perspective to the application of the territoriality principle. But how does ultraterritorial jurisdiction differ from extraterritorial jurisdiction?

The main goal of ultraterritorial jurisdiction is to avoid conflicts and controversies that are usually associated with extraterritorial jurisdiction. Countries tend to regard extraterritorial jurisdiction as an intrusion on their sovereignty. The weaker the country, the greater the possibility that it will consider only the negative impacts from extraterritorial jurisdiction in its internal politics. A change to this perception would come about with co-operation, instead of intervention. Countries affected by a transborder cybercrime should co-operate in order to come to an agreement on how to handle what is surely a potential conflict. In this consensus-building process they should not be concerned with who is going to enforce court rulings abroad, but

---

[49] With the aim of improving mutual legal assistance, countries should be encouraged to adopt mutual legal-assistance agreements and extradition treaties. Extradition treaties can lay down conditions to ensure fair treatment of offenders. Countries should be encouraged to render mutual legal assistance, despite the absence of double criminality.

[50] As regards economic sanctions, it is interesting to note that the United States Trade Act has a provision, s. 301, that requires the United States Trade Representative Office to investigate unfair foreign trade practices. Unless a negotiated settlement is reached, economic sanctions may be applied against a foreign country for unfair foreign trade practices. Some of these practices have already been identified concerning Brazil, India, and Japan. In all cases, a negotiated settlement was reached. Would this kind of measure be effective against countries that become havens for hackers?

[51] See E. Gotkine, 'Venezuela Kidnap Row "Risked War"' (1 February 2005), <http://news.bbc.co.uk/2/hi/americas/4228013.stm>.

rather with devising a common strategy for investigation and prosecution. Ultraterritorial jurisdiction is not intended to favor the exercise of one jurisdiction over another, but rather to combine jurisdictions and law-enforcement authorities from different countries. Together, they can more easily and effectively tackle transborder cybercrimes.

The above-mentioned new perspective that transborder cybercrimes are likely to give to the territoriality principle may result in arbitrary outcomes and deprive suspects of effective protection for their rights. As for Brazil, the immediate consequence of the territoriality principle is that everyone, nationals or foreigners, may be prosecuted and tried for transborder cybercrimes if these have a substantial effect within the national territory (Criminal Code, Arts. 5 and 6). A connection between transborder cybercrimes and the territoriality principle may lead not only to positive conflicts of law, but also to law-enforcement pitfalls. How is Brazil going to conduct, on its own, a transborder cybercrime investigation and prosecution? Other countries may quite probably have the same point of view. Basing themselves on the territoriality principle and believing that the transborder cybercrime had a substantial effect within their national territory, they may all be willing to investigate and prosecute the suspect. Ultraterritorial jurisdiction's solution to this puzzle is to join efforts across national borders in order to achieve a plan of action, based on a rigorous analysis of the transborder cybercrime scenery, aimed at the suspect's prosecution in the country where he is physically located.

To assure this goal, building up a law-enforcement network is an essential factor. The G8 Network of 24-Hour High-Tech Points of Contact is a major example of how such networks should work. Functioning as a platform, they should help to bring law-enforcement authorities together in order to discuss how to tackle transborder cybercrimes, bearing in mind that joint efforts should have as their target, as we have stated above, the suspect's prosecution where he is physically located. Most likely, the place where he is physically located is his homeland or his country of adoption. This means a place with a familiar religion, cultural values, and political system. Pornography is widely available on the Internet. As is widely known, some countries in the Middle East strictly ban pornography. Would it make any sense for a Western citizen who resides in a Western country to be tried for on-line pornography in a Middle Eastern country, in accordance with religious and cultural values of which he presumably has not much knowledge? On the other hand, some countries in the West are highly secularized. Does it sound reasonable for a Middle Eastern resident citizen to be tried for on-line religious proselytism in a Western country?

To avoid impunity on a global scale, the criminalization of cybercrimes should nonetheless be subject to harmonization across the world. Key cybercrime offenses, such as cyberfraud and hacking, should be deemed illegal all over the planet. Treaties could surely play a role in the harmonization of cybercrime legislation, but one should not believe that their ratification would immediately trigger the leveling of legal regimes. The implementation of treaties, as we have had the opportunity to stress, can take years or decades and at the end can be considered unsatisfactory. The exercise of ultraterritorial jurisdiction requires intense international co-operation and favors the suspect's prosecution where he is physically located. To tackle the impunity that perpetrators may enjoy from the absence of an appropriate local cybercrime legislation and the virtual lack of interest in implementing treaties and joining efforts to guarantee the suspect's prosecution, an intergovernmental body should be established to make sure that transborder cybercrimes are adequately dealt with by the international community. We could look to the Financial Action Task Force on Money Laundering (FATF) as a model for such an intergovernmental body. Why the FATF? It is an intergovernmental body that develops and promotes policies, both at the national and the international level, against money laundering. It has the ability to impose sanctions on countries that fail to implement its anti-money laundering recommendations. This ability to impose sanctions confers a binding character to such recommendations. These recommendations often refer back to the content of treaties and establish the duty to fully implement them. A FATF-like intergovernmental body on cybercrime could assist countries in reviewing their laws to ensure that cybercrimes attract appropriate criminal sanctions. Some countries should be chosen, in accordance with their importance in the international community, to become members of this organization. They could make recommendations as regards the criminalization of cybercrimes and the exercise of ultraterritorial jurisdiction. Countries should be regularly assessed and monitored concerning the implementation of these recommendations. Countries failing to comply should be subject to international sanctions on a non-discriminatory basis. A central authority should be structured in each country to provide speedy coordination of mutual legal-assistance and extradition requests as regards transborder cybercrimes.

6.9 Conclusion

International co-operation and consensus-building are the key elements in fighting transborder cybercrimes. If a cybercrime affects several countries, they should co-operate in order to collect evidence. Non-formal mechanisms, such as the G8 Network of 24-Hour High-Tech Points of Contact, can surely prove to be much more effective than what is laid down in treaties concerning the collection of evidence. Administrative contacts, rather than judicial ones, are a much more expeditious way to address this problem. Countries should concentrate all their efforts, on a timely basis, to gathering all evidence of transborder cybercrimes. Law-enforcement authorities, as soon as a cybercrime is committed, should immediately contact each other and formulate a strategy to solve the issue. Offenders should be prosecuted and tried, preferably, in the country where they are physically located.

Consensus-building in cybercrime law enforcement could be attained by means of an intergovernmental body such as the FATF. It should have the ability to regularly conduct and communicate assessments on how effectively its anti-cybercrime recommendations have been implemented by the international community. These recommendations should primarily be based on what is determined in international and regional treaties. If country A has been affected by a cybercrime committed in country B, country A should first contact country B, through the G8 Network of 24-Hour High-Tech Points of Contact, and join efforts to prosecute and try the offender. If efforts fail and the offender goes unpunished, country A should then report what has happened to the FATF-like intergovernmental body. Countries that fail to implement an appropriate cybercrime legislation should be subject to corrective measures by the international community.

The first mission of this FATF-like intergovernmental body should indeed be to stimulate the adoption of cybercrime legislation by the international community. Treaties, such as the Council of Europe's Cybercrime Convention, may have limited reach – notably, a regional one. Some countries may take years to ratify a treaty, and others decades or more to implement it. The FATF periodically issues anti-money laundering recommendations that must be observed by the international community. Similarly, cybercrime recommendations should be made by a FATF-like intergovernmental body, and the implementation of these recommendations should be subject to continuous scrutiny by the international community.

Bibliography

R.C. de Albuquerque, *A Criminalidade Informática* [Computer Crime] (São Paulo, Universidade de São Paulo 2004).

R.O. Blum and J.C. Abrusio, *Crimes Eletrônicos* [Electronic Crimes] (23 December 2002), <http://www.cbeji.com.br/br/novidades/tendencias/main.asp?id=1190>.

R.O. Blum and J.C. Abrusio, *Os Crimes Eletrônicos e seus Enquadramentos Legais* [The Electronic Crimes and their Legal Frameworks] (15 April 2004), <http://www.cbeji.com.br/br/novidades/artigos/main.asp?id=2697>.

S.W. Brenner and B.J. Koops, 'Approaches to Cybercrime Jurisdiction', 4 *Journal of High-Technology Law* (2004) No. 1, pp. 1-46.

M.C.P. Caminha, 'Os Juízes do Mercosul e a Extraterritorialidade dos Atos Jurisdicionais' [Mercosul Judges and the Extraterritoriality of Judicial Acts], 11 *Revista de Direito Constitucional e Internacional* (2003), No. 44, pp. 40-61.

A. Concesi, 'A Jurisdição Universal' [Universal Jurisdiction], *Boletim Científico da Escola Superior do Ministério Público da União* (2003) No. 8, pp. 11-14.

P. Demaret, 'L'Extraterritorialité des Lois et les Relations Transatlantiques: Une Question de Droit ou de Diplomatie?', 21 *Revue Trimestrielle de Droit Européen* (1985) No. 1, pp. 1-39.

M. Diniz, 'Polícia Prende Jovem Acusado de Chefiar Quadrilha de Hackers em MG' [Police Arrests Young Man Accused of Heading a Hacker Gang in MG] (1 December 2004), <http://www1.folha.uol.com.br/folha/cotidiano/ult95u102522.shtml>.

E. Gotkine, 'Venezuela Kidnap Row "Risked War"' (1 February 2005), <http://news.bbc.co.uk/2/hi/americas/4228013.stm>.

J.H. JACOTTET NETO, 'Competência pelo Lugar da Infração dos Crimes Plurilocais e dos Crimes a Distância' [Competence According to the Place of the Offense in Multi-Locational Crimes and Crimes at a Distance], 1 *Revista do Ministério Público do Estado do Rio Grande do Sul* (1992) No. 26, pp. 65-75.

O. KAMINSKI, 'Brasil: Os Vírus de Computador e a Legislação Penal Brasileira' [Brazil: Computer Viruses and Brazilian Criminal Law] (9 February 2004), <http://www.cbeji.com.br/br/novidades/artigos/main.asp?id=2393>.

G.W. KEETON, 'Extraterritoriality in International and Comparative Law', 72 *Recueil des Cours* (1948) No. 1, pp. 283-391.

M. KNOOP, *Análise Forense: Um Mundo sem Fronteiras* [Forensic Analysis: A World without Borders] (7 August 2003), <http://www.cbeji.com.br/br/novidades/artigos/main.asp?id=1841>.

J.C. MAGALHÃES, 'Aplicação Extraterritorial de Leis Nacionais' [Extraterritorial Application of National Laws], 80 *Revista da Faculdade de Direito da Universidade de São Paulo* (1985) No. 80, pp. 157-177.

F.A. PEDROSO, *Competência Penal* [Criminal Competence] (Belo Horizonte, Del Rey 1998).

C. PERANE-MOISÉS, 'O Princípio da Complementariedade no Estatuto do Tribunal Penal Internacional e a Soberania Contemporânea' [The Principle of Complementarity in the International Criminal Court Statute and the Current Sovereignty], 8 *Política Externa* (2000) No. 4, pp. 3-11.

L.C.R. PEREIRA, *Limitação e a Não-Aplicabilidade do Direito: Direito Estrangeiro, Convencional e Comunitário* [Limitation and Non-Applicability of Law: Community, Conventional, and Foreign Law] (Rio de Janeiro, Renovar 2001).

E.S. PODGOR, '"Defensive Territoriality": a New Paradigm for the Prosecution of Extraterritorial Business Crimes', 31 *Georgia Journal of International and Comparative Law* (2002) No. 1, pp. 1-30.

I. STRENGER, *Direito Processual Internacional* [International Procedural Law] (São Paulo, LTr 2003).

Chapter 7
CYBERCRIME AND JURISDICTION IN CHILE

Rodrigo Zúñiga and Fernando Londoño*

7.1 Introduction[1]

Computer and communication developments are strongly challenging our legal systems and jurisdictions. In the context of criminal law, this is quite evident. In fact, new targets of crimes (computer data and computer systems) and new instruments for committing crimes (computers and the Internet) challenge our legal orders at least in four different fields, each one representing a singular problem. First, in accordance with the legality principle, there is the necessity to explicitly criminalize new forms of committing crimes (the pure material problem) and, second, the necessity to implement new investigatory powers or techniques for dealing with cyber-investigations (the pure procedural problem). Third, we have the necessity of resolving the *locus commissi delicti* question and determining jurisdiction (the material jurisdiction problem) and, finally, the necessity of dealing with extraterritorial investigations (the procedural jurisdiction problem). In this report we will principally address Chilean responses to the first three problems (sections 3, 4 and 5). The fourth problem will be considered very briefly (section 6), mainly because it has so far not been a matter of clear legal responses.

* Rodrigo Zúñiga, a graduate in Law (Universidad de Chile), is a lawyer and Legal Adviser at the *Ministerio de Justicia* (Justice Department) of Chile. Fernando Londoño, a graduate in Law (Universidad de Chile), is a lawyer and a lecturer in criminal law at the Universidad de Los Andes, Chile.

[1] The introduction and the conclusion were written by both the authors. The sections dealing mainly with procedural provisions (7.2.2, 7.4, 7.6) were written by Rodrigo Zúñiga. The sections dealing mainly with material provisions (7.2.1, 7.3, 7.5) were written by Fernando Londoño. All translations from Chilean legislation in this chapter are by the authors. We are grateful to Michele Colombo for helpful comments.

B-J. Koops and S.W. Brenner (Eds), Cybercrime and Jurisdiction

7.2 Brief Legislative History

7.2.1 Material provisions

Besides general provisions applicable to cybercrime and cybercrime jurisdiction, Chile has had a specific legal corpus containing penal provisions on cybercrime since 1993: Act No. 19.223 that Establishes Penal Provisions Relative to Informatics (*Ley que tipifica figuras penales relativas a la informática*), most commonly called the Informatic Crimes Act (*Ley de delitos informáticos*). It is a very brief Act – containing just four articles – that specifically sanctions (with imprisonment) offenses such as damage to, alteration or interference of data-processing systems, as well as damage to or alteration of data contained in such systems (Arts. 1 and 3); illegal access to data-processing systems with the purpose of seizing, using, or taking cognizance of data contained in such systems (Art. 2); and the disclosure or spreading of data contained in data-processing systems (Art. 4). Parliament is now studying two important Bills[2] that, if approved, will introduce significant reforms in this field. The criminal provisions punishing cybercrime will be extended to crimes not specifically covered by Act No. 19.223 (such as cyber-fraud).[3] Also, the substantive contents of Act No. 19.223 will be introduced into the Penal Code and thus become a common matter, placed amongst analogous physical-crime provisions, so as to make them more accessible or familiar for judges and lawyers.[4]

7.2.2 Procedural provisions

In June 2005, Chile concluded the process of implementing a new criminal procedure,[5] thus moving from our traditional inquisitorial system[6] to a mainly accusatorial system.

In the new criminal procedure, both investigation and prosecution are subjected to a new administrative power, independent from political or judicial authorities, called the *Ministerio Público* (MP), i.e., the Public Prosecutor. The MP – represented by single prosecutors – is exclusively in charge of directing the investigation. The MP develops its investigative authority with the assistance of the police. Before executing any investigatory power that could affect constitutional rights (such as freedom, privacy, property, etc.), public prosecutors should request judicial authorization from the *juez de garantía* (an investigating judge). This judicial

---

[2] Proposals No. 2974 and No. 3083.

[3] See *infra*, section 7.3.

[4] For a complete description of these proposals, see F. Londoño, 'Los delitos informáticos en el proyecto de reforma en actual trámite parlamentario', *Revista Chilena de Derecho Informático* (Universidad de Chile) (2004) No. 4, pp. 171-190.

[5] This process began in 2000, when the new criminal procedure was implemented in two of the thirteen regions of Chile.

[6] Where the same judge was in charge of investigating, prosecuting, judging, and sentencing.

authority is responsible – among others duties – for protecting the rights of defendants by approving or denying the execution of sensitive investigatory orders requested by the public prosecutors in the context of a formal investigation.

As regards evidence and the system of proof, the new procedure includes an important change: it moves away from a strict system of evidence – in which only certain means of evidence explicitly recognized by law can be used in the investigation and trial – to a free system of evidence, where the parties can present any kind of evidence which is capable of producing a conviction, as long as it is legally produced and introduced at the trial. However, it is important to point out that the results of the investigation stage do not have any evidentiary value in themselves, unless they are presented as evidence during the trial.

7.3 Material Provisions on Relevant Cybercrimes

7.3.1 Provisions within the law

We shall primarily point out that cybercrimes (more precisely, those that will be described in this section) are mainly considered as *simple offenses* – thus, not *crimes* – by the Chilean legal system.[7] As we will see later (section 7.4), this consideration is important when dealing with investigatory powers. As we said above, the main criminal provisions on cybercrime are contained in Act No. 19.223.

Damage to, alteration of or interference with data-processing systems, as well as *damage to and alteration of data contained in such systems* (viruses are tacitly included) are punished with a term of imprisonment for a minimum of 541 days and a maximum of five years (Arts. 1 and 3). Article 1, in particular, provides for imprisonment for someone who willingly destroys or renders useless a data-processing system or its parts or components, as well as for whoever willingly hinders or modifies its operation. Article 3 provides for imprisonment for someone who willingly modifies, damages or destroys data contained in data-processing systems. The criminal provision is all-inclusive (viruses are certainly included), and it is structured as a crime of result (i.e., actual damage is required).

Illegal access to data-processing systems, when committed with the specific intention of possessing, using, or taking cognizance of data contained in such system, is punished with a term of imprisonment from 61 days to three years (Art. 2).

---

7 The Chilean legal system has three degrees of criminal offenses: *misdemeanors*, *simple offenses*, and *crimes*. The division basically corresponds to the length of the terms of imprisonment assigned by law. Offenses punished with a term of imprisonment exceeding five years are considered to be crimes (*crímenes*). Offenses punished with imprisonment exceeding a 60-day but not exceeding a five-year term are considered to be simple offenses (*simples delitos*). Offenses punished with imprisonment not exceeding a 60-day term are considered to be misdemeanors (*faltas*).

Finally, *illegal disclosure or spreading of data contained in data-processing systems* is specifically sanctioned by Article 4. Such conduct is punished with a term of imprisonment from 541 days to five years.

Apart from these specific computer crimes in Act No. 19.223, there are various other cyber-related offenses in Chilean law. We will first look at some relevant *content-based cybercrimes*. In accordance with the United Nations Optional Protocol on the sale of children, child prostitution and child pornography,[8] *child pornography* criminal provisions have been modified, basically in order to include the acquisition and storage of child-porn material, by Act No. 19.927 on Child-Pornography Offenses (January 2004). Now, Article 374bis of the Penal Code punishes with a term of imprisonment from 541 days to five years whoever commercializes, imports, exports, distributes, spreads, or exhibits child-porn material,[9] whatever the carrier of the material. On the other hand, whoever acquires or stores that kind of material is sanctioned with a term of imprisonment for a maximum of three years. As we will explain below (section 7.4), Act No. 19.927 also introduced specific provisions with the purpose of reinforcing powers to collect digital evidence and expanding Chilean jurisdiction in prosecuting and punishing offenses related to child pornography.

Intellectual property violations committed through the Internet are also criminalized. In fact, the criminal provisions included in both laws that protect intellectual property[10] are *technologically neutral*,[11] so as to embrace not only violations committed in the physical world, but also those committed through the Internet.[12] In general, the sanctions are imprisonment for a maximum term of 541 days and moderate fines (in the case of offenses against an author's rights) or harsh fines (in the case of offenses against industrial property). Probably the only infringement not specifically covered by the current intellectual property legislation is unauthorized access to intellectually-protected content included in a web site.[13]

---

[8] See <http://www.unicef.org/voy/explore/rights/explore_157.html>.

[9] Art. 366quinquies of the Penal Code defines child-porn material as 'any representation of any real person younger than eighteen years old in real or simulated explicit sexual activities, or showing his or her sexual parts for primarily sexual purposes.'

[10] Act No. 17.366 on Authors' Rights (specifically Art. 79 in relation to Arts. 1, 3 No. 1, 17 and 18), and Act No. 19.039 on Industrial Property (Art. 28, among others).

[11] For example, through the use of formulas such as 'unauthorized use of protected works' and 'in any way or means'.

[12] A. González (2005), 'Intellectual Property in the Internet', unpublished report for the 2005 LL.M. program on Intellectual Property, Stockholm University, Stockholm. With regard civil-law enforcement, see K. Jadue, 'El derecho de autor en las bibliotecas y galerías virtuales de Internet', *Revista Chilena de Derecho Informático* (Universidad de Chile) (2004) No. 4, pp. 53-79 at p. 54.

[13] H. Hernández, *Informe Definitivo sobre los aspectos penales del anteproyecto de ley que modifica la ley 17.336 sobre propiedad intelectual*, unpublished report prepared for the Chilean Justice Department (Santiago 2001a).

Nevertheless, in almost all such cases, Article 2 of Act No. 19.223 (illegal access to data) would be applicable.[14]

Finally, we can look at some cybercrimes against persons and property. The law-enforcement situation concerning *threats committed through the Internet* is quite similar to that concerning intellectual property violations. Since they are technologically neutral, traditional physical-world criminal provisions (Arts. 296, 297 and 298 of the Penal Code) include all kinds of threats, irrelevant of the means. In these cases, sanctions vary depending on the intensity, the specific means and the consequences of the threat, but they are never lighter than a term of imprisonment for a maximum of five years.

In a similar law-enforcement situation we find *slander* and *offenses against honor*, which are clearly covered by general physical-world criminal provisions:[15] Article 29 of Act No. 19.733 on Mass Media is applicable to offenses committed through on-line mass media, like on-line newspapers, TV, or radio. In other cases (offenses committed through the Internet but not by means of mass media), the traditional provisions contained in the Penal Code, Articles 412 to 431, are applicable. On the whole, the sanctions are imprisonment for a maximum term of three years (in the most serious cases of malicious representation) and a fine, which is higher in the case of offenses committed through on-line mass media.

Cyber-fraud or, more precisely in this context, fraud committed by means of computers, is not specifically regulated by any *direct* criminal provision.[16] In fact, the Penal Code's traditional fraud provision only embraces conduct that misleads human beings, while the legality principle does not allow analogical extension of criminal provisions against defendants. But then again, it is Act No. 19.923, specifically Articles 2 (illegal access) and 3 (alteration of computer data), that – in practice – covers many instances of such conduct.[17] However, such offenses are certainly covered[18] at least in all cases (which are most common) in which computer data are modified, as well as when illegal access to data-processing systems is used in order to commit fraud. However, jurisprudence seems to prefer traditional physical-world criminal provisions, at least when sanctioning the very common cases of cyber-fraud related to the illegal use of data contained in credit and banking cards. In fact, the current case law – motivated by an important decision by the

---

[14] Ibid.

[15] Although considering mainly civil-law enforcement, see Corte de Apelaciones de Temuco, *Ustovic Kaflik* v. *Sáez Infante* (2002); also at <http://www.cedi.uchile.cl/docs/sentenciatemuco.pdf>.

[16] M. Garrido, *Derecho Penal. Parte Especial. Tomo IV* (Editorial Jurídica de Chile, Santiago, 2000) p. 327.

[17] H. Hernández, *Tratamiento de la criminalidad informática en el derecho penal chileno – Diagnóstico y propuestas – Informe Definitivo: 31.12.01*, unpublished report prepared for the Chilean Justice Department (Santiago 2001b); contra, C. Magliona and M. López, *Delincuencia y fraude informático* (Editorial Jurídica de Chile, Santiago, 1999) p. 227.

[18] Although this is not always sound or reasonable in terms of proportionality.

Corte Suprema in 2001[19] – relies on criminal provisions such as aggravated theft[20] or even the counterfeiting of commercial documents.[21] This jurisprudence makes sense – especially by making use of theft[22] – but it could easily go against the legality principle in some cases.[23] Nevertheless, it should be pointed out that the case law on this subject will probably change in the future. In fact, the recent Act No. 20.009 'that limits the liability of legitimate owners concerning transactions made using lost or stolen credit cards' (April 2005) introduces a criminal provision, Article 5, to specifically punish the illegal use of data contained in lost, stolen or counterfeited credit or banking cards; these are data typically used in computer systems, like cash points, web shops, etc. The sanction is a term of imprisonment for a maximum of five years. In spite of the presence of these criminal provisions which are suitable for almost every case of cyber-fraud, the legal situation cannot be considered to be completely satisfactory, at least with regard to consistency, clarity, and strict respect for the legality principle. That is the reason why the approval of Bill No. 3083 is still necessary.[24]

7.3.2 Relevant case law

Undoubtedly the most notorious characteristic of the Chilean substantive jurisprudence on cybercrimes is its scarcity.[25] In this scenario, a relevant case which should

[19] Corte Suprema 08.03.2001, *Revista de Derecho y Jurisprudencia*, Tomo XCVIII (2001) No. 1, sección 4.

[20] Which considers credit or banking cards as *keys* so as to be able to rely on a special criminal provision, Art. 442 No. 3 of the Penal Code, which sanctions (with a more serious penalty) thefts committed by using keys to enter buildings or rooms or to open closets.

[21] Art. 197 of the Penal Code.

[22] Hernández (2001b), op. cit. n. 17.

[23] Especially when the area in question is accessed without the use of a stolen or false card or any means of force, as well as when the card has been completely forged (and not just counterfeited).

[24] As we said above, Bill No. 3083 will – if approved – introduce a provision that specifically criminalizes all kinds of conduct encompassing the notion of cyber-fraud.

[25] Since 1993 – the year in which Act No. 19.223 came into force – we have counted no more than ten decisions regarding violations of this Act. This scarcity is probably due to at least four factors: a) a significant number of cases are not reported by victims in order to avoid loss of reputation or due to feelings of insecurity concerning computer systems. We specifically refer to institutions such as banks and other financial institutions, state departments, hospitals, etc. In short: economic (not loosing customers is a main interest) and security reasons contribute to this field; b) another important factor is uncertainty, among lawyers and judges, about the real goals and possibilities of Act No. 19.223. The difficulties posed by Act No. 19.223 certainly favor this lack of acknowledgment. Nevertheless, we ought to say that in the last five years the significance of this factor has been sensibly reduced by the work of prosecutors (MP) and new judges in the context of the new criminal procedure; c) the use of traditional criminal provisions, especially to resolve some cases that deal with (cyber-)fraud – in part as a consequence of the factor mentioned in b) – is also an important reason for this lack of jurisprudence on cybercrimes. The use of common provisions makes it more difficult for researchers and lawyers to identify and systematize relevant jurisprudence on this subject; and, finally, d) we still believe that cases of cybercrime are not so significant in Chile, at least in comparison with analogous physical-world crimes.

be mentioned is the ATI-Chile case,[26] which ended with a sentence of three years' imprisonment (in probation) being imposed against the perpetrator. The facts are quite simple and represent a central case of hacking into and damaging computer systems and computer data. ATI-Chile was the name of a company that offered computer and web services, such as web hosting and web design. H.M.V.C. – a 21-year old former employee of the company, who had been fired some months previously – accessed ATI-Chile's computer system on at least seven occasions, directly damaging some of the company's data, and obstructing and modifying its computer system. He also accessed and damaged two web sites hosted by the Company. The Court (Juzgado de Garantía from Talca) convicted H.M.V.C. of a series of offenses described in Articles 1, 2, and 3 of Act No. 19.223. The relevance of the sentence lies in the fact that it was one of the first convictions on the subject since the new criminal procedure had entered into force (see section 7.2.2). It was also significant because it allowed for the prosecution of a very central case of cybercrime, testifying to the importance of powers relating to searching computers and networks.

Another relevant case recently took place at Temuco:[27] J.F.G.M. and G.A.C.B. had cloned several banking and credit cards with an electronic device, described in the hearing as a 'little black box', which they had placed on the door of a cash point, covering the device in which customers were supposed to place their cards in order to access the cash point. This electronic device could record the data contained on the magnetic strip of a card. The data were subsequently reproduced by J.F.G.M. and G.A.C.B. on new magnetic strips placed on ordinary plastic cards. They never got to use these cloned cards because they were arrested and prosecuted before they could do so. The court convicted J.F.G.M. and G.A.C.B. of illegal access to information contained in data-processing systems, as described by Article 2 of Act No. 19.223. The decision is important because it considered the magnetic strip of the credit card to be a data-processing system, and because, therefore, it did not equate the expression 'data-processing system', as used in Article 2, with 'computer', which is a very common interpretation among lawyers.

7.4 Procedural Provisions Applicable to Cybercrime Investigations

The Chilean legal system principally contains only general provisions for the investigation of offenses and crimes. Nevertheless, as we will see further, for the investigation of crimes and some special offenses dealing with child pornography, the legislator has included new provisions in order to implement special investigatory powers.

[26] Juzgado de Garantía de Talca, 11 April 2003, unpublished.
[27] Juzgado de Garantía de Temuco, 2 March 2005, unpublished.

With regard to collecting or seizing *stored data*, general provisions on search warrants are certainly adequate for cybercrime-investigation purposes. Thus, Article 217 of the Code of Criminal Procedure (*Código Procesal Penal*, hereafter: NCPP) provides that:

> 'the objects and documents related to the case investigated, those that can be confiscated and those than can be used as evidence, will be seized, after a judicial order requested by the prosecutor, when the person who is in possession of them does not deliver them voluntarily, or when the request for voluntary delivery could place the investigation at risk.'

In the same direction, Article 218 NCPP establishes that:

> '[a]fter a prosecutor's request, the Juez de Garantía can authorize (…) the retention of postal correspondence, telegraph or any other kind of correspondence (…) when, according to well-founded reasons, this is likely to be useful for the investigation. In the same way, [the judge] can authorize the making of simple copies or backup copies of electronic correspondence addressed to the defendant or sent by him.'

Finally, Article 219 NCPP establishes that:

> '[t]he Juez de Garantía can authorize, after a prosecutor's request, the release of copies of communications transmitted or received by any telecommunications company.'

In the current Chilean legal system, the stronger investigatory powers – paradigmatically, the interception of data in transmission – are only applicable for the investigation of crimes and child-pornography simple offenses (content-based offenses). Since 'cybercrimes' are – *in abstracto* – mainly simple offenses,[28] investigations dealing with cybercrimes can rarely rely on strong investigatory powers such as real-time interception of communications.

Our legislation, in the form of Article 222 NCPP, establishes that under certain conditions – investigations dealing with facts that deserve criminal penalties; the plausibility of the charges; and the necessity of the interception warrant – the Juez de Garantía can authorize, after a request by the MP (Public Prosecutor), the interception and recording of telephone communications or other forms of communications, including the Internet. In order to guarantee the real efficacy of this investigatory power, Article 222 NCPP establishes that Internet Service Providers (ISPs) must keep – for the benefit of the MP – an updated list of the IP address ranges allocated to them, and a register of the IP numbers corresponding to the connections made by their customers at least during the last six months. Both the list and the register are confidential.[29]

---

[28] Or, more exactly, facts that *in concreto* deserve *criminal* penalties. Cf., *supra*, section 7.3.1 and n. 7.

[29] Obviously, from a stored-data point of view, the existence of such a list and register does not only benefit investigations involving *crimes* but also investigations involving *simple offenses*.

On the other hand, since Act No. 19.927 came into force, extraordinary investigatory powers can be used in order to prosecute offenses and crimes related to child pornography, the facilitation of prostitution, trafficking in persons with the intention of prostitution, and the commercialization of pornography. In fact, in accordance with the new Article 369ter of the Chilean Penal Code, the interception and recording of telecommunications are always allowed (subject to conditions of plausibility and necessity), no matter what the penalties for the offenses previously mentioned are. Besides, the judicial authority can authorize the use of undercover agents and the controlled delivery of illegal substances (*entrega vigilada*) when required for the investigation of such offenses.

The interception of communications as well as the techniques just mentioned are considered by both case law and scholars to be intrusive techniques. Unlimited or not well-founded interceptions might result in serious breaches of privacy.

> 'Even further, the fear of excessive intrusion on the part of the government can affect the competitiveness of the markets and the economic development of and trust in a judicial system, even affecting foreign investment. For that reason the government should be careful and should create laws that take the nature of the interception into account.'[30]

In order to prevent breaches of privacy when using this investigatory power, Chilean law uses, among others, the following protective criteria:

1. judicial authorization,
2. proof of necessity (the reasonableness criterion),
3. interception for a maximum period of sixty days,
4. interception can only affect specific persons, and
5. persons involved in the interception must keep the information secret.

If the interception does not fulfill the required conditions, the resulting evidence should be considered illegal and thus excluded from any subsequent trial.

7.5 Material Jurisdiction

7.5.1 Legal provisions on jurisdiction concerning cybercrimes

The general provisions within the law on jurisdiction concerning crimes are contained in the Código Orgánico de Tribunales [General Courts Code] (COT)[31] and

[30] R. Downing, *Marcos Jurídicos de la Lucha contra la delincuencia cibernética* (Moscow, 2002).

[31] For an updated version of the COT, see <http://www.bcn.cl/portada.html> (click on 'Leyes Chilenas', then on 'Leyes más solicitadas', and then on 'Códigos de la República').

in Articles 5 and 6 of the Penal Code. The general jurisdiction regime is strongly based on the territorial principle. As Article 6 of the Penal Code establishes:

> 'crimes or simple offenses committed outside the Republic's boundary by nationals or foreigners will not be punished in Chile except in those cases [specifically] determined by law.'

Before considering these specific cases of extraterritorial jurisdiction, we should discuss a fundamental question: if territoriality is the general rule, in what cases should we consider the offense as having been committed on Chilean territory? In asserting the relevant territory, should we just consider the territory where the *activity* took place, or rather only the territory where such activity produced its *results* or effects, or even *both* territories? Obviously, the answer to this question (the *locus commissi delicti* question) will shed a great deal of light on our specific matter.[32] First of all, we should point out that Chilean law does not answer this question (at least not directly), so we must look to the case law and scholars to find an answer. The traditional answer[33] – although no longer the majority – considers the territory where the activity took place as the relevant one for these purposes (the *activity criterion*). In Chile, this theory finds its positive basis in an extensive interpretation of Article 157 of the COT, which supports the activity criterion when deciding on conflicts of competence among national courts belonging to different administrative territories. On the other hand, the pure result criterion has never been considered to be a relevant one, neither by scholars, nor by jurisprudence. Moreover, favored by the co-operation principle and the process of globalization, over the past 50 years both doctrine[34] and jurisprudence[35] have gradually abandoned the activity criterion and strongly embraced the dual activity/result criterion, commonly called the *ubiquity criterion*. Thus, Chilean jurisdiction will be considered to be applicable for the prosecution of any offense when the activity *or* the result[36] has taken place on Chilean territory, no matter what the nationality of the offender is.[37] The

---

[32] The other relevant question to answer in this respect concerns what is to be considered as 'Chilean territory'. In this paper we can only refer to the general provisions and the main doctrine: see Art. 593 Civil Code; Art. 1, 2 and 5 Aeronautic Code; Art. 6 No. 4 COT; Art. 3 and 428 Military Justice Code; among scholars, see S. Politoff, J.P. Matus and M.C. Ramírez, *Lecciones de Derecho Penal – Parte General* (Editorial Jurídica de Chile, Santiago, 2004) pp. 117-120.

[33] A. Etcheberry, *Derecho Penal. Tomo I* (Editorial Jurídica de Chile, Santiago, 1998) p. 72.

[34] In this sense, see the almost unanimous opinion of scholars: Garrido, op. cit. n. 16, p.133; E. Cury, *Derecho Penal. Parte General. Tomo I* (Editorial Jurídica de Chile, Santiago, 1999) p. 193; J. Bustos, *Manual de Derecho Penal. Parte General* (Ariel, Barcelona, 1989) p. 107; Politoff, Matus and Ramírez, op. cit. n. 32, pp. 120-121; E. Novoa, *Curso de Derecho Penal. Tomo I* (Santiago, 1960-1966) p. 162; S. Politoff, et al., *Texto y Comentario del Código Penal Chileno. Tomo I* (Editorial Jurídica de Chile, Santiago, 2002) pp. 72-73.

[35] Corte Suprema 14.09.1964, in *RDJ*, 1964: 363.

[36] Obviously we mean here a relevant activity or result, that is, one embraced or covered by the criminal provision's description of the conduct. See *below*, section 7.5.2.

[37] It is important to underline that the ubiquity criterion revolves around a national – thus non-universal – point of view: it is only a criterion for establishing when crimes shall be considered as

ubiquity criterion is now almost unanimously accepted among Chilean scholars,[38] and, as we will explain below, it has been recently confirmed by the legislator when dealing with conduct related to child pornography.

With respect to cybercrime, the ubiquity criterion would allow, for example, the prosecution in Chile of a person who has spread computer viruses from his computer located in Chilean territory, damaging data-processing systems located abroad. Conversely, the criterion would also allow Chile to prosecute a person who has spread computer viruses from his computer abroad, damaging data-processing systems located within Chilean boundaries.

As we have said above, Chilean law recognizes – as strict exceptions to the territoriality principle – some specific cases of extraterritorial jurisdiction. These exceptions are mainly contained in Article 6 of the COT and most of them have their basis in national interests (the defense or protection principle). None of them deal directly with cybercrimes.[39]

Chilean law includes a single specific provision on jurisdiction for cybercrimes, and it only deals with offenses related to child pornography. The provision was introduced in the Penal Code, as a new Article 374ter, by Act No. 19.927 of January 2004, with the purpose of extending national jurisdiction so as to prosecute crimes related to child pornography committed abroad. The norm provides that conduct such as (1) commercializing, (2) distributing, and (3) exhibiting child pornography should be considered as having been committed in Chile whenever they are perpetrated through any telecommunication system (typically the Internet) that is accessible or available from Chile. That means, for example, that if a person in Europe creates a web site containing child pornography, Chile will consider itself to be competent to prosecute whenever that web site can be reached from computers

---

having been committed in the territory of the state that applies the criterion. In other words, the country considers its jurisdiction to be applicable merely because it considers the crime as having been committed on its territory (and thus because of the *dogma* of state sovereignty within its jurisdiction). In contrast, the universality criterion does not revolve around the national level; here, countries support their jurisdiction because of the type of crime committed (crimes against humanity, in general, and thus recognized by the international community as not being unilaterally subjected to a single state's sovereignty), no matter – at least *prima facie* – where the crime is considered to have been committed.

[38] Despite the importance of the decision taken by the Chilean Supreme Court in 1964 (*supra*, n. 35), the lack of relevant cases on this matter and the relative unpredictability of our jurisprudence prevent us from providing a categorical assessment as to whether or not the ubiquity criterion is dominant in the case law.

[39] The only extraterritorial clause that deserves some consideration in this chapter is the one established by clause 8 of Art. 6 COT, which clearly obeys the universality principle: Chilean jurisdiction is always applicable – no matter what the territory of commission actually is – to 'crimes and offenses laid down in treaties finalized with other foreign powers.' The clause was enacted in the first half of 20th century and its language is rather confusing. That is why it has received little attention among scholars and no direct application by jurisprudence. A strong current doctrine is of the opinion that the clause should only apply if the treaty explicitly imposes a duty to prosecute crimes committed abroad (Politoff, et al., op. cit. n. 34, p. 72; and Politoff, Matus and Ramírez, op. cit. n. 32, at pp. 75-76). Treaties with such clauses currently mainly relate to crimes against fundamental human rights, like genocide, crimes against humanity, and war crimes.

located in Chile! As we can see, the expanding effect of this norm is enormous. Chilean jurisdiction for prosecuting this form of conduct is becoming wider as the Internet grows: the more universal the Internet becomes, the more 'universal' the Chilean jurisdiction becomes. In short: the extension of jurisdiction claims (near universality claims) follows technology's capacity and development.

We can nevertheless appreciate that the provision is nothing more than a strict application of the ubiquity criterion supported by doctrine: in fact, the Chilean legislator did nothing more than to consider (potential) *access* to child pornography as a *result* or the effect of the activity developed abroad.[40] Finally, it is worth considering that, obviously, the concrete effect of this enormous jurisdictional power assumed by Chilean legislation will depend – in actual fact – on practical and political opportunities and considerations. In practice, it will be probably be only effective when the offender is found on Chilean territory.

7.5.2 The reasonableness of claiming jurisdiction for cybercrimes

We consider the ubiquity criterion as a reasonable and efficient solution for claiming jurisdiction concerning cybercrimes. It has been adopted by many legal systems in the past 50 years, now becoming the dominant criterion among countries that belong to the civil-law tradition.[41] The ubiquity principle is based on (1) a national paradigm, but it is completely open to (2) transnational dimensions. For our subject, this is even more evident. (1) Countries will claim jurisdiction only when the fact is somehow related to the territory and thus there is a national interest in prevention or protection:[42] general and special prevention in the case of an *activity* taking place in the country, and the protection of *legal goods*[43] or legal *interests* (property, collective security, or confidence)[44] in the case of *results* affecting certain objects situated within national borders. This may seem to be a purely national criterion. (2) However, with the Internet and information flows, national interests have transnational dimensions.

In the first place, the Internet is the ideal way to reach foreign countries, which is not only a good thing, but also – unfortunately – a bad thing. Crimes can thus attain transnational dimensions. As they attain transnational dimensions, affected foreign

---

[40] See the critics *below*, in section 7.5.2.

[41] Bustos, op. cit. n. 34, at p. 107.

[42] Ibid., at pp. 107-108.

[43] The concept of a *legal good* is not used as that commonly used in private-law contexts. It is used here to represent the *interest* that the criminal provision intends to protect against risky or harmful forms of conduct. It deals with one of the possible meanings of the concept of *bien jurídico*, commonly used by criminal-law scholars belonging to the civil-law tradition.

[44] The legislator, in Act No. 19.223, intended *information* in itself – more properly, the quality, purity and capacity of information – to be the legal good or interest to be (directly) protected by the criminal provisions (congressman José Antonio Viera-Gallo, *Boletín* 412-07, p. 1903). This idea has been criticized by some Chilean scholars who consider traditional legal goods as property or collective confidence as goods to be protected by cybercrime legislation; see Hernández 2001b, op. cit. n. 17.

countries will put pressure on the country where the activity has taken place, so as to have the offense prosecuted. Jurisdictional conflicts will be resolved subsequently, generally in accordance with extradition treaties and principles, but in the meantime we will have at least two interested jurisdictions – activity and result – that are capable of investigating the facts, at least within their boundaries (see section 7.6). In short: the more the Internet grows, the more the ubiquity criterion will entail wider jurisdictional claims (although certainly not universal). This process will probably lead – in the long term, as co-operation and harmonization[45] among national legal systems develop – to more efficient responses against cybercrime.

In the second place, information itself has become – in an economically globalized world – an almost universal good; this is paradigmatically clear in the context of financial markets. That is the reason why the damage, alteration, illegal disclosure, illegal spreading of true information, or the spreading of false information can provoke global damage. In short: since in a global world we are all involved (through information in this case), national interests are no longer only national. The ubiquity criterion should still be dominant in this dimension, but we believe that for an adequate response against information-related cybercrimes affecting information, a more extensive process of legal harmonization might be needed in the future.

Until now, we have only faced the ubiquity criterion as related to *efficiency*. However, that is certainly not enough, and neither is it convenient: there is also (and primarily) a great deal of *justice* to be guaranteed. In fact, the ubiquity criterion is a dangerous weapon against justice when certain aspects of the legality principle are not guaranteed, especially when dealing with cybercrimes. We believe that activity and result – both considered as elements of the concrete fact – must be embraced and strictly described by the legal provision before claiming jurisdiction. Not just any part[46] of the author's activity should take place in a country in order to allow jurisdiction claims by that country; it should at least be a relevant,[47] legally described one. At the same time, not just any consequence or effect of the author's activity should take place in a country in order to allow jurisdiction claims by that country, but at least a relevant, legally described one.

A second consideration deals with the criteria for identifying some relevant results or effects for the purposes of claiming jurisdiction through the ubiquity principle. We are of the opinion that, specifically when dealing with illegal-content cybercrimes, legal systems should avoid considering the single possibility of access to a data-processing system as a 'result' together with the scope of considering the offense as having been committed within national boundaries. In the case of illegal content offenses, the 'availability' of illegal information should not be analo-

[45] Harmonization is essential for the purpose of allowing extradition.

[46] We are of the opinion that is not necessary for the whole activity or the whole result to take place in a single country. Both activity and result (especially activity) can be split for the purposes of answering the *locus commissi delicti* question. See M. Romano, *Commentario Sistematico del Codice Penale. Tomo I* (Milan, Giuffrè Editore, 1995) p. 110, on Art. 6 Codice Penale Italiano.

[47] To become aware of the importance and consequences of this characteristic, see ibid.

gous to results such as damaging a person's security (threats), honor (slander), or property (cyber-fraud, viruses). Otherwise, the ubiquity principle – that has a national basis – would be irrationally extended so as to extend to almost, in practice, the levels of jurisdiction claims favored by the universality principle.[48]

7.6 Procedural Jurisdiction

When addressing the cyber-investigation jurisdiction problem, we will face difficulties that find their origin in the territoriality principle and national sovereignty limitations. Our public prosecutors can only lead investigations within Chilean territory, no matter what kind of offenses they are dealing with. For that reason, law-enforcement officers have encountered serious problems when investigating transnational crimes, for instance, in cases of transnational drug dealing. Until now, useful (but very limited) solutions have been reached through co-operation agreements. Chilean agreements are few and far between (Argentina, Peru, Bolivia, and a few other states) and they merely extend to the Public Prosecutor and police levels (thus, not the judicial level). Co-operation is indeed still very limited: it only allows public prosecutors to obtain certain informal information concerning facts, but not to obtain formal evidence itself. In practice, the Public Prosecutor can only request co-operation through foreign prosecutors in order to obtain a judicial order. Another tool that the Public Prosecutor has used in dealing with extraterritorial investigations is the 'witness-prosecutor'. With the prior approval of the foreign authorities, the Public Prosecutor sends a prosecutor as a 'witness' in order to determine what foreign prosecutors or the foreign police do in a formal context of investigation. Afterwards, the Chilean prosecutor then testifies as to the relevant facts as a witness.

7.7 Conclusion

We have analyzed Chilean responses to four different challenges raised by cybercrimes. First, Chilean responses to the pure material problem of criminalizing cybercrimes are not completely inadequate. Nevertheless, some provisions (especially cyber-fraud provisions) ought to be amended so as to guarantee clarity, coherence, and efficiency. Second, responses to the pure procedural problem of cyber-investigation powers seem to be adequate, at least at the normative level, although judges and prosecutors probably still need to gain more experience in this field. However, Chile has just enacted a wholly new criminal procedure and its implementation will

[48] Perhaps, at least in the case of child pornography, jurisdiction through the ubiquity principle (by considering 'information availability' as a 'result') can be reasonably accepted by additionally requiring the 'presence of the offender' criterion.

demonstrate the weak and the strong points in this field. Third, responses to the material jurisdiction problem deal mainly with the ubiquity principle. We have argued that the ubiquity principle can offer adequate solutions, although harmonization among legal systems might be required in the future in order to guarantee more just and efficient responses. And fourth, adequate responses to the procedural jurisdiction problem are still lacking in the Chilean legal system. Bilateral and multilateral co-operation agreements should be strongly encouraged. In the case of Chile, a more common and challenging transnational crime such as drug-trafficking might pave the way for cybercrime-investigation co-operation agreements. Then again, we hope that the new criminal procedure will represent an ideal field for developing extraterritorial investigation.

Bibliography

J. Bustos, *Manual de Derecho Penal. Parte General* [Criminal Law Manual. General Part] (Ariel, Barcelona, 1989).

R. Downing, *Marcos Jurídicos de la Lucha contra la delincuencia cibernética* [Legal Frameworks for Combating Cybernetic Criminality] (Moscow, 2002).

M. Garrido, *Derecho Penal. Parte Especial. Tomo IV* [Criminal Law. Special Part. Vol. IV] (Editorial Jurídica de Chile, Santiago, 2000).

H. Hernández, *Informe Definitivo sobre los aspectos penales del anteproyecto de ley que modifica la ley 17.336 sobre propiedad intelectual* [Definitive Study on the Criminal Aspects of the Pre-Draft Law to Modify Law 17.336 on Intellectual Property], unpublished report prepared for the Chilean Justice Department (Santiago 2001a).

H. Hernández, *Tratamiento de la criminalidad informática en el derecho penal chileno – Diagnóstico y propuestas – Informe Definitivo: 31.12.01* [Treatise on Informatics Crime in Chilean Penal Law – Diagnosis and Proposals – Definitive Study: 31.12.01], unpublished report prepared for the Chilean Justice Department (Santiago 2001b).

K. Jadue, 'El derecho de autor en las bibliotecas y galerías virtuales de Internet' [Copyright Law in Internet Libraries and Virtual Galleries], *Revista Chilena de Derecho Informático* (Universidad de Chile) (2004) No. 4, pp. 53-79.

F. Londoño, 'Los delitos informáticos en el proyecto de reforma en actual trámite parlamentario' [Informatics Crimes in the Reform Bill Currently before Congress], *Revista Chilena de Derecho Informático* (Universidad de Chile) (2004) No. 4, pp. 171-190.

C. Magliona and M. López, *Delincuencia y fraude informático* [Criminality and Informatics Fraud] (Editorial Jurídica de Chile, Santiago, 1999).

S. Politoff, J.P. Matus and M.C. Ramírez, *Lecciones de Derecho Penal – Parte General* [Lectures in Criminal Law – General Part] (Editorial Jurídica de Chile, Santiago, 2004).

S. Politoff, et al., *Texto y Comentario del Código Penal Chileno. Tomo I* [Text and Commentary on the Chilean Criminal Code] (Editorial Jurídica de Chile, Santiago, 2002).

Chapter 8
CYBERCRIME AND JURISDICTION IN DENMARK

Henrik Spang-Hansen*

8.1 INTRODUCTION

The law of Denmark is part of the family of Nordic law that belongs to the civil-law tradition, although this group must undoubtedly be considered to form a special legal family, alongside the Romanist and German legal families. Roman law played a smaller role in the legal development of the Nordic countries than in Germany. Nordic law has few, if any, of the 'stylistic' hallmarks of the common-law tradition. Also, it should be noted that political and cultural ties between the Scandinavian countries have always been very close. Thus, what is written here on Danish Law covers, to a certain extent, the other Nordic countries as well – several special conventions are in existence between the Nordic countries, some of which will be mentioned in this chapter.

Furthermore, it should initially be pointed out that Denmark does not make use of the doctrine of *stare decisis*, and only a modest selection of cases are published in the (only) Danish Case Reporter (Part A) (*Ugeskrift for Retsvæsen*, hereafter: UfR).[1] Additionally, it should be pointed out that most of the Danish legislation on cybercrime has been changed in the last couple of years; therefore, many old cases are not worth mentioning here.

8.2 SUBSTANTIVE CYBERCRIME LEGISLATION

8.2.1 General issues

In Denmark, cybercrime is referred to as IT crime (*IT-kriminalitet*) or data crime (*datakriminalitet*). However, there is no exact definition of this term in the Penal

* Henrik Spang-Hanssen is Attorney-at-Law at the Danish Supreme Court and a Senior Researcher in Silicon Valley, California.

[1] Danish Case Reporter (Part A) or Journal of Law (Part B) (*Ugeskrift for Retsvæsen*). Cases are indicated as UfR year.page + nothing (Lower Court), or Ø (Court of Appeals, Eastern Division), or V (Court of Appeals, Western Division), or H (The Supreme Court).

B-J. Koops and S.W. Brenner (Eds), Cybercrime and Jurisdiction

Code (*Straffeloven*)[2] and, to some extent, the various terms are used differently in the Penal Code and in special legislation. In this chapter, the term 'cybercrime' will be used.

Can previous statutes be applied analogously to new cybercrimes? The principle in Danish law is that a penalty can only be imposed for a certain form of conduct if a statute declares that this conduct is a crime or if it can be considered as being totally equivalent to a statutory crime ('absolute analogy').[3] Furthermore, there is a prohibition on analogizing, which follows from Article 7 paragraph 1 of the European Convention on Human Rights,[4] of which Denmark is a party: 'No one shall be held guilty of any criminal offence on account of any act or omission, which did not constitute a criminal offence under national or international law at the time when it was committed.' The practice of the courts in Denmark is somewhat ambiguous. In cases such as UfR 1940.156Ø and UfR 1996.356Ø, an extensive analogy was used, but not in UfR 1990.70H. It is the overwhelming opinion that clear authority in the law is to be preferred, rather than legislation which tries to cover all the prospects for future technology.

Pursuant to §21 Penal Code, conduct which promotes or leads to a crime is criminalized as an attempt when the offense is not completed. The starting point in Danish law is that, ordinarily, preliminary actions cannot be regarded as a criminal attempt, unless they have a certain gross or dangerous nature.

Under §23 Penal Code, if someone through incitement or by word and deed has contributed to the crime, he is aiding and abetting – and is thus a criminal accessory. The overall principle is that there has to be evidence of an intentional criminal act. Pursuant to §2 Penal Code, §23 also covers violations of special legislation. However, certain statutes also make gross negligence a crime, e.g., a violation of §76 of the Danish Copyright Act. The technical nature of the Internet has brought into focus the question of aiding and abetting, since it is often impossible to determine who has produced or forwarded defamatory information. At this point, it should be pointed out that the immunity of Internet Service Providers in the United States is wider than the one provided in Article 12 of the EC Directive on electronic commerce, which covers only purely aiding ('mere conduit').[5]

As for criminal intent, it should be pointed out that it is not sufficient to prove, for instance, that a person who is found to have a non-activated virus in his possession, has previously carried out similar destructive acts. Intent requires proof of acts of further preparation than the pure act of constructing the virus. Finally, it should be noted that with regard to punishment, a Danish court will take all the

---

[2] Note that the *Straffeloven* covers general or civil crimes only, and not military crimes, so that, strictly speaking, it might be termed more precisely the Civil Penal Code.

[3] Penal Code § 1. The latest consolidated version of the law is published as No. 960 of 21 September 2004.

[4] Convention for the Protection of Human Rights and Fundamental Freedoms of 4 November 1950 (Council of Europe, *ETS* 5).

[5] Directive 2000/31/EC on electronic commerce, *OJ* L178, 17/07/2000, pp. 1-16.

crimes into consideration and impose a combined sentence, rather than just add up all the singular penalties.

8.2.2 Provisions relating to cybercrimes

Statutes on crime can be found in both the Penal Code and special legislation, for example the Copyright Act. In 1985, the first law was enacted on 'data crime' in order to amend the Penal Code, thereby penalizing a number of cybercrimes.[6] The Penal Code was subsequently amended several times in the 1990s, e.g., by Law No. 388 of 22 May 1996, and major amendments relating to cybercrime were enacted by Law No. 352 of 19 May 2004, which came into force on 1 July 2004. Different amendments in 2004 now allow Denmark to ratify the Cybercrime Convention,[7] which it signed on 22 April 2003.[8] Ratification took place on 21 June 2005,[9] with reservations to Articles 9, 14 and 38 of the Convention,[10] and to Articles 3, 5, 6 and 14 of the Additional Protocol to the Cybercrime Convention concerning the criminalization of acts of a racist and xenophobic nature committed through computer systems.[11]

Crimes related to gaining profit

Hacking can be used to steal, destroy, or change information or software on computers or networks. These crimes are dealt with in the following provisions in the Penal Code.

Theft is dealt with by §276: 'Any person, who, without the consent of the possessor, removes a foreign tangible movable with the intent of obtaining for himself or for others an unjustifiable gain by its misappropriation, is guilty of theft.' A 'tangible movable' in this context also includes electricity, which is made, stored, or used to produce light, heat, power, or movement or for any other economic purpose. The last sentence does not cover electronic data transmission or network communications. The statute thus only covers computer or data theft if this is done by the use of a tangible medium, for example, removal of data to a diskette that is used for transporting the information to another computer. Where the offence is of a particularly destructive nature or is carried out by a group of persons, the maximum

[6] Law No. 229 of 6 June 1985. See also the Danish Recommendation Report 1032/1985 on cybercrime.

[7] Council of Europe, Convention on Cybercrime, Budapest 23 November 2001 (CETS 185).

[8] See section 1.1 of Remarks to Bill L 55 of 5 November 2003, enacted as Law No. 352 of 19 May 2004 (in force since 1 July 2004).

[9] Council of Europe, Convention on Cybercrime, Chart of signatures and ratifications, at <http://conventions.coe.int/Treaty/Commun/ ChercheSig.asp?NT=185&CM=11&DF=22/08/2005&CL=ENG>.

[10] See the text of the reservations (forthcoming), available through <http://conventions.coe.int/> (click on 'Reservations and Declarations' and search for CETS 185).

[11] Ibid.

penalty is eight years' imprisonment – the normal maximum is 1½ years' imprisonment.

Data fraud is defined as follows in §279a: any person who unlawfully changes, adds, or deletes information or programs related to electronic-data processing or in any other possible way unlawfully tries to influence the result of such data processing, with the intent to gain unjustifiable profit for himself or others, is guilty of data fraud. The statute requires that the offender has broken into (i.e., interfered with) the data process. The penalty is the same as for theft. The use of false electronic money is regarded as either fraud (§279) or data fraud (§279a).[12] Acquiring or spreading false electronic money is penalized under §169a; paragraph 2 defines false electronic money as electronic money that, without being genuine, can nevertheless be used as such.[13]

Theft carried out through electronic data transmission is covered by §293, which deals with the issue of the unlawful use of something that belongs to someone else (taking without the owner's consent). Where the crime is more systematic or is of an organized nature, or where the 'borrowed' item is not returned after use, the maximum penalty is two years' imprisonment; the normal maximum is one year.[14] §293 is also used in situations of misusing such telecommunications that require a physical connection to other equipment. In the case of using a cellular phone, the illegal act is regarded as data fraud, §279a.

Illegal acts relating to data transmission can also be punished pursuant to other provisions. A person who destroys, damages, or removes things belonging to others can be punished pursuant to §291 for criminal damage. An example would be to change the content of a web page. If the damage is substantial and is carried out with intent, a sentence of six years' imprisonment can be imposed (para. 2); if the act is not intentional but concerns gross negligence, the maximum penalty is six months in prison (para. 3). This provision covers incidents where a person willfully spreads virus software via the Internet, Denial-of-Service (DoS) attacks, the 'Ping of Death',[15] and situations where data have been made inaccessible to the user.[16] It

---

[12] Section 3.1.1 of Remarks to Bill No. L 55 of 5 November 2003, enacted as Law No. 352 of 19 May 2004.

[13] Cf., UfR 2000.1181 (Court of Appeals for Eastern District, 2000): attempted data fraud pursuant to §279a relating to 22 withdrawals and attempted withdrawals over a period of 2½ hours and in connection with being in possession of 123 false debit cards, all the cards relating to a bank in Moscow.

[14] Cf., UfR 1978.1003 (Court of Appeals for Eastern District, 1978): conviction pursuant to §293 for an illegal connection to a community antenna (by taking without the owner's consent), since such a connection could only be motivated by the aim of obtaining free access to programs, that is, the information transmitted by the system.

[15] 'A ping of death is a type of attack on a computer that involves sending a malformed or otherwise malicious ping [a computer network tool] to a computer. A ping is normally 64 bytes in size; many computer systems cannot handle a ping larger than 65,536 bytes. Sending a ping of this size often crashes the target computer' (<http://en.wikipedia.org/wiki/Ping_of_death>) [editors' note].

[16] Remark No. 13 to Bill No. L 55 of 5 November 2003, enacted as Law No. 352 of 19 May 2004. Cf., UfR 1987.216 (Court of Appeals for Eastern District, 1987): media for carrying data and stored

also covers incidents of deleting data or software. A panel of experts who drafted White Paper No. 1032/1985 were not sure whether §291 could be used where the unlawful act is the distortion of data while they are being transmitted.[17]

If an electronic data-related act causes interference in the operation of public communications, public mail-delivery, telegraph or telephone installations, radio or TV installations, or information systems or installations, which provide the public supply of water, gas, electricity, or heating, §193 applies, with a maximum penalty of six years' imprisonment. In a case of gross negligence, the maximum penalty is six months in prison. This provision includes computer systems or installations that are of importance for public use, for example attacks against central functions on computer networks, host servers, and bank computer systems.[18]

Crimes related to peace, privacy, and honor

Pursuant to §263 paragraph 2, a person who unlawfully gains access to information or programs of others, which are intended for use in an information system, will be punished with up to 1½ years' imprisonment.[19] The provision includes incidents where a person unlawfully opens an electronic message. If the intention is to gain access to a firm's business secrets, or in other important circumstances, or where criminal acts are of a more 'systematic or organized nature', the maximum penalty is six years in prison (para. 3). The provision cannot be used where the criminal has misused his lawfully achieved access to the (confidential) information, or in cases where, for example, someone opens an e-mail message that was meant for someone else but was accidentally sent to him.[20]

Whether the crime is of a 'systematic or organized nature' will depend on the situation and the facts. The term is related to Article 7 of the Council Framework

---

data were regarded as 'things'. T. had committed criminal damage pursuant to §291, not by deleting a user file directory (UFD), but by removing it to another master file directory (MFD) and changing the name of the UFD, which meant that the file could not be printed. The court did not distinguish between the physical media and the content, but came to its decision on the basis of all the facts. It pointed out that an aggravating circumstance was the fact that to undo the criminal acts, external computer expertise had been required. The principal criminal was also sentenced for having laid 'logical bombs' that deleted all relevant user files. They received six years in prison pursuant to §291 para. 2.

[17] The panel held that § 263 (closed content) could be used. Justice Department's Expert panel on economic and data crimes, *White Paper 1417 of 2002 on IT-Crimes* (2002), available at <http://www.jm.dk/wimpdoc.asp?page=document&objno=64938>.

[18] Ibid.

[19] Cf., UfR 2000.1450 (Court of Appeals for Eastern District, 2000): a sentence pursuant to §263 para. 2 for having attempted to install a program, which failed because of an installed anti-Back Orifice program, and for having taken possession of another person's user-ID and password. The computer was confiscated.

[20] Cf., UfR 1996.979 (Court of Appeals for Eastern District, 1996): a bank clerk was acquitted on charges under §263 para. 2 for having accessed the bank's computer system and thereby acquiring certain business secrets. He had used his own password but accessed information not relating to his job, from which he had been dismissed.

Decision on attacks against information systems,[21] which lists participation in a criminal organization as an aggravating circumstance, except that no use is made of the maximum sentence. However, the term in the Danish provision is not limited to activities done by a criminal organization as defined in EU law. Other forms of systematic or organized hacking can be regarded as an aggravating circumstance that will allow the use of paragraph three.[22]

A person who unlawfully and commercially sells or informs a group of persons of a code or other means of access to a non-commercial information system that is access-protected by a code or other special feature, can be sentenced to up to 1½ years' imprisonment (§263a). The same punishment can be imposed for non-commercial actions if 'a large number' of codes are passed on (para. 2); this is presumed to be at least ten codes. In circumstances where the dissemination has been done several times but by less than ten codes at a time, the use of paragraph 2 will require that there is such a close connection in time that the successive acts can be regarded as one. In serious cases, for example where the code is passed on 'on a large scale' or causes a major risk of large-scale damage, the maximum penalty is six years in prison (para. 4). The provision includes private PCs and systems that are intended for single users or a small user group, as well as company internal information systems and central systems.

The use of §263a is precluded in instances of possession or acquisition of codes or other means of access, and for non-commercial dissemination of only a few codes. Such acts might, however, be penalized as an attempt or aiding and abetting hacking.[23]

Where a person unlawfully achieves or spreads a code or other means of access to a commercial information system, whereby access is reserved for paying subscribers, the normal maximum penalty is 1½ years' imprisonment (§301a). In serious cases, the maximum penalty is six years in prison; 'serious cases' are considered to be incidents where dissemination takes place via the Internet to a larger closed group of people, for example a club on the Internet with a large number of members.[24] The pure possession of such means of access is not covered by §301a.[25] The provision includes all means of access to commercial information systems, for example decoder cards, calling cards (phone pin codes), NUI codes, etc. Acquiring or disseminating one single code or means of access is enough to trigger the provision.

Pursuant to §264c, a person risks the same penalty as under §263 if he, without having been an accessory to the main crime, acquires or unlawfully uses informa-

---

[21] Council Framework Decision 2005/222/JHA on attacks against information systems, *OJ* 16.3. 2005, L69/68-71.

[22] Remark No. 9 to Bill L 55 of 5 November 2003, enacted as Law No. 352 of 19 May 2004.

[23] See §263 para. 2 in conjunction with §21 or §23. Remark § 1 No. 10 to Bill L 55 of 5 November 2003, enacted as Law No. 352 of 19 May 2004.

[24] Remark § 1 No. 16 to Bill L55 of 5 November 2003, enacted as Law No. 352 of 19 May 2004.

[25] *White Paper 1417*, op. cit. n. 17.

tion that has been gained by a crime as mentioned in §263, for example hacking.[26]

§264d criminalizes a person who unlawfully distributes messages or pictures that relate to another person's private sphere, or pictures of a person taken under circumstances that obviously require such images to be kept from the public.[27] The provision includes messages or pictures relating to deceased persons and carries a maximum penalty of six months' imprisonment.

§163 criminalizes the making of a false written statement. By a 1996 amendment, the criminal provision was expanded to include statements given 'through another readable medium.'[28]

Piracy

The Danish Copyright Act (*Lov om ophavsret*),[29] in §76 paragraph 1, penalizes, with a fine, a person who with intent or gross negligence violates the Act's provisions on copyright protection or neighboring rights. If the crime is carried out with intent and in 'serious cases', the maximum penalty can rise to 1½ years' imprisonment (para. 2) – or even higher if §299b Penal Code is applicable (see below).

'Serious cases' are especially if the crime is part of a business, if a significant number of copies are produced or spread to the public, or if creations or productions are reproduced in such a manner that the public has access to the reproductions at an individually chosen place and time (§76 para. 2 Copyright Act). The violation of the exclusivity of copyright by making a work available is in itself a serious case. The making available of copyrighted works, for example, via uploading to a homepage or other kinds of distribution via open computer networks such as the Internet, so that the public obtains access, is covered by paragraph 2, even if the dissemination is non-commercial.[30]

If the reproduction is done outside Denmark under such circumstances that in Denmark it would violate the Act, then a person who imports such reproductions intending to give the public access thereto, can be punished with a fine pursuant to §77 Copyright Act.[31] In serious cases, the penalty can rise to 1½ years' imprisonment.

§299b Penal Code penalizes certain cases of severe copyright infringement: a person who, for profit for himself or others or in especially serious cases, severely

---

[26] Cf., UfR 1996.1538 (Court of Appeals for Eastern District, 1996): a law firm had sent a hard disk for destruction at a burning plant without effectively having deleted personal information on the hard disk. The information came into the possession of a journalist who wrote about data security and who used the information as an example. A court decision relying on §264c ordered the hard disk and the diskettes on which the information had been copied to be handed over to the law firm.

[27] Cf., UfR 1999.177V (spiteful act through the Internet), see *infra*, n. 35.

[28] Law No. 388 of 22 May 1996 concerning Penal Code §163.

[29] The latest consolidated version of the Copyright Act is published as No. 710 of 30 June 2004, amended by Law No. 1440 of 22 December 2004.

[30] Section 2.3.3.1 and § 4 No. 1 of Remarks to Bill L 55 of 5 November 2003,.

[31] Section 2.3.3.1 of Remarks to Bill L 55 of 5 November 2003.

infringes a copyright (cf., §76 para. 2 Copyright Act), or who participates in an illegal import of a serious nature (cf., §77 para. 2 Copyright Act), can be sentenced to a term of imprisonment for up to six years. The provision requires the crime or import to be of a severe, gross nature, which is especially the case if the act is carried out with the purpose of making an unlawful profit for himself or others. Other serious, gross copyright violations can also lead to the use of §299b, for example, because the violation is on such a scale that the copyright owner has suffered extreme losses, or risks an extreme loss. §299b is presumed to be used where the violation is deemed to be so gross that the reaction of the public should require the Penal Code to be used rather than the Copyright Act, or where the violation relates to unique, very expensive software or systems, which, for example, have been developed for one or more businesses.[32]

Copyright-protection (or Digital Rights Management) systems are dealt with in §78 Copyright Act, which penalizes, with a fine, a person who:

> '(A) with intent or gross negligence, sells or for commercial purposes possesses means, the sole purpose of which is to make it easier to remove or circumvent technical devices that protect software (§75b);
>
> (B) with intent or gross negligence, and without permission, circumvents effective technical devices, or produces, imports, spreads, sells, leases, advertises for sale, rent, or for commercial purposes possesses devices, products, or components that circumvent technical devices, including services, but excluding software and encryption-research tools (§75c);
>
> (C) without permission, removes or changes electronic information about the administration of rights, or distributes, imports with the purpose of distributing or transferring to the public, copies of creations or other products where the electronic information of the owner's rights have been removed or changed without permission and if the person knew or should have known that the act was a violation of the Copyright Act (§75e).'[33]

Forgery

Forgery is penalized in §171, by a term of imprisonment for up to two years or, in serious cases or with a larger amount of forgeries, six years. Paragraph 2 defines a

---

[32] Section 2.2.3 and § 1 No. 14 of Remarks to Bill L 55 of 5 November 2003.

[33] As Norwegian legislation to a very large extent copies EU legislation with a Nordic 'stamp', it is worth mentioning here the case of a Norwegian teenager, Jon Lech Johansen, who has been sued both in Norway and in the U.S. in connection with his participation in developing circumvention software that allows DVDs to be shown in the Linux operating system. The civil case in the U.S. is *DVD Copy Control Association* v. *Andrew Brunner, Jon Lech Johansen, Masters of Reversed Engineering (MoRE), et. al.*, 10 Cal.Rptr.3d 185, 116 Cal.App.4th 241 (Cal.Ct.App.6.Dist., February 27, 2004). The criminal Norwegian case can be found, in an unofficial English translation, at <http://www.geocities.com/hssph/DVDjon1.pdf and http://www.geocities.com/hssph/DVDjon2.pdf>. Johansen was acquitted of all charges in Norway in both the trial and the appeal court.

document as a written or electronic statement bearing the name of the author, which appears to be intended to serve as evidence. The provision does not require any specific security means as is the case for the electronic statement, such as an electronic signature.[34] Neither does the provision require that the issuer's manifestation has the characteristic of a signature. The provision only covers documents that have the purpose of expressing legal intent, in other words they can serve as evidence. However, the provision does not cover documents dealing with rights.

Means of payment

§301 penalizes, with up to 1½ years' of imprisonment, a person who with intent of illegal use produces, achieves, possesses, or disseminates (a) information that identifies means of payment issued to others, or (b) generated debit card numbers. The provision does not include real credit cards. It includes all debit cards, no matter how the necessary information on payment has been achieved. If the dissemination is to a larger group of people, for example to a larger Internet group, or in other serious cases, the maximum sentence can be six years in prison.

Crime related to sexual morality

A person who, through indecency, outrages public decency or who is guilty of a public nuisance, can be sentenced to up to four years in prison (§232).[35] Furthermore, the court can issue a restraining order prohibiting the offender from visiting public parks, schools, playgrounds, reformatories, mental hospitals and institutions for handicapped persons, and specifically mentioned woods, swimming pools, and beaches (§236). Disobeying the order can be penalized with up to four months in prison.[36] If a person sells indecent images to a person under sixteen of age, the offender can be fined, but not imprisoned, pursuant to §234.

Pornography as such is not punishable; by a 1969 amendment to the Penal Code, the provision penalizing pornographic images was abolished. That provision had also made it illegal to make public or disseminate child pornography. However, the

---

[34] Section 4.3.1. of Remarks to Bill L 55 of 5 November 2003, enacted as Law No. 352 of 19 May 2004.

[35] Cf., UfR 1999.177V (Court of Appeals for Western District, 1999): a scorned husband T. published on his web site seven nude pictures of his ex-wife, each with an offending text, together with her social security number, address, and phone number. For this spiteful spreading of information on the Internet, T. was sentenced to 20 days of mitigated imprisonment pursuant to §264d and §232.

[36] Cf., UfR 2001.2573 (Court of Appeals for Eastern District, 5 September 2001): 24-year old T. was charged with a violation of §264d and §232, because he had put a text on a web site under the profile 'Lovers', according to which a 15-year old female, with a given nickname and address, wanted different kinds of sex with experienced men. This had the effect that a 13-year old girl, whose name and address were very similar, received sexual enquiries from several men. This violated §264d, even though the information concerning the girl was untrue. By uploading the text, T. could expect the 13-year old girl to be contacted by men with offers of sexual behavior, including anal sex, that are unusual for a young girl. T. was therefore regarded as an accessory to the violation of her decency (§232 *juncto* §23), and he was sentenced to twenty days in prison and ordered to pay 3,000 Euros in damages.

making of child pornography has always been illegal pursuant to chapter 24 of the Penal Code.

Child pornography is dealt with in §235, which was last amended in 2003,[37] with the purpose of, amongst other things, making the necessary amendments for Denmark to be able to participate in the EU Framework Decision on combating the sexual exploitation of children and child pornography, to which the Commission had put forward a proposal in January 2001.[38] Paragraph 1 of §235 states that someone who distributes obscene pictures, film, or other obscene visual presentations 'or similar' of persons under the age of eighteen, can be punished with a fine or a term of imprisonment for up to two years or, in serious cases, up to six years. 'Serious cases' especially relate to cases where the child's life is put in danger, where gross violence is used, where the child is seriously injured, or where the dissemination is of a more systematic or organized nature. Paragraph 2 adds that someone who possesses or for payment makes himself familiar with child pornography can be punished with a fine or a term of imprisonment for up to one year. This does not cover possession of obscene images of a person over the age of fifteen, if that child has permitted such possession. 'Or similar' covers commercial presentation or the leasing of child pornography.[39]

§235 only deals with real photographs or films; cartoons, computer-produced images, and other productions that depict sexual attacks on a child but which did not happen in reality, is not made a crime.[40] If a photograph or similar has an artistic value, this might legitimize it and thus exclude it from §235.[41]

Pursuant to the commentary to the Bill that amended §235, a person is not regarded as having possession of an image that is momentarily moved from a database to the person's own computer. However, if the person stores the image on a hard disk or diskette, so that he can view it again, then the image is regarded as being in the possession of the person in question.[42] More accidental situations, where an Internet user accesses network areas or web sites with free access to child pornography, are not covered by §235.[43]

---

[37] Law No. 228 of 2 April 2003, based on the Justice Department's Expert panel on economic and data crimes, *White Paper 1377 of 1999 on Child Pornography and IT-investigations* (1999).

[38] *OJ* C062 E, 27/02/2001, pp. 0327-0330. This became Council Framework Decision 2004/68/JHA of 22 December 2003, *OJ* L13, 20/01/2003 pp. 4-48.

[39] Section 2.1.4 of Remarks to Bill No. L 117, enacted as Law No. 228 of 30 September 2003.

[40] Ibid.

[41] See pp. 40-41 of *White Paper 435/1966 on penalties for pornography* and F.T. 1999-2000, Supplement A, column 7800.

[42] F.T. 1994-95, Supplement A, column 473. See also *White Paper 1377*, op. cit. n. 37, at p. 57.

[43] Section 2.1.5 of Remarks to Bill No. L 117, enacted as Law No. 228 of 30 September 2003.

8.3 Procedural Provisions

8.3.1 Investigation powers

The general Danish rules on investigations which are relevant for this chapter are found in Chapters 67 and 71 of the Procedure Code (*Retsplejeloven*).[44] They state that the police can initiate an investigation after receiving information of a violation or on their own initiative when there is a presumption that a crime has been committed. Upon request, a court determines the limitation of an investigation, the rights of the suspect and it can appoint an attorney on his behalf. The Danish Constitution states that any suspect has to be brought before a court within 24 hours of being taken into custody.

An investigation can only be initiated if a charge can be brought. However, the police may take urgent actions when it can fairly be presumed that the interested private party, if he knew of the violation, would bring a charge.[45] The general rule in the Penal Code is that the police can bring a charge, unless a provision requires a charge to be brought by the interested private party. However, if a provision so allows and if public interest is at stake, the police can bring a charge themselves.

Chapter 71 of the Procedure Code (§780 et seq.) deals with encroachments on the right to the secrecy of messages. It deals with observation and data readings and allows the police, pursuant to a written court order and after appointing an attorney for the suspect, to infringe the secrecy of messages by:

a. wiretapping;
b. monitoring other conversations or statements with the use of a device for that purpose;
c. recovering information concerning phones and similar communication devices that have been connected to a certain phone or device, even if the owner has not given permission ('teleinformation');
d. recovering information concerning phones and similar communication devices that are in a certain specific area, and have had a connection to other phones or devices ('extended teleinformation');
e. retaining, opening, and acquainting oneself with the content of letters, telegrams, and other mail;
f. blocking the delivery of mail mentioned under e.[46]

---

[44] The *Retsplejeloven* contains provisions on both criminal procedure and civil procedure. The latest consolidated version of the Danish Procedure Code is published as No. 961 of 21/09/2004, amended by Law No. 1436 of 22 December 2004 §2. An unofficial translation by Henrik Spang-Hanssen of chapter 22 on civil jurisdiction is available at <http://www.geocities.com/hssph/Chapter22.htm>.

[45] §720 Procedure Code.

[46] §780 Procedure Code. Cf., UfR 1999.178 (Court of Appeals for Western District, 26 October 1998): the police asked for an order compelling a telecompany to save copies of incoming e-mails from a specific account belonging to T. and to hand over the e-mails for investigation purposes. The court

Mailing companies and the suppliers of telenet and teleservices are obliged to co-operate with the police. Moreover, suppliers have to register and store information on teletraffic for one year for investigation and prosecution purposes.[47] The provision only requires the registration and storage of traffic data, not the content of the communication itself.[48]

The police can, as part of an investigation in which electronic evidence can be of significance, order the suppliers of telenet and teleservices to store electronic data as a matter of urgency, including traffic data, for a necessary period of up to ninety days. The suppliers of telenetwork and teleservices have to pass on without delay the traffic data of other suppliers whose network or services have been used in connection with electronic communications that can be of significance for the investigation.[49] This is regulated in §786a, which was added to the Procedure Code in 2004 in order to conform to Articles 16 and 17 of the Cybercrime Convention. The use of the provision does not depend on whether the provider in question has chosen to store the information. The decisive issue is whether the data is in the possession of the provider at the time when the order is given and whether or not the keeping thereof is only temporary. Thus, an order can be issued to cover, for example, e-mails that are normally only kept by a provider until such a time when the customer downloads his e-mail to his computer. The order cannot cover a customer's future e-mail correspondence – it only covers past correspondence.[50]

Reading non-publicly accessible information in an information system by the use of programs or other devices ('data reading') can be done, provided that a court determines the following: (1) there is a presumption that the information system has been used by a suspect for a crime or will be used for a planned crime, (2) the intervention is presumed to be vital for the investigation, and (3) the crime can be punished with six years' imprisonment or more, or involves national security (§791a Procedure Code).[51]

---

held that an ingoing e-mail could be regarded as 'other similar telecommunication' in §780 Procedure Code on teletapping. In UfR 2005.777 (Court of Appeals for Western District, 3 November 2004), the police asked for an order compelling an ISP to divulge who at a certain time had been logged on to the Internet by using a certain IP address. The court pointed out that the required information was equivalent to information about who owned a known e-mail address or which person has a confidential phone number. As such, it could not be required that the conditions for infringing the secrecy of (the contents of) messages should be fulfilled.

[47] §786 Procedure Code.

[48] Remark 7.3.3 to Bill L 55 of 5 November 2003, enacted as Law No. 352 of 19 May 2004.

[49] §786a Procedure Code.

[50] Remark 7.3.3. to Bill L 55 of 5 November 2003, enacted as Law No. 352 of 19 May 2004.

[51] Cf., UfR 2001.1276 (Supreme Court, 18 March 2001): in connection with an investigation into the narcotics trade, the police requested a court's permission to install certain software ('sniffer program') in a suspect's computer system with the purpose of obtaining knowledge as to what had been written on the computer, which was installed in a certain apartment. The Supreme Court held that the requested arrangement was equivalent to repeated confidential search warrants and affirmed the Court of first instance's decision, which denied the request, since §791a para. 3 Procedure Code only deals with observations of persons who are present in a dwelling, and the request did not relate to this.

Pursuant to §804 Procedure Code, a person who is not a suspect, in the case of an investigation into a crime for which a public charge is required, can be ordered to show or hand over objects or information ('edition'), if there is reason to believe that the object which the person in question has in his possession can be used as evidence, should be confiscated, or has been removed by means of the crime from a third party who can reclaim it. This provision can be used for acquiring electronic information from Internet access providers or telecompanies concerning customers' names and addresses.

8.3.2 International co-operation

Denmark has no special legislation on international assistance in criminal cases. Foreign requests, for example, seizure of evidence for use in a criminal case in a foreign state, can – according to practice and as confirmed by case law – be initiated pursuant to the Procedure Code or by analogy to it, as long as the requested measure can be used in a similar criminal case in Denmark.[52]

Denmark has ratified:

- the Council of Europe's Convention of 13 December 1957 on Extradition;[53]
- the Council of Europe's Convention of 20 April 1959 on Mutual Assistance in Criminal Matters and the Protocols of 17 March 1978 and 21 November 2001;[54]
- the European Convention of 28 May 1970 on the International Validity of Criminal Judgments;[55] the Danish law implementing this convention does not cover co-operation between the Nordic countries and the EU countries, which is covered by special laws;
- the Council of Europe's Convention of 8 November 1990 on Money Laundering, Search, Seizure and Confiscation of the Proceeds from Crime;[56]
- the Council of Europe's Convention of 21 March 1983 on the Transfer of Sentenced Persons (Strasbourg);[57]

---

[52] See the cases published in UfR 1972.600 H and UfR 1988.203 V.

[53] Incorporated into the Danish Law on Extradition of Criminal Offenders (*Udlevering af lovovertrædere*). The latest consolidated version of the law is published as No. 110 of 18 February 1998, later amended by Law 280 of 24 April 2001, No. 378 of 6 June 2002, No. 433 of 10 June 2003 and No. 1160 of 19 December 2003. Treaty text in English at <http://conventions.coe.int/treaty/en/Treaties/Html/024.htm>.

[54] The European Convention on Mutual Assistance in Criminal Matters, treaty text in English at <http://conventions.coe.int/treaty/en/Treaties/Html/030.htm>. Ratifications include all EU Member States.

[55] European Convention on the International Validity of Criminal Judgments, treaty text in English at <http://conventions.coe.int/treaty/en/Treaties/Html/070.htm>. Ratified by Austria, the Netherlands, Spain, Sweden, Cyprus, Estonia, Latvia, and Lithuania.

[56] Treaty text in English at <http://conventions.coe.int/treaty/en/Treaties/Html/141.htm>.

[57] Convention on the Transfer of Sentenced Persons, treaty text in English at <http://conventions.coe.int/treaty/en/Treaties/Html/112.htm>.

- the UN Convention of 20 December 1998 against illicit traffic in narcotic drugs and psychotropic substances.

The last five of this list have been incorporated into the Danish Act on International Enforcement of Punishment, etc. (*International fuldbyrdelse af straf mv*).[58] By an amendment of December 2004, this Act has been changed so that it now covers, as of 1 January 2005, only states outside the Nordic and the European Union areas.[59]

On 23 September 1997, Denmark ratified the Schengen Convention.[60] Pursuant to Article 51, the requested state can deny a seizure request if enforcement is inconsistent with its legislation. A similar right is given in Article 18 of the above-mentioned CoE Convention of 8 December 1990.

Denmark has ratified the Cybercrime Convention, which in Article 32 deals with the regulation of transborder access to data and where mutual assistance is not required. Article 20 of the latter convention deals with the tapping of telecommunications without assistance from another state. A Danish expert panel on cybercrime has noted that, for computer crime, the required investigation powers should be more characterized as infiltration than as agent operations. Further, administrative rules for computer infiltration by the police should be drafted. The panel also pointed out the necessity of international rules that allow flexible cross-border investigations.[61]

8.3.3 Co-operation with EU countries

Pursuant to reservations to some principal EU treaties, Denmark is not fully 'covered' by the EU legislation that is valid in other Member States; among such reservations are investigation issues. However, as far as mutual assistance between EU countries is concerned, as a result of the latest amendment, Denmark can now be regarded as a 'full' member. Denmark has ratified the Convention on Mutual Assistance in Criminal Matters between the Member States of the European Union of 29 May 2000.[62]

---

[58] Law No. 323 of 4 June 1986, amended by Law No. 291 of 24 April 1996, Law No. 280 of 25 April 2001, Law No. 258 of 8 May 2002, and Law No. 1434 of 22 December 2004.

[59] Law No. 1434 of 22 December 2004, inserting a new paragraph 3 in §1 of Law No. 323 of 4 June 1986 on International Enforcement of Punishment.

[60] Law No. 418 of 10 June 1997 and Agreement concluded between the European Council, Ireland, and Norway on the Schengen acquis, *OJ* L176, 10/07/1999, pp. 0036-0049.

[61] Section 7.2 in *White Paper 1417* of 2002 from the Justice department's Expert panel on economic and data crimes, available at <http://www.jm.dk/wimpdoc.asp?page=document&objno=64938>. See further Interpol's contribution to combating Information Technology Crime, at <www.interpol.int/Public/TechnologyCrime/default.asp>, and EISIL Cybercrime and Protection of communication at <http://www.esil.org>.

[62] *OJ* C197, 12/07/2000, pp. 0001-0023. Explanatory report at *OJ* C379, 29/12/2000, pp. 0007-0029.

In December 2004, Denmark made amendments[63] to its law on the Europol Convention,[64] by which the Danish Act is updated so that it is in accordance with the Convention that established the European Police Office,[65] in force since 1 July 1999. Protocols have extended the scope and subject-matter of this convention, for example, by establishing databases for analysis and control.

For jurisdiction with respect to the Europol Convention (see Art. 39), it should be pointed out that §1 paragraph 1 of the Danish Europol Act allows the use of EU Council Regulation 44/2001 of 22 December 2000 on jurisdiction and the recognition and enforcement of judgments in civil and commercial matters, even though the Regulation is not valid for Denmark (see below). Also, in December 2004, a law was enacted on the Execution of Certain Criminal Decisions, in force since 1 January 2005.[66] This makes it possible, with a few and simple formalities, to allow the enforcement of decisions from the most common criminal courts of other Member States. The Minister of Justice remarked that this framework, to a much larger extent than other procedures, commits the enforcing state to fulfill a decision from another EU Member State without testing the basis of the foreign decision, and without the condition that the act is also an offense pursuant to the law of the enforcing state. Denmark has chosen to use all possible facultative exception options – as is the case for Denmark's implementation of the European Arrest Warrant.[67] Special rules are in force between the Nordic members of the EU.

As for the so-called positive list in the framework, it was pointed out that it is the law of the issuing state that determines whether the act in question is covered by the list. Moreover, although the Penal Code does not contain the term 'Participation in a criminal organization' (conspiracy), such an act might be punished as aiding and abetting a crime pursuant to §23 of the Code.[68]

---

[63] Law No. 1435 of 22 December 2004 on the implementation of supplementary Protocols to the Convention on the establishment of a European Police office (Europol Convention). See also Remark to Bill L 6 of 6 October 2004. Denmark ratified the Convention by Law No. 415 of 10 June 1997.

[64] Denmark incorporated the Convention into Danish law by Law No. 415 of 10 June 1997.

[65] *OJ* C316, 27/11/1995, pp. 0002-0032, Council Act of 30 November 2000, *OJ* C358, 12/12/2000, pp. 0001-0007, Council Act of 28 November 2002, *OJ* C312, pp. 0001-0007, Council Act of 27 November 2003, *OJ* C2, 06/01/2004, pp. 0001-0012.

[66] Law No. 1434 of 22 December 2004. See also Remarks to Bill No. 5 of 6 October 2004. The basis for this Law was the Council Framework Decision 2003/577/JHA of 22 July 2003 on the Execution in the European Union of Orders Freezing Property or Evidence, *OJ* L196, 02/08/2003, pp. 0045-0050; Proposal on Council Framework Decision on the Execution in the European Union of Confiscation Orders, agreed upon at the Council meeting of 29 April 2004 (see the initiative by the Kingdom of Denmark, *OJ* C184, 02/08/2002, pp. 0008-0014); and Proposal to Council Framework on the application of the principle of Mutual Recognition to Financial Penalties, agreed upon at the Council meeting of 8 May 2003 (see *OJ* C278 02/10/2001, pp. 0004-0008).

[67] Law No. 433 of 10 June 2003. See also Council Framework Decision of 13 June 2002 on the European arrest warrant and the surrender procedures between Member States, *OJ* L190, 19/07/2002, pp. 0001-0055 and Denmark's statement at *OJ* L246 29/02/2003, p. 0001.

[68] Remark to § 5 to Bill No. 5 of 23 October 2004, enacted as §5 in Law No. 1434 of 22 December 2004.

The Minister of Justice also remarked on the bill that the execution of foreign decisions must not violate Denmark's international obligations, including the European Convention on Human Rights. Such obligations did not need to be written into the law.[69] Since the preambles of the framework do not prohibit execution if the requesting state aims to prosecute someone on discriminatory grounds, a provision was inserted allowing Danish courts to re-examine a foreign decision.[70] Furthermore, the execution of a foreign fine can be refused, if the decision is related to an act committed outside the requesting state's territory, and if a similar act carried out outside Danish territory is not included in the Danish rules on punishment.[71]

The competence to decide on the execution of foreign decisions on seizure lies in the hands of the courts. As for foreign decisions on the execution of financial penalties and confiscation, the competence in Danish law lies with the Minister of Justice, with a possible appeal to the courts.

Finally, it should be mentioned that Denmark has enacted a law on the extradition of offenders to other EU Member States.[72] The law does not cover extradition between the Nordic countries.

8.3.4 Co-operation with the Nordic countries

Co-operation in the enforcement of criminal-law decisions taken by Nordic countries (Denmark, Finland, Iceland, Norway, and Sweden) covers confiscation and seizure, as well as imprisonment.[73] There exists a Nordic Agreement of 26 April 1974 on Mutual Assistance. Furthermore, there is co-operation concerning legal assistance, but only between Denmark, Norway, and Sweden.[74] Besides, the Nordic countries recognize and enforce Nordic decisions relating to certain civil claims decided in a civil or criminal case.[75]

These agreements extend the scope of similar agreements with other countries; for example, in some cases a request cannot be denied. In most respects, the uniform legislation in force between the Nordic states allows the provisions of the EU Framework Decisions to be extended and enlarged and helps to simplify and facilitate the procedures more than EU legislation does. Denmark, Finland, and Sweden will therefore continue to apply the uniform legislation in force between them. For

[69] Remark 1.4 to Bill No. 5 of 6 October 2004, enacted as Law No. 1434 of 22 December 2004.

[70] §§ 7, 20, 33 of Law No. 1434 of 22 December 2004.

[71] § 21 para. 1(2) of Law No. 1434 of 22 December 2004.

[72] Law No. 433 of 10 June 2003.

[73] Law No. 214 of 31 May 1963, amended by Law No. 323 of 4 June 1986, Law No. 291 of 24 April 1996 and Law No. 280 of 25 April 2001 on Co-operation between Denmark, Finland, Iceland, Norway and Sweden concerning the execution of penalties, etc., upon application concerning the execution of decisions on fines and confiscation between the Nordic countries.

[74] See Justice Department Circular No. 160 of 14 November 1958.

[75] The latest consolidated version of the law is published as No. 635 of 15 September 1986 (*Lov om anerkendelse og fuldbyrdelse af nordiske afgørelser*), amended by Law No. 209 of 29 March 1995 and Law No. 389 of 14 June 1995.

example, in Denmark, the Nordic Extradition Act[76] goes further than the Framework Decision in its procedures for the surrender of persons who are the subject of European arrest warrants.[77]

8.4 Jurisdiction Concerning Cybercrime

Denmark does not make use of a distinction, as the United States does, between general and specific personal jurisdiction. The personal jurisdictional and venue question is linked to (determined by) the subject-matter question.

General rules on the right of punishment (jurisdiction competence) are laid down in the §§ 6-12 Penal Code, which positively describe the extent of Danish jurisdiction in criminal matters. Pursuant to the basic rule in §6 Penal Code, Danish criminal jurisdiction covers acts carried out:

1. in the Kingdom of Denmark (the principle of territorial jurisdiction);
2. on a Danish vessel that is outside any states' territory as recognized by public international law; or
3. on a Danish vessel that is in a foreign territory as recognized by public international law, by persons who belong to the vessel or are traveling as passengers on board.

Furthermore, pursuant to §7 (the personality principle), Danish criminal jurisdiction applies to acts that a person with Danish citizenship or domicile has committed outside Denmark, (1) as far as the act was carried out outside any state territory recognized by public international law, if the crime, pursuant to Danish law, carries a maximum penalty of four months of imprisonment or more, or (2) as far as an act is carried out inside such a territory, if it is punishable also pursuant to the legislation of that territory ('double criminality') (§7 para. 1). Paragraph 2 states that paragraph 1 also covers acts carried out by a person having the citizenship of Finland, Iceland, Norway, or Sweden and staying in Denmark.

In addition, pursuant to §8, Danish criminal jurisdiction covers acts perpetrated outside Danish territory,[78] without considering to which state(s) the perpetrator is related to:

---

[76] Law No. 27 of 3 February 1960, as amended by Laws No. 251 of 12 June 1975, No. 433 of 31 May 2000, No. 378 of 6 June 2002, and No. 433 of 10 June 2003.

[77] Denmark's statement to the Council Framework Decision of 13 June 2002 on the European arrest warrant and the surrender procedures between Member States, *OJ* L246, 29/02/2003, p. 0001.

[78] It is, however, a precondition for acts carried out outside Denmark that the Danish provision in question is not limited to acts carried out on Danish territory. See UfR 1998.1027 H.

1. when the act violates the independence, security, Constitution, or public authorities of Denmark, official duties in relation to Denmark, or such Danish interests as require legal protection by Denmark;
2. when the act violates an obligation that the offender, pursuant to the law, has to observe abroad, or a duty towards a Danish vessel;
3. when an act carried out outside state territory violates a person with Danish citizenship or residence, and the crime pursuant to Danish legislation can be punished by up to four months' imprisonment or more;
4. in the case of hijacking a plane, ship or other means of collective transport (§183a);
5. when the act is covered by an international instrument obliging Denmark to prosecute; or
6. when extradition to a foreign state is denied, and the act fulfills the double-criminality requirement and the crime, pursuant to Danish law, can be punished with more than one year in prison.

Furthermore, §9 states that in the case of a result crime,[79] the crime is also considered to have been carried out at the place where the consequence has taken place or is expected to take place.

If action pursuant to these rules is taken in Denmark, the decision has to follow Danish law, both in terms of the penalty and in terms of other legal consequences. If the incident is covered by §7 and the crime is carried out in a foreign state, then the punishment cannot exceed the maximum penalty pursuant to the legislation of the territory of the place where the crime was committed (§10). This limit not exceeding the maximum penalty of the state where the criminal act was perpetrated, presumably also applies to incidents where the basis of Danish jurisdiction is §8 *sub* 6.

The Danish Justice Department is of the opinion that §6 and §7 paragraph 1 fulfill the requirements of Article 22 of the Council of Europe Convention on Cybercrime.[80]

8.5 Analysis and Opinion

Denmark, like the other Nordic countries, and especially after the new legislation of December 2004, has fairly detailed provisions as to when Denmark can claim jurisdiction for cybercrimes so as to deal with cyber-investigation jurisdiction. Time can only tell how all these new provisions related to cybercrime will work; only in

[79] A result crime can be described as a crime which causes 'actual harm' (e.g., murder, robbery, etc.), as opposed to 'danger' crimes (e.g., endangering someone's life, regardless of whether someone is actually killed or not) [editors' note].

[80] Remark No. 7.1 to Bill L 55 and Memorandum on the consequences of the convention from the Danish Ministry of Justice to the Justice Committee of the Danish Parliament, General Part – exhibit 294 – EU assembly 2002-03, <http://www.folketinget/dk/Samling/20012/ udvbilag/REU/ Almdel_bilag294.htm>.

time will there be a basis for making an analysis of the provisions. Thus, the following will be the opinion of the author.

When dealing with the subject of cybercrime jurisdiction, one should not overlook the importance of principles on jurisdiction in public international law, as both national law and private international law have to comply with public international law. This point is often overlooked when legislatures, courts, the police, and scholars deal with rulings on international computer networks. The schism between France and the United States in the Yahoo case – the 'S.S. Lotus case[81] for the Internet' – is an excellent case in point.[82]

Also, it should be remarked that an international governmental group recommended in June 2005 to 'ensure that all measures taken in relation to the Internet, in particular those on grounds of security or to fight crime, do not lead to violations of human rights principles', including freedom of expression.[83]

8.5.1 **What is a cybercrime?**

First, one has to ask what should establish a cybercrime. There is no doubt that spreading a virus in a computer network is not desirable for anyone, but this does not necessarily make it a crime, as it can also be a weapon in any future warfare ('Information Warfare').[84]

Many military officers and at least one President's Directive acknowledge that future wars will not be won with the use of conventional weapons, but by the country that has the best computer experts. Thus, the military in different nations are employing people to attack other countries' computer networks, so that other countries' main computers can be infiltrated or networks can be destroyed or made useless by a denial-of-service attack or a Ping of Death. One scholar has even suggested that a state can enforce its decisions and sanctions by hacker tools like viruses and worms against 'offenders' in foreign states.[85] However, this suggestion goes far beyond what is legal under public international law.[86]

The situation is a little different with regard to hacking, as this phenomenon can be considered to be a crime, a military weapon, or a means for supporting human rights. In the case of the last mentioned, it should be remarked that, recently, many

---

[81] *S.S. Lotus case* (*France* v. *Turkey*), 1927 PCIJ (Ser. A) No. 10, p. 28, available at <www.geocities.com/hssph/Lotus.pdf>. Cf., section 5.6.1 of this book.

[82] Henrik Spang-Hanssen, *Cyberspace & International Law on Jurisdiction* (DJØF Publishing, Copenhagen, 2004), pp. 184-188, 463-466, and 483-518.

[83] Working Group on Internet Governance, *Report of the Working Group on Internet Governance*, June 2005, p. 18 # 81, available at <http://www.wgig.org>.

[84] Spang-Hanssen, op. cit. n. 82, chapter 14.

[85] Joel Reidenberg, *Technology and Internet Jurisdiction*, 153 *University of Pennsylvania Law Review* (2005) p. 1951, at p. 1963.

[86] Case concerning Military and Paramilitary Activities in and against Nicaragua (*Nicaragua* v. *United States of America*) of 27 June 1986, 1986 ICJ 14.

people have realized that an extremely important weapon in the struggle for human rights is computer codes. Thus, 'hacktivism' has turned up in the shape of elite computer experts – the 'original' hackers, not crackers – who have set their sights on ways to help human rights causes and are trying to provide activists with electronic means to circumvent government surveillance and information management.[87] Such humanitarian help probably does not qualify as a crime – at least, there is a lack of the necessary criminal intent.

Finally, as for on-line content, it should be pointed out that what in one country might be illegal, can be completely legal in another.

From the perspective of having previously worked as a district attorney, it is of course preferable for the police and prosecution to have jurisdiction over any crime pursuant to one's own laws. Furthermore, there is no doubt that computers and their networks have provided law-enforcement tools which they have never previously had in history. However, aspects such as privacy should limit the extent to which a country can claim jurisdiction for acts legally carried out abroad. Additionally, due process requires that a cybernaut can predict in which jurisdiction he can be sued. In this respect, it should also be remembered that many cybercrimes are committed by minors who have no expectation of criminal prosecution in foreign countries and who often lack legal capacity with respect to criminal provisions. Finally, it is questionable whether a foreign country should have criminal jurisdiction over an alien who for human rights reasons circumvents the foreign government's surveillance and information management, as long as he does not enter that foreign country and the acts are legal in the country where the act is carried out; claiming jurisdiction would be against the UN Universal Declaration of Human Rights.

As for copyright infringement and circumventing the zoning feature in DVD hardware, it can be questioned whether this should be illegal in all countries, as the Hollywood DVD zones, after the extension of the EU in May 2004, no longer correspond to the European Single Market; the three Baltic states are in another DVD zone than the rest of the EU Member States. Thus, EU consumers have to check carefully whether the DVD they buy can be played on their DVD player. This situation is contrary to the Single Market and it can be questioned whether consumers are allowed to circumvent the DVD feature on DVDs bought in the EU Single Market. Thus, the extension of the EU has made present DVD copyright-protection provisions contrary to principal and essential articles in the main EU treaties.[88]

Spam and cookies can be very annoying, but it is questionable whether they always imply a crime. Spam from one person targeted at a certain individual or company can be a crime. On the other hand, spam can be regarded as electronic

---

[87] Spang-Hanssen, op. cit. n. 82, at p. 102.

[88] Henrik Spang-Hanssen, 'Hollywood puts 3 Baltic countries into a Second Class of E.U. or Hollywood does not recognize E.U.'s single market from May First 2004', available at <www.geocities.com/hssph/articles>.

unsolicited advertising and thus an on-line business method and not a crime. So far, many court decisions have relied on the fact that the cybernaut knew that a certain network or nodes would have great difficulties in handling the amount of unsolicited advertising. But is it a crime when a delivering system is 'overwhelmed' with unsolicited advertising? Furthermore, in some countries (the US, for example), certain kinds of spam and cookies are allowed, whereas it is illegal in other countries (such as the EU) without prior permission by the receiver. For spam and cookies, which are usually computer-generated and thus without human interference, it is questionable for the country wanting to claim jurisdiction whether the necessary criminal intent by a person can be proved.

8.5.2 Cybercrime jurisdiction and public international law

For acts carried out purely on-line on international computer networks – where anything first uploaded can be accessed by anyone connected to the Internet – it should be considered whether the requirements of a close connection and reasonableness, made in the international law on jurisdiction, are fulfilled.[89] In relation to acts carried out on international computer networks, a restricted interpretation of provisions should be made; so, it is required that the act has been aimed at the country claiming jurisdiction and that it is reasonable pursuant to the basic international law on jurisdiction that, for example, a Danish court deals with the case.[90] Maybe, a distinction should also be made between incidents where the damage is related to a natural person and incidents concerning a business.[91]

Public international law only allows states to exercise universal jurisdiction concerning incidents where international law grants universal jurisdiction, that is, a state exercises universal jurisdiction on behalf of the international community.[92] It would bring chaos to international computer networks if every state could legislate concerning content on foreign web sites and, through its courts, deliver judgments against aliens considered to violate that state's law. As for the Danes, it would, for example, imply that the content of Danish web sites that is in accordance with Danish law (e.g., after the liberalization of some pornography provisions) but that

[89] See Henrik Spang-Hanssen, 'Danmarks værnetingsregler & "ren" online handlen uden for E.U. på internationale computer netværk' [forthcoming as 'Jurisdiction Rules of Denmark & "pure" online dealings outside the European Union on international computer networks'] (2004), available at <www.geocities.com/hssph/DK_Verneting.pdf>.

[90] Spang-Hanssen, op. cit. n. 82, sections 32.1.1.1 and 32.2 and chapter 34.

[91] Cf., UfR 2002.405 (Supreme Court of Denmark, 27 November 2002, *Viasat A/S and Canal Digital Danmark A/S* v. *A*: a Danish citizen residing in Columbia and without any location in Denmark edited the web site <http://www.piratdk.com>, located on a server outside Denmark. From the web site certain material could be downloaded that was illegal in Denmark. The web site was in the Danish language and concerned Danish encryption keys. The court held that §243 Procedure Code cannot be used in cases where an injunction is sought. Similarly, UfR 2001.2186 (Easter Appeal Court 26 June 2001).

[92] Spang-Hanssen, op. cit. n. 82, pp. 252-254.

constitutes a violation in foreign countries, could be punished there.[93] If so, Danes could be arrested at (catholic) southern European holiday destinations or in the United States on the basis of their web site content, which foreigners cannot be prevented from viewing (unless access is prevented, which is very costly). In this context, it is troubling that the United States considers that it has personal jurisdiction over circa 70 per cent of what occurs on international computer networks, because circa 70 per cent of network servers are located in the United States.[94] Furthermore, does this allow the United States to monitor e-mail correspondence or to claim jurisdiction? It is doubtful whether a cybernaut has had any thoughts about US-located servers and thus has had the necessary criminal intent related to the United States. A citizen in the EU might very possibly rather have in mind Article 25(1) of the EC Data Protection Directive, which provides that personal data may be transferred to a non-EU third country only if that country ensures an adequate level of protection for personal data.

It should be pointed out that legal scholars and politicians have not been able to find a solution[95] concerning jurisdiction and enforcement. A workable solution related to cyberspace can only be achieved if technical network aspects are taken into account; therefore, the participation of computer experts in drafting jurisdictional rules related to Cyberspace is required[96] – no government has ever legislated on cars without thoroughly consulting car experts, but as to cyberspace legislation, experts have so far not been invited. It is characteristic of conferences dealing with the international public networks that they lack the participation of both computer experts and public international law scholars. For example, an attempt to draft a Convention on Jurisdiction and Enforcement has only been undertaken by national government officials or private international law scholars.[97] Before computer experts and public international law scholars are invited to the same table, it is unrealistic to presume that fair cross-border rules will be accepted by the international community.

Parts of the cybercrime conventions are in direct violation of common public international law and several fundamental statements by the international community. I expect that countries will make many reservations when signing the Cybercrime Convention, so that their citizens still have the protection that public international law gives them. To require every citizen in the world to keep an eye on the law in every foreign country and to obey these laws is fundamentally contrary to the public international law principle that a citizen, being in his own country, has

[93] Another example is the French-US Yahoo! case, which is thoroughly considered in Spang-Hanssen, op. cit. n. 82, pp. 184-189, 463-466, and 483-517.

[94] Compare the legislation related to the USA Patriot Act (Uniting and Strengthening America by providing appropriate tools required to intercept and obstruct terrorism) of 26 October 26, 2001, 2001 PL 107-56 (HR 3162).

[95] See Spang-Hanssen, op. cit. n. 82, section 33.6.

[96] Ibid., chapter 35.

[97] Idem, section 33.5.

to obey the laws of his own country. It is even possible that an international tribunal, which in the last couple of years has had increasing success, will reject parts of the Cybercrime Convention after human-rights advocates have brought a case before it. Neither should it be forgotten that national courts in the past couple of years have to a large extent overruled previous court decisions because of principles contained in human rights instruments.

The trend in the Cybercrime Convention and in several EU legislative instruments to extend the reach of a state's legislation to aliens is a fearful trend, as it allows, in combination with the European arrest warrant, a EU country to arrest a non-EU citizen upon his arrival in another EU country. Thus, for that non-EU citizen, the whole EU territory might be a 'closed territory', if the cybernaut has done something at home that is illegal in one – but possibly not all – of the EU countries. Furthermore, a person can have his property seized or confiscated, or be fined, for acts that are not illegal in his own country, if the act is only on the 'positive list', since it is the requesting state's legislation that determines whether an act is on that list; the requested state does not even have to really check whether the act is in fact illegal in the requesting EU state.

8.5.3 Cyber-investigation jurisdiction

As previously mentioned, Denmark has ratified and enacted several instruments that regulate cyber-investigation jurisdiction. In Denmark, this jurisdictional question is dealt with in provisions in the Procedure Code (see section 8.3.1). The Danish police are generally required to obtain a court order before initiating a cyber-investigation, and if investigative acts are cross-border, consent from a foreign country is required. The Danish police have very limited possibilities to use agents.

The Danish Committee for IT security has recently suggested that a special District Attorney's Office for cybercrime should be established, since cybercrime is so complicated that it requires special expertise. At present, a new special cybercrime unit is being established at the National Commission of the Danish Police (since cybercrimes mostly cross borders and cover several local districts), which assists local police authorities.[98] This does not mean that the Danish police were previously inefficient – quite the opposite in fact. Danish police have been participating in several cross-border cyber-investigations in order to, for example, crack down on pedophile groups. Because of their high success rate in solving cases, officers from the National Commission of the Danish Police have on several occasions been 'borrowed' by foreign police forces to assist with Danish investigation methods. The Danish police have been provided with high technology, just as nearly 80 per cent of the Danish population have Internet access and thus access international

[98] Dorte Toft, 'Politiet skal oppe sig i jagt på it-kriminelle', *Computerworld DK* (4 March 2005), available at <http://www.computerworld.dk/default.sap?Mode=2&ArticleID=27289#>.

public computer networks. This, of course, does not mean that the police would not like to have even better equipment.

Europol offers special tools to each Member State's police and it further offers co-operation from other countries' police forces, as does Interpol. As far as jurisdiction is concerned, these instruments all seem to be based on co-operation and thus consent from a foreign state, which is in accordance with the principles of public international law on jurisdiction.

8.5.4 **Conflicts in cybercrime jurisdiction**

As mentioned above in section 8.2.2, the Danish Parliament in December 2004 enacted legislation to allow Denmark to ratify the Cybercrime Convention, which it did in June 2005. Thus, the jurisdictional rules in that Convention will solve most cybercrime jurisdiction conflicts between the parties to that convention.

Between the Nordic countries, legislation makes it nearly impossible that conflicts can occur. Between EU Member States, different legislation will solve most cybercrime jurisdiction conflicts. Mention can be made of, among other instruments, the Convention on Mutual Assistance in Criminal Matters between the Member States of the European Union.[99] In 2004 the European Commission issued a report,[100] which explains the present situation pursuant to mutual assistance in criminal matters between the EU Member States.

To a certain degree, the Agreement between the European Union and the United States on extradition and mutual legal assistance in criminal matters[101] also solves some conflicts in cybercrime jurisdiction. Also, it should be mentioned that Denmark, subject to the Council Decision of 6 June 2003 concerning the signing of this Agreement, had an obligation to enact legislation to implement the Council Decision. This must be regarded as having been achieved by the new Danish legislation of December 2004 (see section 8.3.2). As Denmark has chosen to implement the EU Frameworks as general rules in its Procedure Code, it can be expected that Denmark will not differentiate between EU countries and other countries.

Besides these instruments, Denmark also has special agreements with certain countries. Nevertheless, the overall issue is that conflicts in cybercrime jurisdiction – adjudication and enforcement – must be determined by public international law[102] and Danish private international law.

---

[99] *OJ* C197, 12/07/2000, pp. 0001-0024, Protocol of 16 October 2001, *OJ* C326, 21/11/2001, pp. 0001-0008.

[100] Report of 5 April 2004 from the Commission, COM(2004) 230final.

[101] *OJ* L181, 19/07/2003, pp. 0025-0026. Norway has also entered into an agreement with the EU: *OJ* L26, 29/01/2004, pp. 0001-0002.

[102] Spang-Hanssen, op. cit. n. 82, pp. 258-291, 381-424, and 437-462.

8.6 Conclusion

Cybercrime nearly always involves cross-border acts, thus public international law is involved. There does not yet exist any customary international law specifically related to international computer networks, and the Cybercrime Convention is a treaty which has only been ratified by a small group of nations. Thus, it will have to be seen what public international law, including international tribunals, will make of limits to or rejections of national laws or the private international law (choice of law) of each nation in the world.

To the extent that such laws – including the implementation of provisions in the Cybercrime Convention – are legal under public international law, each nation will have some new tools to punish acts committed on international computer networks and to enforce these decisions. The international computer networks and increased international police co-operation have created new tools to fight crimes, including cybercrimes. Danish legislation and law-enforcement agencies can be said to be fairly up to date in fighting cybercrime internationally.

Bibliography

Folketinget [Danish Parliament], <www.folketinget.dk>.

Justice Department's Expert panel on economic and data crimes, *White Paper 1377 of 1999 on Child Pornography and IT-investigations* (1999).

Justice Department's Expert panel on economic and data crimes, *White Paper 1417 of 2002 on IT-Crimes* (2002), available at <http://www.jm.dk/wimpdoc.asp?page=document&objno=64938>.

Lars Bo Langsted, Peter Garde and Vagn Greve, *Criminal Law – Denmark*, 2nd edn. (Copenhagen, DJØF Publishing, 2004) [note: published before major changes in the cybercrime legislation of December 2004]

Retsinformation [Danish legislation], <http://www.retsinfo.dk>.

Henrik Spang-Hanssen, *Cyberspace & International Law on Jurisdiction* (Copenhagen, DJØF Publishing, 2004).

Henrik Spang-Hanssen, 'Danmarks værnetingsregler & "ren" online handlen uden for E.U. på internationale computer netværk' [forthcoming as 'Jurisdiction Rules of Denmark & "pure" online dealings outside the European Union on international computer networks'] (2004), available at <www.geocities.com/hssph/DK_Verneting.pdf>.

Henrik Spang-Hanssen, 'Hollywood puts 3 Baltic countries into a Second Class of E.U. or Hollywood does not recognize E.U.'s single market from May First 2004', available at <www.geocities.com/hssph/articles>.

Chapter 9
CYBERCRIME AND JURISDICTION IN GERMANY. THE PRESENT SITUATION AND THE NEED FOR NEW SOLUTIONS

Ulrich Sieber*

9.1 Introduction

9.1.1 The new challenges of cybercrime

In the past fifty years, the technological development of computer systems and computer networks has created new forms of Internet-based transnational crime. This evolution has led to a multitude of new problems for traditional criminal law, which stem primarily from two fundamental characteristics of cybercrime. First, the growing importance of incorporeal objects raised many new questions with respect to the legal status of incorporeal objects, for both substantive and procedural criminal law. Second, the technological possibilities of the Internet for committing a crime in one country with disastrous consequences in many other countries led to new questions of transnational crimes for procedural law, for international co-operation as well as for substantive and procedural jurisdiction.[1]

9.1.2 The new responses of the international community

The international community has rapidly reacted to these new developments in many areas by means of different instruments for the evolution and the harmonization of criminal law.

In the field of *substantive criminal law*, as early as 1986, the OECD[2] developed detailed solutions which were subsequently further developed by various commit-

* Prof. Dr Ulrich Sieber is Director of the Max Planck Institute for Foreign and International Criminal Law, Freiburg, Germany. He would like to thank Mrs. Indira Tie for translating and proof-reading this text.

[1] See Sieber, The Emergence of Information Law, in E. Lederman & R. Shapira, eds., *Law, Information and Information Technology* (The Hague 2001), pp. 1-29.

[2] See Organisation for Economic Co-Operation and Development (OECD), *Computer-related Crime – Analysis of Legal Policy in the OECD-area* (Paris 1986). For an overview on the relevant

B-J. Koops and S.W. Brenner (Eds), Cybercrime and Jurisdiction

tees of the Council of Europe and other international organizations. These general solutions, especially with respect to hacking, sabotage, fraud, forgery, etc., were later complemented by international solutions in specific areas, such as child pornography, xenophobia, and the liability of Internet providers.

In the field of *procedural law and international co-operation*, it was especially the Council of Europe's Convention on Cybercrime (CCC)[3] that created the first detailed international solutions with respect to questions such as search and seizure, wiretapping, expedited preservation of stored data, and collecting traffic data.[4]

Contrary to the situation in the field of substantive and procedural law, little attention has so far been paid to the field of *jurisdiction in criminal matters* and the implications that the incorporeal and transnational nature of cybercrime entails in this field of law. This is not only true with respect to the issues of substantive jurisdiction (i.e., the question of whether the courts of a certain state will hear a certain case), but also in relation to procedural jurisdiction. The CCC contains only practical solutions for mutual assistance and ensures that no negative conflicts of jurisdiction arise; however, most problems of procedural jurisdiction are left unanswered.[5]

9.1.3 The situation in Germany

The situation of German legislation can be seen as a reflection of this international development. In the field of *substantive criminal law*, new provisions were created in 1986 in the *Strafgesetzbuch* [Criminal Code] (hereafter: *StGB*).[6] These concerned hacking (s. 202a), alteration of data (s. 303a), computer sabotage (s. 303b), computer fraud (s. 263a), and forgery (s. 269).[7] As a result of this early legislation, German law meets most of the demands of the CCC with respect to substantive criminal law and will require only a few amendments. Most notably, the manufacture, distribution, and possession of hacking tools is not yet an offense under Ger-

---

international activities see Sieber, 'Computer Crimes, Cyber-Terrorism, Child Pornography and Financial Crimes. General Report for Round Table II of the 17th International Congress of Penal Law, Beijing 2004', in Spinellis, ed., *Computer Crimes, Cyber-Terrorism, Child Pornography and Financial Crimes: Reports presented to the Preparatory Colloquy for the Round Table II of the 17th International Congress of Penal Law (Beijing 2004)* (Athens, Ant. Sakkoulas 2003).

[3] Council of Europe, Convention on Cybercrime, Budapest, 23 November 2001 (CETS 185), available at <http://conventions.coe.int/Treaty/en/Treaties/Html/185.htm>.

[4] A brief account of the history of the Convention is given in the *Explanatory Report*, available at <http://conventions.coe.int/Treaty/EN/Reports/Html/185.htm>. See also chapter 2 of this book.

[5] At least, Art. 32 CCC clarifies two disputed questions, namely (1) whether investigative measures involving access to publicly available data stored in a foreign state violate that state's sovereignty, and (2) whether the consent of the person affected by the investigation substitutes the consent of the competent authority of the foreign state affected by the investigation.

[6] The provisions from the German *Srafgesetzbuch* (Criminal Code) can be found, in a translation provided by the German Federal Ministry of Justice of the version promulgated on 13 November 1998, at <http://www.iuscomp.org/gla/statutes/StGB.htm>.

[7] *Zweites Gesetz zur Bekämpfung der Wirtschaftskriminalität* (Second Act Combating Economic Crime), *Bundesgesetzblatt* (Federal Law Gazette) (hereafter: *BGBl.*) I 1986, p. 721.

man law.[8] In addition, minor changes will affect the scope of the current statutes on hacking,[9] interception,[10] computer sabotage,[11] and the definition of child pornography.[12]

Contrary to the situation in the substantive criminal-law area, the problems of *procedural law* are not adequately solved by German legislation. In academic discourse, possible loopholes of the present coercive powers with respect to investigations in cybercrime have been discussed. However, concrete and systematic solutions for a reform of the German Criminal Procedure Code have not yet been developed by academics or legislators.[13]

In the field of *jurisdiction* (particularly in the field of substantive jurisdiction), the legal situation is less satisfactorily settled in Germany. *Procedural jurisdiction* has not yet been sufficiently analyzed with respect to the question of whether investigations on the Internet concerning computer systems on foreign territory violate international law.[14] With respect to *substantive jurisdiction* in cyberspace, the situ-

---

[8] At present, there are only three related offenses with a much narrower scope. S. 5 *Zugangskontrolldienstegesetz* (Conditional Access Services Act) criminalizes the manufacture, import and distribution for commercial purposes of equipment or software designed or adapted to give unauthorized access to a protected service (cf., Directive 1998/84/EC, *OJ* L320 of 28 November 1998). Secondly, in accordance with Art. 6(2) Directive 2001/29/EC, *OJ* L167 of 22 June 2001, s. 108b *Urheberrechtsgesetz* (Copyright Act) makes it an offense to manufacture, import, distribute, sell, or rent for commercial purposes a device designed to circumvent copy protection. The third example is s. 263a *StGB*, which provides that whoever prepares an act of computer fraud by manufacturing, procuring, offering, storing or committing to another person computer programs, the purpose of which is to commit an act of computer fraud, shall be punished (cf., Art. 4 EU Council Framework Decision 2001/413/JHA, *OJ* L 149 of 2 June 2001).

[9] In contrast to Art. 2 CCC, s. 202a *StGB* ('data espionage') requires that the offender obtains data. Illegal access to a computer system as such was deliberately not criminalized. It can be argued, however, that this distinction is merely theoretical, since in practice, an offender who has gained access to a computer system will not stop short of retrieving at least some data.

[10] Besides the above-mentioned provision on data espionage in s. 202a *StGB*, currently only the interception of radio transmissions not intended for the perpetrator is an offense under s. 148 *Telekommunikationsgesetz* (Telecommunication Act). Illegal access to a service based on conditional access is not a criminal offense, but only a regulatory offense.

[11] In its current form, s. 303b *StGB* covers only data processing within business enterprises and public agencies, but not private computer systems.

[12] S. 184a *StGB* ('distribution, obtaining and possession of child pornography') refers to the definition of 'child' for the purpose of the offense of sexual abuse of children in s. 176, thus covering persons under fourteen years of age. The CCC demands that the age limit be raised to at least 16 years.

[13] For an overview, see M. Gercke, 'Analyse des Umsetzungsbedarfs der Cybercrime Konvention. Teil 2: Die Umsetzung im Bereich des Strafverfahrensrechts' ['Analysis of the need for legal reform in implementing the CCC. Part 2: Transposition in Procedural Law'], *Multimedia-Recht* (2004) pp. 801-806; T. Böckenförde, 'Die Ermittlung im Netz' ['Investigation on the Net'] (Tübingen, Mohr Siebeck 2003); W. Bär, chapter 24 (Criminal Procedure), in H.B. Wabnitz and T. Janovsky, eds., *Handbuch des Wirtschafts- und Steuerstrafrechts* [Handbook of Economic and Tax Criminal Law] (Munich, Beck 2004).

[14] The best overview is given by N. Seitz, 'Transborder Search: A new perspective in law enforcement?', *International Journal of Communications Law and Policy* (2004), Web-Doc 2-Cy-2004, available at <http://www.digital-law.net/IJCLP/Cy_2004/ijclp_webdoc_2_Cy_2004.htm>; W. Bär, loc. cit. n. 13, margin Nos. 21-25.

ation is even less clear. Not only on the international stage, but also in Germany, there are no convincing solutions for applying criminal sanctions concerning the Internet. Legal scholars scrutinize the problems of the international application of German criminal law in detail,[15] but have not yet developed strategies for new legislation.

9.1.4 **The need for new solutions in the field of jurisdiction**

As a consequence, one of the major needs for a deeper academic discussion in the field of cybercrime and one of the most interesting questions for information law lies in the area of *substantive jurisdiction* in cyberspace. In this area, serious problems exist, since the concept of criminal jurisdiction in Germany – as in most other countries – is based mainly on the principle of territoriality, whereas cyberspace seems to concern a global space where territorial frontiers have no significance. Thus in some cases, especially with respect to illegal content on the Internet, the question arises whether cybercrimes are not covered by any national jurisdiction or whether they should fall under the jurisdiction of approximately 190 national legal systems, if, for example, the illegal contents of a server on the Internet can be accessed in all countries of the world.

In practice, this question of substantive jurisdiction is particularly important, as many crimes in cyberspace are judged differently by the various legal systems. This is not only true with respect to different cultures, for example, the question as to whether web sites originating from countries with a Christian culture are covered by the criminal law of Islamic states where they can be accessed. There are also considerable differences between the laws of various Western democracies with similar political and cultural standards. Disseminating Nazi propaganda, for instance, is criminalized in Germany and Austria but may be protected by the constitutional freedom of expression in the United States and Canada. Even child pornography, which in the meantime is banned internationally, is covered by different statutes, especially with respect to the age limit of the children to be protected, the criminalization of mere possession of child pornography, as well as the legality of virtual child pornography.[16]

These legal differences have already caused problems and questions in various cases. In one German case, German prosecutors charged an Australian national with publishing materials denying the Holocaust on his Australian web server, despite the fact that his web site was not criminalized under Australian law.[17] In another case, a French Internet vendor offering ladies' underwear asked whether his

---

[15] See *infra*, section 9.2.

[16] For a comparative analysis of the criminal law on child pornography, see U. Sieber, *Kinderpornographie, Jugendschutz und Providerverantwortlichkeit im Internet* [Child pornography, the protection of minors, and the liability of Internet providers] (Mönchengladbach, Forum Verlag 1999).

[17] For a discussion of the *Toben* case see *infra*, section 9.3.3.

web site in France was in compliance with German pornography legislation. Similarly, a producer of German web sites was concerned whether its publicity for alcoholic beverages was subject to the criminal statutes of Muslim countries in which the respective web sites could be accessed. Since data on the Internet can be accessed with a simple click of the mouse from nearly anywhere in the world, the question arises as to whether someone who runs a web site needs to be aware of more than 190 criminal law jurisdictions.[18]

The aim of this chapter is to answer these questions of substantive jurisdiction for German law and to develop some ideas for future international solutions to cybercrime jurisdiction.

9.2 Traditional Approaches in German Criminal Law

9.2.1 The need for differentiation

Offense-specific and legal differentiation
The question of how German criminal law applies to the Internet cannot be answered in general according to the German legal system, since different offenses are concerned and the German law on jurisdiction contains special provisions for specific offenses. In addition, there is a wide range of phenomena with different starting points for the determination of the *locus criminis*. Problems of cybercrime range from the targeted destruction by offenders abroad of data stored on German computers to the active worldwide distribution of criminal content in Internet news groups or on web servers. The particular difficulty with the latter example is that while the physical location of the hosting server may be 'passively' situated in a foreign country, the data contained may be 'actively' accessed by German users with the mere click of a mouse. For this reason, a comprehensive survey of the legal situation calls for offense-specific differentiation before the truly interesting and decisive questions can be clarified.

Non-territorial rules of jurisdiction
The applicability of German criminal law to the Internet is unproblematic for those offenses that are covered not only by the *principle of territoriality* (which is the basic and general principle of jurisdiction in Germany), but also by the *active personality principle*, the *universality principle*, or the *protective principle* (which supplement the principle of territoriality in specific cases). For example, this is the case according to section 7 *StGB*, when the offender or the victim is a German citizen and the offense is punishable according to the law of the jurisdiction where it was allegedly committed. In addition, according to section 6 paragraphs 4-7 *StGB*,

[18] Cf., U. Sieber, 'Die Bekämpfung von Hass im Internet' [Combating Hate on The Internet], *Zeitschrift für Rechtspolitik* (2001), pp. 97-103 at p. 101.

German criminal law prohibits slave trading, the distribution of narcotics, the dissemination of child pornography, and the forgery of payment cards, regardless of the *locus criminis*.[19] The same is true for the violation of company or trade secrets belonging to German businesses or – as has meanwhile also been detected on the Internet – organ trading, to which section 5 paragraphs 7 and 12 *StGB* apply. These non-territorial principles of jurisdiction[20] do not pose any problems that are specific to cybercrime.

The basic rule of territorial jurisdiction

Barring such special cases, the applicability of German criminal law is governed by the principle of territoriality as regulated in section 3 *StGB* and the 'theory of ubiquity' (*Ubiquitätstheorie*) which is regulated in section 9 *StGB*. According to section 3 *StGB*, German criminal law applies to offenses 'which are committed *domestically*'. According to section 9(1) *StGB*, an 'act is committed at every location at which *the offender acted* or, in the case of omission, should have acted, or at which *the result inherent to the offense occurred* or was expected to occur according to the intention of the offender' [emphasis added].[21] Thus, the prerequisite for criminal jurisdiction in Germany is, as a rule, either the act which is an offense (s. 9(1) 1st alternative *StGB*) or its result (s. 9(1) 3rd alternative *StGB*) having occurred on German territory. This twofold approach of combining the location of the act and the location of the result is called the 'theory of ubiquity'.

Clear cases of the territoriality principle

In certain cases, it is easy to apply the principle of territoriality and the 'theory of ubiquity' of section 3 in conjunction with section 9(1) *StGB* to the Internet. This is especially so when the offender operates from within Germany, by manipulating, for example, a computer located in a foreign jurisdiction. In this case, Germany is clearly 'the location of the criminal act' in the legal sense as stipulated by section 9(1) 1st alternative *StGB*. Moreover, cases of typical result crimes are also not problematic if the result of the offense occurs in Germany; for instance, if, according to section 303a *StGB*, an offender operating from abroad destroys computer data on a computer located in Germany via the Internet. In this case, Germany is the 'location of the criminal result' in the legal sense of section 9(1) 3rd alternative *StGB*.

---

[19] In addition to requirements set forth in statutory law, the courts would always apply a reasonableness standard requiring a sufficient link that warrants domestic prosecution. With regard to crimes against international law, s. 153f *Strafprozessordnung* (Code of Criminal Procedure), which was created in 2002, gave law-enforcement authorities the discretion not to prosecute. See BGH, *Neue Zeitschrift für Strafrecht* 1994, 232 with further references.

[20] For a discussion of the principles underlying the German rules of jurisdiction, see H. Jescheck and T. Weigend, *Lehrbuch des Strafrechts. Allgemeiner Teil* [Textbook on Criminal Law, General Part], 5th edn. (Berlin, Duncker & Humblot 1994), pp. 167-171.

[21] 'Eine Tat ist an jedem Ort begangen, an dem *der Täter gehandelt* hat oder im Falle des Unterlassens hätte handeln müssen oder an dem *der zum Tatbestand gehörende Erfolg eingetreten* ist oder nach der Vorstellung des Täters eintreten sollte' [emphasis added].

Special territorial problems with action crimes and abstract endangerment offenses
Difficulties arise, however, with 'Tätigkeitsdelikte' (action crimes)[22] and 'abstrakte Gefährdungsdelikte' (abstract endangerment offenses).[23] Examples are dissemination offenses and speech offenses, such as making accessible pornography, glorifications of violence, or racist or national-socialist hate speech.[24] The prevailing opinion is that these offenses are to be considered 'abstract endangerment offenses',[25] which are widely thought to lack a 'location of the criminal result' in the legal sense. This leads to problems if the criminal acts are carried out in a foreign country and Germany is only subjected to an abstract and intangible danger. These problems have occurred in real-life situations, especially in cases when offenders abroad made pornographic or national-socialist material available on foreign web servers and this material was easily accessible to German users.[26] The following comments deal with the applicability of German criminal law to such problematic and topical present-day cases of dissemination offenses and speech offenses.

9.2.2 The traditional approaches to action crimes and abstract endangerment offenses

The applicability of the principle of territoriality according to sections 3 and 9 *StGB* to the dissemination of illegal content or hate speech originating from foreign countries is extremely controversial in the literature due to the classification of such actions as abstract endangerment offenses. Because the location of the criminal act in the legal sense of section 9(1) 1st alternative *StGB* is thought to depend on the physical location of the offender,[27] the different solutions depend especially upon

---

[22] An offense is categorized as 'Tätigkeitsdelikt' if a mere action suffices to complete the offence and no result whatsoever is an element of the offense.

[23] An offense is categorized as 'abstraktes Gefährdungsdelikt' if it makes a conduct punishable because it is inherently dangerous while it is not relevant for the completion of the offense that the offender actually harmed or endangered specific persons or objects. Where a specific endangerment of property or persons is an element of the offense, such an offense is called 'konkretes Gefährdungsdelikt' (specific endangerment offense).

[24] Relevant offences are ss. 74d, 80a, 86, 86a, 90-90b, 103, 111, 130, 130a, 131, 140, 164, 166, 184-184c, 185-189, 194, 200, 219a *StGB*; for an overview, see U. Sieber, 'Strafrecht und Strafprozeßrecht' [Criminal Law and Criminal Procedure], in T. Hoeren and U. Sieber, eds., *Handbuch Multimedia-Recht* [Handbook on Multimedia Law] (Munich, Beck 1999), part 19, margin Nos. 600 et seq.

[25] See M. Kienle, *Internationales Strafrecht und Straftaten im Internet* [Criminal Jurisdiction and Offenses on the Internet] (Constance, Hartung-Gorre 1998), p. 67 et seq. and p. 83 et seq.

[26] For the technical aspects, see U. Sieber, 'Criminal Liability for the Transfer of Data in International Networks – New Challenges for the Internet', 13 *Computer Law & Security Report* (1997), pp. 151-157, 223-233, 312-318, and 413-418; 14 *Computer Law & Security Report* (1998), pp. 22-28, and U. Sieber, 'Control Possibilities for the Prevention of Criminal Content in Computer Networks', 15 *Computer Law and Security Report* (1999), pp. 34-39, 90-100, and 168-180.

[27] G. Gribbohm, Commentary on s. 9 *StGB*, in B. Jähnke, ed., *StGB. Leipziger Kommentar* [Criminal Code. Leipziger Commentary], 11th edn., (Berlin, de Gruyter 1992 et seq.); contra, K. Cornils, 'Der Begehungsort von Äußerungsdelikten im Internet' [The *Locus Criminis* of Speech Offenses on the Internet], *Juristenzeitung* (1999), pp. 394-398.

answering the question of how the 'location of the criminal result' of an abstract endangerment offense is to be defined according to section 9(1) 3rd alternative *StGB*.

Restrictive approach

A 'restrictive' approach assumes that abstract endangerment offenses do not have a 'location of criminal result' in the legal sense of section 9(1) 3rd alternative *StGB* but instead have only a 'location of criminal act' in the sense of section 9(1) 1st alternative *StGB*.[28] This would mean that, according to the principle of territoriality stated in German criminal law, an actor would not be subject to criminal liability simply for placing pornographic or national-socialist material on a foreign web server, for posting the material in newsgroups on a German server, or for forwarding such material to Germany in e-mails via mailing lists. This assumption leads to an extremely far-reaching restriction of the area of applicability of German criminal law.[29]

Extensive approach

The opposing 'extensive' view presumes that a 'location of the criminal result' is given at *all* places where the abstract danger could materialize.[30] According to this view, a person acting in a foreign country would not only be liable under German law for mailing pornographic or national-socialist material or insulting comments to Germany, but also if this content could be accessed on a foreign server even though the material has no connection whatsoever with Germany. Because of the international interaction of computer networks brought about by the advent of the Internet, the mere possibility that such material could be accessed from within Germany would be sufficient to constitute a *locus criminis* in Germany in the case of 'abstract endangerment offenses' as described above.

If this 'extensive' theory were to be consistently followed, the corollary would be that practically all material available on the Internet would be subject to German

---

[28] See Gribbohm, loc. cit. n. 27, margin No. 20; C. Pelz, 'Die strafrechtliche Verantwortlichkeit von Internet-Providern' [The Criminal Liability of Internet Providers], *Zeitschrift für Urheber- und Medienrecht* (1998), pp. 530-534 at p. 531; H. Satzger, 'Die Anwendung des deutschen Strafrechts auf grenzüberschreitende Gefährdungsdelikte' [The Application of German Criminal Law on Transborder Endangerment Offenses], *Neue Zeitschrift für Strafrecht* (1998), pp. 112-117 at p. 115.

[29] M. Kienle, op. cit., n. 25, p. 173 et seq., even argues for the additional requirement that the act is punishable at the location of the act, according to s. 7 *StGB*, which provides that: 'German criminal law shall apply to acts, which were committed abroad against a German, if the act is punishable at the place of its commission (...).'

[30] See B. Heinrich, 'Der Erfolgsort beim abstrakten Gefährdungsdelikt' [The Location of the Criminal Result in Abstract Endangerment Offenses], *Goltdammer's Archiv für Strafrecht* (1999), pp. 72-84 at p. 83 et seq.; C. Kuner, 'Internationale Zuständigkeitskonflikte im Internet' [Jurisdictional Conflicts on the Internet], *Computer und Recht* (1996), pp. 453-458 at p. 456; M. Löhnig, '"Verbotene Schriften" im Internet' ['Illegal Writings' on the Internet], *Juristische Rundschau* (1997), pp. 496-498 at p. 496; H. Jescheck and T. Weigend, op. cit. n. 20, p. 179.

criminal law. This is indeed accepted by several academics.[31] However, it leads to a very broad application of German criminal law, which is problematic not only with regard to the corresponding 'global' prosecutorial obligation that it places upon the German authorities,[32] but also in relation to international law *per se*. In addition, if other legal systems were to adopt this approach, then all material on the Internet would be subject to a multitude of criminal jurisdictions. This would lead – at least in theory – to the Internet being governed by the strictest national criminal-law jurisdiction.

Compromises

In order to avoid the far-reaching consequences that are brought about by equating the 'location of the criminal result' with the 'location of the abstract endangerment', many authors apply additional subjective or objective criteria.[33]

- For example, some apply a subjective criterion to the extensive view, requiring that the alleged offender must either have knowingly risked that illegal contents could be accessed in Germany or must have intentionally acted, 'aiming at' users in Germany actually accessing the data.[34]
- Others require a territorial link as an objective criterion.[35]
- Some authors argue for criteria such as the language in which the material is made available to specify the territorial link.[36]
- Such an objective link is also seen, by others, if the offender is a German national: By means of the cumulative application of sections 9 and 7 *StGB*,[37] a specific objective link to the Federal Republic of Germany could be ascertained, thereby enabling a resulting restriction of section 9 *StGB* beyond its actual wording.[38]

---

[31] See B. Heinrich, loc. cit. n. 30, pp. 76 and 82; N.P. Flechsig and D. Gabel, 'Strafrechtliche Verantwortlichkeit im Netz durch Einrichten und Vorhalten von Hyperlinks' [Criminal Liability on the Net for Providing Hyperlinks], *Computer und Recht* (1998), pp. 351-358 at p. 352.

[32] See *infra*, n. 93.

[33] See Kienle, op. cit. n. 25, p. 159 et seq., especially the references in notes 534 and 535, for an overview of approaches developed long before the advent of the Internet.

[34] See M. Collardin, 'Straftaten im Internet' [Criminal Offenses on the Internet], *Computer und Recht* (1995), pp. 618-622 at p. 621; C. Engel, 'Inhaltskontrolle im Internet' [Controlling Content on the Internet], *Archiv für Presserecht* (1996), pp. 220-227 at p. 226. D. Oehler, *Internationales Strafrecht*, 2nd edn. (Cologne, Heymann 1983), margin No. 253 et seq. requires that the occurrence of the result in a foreign jurisdiction was at least foreseeable for the offender.

[35] B. Breuer, 'Anwendbarkeit des deutschen Strafrechts auf extraterritorial handelnde Internet-Benutzer' [Applying German Criminal Law to Internet Users Acting Extraterritorially], *Multimedia-Recht* (1998), pp. 141-144 at p. 144; E. Hilgendorf, 'Überlegungen zur strafrechtlichen Interpretation des Ubiquitätsprinzips im Zeitalter des Internet' [Thoughts on the Interpretation of the Ubiquity Principle of Criminal Law in the Internet Era], *Neue Juristische Wochenschrift* (1997), pp. 1873-1878 at p. 1876.

[36] E. Hilgendorf, loc. cit. n. 35, p. 1876.

[37] Cf., n. 29.

[38] See B. Breuer, loc. cit. n. 35, p. 144.

In the development of such theories, the discussions on criminal jurisdiction often use criteria that can also be found in civil law in the context of the *locus delicti* with regard to violations of competition law.[39]

Criticism

The aforementioned views are not convincing, because of their dogmatic approach. This is particularly true of the 'extensive' theory, which seeks to equate the 'location of the criminal result' with the 'location of the abstract endangerment'. In the case of abstract endangerment offenses, the wording of section 9 *StGB* does not allow for an interpretation according to which the 'result inherent to the offense' is taken to occur at all locations where the danger caused by an abstract endangerment offense can be realized. The characteristic attribute of abstract endangerment offenses is the very fact that no result has to occur for the offense to be completed. In addition, in many cases, it is unclear where the offense amounts to an 'abstract danger'. The 'entire endangered radius surrounding the source of danger'[40] that is drawn upon for this purpose is unclear – a point indicated by the previous examples regarding the dissemination of offensive material. Moreover, the hypothetical scenario in which Germany would act as a 'global police officer' managing all Internet content the world over is highly unconvincing. Since the Internet facilitates the accessibility of data across the globe, the potential availability of Internet-based material provides no suitable connecting link for any specific application of national criminal law.

To some extent, the subjective and objective restrictions mentioned above lead to more reasonable results from a policy point of view than the underlying 'purist' theory. However, these approaches are also subject to the same misgivings as the fundamental theory. Indeed, as the multitude of factors mentioned demonstrates, the different restrictions cannot be dogmatically justified, they are sometimes almost arbitrary in nature, and they are generally difficult to manage.

On the other hand, the 'restrictive' approach is too narrow because it unjustly equates 'result' in the legal sense of section 9(1) *StGB* with 'result' in the sense of the dogmatic category of *Erfolgsdelikte* (result crimes)[41] as developed in the *Tatbestandslehre* (the general theory of the definition of criminal offenses). However, as will be discussed below, this equation is by no means convincing.

---

[39] For civil law, cf., J. Dieselhorst, 'Anwendbares Recht bei internationalen Online-Diensten' [Applicable Law in International On-line Services], *Zeitschrift für Urheber- und Medienrecht* (1998), pp. 293-300; for a discussion of these principles from a criminal-law point of view, see Kienle, op. cit. n. 25, p. 177 et seq.

[40] Heinrich, loc. cit. n. 30, p. 82.

[41] An offense is categorized as 'Erfolgsdelikt' if the definition of the offense requires a result (especially damage) that is causally connected to the offender's act or omission.

9.3 New Solutions

9.3.1 The autonomous interpretation of the concept of result

The concept of 'result' in different contexts

The starting point for finding solutions to the problems at hand must be a clarification of the meaning of section 9 *StGB*, more specifically, the meaning of the phrase 'result inherent to the offense' (*zum Tatbestand gehörender Erfolg*) as stated in section 9 *StGB*. This definition cannot be equated with the concept of result found in the *Tatbestandslehre* – as has been done by most authors up to now – in a narrow-minded terminology-oriented style of legal thought ('*Begriffsjurisprudenz*'). A systematic and contextual interpretation of the Criminal Code shows that the result concept in criminal law can be interpreted much more broadly than in the case of result crimes, not only according to section 13 *StGB* and section 78a *StGB* but also according to section 9 *StGB*.

In the case of crimes by omission, the prevailing opinion holds that a 'result' in the legal sense of section 13 *StGB*[42] can be realized by a simple action crime or abstract endangerment offense.[43] The same is true for 'result' in the legal sense of section 78a *StGB*,[44] which case law shows can even be constituted by an abstract danger.[45] In part, the literature on the subject has asserted that every committed offense leads to a result; however, the literature also distinguishes between the result that must exceed the act of commission in some way and the result that entails the act of commission itself.[46] Even in the case of the common legal definition of a result according to section 9 *StGB* as given here, prevailing opinion also overcomes the narrow interpretation (in the context of the dogmatic category of result crime) by assuming that a 'result' occurs in the form of specific endangerment with regard to specific endangerment offenses and furthermore by assessing that *objektive Bedingungen der Strafbarkeit* ('objective conditions for criminal liability' which are not an element of the *actus reus*) or aggravating circumstances are a 'result' in the legal sense of section 9 *StGB*.[47]

For these reasons, regarding the wording of the provision, as well as its systematic interpretation in the context of the Criminal Code, no qualifications are necessary when individually interpreting 'result' and including the *Tathandlungserfolg*

---

42 In s. 13(1) *StGB*, omission is defined as the failure to avert a result.

43 See Satzger, loc. cit. n. 28, p. 177; G. Jakobs, *Strafrecht. Allgemeiner Teil* [Criminal Law. General Part], 2nd edn. (Berlin, de Gruyter 1993), chapter 29 margin No. 2.

44 Section 78a *StGB* stipulates that statutory limitation shall commence as soon as the act is completed or, if the result occurs later, as soon as the result occurs.

45 See *BGHSt* 32, 293, 294; *BGHSt* 36, 255, 257.

46 H. Maurach and H. Zipf, *Strafrecht Allgemeiner Teil, Ein Lehrbuch. Grundlehren des Strafrechts und Aufbau der Straftat* [The General Part of Criminal Law. A Textbook on the Principles of Criminal Law and the Structure of Criminal Offenses] (Heidelberg, Müller 1992), chapter 20 margin No. 27.

47 See *BGHSt* 42, 235, 242.

('effect of the criminal act') as a 'result' in the legal sense of section 9(1) 3rd alternative *StGB* if the offender acts from a foreign country, yet his action has an effect in Germany. This means that if an offender forwards illegal material from a foreign country to Germany by mail, then the requirement that such material be 'distributed' in Germany is fulfilled, regardless of whether the corresponding criminal act (e.g., the distribution of pornographic material) is classified as an abstract endangerment offense or result crime in the context of the general theory of the definition of criminal offenses.

The Historical Background of the Ubiquity Theory

This broader definition of 'result', which also includes a *Tathandlungserfolg*, can be substantiated by way of historical interpretation. The definition proposed here is in agreement with a leading case of the Reichsgericht (Supreme Court of the German Reich) which, when interpreting section 3 *Reichsstrafgesetzbuch (RStGB)* (Criminal Code of the German Reich) of 15 May 1871,[48] had to start from the general formulation describing the commission of 'punishable acts'.[49] According to the Reichsgericht, an 'act' was not just defined as a 'personal action' but also included 'an effect gained and intended by the action, calculated as part of the punishable act inherent to the offense, and incorporated into the definition of the same.'[50] The Reichsgericht thus combined the 'theory of action or location' (the location where the offender committed the action was seen as decisive in the prevailing interpretation of section 3 *RStGB* at the time) with the 'result theory' (the location of the result or any *interim* result being the relevant location, a view propagated by a minority opinion), thus forming a 'unified theory' in which the two criteria of 'action and result' were combined.[51] This two-pronged approach of 'action' and 'result' – which forms the underlying principle of the ubiquity theory today – was justified by the Reichsgericht from a naturalistic viewpoint in the sense of 'action and effect', but not in the sense of 'the criminal act' and 'the concept of "result" as in "result crime".'

The ubiquity theory in statutory law

New legislation on the territorial application of criminal law of 6 May 1940,[52] which introduced the principle of personality in section 3(1) *StGB*, adopted this interpretation of the location of the criminal act in section 3(3) of the *RStGB*. The basic distinction between the location of the criminal act and the location of the criminal result was confirmed and retained in the course of subsequent legal re-

[48] *RGBl.* (*Reich Law Gazette*) 1871, p. 127 et seq.

[49] There was no provision like section 9 *StGB* to define the legal meaning of 'act' in s. 3 *RStGB*.

[50] Cf., s. 3 *Reichsstrafgesetzbuch*: 'The criminal law of the German Reich shall be applied to all criminal acts committed on its territory, even if the offender is a foreigner.'

[51] *RGSt* 1, 274, 276.

[52] *RGBl.* 1940 I, p. 754 et seq. Cf., E. Mezger, 'Der Anwendungsbereich des deutschen Strafrechts' [The Scope of Application of German Criminal Law], *Deutsches Recht* (1940), pp. 1076-1079.

form. According to section 3(3) *RStGB*-1940, an act was 'committed at any place at which the offender acted (...) or at which the result was effected or intended to occur.' Unaltered even in the new version of the Criminal Code of 1 September 1969, this wording of section 3(3) *StGB*[53] was later limited, in accordance with the suggestions of the *Große Strafrechtskommission* (Criminal Law Reform Commission) and the '*Entwurf 1962*' (the draft Criminal Code of 1962), to the location 'at which the offender acted (...) or at which the *result inherent to the offense* occurred' by the *Zweites Strafrechtsreformgesetz* (Second Criminal Law Reform Act) of 4 July 1969.[54] This is the version of section 9(1) *StGB* that has been in force since 1 January 1975.[55]

According to the comments of the Criminal Law Reform Commission, the restriction of the scope of the wording 'result inherent to the offense' was merely intended to clarify 'that the occurrence of the result should be seen as being closely connected to the criminal offense.'[56] This interpretation – which is fully compatible with the case law of the Reichsgericht – becomes even clearer when read in conjunction with the reasoning of section 8 of the *Alternativentwurf eines StGBs* (Alternative Draft of a Criminal Code, authored by a group of academic lawyers). According to section 8 *Alternativentwurf*, a result, as intended in the provision, should be 'solely limited to the particular effect of a criminal conduct described in the definition of the offense, which Mezger called an "external result".'[57] From the Explanatory Memorandum of the Second Criminal Law Reform Act of 1969, it also appears that the legislature was concerned with the continuity of the hitherto existing legal situation.[58] Approaches that seek to restrict the operation of section 9(1) 3rd alternative *StGB* to the category of 'result crimes' are nowhere to be found. After a corresponding decision by the Bayerisches Oberstes Landesgericht (Bavarian Supreme Regional Court) relating to sections 99 and 100(1) *StGB*, an independent interpretation of the concept of result in section 9 *StGB* – which follows the previous case law of the Reichsgericht on the 'effect of a criminal act' – was proposed by the Bundesgerichtshof (Federal Supreme Court, hereafter: BGH) in a recent decision on section 323a *StGB*, stating that the result concept of section 9 *StGB*

---

[53] *BGBl.* I, p. 1445 et seq.

[54] *BGBl.* 1969 I, p. 717 et seq.

[55] *BGBl.* 1973 I, p. 909.

[56] G. Kielwein, 'Räumliche Geltung; Ort der Tat' [Territorial Jurisdiction. The locus criminis], *Niederschriften über die Sitzung der Großen Strafrechtskommission IV, AT, 38. bis 52. Sitzung* [Proceedings of the Session of the Criminal Law Reform Commission IV, General Part, 38th to 52nd Session] (Bonn, Ministerium der Justiz 1958), p. 20.

[57] J. Baumann, et al., *Alternativentwurf eines Strafgesetzbuches. Allgemeiner Teil* [Alternative Draft for a Criminal Code. General Part], 2nd edn. (Tübingen, Mohr 1969), p. 39, with reference to E. Mezger, loc. cit. n. 52, p. 1078.

[58] See German Bundestag, ed., *BT-Dr.* V/4095, p. 7, citing from the *Explanatory Memorandum* of the 1962 draft, German Bundestag, ed., *BT-Dr.* IV/650, p. 113: 'Subsection (1) [of s. 9 *StGB*] is merely an explicit statement of the current legal situation.'

'cannot be derived from the concepts found in the general doctrine of the definition of criminal offenses.'[59]

Other considerations in support of the new approach

Furthermore, the aspects of legal certainty and manageability of section 9 *StGB* also support interpreting the result clause of section 9 *StGB* to mean any *Tathandlungserfolg* (effect of the criminal act), as it has been justified by the wording, a systematic interpretation, and the historical background of the legislation. A strong argument is the fact that the controversial distinctions between result crimes, specific endangerment offenses, abstract endangerment offenses, and mere action crimes lead to considerable classification difficulties.[60] For this reason, the long-term, seldom questioned restriction of the 'result inherent to the offense' to 'results' as specified in the category of result crimes is not only superfluous as regards the wording of section 9 *StGB*, but it is also vague and misleading.

In fact, in many cases, the classification of a particular offense as one of abstract endangerment in order to protect individual legal interests is interchangeable with the qualification of an offense as a result crime protecting a collective legal interest. For example, section 324(1) *StGB* reads: 'Whoever, without authorization, pollutes a body of water or otherwise detrimentally alters its quality (...).' This can be interpreted both as an abstract endangerment offense protecting the individual legal interest of human health and as a result crime protecting the collective legal interest to non-contaminated water as a natural resource.[61] In such a case, the applicability of sections 3 and 9 *StGB* should not have to rely on dogmatic classifications if, for example, an offender in a foreign country contaminates a river that subsequently flows into Germany. Thus, just as the contamination of the water can be a 'result inherent to the offense', so too could the distribution or making accessible of pornographic material. In cases in which pornographic or national-socialist material is forwarded to Germany, such an interpretation avoids the less plausible conclusion that German criminal law should not be applicable (in contrast to the case of an insulting letter forwarded to Germany, for example) just because the respective criminal offenses are classified as abstract endangerment offenses.

Arguments against an extensive interpretation of the offender's conduct

Following the aforementioned case law of the Reichsgericht, the above conclusion could also be justified by means of an extensive interpretation of the 'location at which the offender acted' in the legal sense of section 9(1) 1st alternative *StGB* instead of the interpretation given here of the 'location of the result inherent to the

---

[59] See Bayerisches Oberstes Landesgericht, *Neue Juristische Wochenschrift* 1957, 1327; *BGHSt* 42, 235, 242.

[60] Cf. F. Zieschang, *Die Gefährdungsdelikte* [Endangerment Offenses] (Berlin, Duncker & Humblot 1998), p. 214 et seq.

[61] Ibid., p. 222.

offense' in the legal sense of section 9(1) 3rd alternative *StGB*.[62] However, the fact that the legislature has deliberately extended the *locus criminis* to include the 'result' of a conduct places particular emphasis on the historical and systematic interpretation. In conformity with prevailing opinion, the literal meaning of section 9(1) 1st alternative *StGB* suggests that the conduct of an offender can only take place at the location of his physical presence and not at a number of locations, e.g., in the case of a web server of which the pages can be accessed from many locations. An extensive interpretation, which would also stretch the temporal extension of the offender's 'action' indefinitely, is no longer necessary following the introduction of section 9 *StGB* in 1969. It would make superfluous the legislative inclusion of the result principle in section 3 *StGB* in 1940 that was retained in the amendment of section 9(1) *StGB*. Also, the differentiation of criminal conduct and criminal result according to section 9 *StGB* would be lost. Replacing the 'result inherent to the offense' with the criminal conduct supplemented by all its effects also entails the risk of bypassing the limitation of section 9 *StGB* intended by the Criminal Law Reform Commission, since the broader term for criminal conduct in section 9(1) 1st alternative *StGB* would not be restricted to a criminal effect 'inherent to the offense'.

In addition, difficulties in differentiation would arise, both when determining the location of the criminal conduct and the location of the criminal result. For example, in the context of the suggested extensive interpretation, the location of the criminal conduct could no longer be determined in agreement with prevailing opinion (based on the 'behavior-oriented' concept of criminal conduct) simply in the sense of the bodily motion of the offender at a certain location (or, in the case of omission, non-motion).[63] Instead it would require a separate definition – for instance using criteria such as causation or control.[64]

As a basis for further analysis, the following conclusion can be stated. A 'result' in the legal sense of section 9(1) 3rd alternative *StGB* is not limited to result crimes, but must be defined independently. This approach includes the *Tathandlungserfolg* (effect of the criminal act) and comprises every result caused by and attributable to the offender that constitutes the offense.

---

62 See Cornils, loc. cit. n. 27. See also T. Weigend, 'Strafrechtliche Pornographieverbote in Europa' [Criminal Prohibitions of Pornography in Europe], *Zeitschrift für Urheber- und Medienrecht* (1994), pp. 133-140 at p. 134, who fails to substantiate his opinion. Cornils takes a different approach, but agrees with the conclusions reached at here, which were outlined in U. Sieber, loc. cit. n. 24, margin Nos. 397 et seq.

63 See Jakobs, op. cit. n. 43, ch. 6 margin No. 1.

64 Cf., Cornils, loc. cit. n. 27, p. 397 for the use of 'control' as a criterion to limit the location of the criminal act according to her approach. This criterion might be narrower than the criterion of attribution (of results to the offender) that is proposed here.

9.3.2 Dissemination of illegal content: distinction between push and pull

The consequences of the approach outlined above will be demonstrated by discussing one of the most important problem areas of application, namely the distribution of illegal content.

Starting point

If the 'result inherent to the offense' can also be a *Tathandlungserfolg* (effect of the criminal act), it follows that the applicability of German criminal law depends – as the very wording 'result inherent to the offense' indicates – on the structure of the respective criminal offenses. This will be demonstrated by analyzing two of the most significant definitions of criminal conduct pertaining to the dissemination of illegal material– namely the acts of 'distributing' (*verbreiten*) and 'making accessible' (*zugänglich machen*) such content.[65]

The 'distribution' of illegal content requires – at least according to the commonly held opinion prior to the most recent case law of the BGH[66] – the passing on of a physical copy of a written document or similar objects.[67] Distributing a document in Germany therefore requires that a physical copy containing illegal content enters Germany for the criminal act to be completed. Regardless of the classification of the respective criminal offense, such a *Tathandlungserfolg* (effect of the criminal act) occurs, for example, when the originator of a document sends it from a foreign country to Germany by mail. However, if the originator distributes the document abroad only, and it is subsequently brought into Germany unknowingly by a tourist, it is not the originator but the tourist who distributes the document in Germany. It is generally accepted in German criminal law, that such an involvement of a third party who is personally responsible for his own conduct limits the attribution of results to the originator (as long as the originator is not a participant in

[65] See U. Sieber, loc. cit. n. 24, part 19, margin Nos. 608 et seq. for the interpretation of 'distributing' and 'making accessible'.

[66] In *BGHSt* 47, 55 (59), the BGH – if only *obiter dictum* – departed from the hitherto common opinion and held that the term 'distribution' with regard to the Internet is to be 'specifically' applied, such that it includes (non-corporeal) data transmission. In the particular case, an on-line dissemination of documents containing child pornography was concerned. The BGH argued that a data carrier (the offender's local hard drive on which the material was stored) could also be 'distributed' by virtue of its contents arriving at the working memory of a computer or a permanent storage medium. This decision should be rejected for a number of reasons. Firstly, it equates the difference between 'distributing' and 'making accessible'; in the case at hand, the interpretation of 'distribution' was not at all relevant since a case of 'making available' was clearly given. Secondly, the BGH failed to acknowledge that s. 11(3) *StGB* includes the term 'data carrier' (i.e., a physical representation of data) along with the terms documents, audio and video recordings and depictions, and does therefore not refer to the contents of the data carrier, i.e., the (non-corporeal) data, as such. For detailed criticism of this decision, see the comments by M. Gercke, *MultiMedia und Recht* 2001, pp. 678-680 and H. Kudlich, *Juristenzeitung* 2001, pp. 310-312.

[67] U. Sieber, loc. cit. n. 24, margin Nos. 608 et seq.

the act of the third party).[68] This means in the present context: future distribution activities by third parties cannot be attributed to the originator.

The same principle is true for the 'making accessible' of illegal content, which is relevant with regard to on-line dissemination of materials on the Internet. The interpretation of this element of an offense creates greater problems than the interpretation of 'distribution', because the non-physical nature of accessibility is much harder to define. The 'accessibility' of a document does not necessarily require that its substance enters the recipient's sphere of perception or sphere of control. Rather, according to prevailing opinion, accessibility also occurs when it is possible for the recipient (even if he does not have a physical copy of the document in his possession) to obtain knowledge of the document's contents. Thus, if a document is mailed to a computer system in Germany by means of an individual e-mail or a mailing list, it is made accessible in Germany in a non-physical form. The *locus criminis* of dissemination offenses and speech offenses on the Internet is therefore not only in Germany if the offender acts there (in the sense of physical presence), but also if he purposefully transmits data from a foreign country to a computer located in Germany. However, if the originator of the document stores it on an Internet server located abroad and the document is then retrieved by users in Germany acting in their own personal responsibility, then the document has been made accessible only in the foreign country and not in Germany by the originator. Although this definition of 'making accessible' – which has been developed by legal doctrine, but is not explicitly stated in the Criminal Code – emphasizes the possibility of obtaining knowledge,[69] it must not be forgotten that the 'result inherent to the offense' does not occur where some recipient actually obtained knowledge (which is irrelevant, as only the *possibility* is required), but rather *where the offender created the possibility* of other persons obtaining knowledge of the contents. When determining the location of the criminal result, the personally responsible retrieval of data on the part of the German user cannot be attributed to the operator of the foreign server just as the subsequent distribution of a physical document by a third party (as described in the above-mentioned example) cannot. The location of the conduct of the offender and the location of the effect of the criminal act can therefore differ from the location at which a document is made discernable through the willful conduct of a third party.

---

[68] See W. Frisch, *Tatbestandsmäßiges Verhalten und Zurechnung des Erfolgs* [Criminal Conduct and Attribution of the Criminal Result] (Heidelberg, C.F. Müller 1988), p. 230 et seq.; Jakobs, op. cit. n. 43, ch. 24 marginal Nos. 13 et seq.; C. Roxin, *Strafrecht – Allgemeiner Teil* [Criminal Law – General Part], Vol. 1, 3rd edn. (Munich, Beck 1997), chapter 24 margin Nos. 26 et seq. There is some controversy on the special circumstances in which the third party's conduct is still attributable. Eliminating results by negating their attributability according to the view proposed here will exclude from criminal jurisdiction most of the cases for which other authors mention criteria specifying the foreseeability of criminal jurisdiction in a certain country. Cf. Kienle, op. cit. n. 25, p. 102 et seq.

[69] See H. Lenckner and W. Perron, commentary on s. 184 *StGB*, in A. Schönke and H. Schröder, eds., *StGB. Kommentar* [The Criminal Code. A Commentary], 26th edn. (Munich, Beck 2001), margin No. 9.

An expansion of the 'result inherent to the offense' beyond the location of the server cannot be argued for by liberally interpreting the term 'making accessible' on account of the easy accessibility of data in global cyberspace. The above-mentioned aspects of attribution and the parallel with the distribution of physical documents run contrary to such reasoning. Indeed, if one were to include the location of retrieval by a third party as the location of the act of 'making accessible', it would follow that the operator of a newspaper standing just beyond the German border would also be liable for making pornography accessible if crossing the border and obtaining pornographic material from him is 'easily' possible from Germany. A document is therefore only made accessible at a location where the offender reproduces it – be it in corporeal or incorporeal form. Along the lines of an old decision by the Reichsgericht, an incorporeal communication occurs at any location where the sound waves of a shout are audible or the electromagnetic waves of a broadcasting station can be received.[70] In contrast, no communication occurs in Germany if data has to be obtained from a foreign country by corporeal transport or incorporeal retrieval. An expansive interpretation of 'making accessible' would also mean that the German law-enforcement authorities would be forced to prosecute any illegal content located anywhere in the world just because it is accessible from Germany.[71]

Distinction between push and pull techniques

The technical distinction between 'push techniques', in which data from a foreign country are actively transmitted to a computer system in Germany, and 'pull techniques', in which data are 'fetched' from a foreign country,[72] is essential for determining the location where Internet documents are 'made accessible'.[73] This difference between push and pull techniques is decisive in the area of speech of-

---

[70] See *RGSt* 20, 146, 147 et seq. In 1889, the Reichsgericht had to adjudicate a case in which the 'seditious' shout 'Vive la France' was uttered in France and could be heard some 200 meters away on the other side of the German border.

[71] Cf., *infra*, section 9.4.3.

[72] It is worth noting that the EU Court of Justice made the same distinction in the definition of 'transfer' (of personal data into third countries). In *Lindqvist* (judgment of 6 November 2003, C-101/01 at No. 71), the Court held 'that there is no transfer [of data] to a third country within the meaning of Article 25 of Directive 95/46 where an individual in a Member State loads personal data onto an internet page which is stored with his hosting provider which is established in that State or in another Member State, thereby making those data accessible to anyone who connects to the internet, including people in a third country.'

[73] In the BGH decision already mentioned (*BGHSt* 47, 55 (59), n. 66), the court explicitly overruled the distinction between 'push' and 'pull', arguing that for an 'Internet-specific definition of "distribution"', no differentiation should be made between the transmission of data into the storage medium of a user by a vendor and the potential access to the data on the part of the user. Without any further reasoning, the court stated that the technical processes of uploading data by the vendor on the part of the user (push) and downloading the data being offered by the user himself (pull) 'are inextricably linked' and can therefore 'hardly be differentiated from one another'. As a rule, however, it can be clearly determined who initiates some data transmission. The purported area of transition does not exist.

fenses, especially as regards the basic premise that the battle against illegal content in computer networks can only be conducted in the country where the respective server is located. An application of German criminal law to foreign providers of web pages, located for instance on American servers, would not be reasonable. As no influence upon the providers of such contents could be exerted from Germany, criminal law would fail to effect behavioral control.

Therefore, a broader application of German criminal law can only be assumed if, in individual cases, the prerequisites exist for the participation of a person acting from a foreign country in a German domestic offense in accordance with section 9(2) clause 1 *StGB*.[74] The 'intentional action' or 'vested interest' of an offender acting from a foreign country must be taken into consideration here, for example, and not in the unsubstantiated limitation of a too widely conceived result theory of abstract endangerment offenses. In a considerable overexpansion of the principle of territoriality, German criminal law is applicable, according to section 9(2) clause 2 *StGB*[75] with regard to transnational participation, even if the act is not punishable in the foreign jurisdiction.[76] Bypassing German criminal law by relocating servers to 'legal oases' can therefore be effectively counteracted without forcing German criminal-prosecution agencies to play the role of 'global police officers' in the world of cyberspace by extending the application of German criminal law across-the-board to all globally retrievable content in the Internet.

9.3.3 The BGH decision in the *Toben* case

The facts of the case and the court's analysis

The BGH followed at least the basic approach of this newer conception in its first and only decision regarding cybercrime jurisdiction.[77] As already mentioned above, this decision concerned the case of an Australian citizen, Fredrick Toben, who posted web pages on his Australian web server in which he denied the Holocaust. Such material is punishable in Germany – and, similarly, according to Swiss[78] and Aus-

[74] 'Incitement or accessoryship is committed not only at the place where the act was committed, but also at every place where the inciter or accessory acted or, in case of an omission, should have acted or where, according to his understanding, the act should have been committed.'

[75] 'If the inciter or accessory in an act abroad acted domestically, then German criminal law shall apply to the incitement or accessoryship, even if the act is not punishable according to the law of the place of its commission.'

[76] For criticism of this provision, see H. Jung, 'Die Inlandsteilnahme an ausländischer strafloser Haupttat' [Domestic Participation in a Non-Criminal Extraterritorial Act], *Juristenzeitung* (1979), pp. 325-332.

[77] Judgment of 12 December 2000 – 1 StR 184/00, *BGHSt* 46, 212, available at <http://www.oefre.unibe.ch/law/dfr/bs046212.html>.

[78] Art. 261bis *Swiss StGB* (Criminal Code), available at <http://www.admin.ch/ch/d/sr/311_0/a261bis.html>. Art. 171c Swiss *MilitärStGB* (Military Criminal Code) contains a similarly worded prohibition for persons subject to military law.

trian[79] law – not only because it disparages the memory of the victims of the Holocaust (s. 189 *StGB*) and insults its survivors (s. 185 *StGB*), but also because the denial of the Holocaust may threaten public peace as proscribed by section 130(1) paragraph 2 and/or section 130(3) *StGB*. Section 130 *StGB* provides, with reference to the definition of genocide contained in section 6(1) *Völkerstrafgesetzbuch* (Code of Crimes Against International Law), that:

> '(1) Whoever, in a manner that is capable of disturbing the public peace:
> 1. incites hatred against segments of the population or calls for violent or arbitrary measures against them; or
> 2. assaults the human dignity of others by insulting, maliciously maligning, or defaming segments of the population,
> shall be punished with imprisonment from three months to five years. (...)
>
> (3) Whoever publicly or in a meeting approves of, denies or renders harmless an act committed under the rule of National Socialism of the type indicated in section 6(1) *VölkerStGB*, in a manner capable of disturbing the public peace shall be punished with imprisonment for not more than five years or a fine.'

In Australia, at the time at which Toben was being prosecuted in Germany, the denial of the Holocaust was merely 'unlawful' and subject to administrative-law sanctions, but not criminal.[80] Despite this legal situation in his home country, Toben was taken into pre-trial custody during a stay in Germany and convicted on three counts by the Landgericht (District Court) of Mannheim.[81]

- On the basis of an open letter sent to German addressees, he was convicted of 'agitation of the people' in coincidence with 'insult' and 'disparagement of the memory of deceased persons'.
- On the basis of two on-line publications stored on the Australian web server, he was only convicted of 'insult' in coincidence with 'disparagement of the memory of deceased persons'. With regard to the offense of 'agitation of the people', the Court denied jurisdiction, since the crimes were committed outside of Germany: Toben had acted in Australia and no result had occurred in Germany.

Both Toben and the prosecutor filed an appeal against this conviction. The BGH held, contrary to the opinion of the trial court, that the 'result inherent to the offense' of section 130(3) *StGB* in the legal sense of section 9(1) 3rd alternative *StGB* could not be equated with the definition of 'result' found in the *Tatbestandslehre*,

[79] S. 3h *Verbotsgesetz* 1947 (Prohibition Act), outlawing Nazi organizations and associated activities.

[80] See chapter 4, section 4.2.3.

[81] Landgericht Mannheim, 11 November 1999, Az. 5 KLs 503 Js 9551/99, available at <http://www.afs-rechtsanwaelte.de/urteile84.htm>.

but must rather be reasoned according to the *ratio legis* of section 9 *StGB*.[82] According to the BGH, the purpose of this provision was that – even when a criminal act has been committed in a foreign country – German courts should have jurisdiction if domestic legal interests protected by the offense in question have been damaged or endangered.[83] The BGH left open the question of where the location of the criminal result should be generally localized in the case of abstract endangerment offenses. Instead, it classified sections 130(1)-(2) *StGB* as *abstrakt-konkrete Gefährdungsdelikte* ('abstract-specific endangerment offenses'), because it is an element of both offenses that the offender incites hatred (para. 1) or approves, denies, or renders harmless the Holocaust (para. 3) 'in a manner capable of disturbing the public peace.' According to the BGH, the wording of the statute requires a 'specific capability of disturbing the public peace in the Federal Republic of Germany', which the court qualified as a 'result inherent to the offense' in the legal sense of section 9(1) 3rd alternative *StGB*.[84]

Although the web pages that formed the basis of the charge had been published exclusively in English and it was obvious that Toben had not purposefully forwarded ('pushed') the material from Australia to German Internet users (as opposed to the above-mentioned letters), but had merely enabled German Internet users to download them from his Australian web server, in the opinion of the BGH, the reference to the Holocaust as a part of German history and the corresponding link to public peace especially in Germany was sufficient to provide legitimate grounds for jurisdiction.[85] The BGH thus rejected the differentiation between 'push' and 'pull' techniques, the application of which would have had to result in an acquittal of the accused.[86] With regard to the other two offenses – insulting and disparagement of the memory of deceased persons – the BGH only briefly stated that a location of criminal result was given in Germany, at least since the investigating police officers had gained knowledge of the web site's contents.[87]

---

[82] In this respect, the BGH explicitly agreed with my approach set forth in Sieber, 'Internationales Strafrecht im Internet' ['Criminal Law Jurisdiction and the Internet'], *Neue Juristische Wochenschrift* (1999), pp. 2065-2073 at pp. 2068-2069.

[83] *BGHSt* 46, 212, 220.

[84] Ibid., 212, 221.

[85] Idem, 212, 224. Unfortunately, it is not clear whether these remarks were intended to support the *ratio decidendi* – the reasoning that the capability to disturb public peace in Germany qualifies as a 'result' (which, of course, occurred in Germany) – or whether these remarks form an additional argument because it was felt that the other argument was too weak.

[86] The BGH expressly mentioned my approach (cf., n. 82) and stated that, in the case at hand, it would have led to answering the question of a German location of the criminal result in the negative.

[87] It is generally agreed that for an insult (or disparagement) to be completed, the speech must be noticed. This qualifies as a *Tathandlungserfolg* (effect of the criminal act), which would – if a 'push' technique had been employed – constitute a *locus criminis*.

Criticism

The decision might be acceptable if the definition of the offense in sections 130(1) and (3) *StGB* in fact required a *Tathandlungserfolg* (effect of the criminal act) of disturbing public peace in Germany (and if, of course, such a disturbance of public peace had occurred). This would be the case if it was required that (1) the offender denies the Holocaust and *by so doing* (2) *actually* disturbs public peace in Germany. However, the actual wording of the statute does not mention a disturbance of public peace as an element of the offense; rather, it requires, as an attribute of the criminal act, that the denial occurs *in such a way as to be capable of* disturbing public peace. This describes an attribute of the criminal act and, as a *restriction* of the criminalized conduct, is intended to eliminate harmless speech, but it cannot be interpreted to constitute a 'result' of the criminal act even in the broadest sense.[88]

One of the justices who passed the judgment in *Toben* told the author of this chapter in a personal conversation that the line of reasoning followed in this specific case involving section 130 *StGB* was not intended to serve as a general rule for future cases of dissemination or speech offenses. Indeed, there are other relevant offenses where even such 'workarounds' would not be possible. When a mere action like 'making accessible' some material or 'using symbols' of unconstitutional organizations constitutes the offense (*Tätigkeitsdelikt*), there is no element of the offense beside the offender's conduct that could be construed to be some form of 'result inherent to the offense' of that conduct.[89] For example, the Kammergericht (Regional Court) of Berlin had to adjudicate a case where German hooligans displayed the so-called Hitler salute at a soccer match in Poland that was broadcast on German TV.[90] The court recognized that the wording 'use' does not entail any result and accordingly argued by way of an extension of the location of the criminal act to all places where the Hitler salute in question could be seen on TV, which was of course also the case in Germany.[91]

9.4 Results and Consequences

9.4.1 **Result with respect to present law**

As seen above, according to sections 5-7 *StGB*, German criminal law applies to specific offenses regardless of the *locus criminis*. Apart from these special cases, however, the applicability of German law according to sections 3 and 9 *StGB* depends on whether the offender 'acted' from within Germany (s. 9(1) 1st alternative

---

[88] See H. Kudlich, *Strafverteidiger* (2001), pp. 397-399.

[89] Using a symbol implies that it can be perceived optically or acoustically, while it is not relevant whether anybody actually perceived the display or utterance, see *BGHSt* 23, 267, 268.

[90] Kammergericht, *Neue Juristische Wochenschrift* (1999), 3500 et seq.

[91] The BGH did not overrule this decision, but expressed clear skepticism towards such an extensive interpretation of the criminal act in *BGHSt* 46, 212, 224 et seq.

StGB) or whether the 'result inherent to the offense' (s. 9(1) 3rd alternative *StGB*) occurred within Germany. If the location of the criminal act continues to be defined as the physical location of the offender (in accordance with prevailing human thought), then the scope of the German criminal law with regard to cases of dissemination offenses and speech offenses carried out in foreign countries will be determined by how the 'result inherent to the offense' in the legal sense of section 9(1) 3rd alternative *StGB* is interpreted.

In determining the location of the criminal result in accordance with section 9 *StGB*, any attempt to understand the term 'criminal result' in the sense of result crimes and then to contrive exceptions to the rule (which are not further substantiated for abstract endangerment offenses lacking such a tangible result), in order to arrive at a location of the criminal result for such offenses is unsustainable. The ensuing discussion on the location of the criminal result of abstract endangerment offenses – however they are defined – is a superfluous detour caused by '*Begriffsjurisprudenz*'.

In fact, as with other provisions in the Criminal Code, the criminal result in the legal sense of section 9(1) 3rd alternative *StGB* should be determined individually and independently from the *Tatbestandslehre* (general theory of the definition of criminal offenses). According to the wording and *ratio legis* of sections 3 and 9 *StGB* and the subjective goal of the legislators, this definition of criminal result would incorporate every offense-related consequence of criminal conduct that is inherent to the offense activities and that can be attributed to the offender. Therefore, in cases in which the offender acts outside Germany, the question whether an offense falls within the jurisdiction of German criminal law is not dependent on the shaky classification of an offense as a result crime or abstract endangerment offense. Rather, the crucial point is if a *Tathandlungserfolg* (effect of the criminal act) occurs that is inherent to the offense. Such a *Tathandlungserfolg* occurs on the Internet when the 'making accessible' of documents in the context of the abovementioned dissemination and speech offenses is effected by using push technologies to transmit data to Germany. No such *Tathandlungserfolg* exists, however, if the data are only stored on foreign servers and can be retrieved by third parties in Germany by means of pull technologies.

9.4.2 **Evaluation of the present legal situation**

The result at hand is based primarily on the fact that – at least *de lege lata* – the territoriality principle restricts the possibility of criminal prosecution to cases in which the offender himself commits criminal acts or brings about a criminal result within the territory of a given jurisdiction. This interpretation of the 'making accessible' of illegal contents is advantageous, because the application of criminal sanctions cannot be extended to cases in which the relevant technical processes occur abroad and where it is therefore unfeasible to implement effective national criminal prosecution.

However, this interpretation of the territoriality principle does not lead to satisfactory results at present. It enables offenders to provide content that is illegal according to domestic law, on foreign servers without risking punishment, even though the specific nature of the Internet makes the content just as accessible as if it were stored on a domestic server. Such a general rejection of any domestic jurisdiction in these cases is not convincing, because the relationship to protected national interests can be so close that a reaction on the part of domestic criminal law is warranted and appropriate. This would be the case, for example, if the offender used a foreign web site purposefully to address domestic Internet users with native-language content, even if he does not cause an attributable *Tathandlungserfolg* (effect of the criminal act) in the sense of the approach expounded above.

If the reasons for the unsatisfactory present situation are analyzed, it becomes apparent that they stem from the fundamental incompatibility of the Internet's global nature with the traditional notions of state territoriality in the concept of jurisdiction: The most relevant provisions in sections 3 and 9 *StGB* are based on the concept of a corporeal world in which objects, actions, and changes can be clearly allocated to a particular territory under the sovereignty of a particular state. This concept can include cross-border acts and acts affecting several countries, so long as they have a physical effect and lead to specific determinable changes. However, this concept is no longer suitable for global cyberspace.[92] While the 'virtual' space of the Internet can still be attributed to individual state territories upon an analysis of its physical components (computer systems, network nodes, and circuitry), these physical classifications lose their meaning when viewed functionally. When viewing a web page or downloading data from an FTP server, it is irrelevant whether the server storing the data is located domestically or in a foreign country. The transmission of an e-mail is also arbitrary and may be routed via foreign territory by the transmission technology just as arbitrarily; the mail server from which the recipient eventually retrieves the message need not be located within the recipient's own country. In peer-to-peer networks, a document may even be stored on a number of computer systems all over the world without making any difference to the user. As a consequence, any 'localization' of this 'virtual' space that is not linked to tangible effects outside of the network but only to its physical components (e.g., servers or routers) is thus only a constructed aid. Thus, the traditional law on jurisdiction,

[92] The problem is not confined to the Internet – it already occurs in relation to conventional radio and television broadcasts. However, with regard to these services, adequate and feasible legal solutions have already been found at a supranational and international level. See in particular the European Directive 89/552/EEC 'Television without Frontiers' (*OJ* L298, 16 November 1989) amended by Directive 97/36/EC (*OJ* L202, 30 July 1997). This directive stipulates that broadcasts must be in compliance only with the country of transmission's legal regime. It also establishes minimum standards for advertising, teleshopping, the protection of minors, etc. Similar provisions can also be found in the European Convention on Transfrontier Television by the Council of Europe of 5 May 1989 (CETS 132).

which is based upon the principle of territoriality, can no longer provide satisfactory answers to the relevant issues.

For this reason, in order to change the situation, additional and specific rules of jurisdiction for the Internet and the global realm of cyberspace must be established, which, for example, are based on the aspect of specific endangerment to national interests. However, so far as such regulations are enforceable in practice and do not create international conflicts of laws, they must become part of a solution that goes far beyond the definition of the sovereign territorial right of states to apply sanctions to Internet crime. Space constraints allow for such a solution only to be touched upon in the outlook of the present chapter.

9.4.3 Basic principles for the future development of jurisdiction in cyberspace

The development of appropriate regulations for jurisdiction in cyberspace must assume that the Internet poses a series of new, Internet-specific challenges to the traditional approach of the law of jurisdiction. The distribution of illegal content shows that the national interest of a country is not only hampered or endangered by certain criminal acts committed on its territory or causing results on its territory, but that the same dangers are also present through criminal conduct, in which both the act and the result take place solely in a foreign country. As the Internet enables quick and uncomplicated access to content stored both locally and abroad, it is immaterial for the threat to national interests whether the on-line content is made available on local or foreign servers.

Against this backdrop, it is understandable and indeed justifiable that national legal systems *de lege ferenda* wish to extend their jurisdiction to data located on foreign servers accessible via the Internet. If one attempts to understand these cases as an 'extraterritorial' application of national law, then one should strive to narrow them down to situations involving specific endangerments to national states, for example, if according to objective external circumstances or the subjective goals of the offender, the content placed on the Internet is specifically targeted at recipients in a particular country. By methodically following the universality principle, restrictions of jurisdiction to particularly serious offenses (like the dissemination of child pornography) are also possible. In order to avoid overloading national prosecution authorities, the principle of discretionary prosecution and not the principle of mandatory prosecution should apply to such cases.[93] In addition, the distribution

[93] In Germany, discretionary prosecution is limited to exceptional circumstances. According to s. 153 *Strafprozessordnung* (*StPO*, Code of Criminal Procedure), the public prosecutor may refrain from prosecuting a misdemeanor if the guilt of the offender may be considered minimal and prosecution is not in the public interest. If the effects of the crime are not limited to German territory, further narrowly defined exceptions apply: s. 153c para. 2 *StPO* permits the prosecution to cease further criminal proceedings if the offender has already been tried in a foreign jurisdiction. In accordance with s. 153c para. 3 *StPO*, prosecutorial restraint may also be exercised if the result inherent to the offense occurs in

of illegal content through the Internet as well as the spreading of viruses and worms and denial-of-service attacks make it glaringly apparent that cybercrime offenses affect a plethora of countries in exactly the same way. This requires additional regulations for avoiding conflicts with a multitude of applicable laws. As a consequence of all these special questions, the Internet-specific rules of jurisdiction can no longer be justified on the basis of existing law in many legal systems, but rather must be developed on the basis of new Internet-specific laws.

However, in these cases, not only questions of substantive jurisdiction arise. Abstaining from excessive extraterritorial prosecution – which exists extensively on paper but is hardly enforceable in practice – will only be truly possible if it can be ensured that another country will effectively prosecute the alleged criminal offense. In many cybercrime cases, only one or a few countries may be in a position to prosecute effectively, and enforcing national laws in a foreign country remains particularly problematic. Therefore, aside from regulating a country's sovereign right to apply criminal sanctions, a system ought to be created that would enable a prosecution worldwide (where feasible) for serious forms of Internet crime. For that reason, serious Internet-related crime should be subject to international minimum standards of substantive law and to internationally defined criminal coercive powers and other procedural rules, as well as provisions of international co-operation. In augmenting this process, care should be taken to ensure that these regulations are effective in practice (as is the case in the campaign against money laundering via peer-review methods by the Financial Action Task Force). To this end, the normative approaches of the Convention on Cybercrime of the Council of Europe and the practice-oriented work of the G8 Work Group on High-Tech Crime could possibly be merged and further developed.

9.4.4 Conclusions for legal policy

The subject-matter discussed here does not only affect the possibilities of applying criminal sanctions; it goes much deeper. The difficulties posed by dissemination of illegal content and speech offenses, and by many other computer-crime offenses that occur in the global arena of cyberspace are derived from the facts that national borders have become meaningless in the technical reality of the Internet, and that border controls to fend off illegal content are presently impossible, both for technical and policy reasons. Because traditional territorial borders can no longer ward off harm, global cyberspace cannot be regulated solely by national laws. Today, neither comprehensive control measures nor extensive legal provisions in the area

---

Germany, but the act is initiated in a foreign country and the conduct of proceedings would pose the risk of serious detriment to the Federal Republic of Germany, or if other predominant public interests present an obstacle to prosecution. The legislative intent of this provision was to deal with extraordinary situations, such as the liberation of hostages, which should not be endangered by prosecution. If none of these exceptions apply, the prosecution of all triable offenses is mandatory in accordance with s. 152 para. 2 *StPO*.

of jurisdiction can, for example, prevent a German user from downloading Internet content that is legal in the United States but illegal in Germany, from an American server.[94] As a consequence, the accessibility of content considered legal in foreign countries cannot be prevented in any corner of the globe today without internationally recognized minimum penal standards, adequate provisions of procedural law, and the implementation of these with the help of international agreements. Thus, aside from the adequate right of sovereign states to apply penal sanctions, global cyberspace – established by the worldwide reach of computer networks – requires a global criminal-law response in which Internet-specific regulations governing the scope of individual national criminal jurisdictions are complemented by minimum standards of substantive and procedural criminal law as well as by provisions of international co-operation.[95]

Bibliography

K. Bremer, *Strafbare Internet-Inhalte in internationaler Hinsicht* [Illegal Internet Content from an International Perspective] (Frankfurt, Peter Lang 2001).

B. Breuer, 'Anwendbarkeit des deutschen Strafrechts auf extraterritorial handelnde Internet-Benutzer' [Applying German Criminal Law to Internet Users Acting Extraterritorially], *Multimedia-Recht* (1998), pp. 141-144.

K. Cornils, 'Der Begehungsort von Äußerungsdelikten im Internet' [The *Locus Criminis* of Speech Offenses on the Internet], *Juristenzeitung* (1999), pp. 394-398.

R. Derksen, 'Strafrechtliche Verantwortung für in internationalen Computernetzen verbreitete Daten mit strafbarem Inhalt' [Criminal Liability for the Dissemination of Illegal Data in International Computer Networks], *Neue Juristische Wochenschrift* (1997), pp. 1878-1885.

C. Engel, 'Inhaltskontrolle im Internet' [Controlling Content on the Internet], *Archiv für Presserecht* (1996), pp. 220-227.

B. Heinrich, 'Der Erfolgsort beim abstrakten Gefährdungsdelikt' [The Location of the Criminal Result in Abstract Endangerment Offenses], *Goltdammer's Archiv für Strafrecht* (1999), pp. 72-84.

E. Hilgendorf, 'Überlegungen zur strafrechtlichen Interpretation des Ubiquitätsprinzips im Zeitalter des Internet' [Thoughts on the Interpretation of the Ubiquity Principle of Criminal Law in the Age of The Internet], *Neue Juristische Wochenschrift* (1997), pp. 1873-1878.

---

[94] For technical details, see U. Sieber, *Verantwortlichkeit im Internet* [Liability on the Internet] (Munich, Beck 1999), margin Nos. 399 et seq. For this reason and in order to create a common market within the EU, national preventative measures and the extensive application of national criminal law are being replaced by new substantive legal regulations based on the 'country of origin' principle in the E-Commerce Directive. See Art. 3 of the Directive 2000/31/EC (*OJ* L178, 17 July 2000).

[95] For such approaches, cf., U. Sieber, 'Auf dem Weg zu einem europäischen Strafrecht' [En-Route Towards a European Criminal Law], in M. Delmas-Marty, ed., *Corpus Juris der strafrechtlichen Regelungen zum Schutz der finanziellen Interessen der Europäischen Union* [Corpus Juris of Penal Provisions for the Protection of European Union Finances] (Cologne etc., Heymann 1999).

J.D.W. Klengel and A. Heckler, 'Geltung des deutschen Strafrechts für vom Ausland aus im Internet angebotenes Glücksspiel' [German Criminal Jurisdiction over Online Gambling Offered on the Internet from Abroad], *Computer und Recht* (2001), pp. 243-249.

M. Kienle, *Internationales Strafrecht und Straftaten im Internet* [Criminal Jurisdiction and Offenses on the Internet] (Constance, Hartung-Gorre 1998).

F. Körber, *Rechtsradikale Propaganda im Internet – der Fall Töben* [Right Wing Extremist Propaganda on the Internet – The Toben Case] (Berlin, Logos Verlag 2003).

C. Kuner, 'Internationale Zuständigkeitskonflikte im Internet' [Jurisdictional Conflicts on the Internet], *Computer und Recht* (1996), pp. 453-458.

T. Lehle, *Der Erfolgsbegriff und die deutsche Strafrechtszuständigkeit im Internet* [The Concept of Result and German Jurisdiction on the Internet] (Constance, Hartung-Gorre 1999).

E. Mezger, 'Der Anwendungsbereich des deutschen Strafrechts' [The Scope of Application of German Criminal Law], *Deutsches Recht* (1940), pp. 1076-1079.

K. Ringel, 'Rechtsextremistische Propaganda aus dem Ausland im Internet' [Right-Extremist Propaganda from Abroad on the Internet], *Computer und Recht* (1997), pp. 302-307.

H. Satzger, 'Die Anwendung des deutschen Strafrechts auf grenzüberschreitende Gefährdungsdelikte' [The Application of German Criminal Law to Transborder Endangerment Offenses], *Neue Zeitschrift für Strafrecht* (1998), pp. 112-117.

U. Sieber, 'Strafrechtliche Verantwortlichkeit für den Datenverkehr in internationalen Computernetzen', *Juristenzeitung* (1996) pp. 429-442 and 494-507; English translation: 'Criminal Liability for the Transfer of Data in International Networks – New Challenges for the Internet', 13 *Computer Law & Security Report* (1997), pp. 151-157, 223-233, 312-318, and 413-418; 14 *Computer Law & Security Report* (1998), pp. 22-28.

U. Sieber, 'Kontrollmöglichkeiten zur Verhinderung rechtswidriger Inhalte in Computernetzen', *Computer und Recht* (1997), pp. 581-598 and 653-669; English translation: 'Control Possibilities for the Prevention of Criminal Content in Computer Networks', 15 *Computer Law and Security Report* (1999), pp. 34-39, 90-100, and 168-180.

U. Sieber, *Legal Aspects of Computer-Related Crime in the Information Society. COMCRIME Study*, version 1.0, January 1, 1998, available at <http://www.jura.uni-muenchen.de/einrichtungen/ls/sieber/article/comcrime/comcrime_www.pdf>.

U. Sieber, 'Strafrecht und Strafprozeßrecht' [Criminal Law and Criminal Procedure], in: T. Hoeren & U. Sieber, eds., *Handbuch Multimedia-Recht* [Handbook on Multimedia Law] (Munich, Beck 1999).

U. Sieber, *Verantwortlichkeit im Internet* [Liability on the Internet] (Munich, Beck 1999).

Comments on BGH 12 December 2000 – 1 StR 184/00 (the *Toben* case)

F. Clauss, *MultiMedia Recht* (2001), pp. 232-233.

T. Hörnle, *Neue Zeitschrift für Strafrecht* (2001), pp. 309-311.

F. Jessberger, *Juristische Rundschau* (2001), pp. 432-435.

A. Koch, *Juristische Schulung* (2002), pp. 123-127.

H. Kudlich, *Strafverteidiger* (2001), pp. 397-399.

O. Lagodny, *Juristenzeitung* (2001), pp. 1198-1200.

I. Vassilaki, *Computer und Recht* (2001), pp. 262-265.

M. Vec, *Neue Juristische Wochenschrift* (2002), pp. 1535-1539.

Chapter 10
CYBERCRIME AND JURISDICTION IN INDIA

Pavan Duggal*

10.1 Introduction

India is a land of unity and diversity and has a culture that spans over thousands of years. In the modern age, India achieved independence from the British on 15th August 1947. The Preamble to the Constitution of India has declared India as a 'sovereign, socialist, secular, democratic, republic'.

A commercial Internet service was introduced on 15th August 1995 by the state-owned Videsh Sanchar Nigam Limited (VSNL). The beginnings of Internet in India were small and the pace of growth slow. It took time for Internet to really catch on with the people.

In the beginning, the growth of Internet use was very slow. However, the late 1990s saw a spurt in the number of cyber-cafes in the country. Thus, with increasingly cheap access to the Internet available through cyber-cafes in India, the number of Internet users in India has grown remarkably. At this juncture, let us look at the facts and figures concerning PC penetration in India in the past decade.[1]

Table 10.1 – *PC Penetration in India*

	Mar-97	Mar-98	Mar-99	Mar-00	Mar-01	Mar-02	Mar-03	Mar-04	Mar-05
Population (million)	961	977	993	1010	1027	1089	1156	1226	1301
(PC penetration) per 1,000 population	1.63	2.17	2.83	3.72	4.94	5.38	7.16	9.19	12.72

The growth in Internet use in India and its ready adoption by Indians has meant a significant advancement, given a strong Information Technology and software in-

* Pavan Duggal is an Advocate at the Supreme Court of India, the Founder and President of Cyberlaw Asia, and the President of Cyberlaws.Net.

[1] <http://www.nasscom.org/it_industry/internet_trends.asp>.

B-J. Koops and S.W. Brenner (Eds), Cybercrime and Jurisdiction

dustry in India. However, the other side of the coin is that Indians, like citizens of other countries, are beginning to use the Internet and the electronic medium for unauthorized access and new categories of cybercrimes.

It is important to note that cybercrimes in India are on the increase with each passing day. According to one estimate by Project India Cracked, between February 2000 and December 2002, Indian government and corporate web sites have been hacked and defaced about 780 times.[2] However, the problem area is the great amount of under-reporting of cybercrimes in India. This is the main reason why no study on cybercrimes really reflects the correct picture of the exact extent of cybercrimes in India.

A large number of cybercrimes have been reported in the media. It is pertinent to note that the Indian press appears to have a fondness for reporting cybercrimes. The early cases of Internet crimes in India were reported extensively and gained a lot of attention. The early days of cybercrimes reporting also jolted the conscience of the lawmakers. Thus, there was felt to be a need to legally regulate cybercrime.

10.2 Indian Cybercrime Legislation

India has a very comprehensive system of penal legislation, namely, the Indian Penal Code of 1860.[3] Understandably, given the era during which it was adopted, the Indian Penal Code does not specifically cover cybercrimes. It was drafted by the British, who then occupied India, three years after the First War of Indian Independence in 1857. At that time, the legislators could not be faulted for not having thought of the Internet, since the Internet could not have been visualized at that point of time. The various challenges that criminal exploitation of computer networks and the Internet throws up are not, therefore, effectively addressed under the Penal Code of 1860.

The Penal Code has been amended by the Indian Information Technology Act, 2000. However, the said amendments are purely related to making certain categories of offences under the Indian Penal Code applicable to electronic records. This is the reason why there was felt to be a need for including a distinct chapter on cybercrime in India's first cyberlaw.

India's first cyberlaw was enacted in 2000. This is the Indian Information Technology Act, 2000 (hereafter: IT Act).[4] This was passed by both Houses of Parliament on 17th May 2000. It received the assent of the President on 9th June 2000 and was finally implemented on 17th October 2000.

[2] See Project Indian Cracked, <www.srijith.net/indiacracked/stats/index.shtml>.

[3] The Indian Penal Code (Act No. 45 of 1860), available at <http://www.indialawinfo.com/bareacts/ipc.html>.

[4] The Information Technology Act, 2000 (No. 22 of 2000), available at <http://www.mit.gov.in/itbill2000.pdf>. The Indian Information Technology Rules, 2000 can be found at <http://www.mit.gov.in/rules/act2000.pdf>.

The Indian cyberlaw embodies the Indian legal response to the emerging challenges of cybercrime. Chapter XI of the IT Act, entitled 'Offences', is the relevant chapter that deals with cybercrimes and investigation powers.[5] This chapter details certain specified kinds of acts that have been designated as cybercrimes. These acts have been declared penal offences, which are made punishable with imprisonment and fines (the fines declared are in the Indian denominations, one lakh rupees being Rs 100,000 – approximately US$ 2,380).

Let us now examine the relevant provisions of Chapter XI of the Information Technology Act, 2000.

10.2.1 Substantive law

Chapter XI of the IT Act addresses only certain kinds of cybercrimes. The first category of cybercrimes which it addresses deals with the issue of unauthorized access and hacking. As in other countries, the criminalizing of such conduct is to emphasize the need to protect the integrity of computer systems and the data resident therein.

Causing damage to a computer source code is an offence under section 65 IT Act. Anyone who knowingly or intentionally conceals, destroys, or alters any computer source code, when the source code is required to be kept or maintained by any law currently in force, is brought within the ambit of the penalty. This offence is made punishable with imprisonment for up to three years, or with a fine of up to two lakh rupees, or with both.

As noted above, hacking is criminalized by section 66 IT Act. This offence involves the following elements:

1. there should be intent on the part of the accused to cause wrongful loss or damage to the public or any person, or
2. there should be knowledge of or attributable to the accused that he is likely to cause wrongful loss or damage to the public or any person. Moreover,
3. the accused must destroy or delete or alter any information residing in a computer resource, or
4. the accused must diminish the value or utility of any information residing in a computer resource, or
5. the accused must affect any information residing in a computer resource injuriously by any means.

If one of the first two *and* one of the last three of these conditions are satisfied, then that constitutes the offence of hacking within the meaning of section 66 IT Act.

Any person who breaches a protected system leaves himself open to criminal liability under section 70 IT Act. Anyone who accesses or attempts to access a

[5] Information Technology Act, 2000 at pp. 20-23.

protected system commits an offense and can be punished with imprisonment for a term of up to ten years and can also be fined.

On-line obscenity is addressed in section 67 IT Act. This provision deals with the offence of publishing or transmitting obscene electronic information. Even causing obscene electronic information to be published is criminalized. The punishment for this offence on first conviction is imprisonment for a term of up to five years and with a fine of up to one lakh rupees. In the event of a second or subsequent conviction, the quantum of imprisonment and fine are both doubled.

The law also criminalizes some acts relating to Digital Signature Certificates. Section 68 IT Act criminalizes a failure to comply with the orders of the Controller of Certifying Authorities. The Controller may direct a Certifying Authority or any employee of such authority to take measures or to cease carrying on such activities as are specified in the Controller's order, if those are necessary to ensure compliance with the provisions of this Act, rules or any regulations made thereunder. Any person who fails to comply with the order passed under section 68 can be held liable for an offence and sentenced to imprisonment for a term not exceeding three years or to a fine not exceeding two lakh rupees or both.

Section 71 IT Act deals with misrepresenting or suppressing a material fact from the Controller of Certifying Authorities in order to obtain any license or Digital Signature Certificate. Section 73 criminalizes the publication of a Digital Signature Certificate that is false concerning certain particulars. Section 74 deals with the offence of publication of a Digital Signature Certificate for fraudulent or unlawful purposes. The punishment for all of these offences is imprisonment for up to two years, a fine of up to one lakh rupees, or both.

Breach of confidentiality and privacy by an authorized official under the IT Act is made punishable with imprisonment for a term of up to two years, with a fine of up to one lakh rupees, or with both (section 72 IT Act).

Finally, section 77 IT Act elaborates the issue of non-interference of penalties with other punishment. It provides that no penalty imposed or confiscation made under the Act shall prevent the imposition of any other punishment to which the person affected is thereby liable under any other law currently in force.

10.2.2 **Procedural law**

Section 78 IT Act deals with the power to investigate offences under the Indian cyberlaw. Section 78 provides that notwithstanding anything contained in the Code of Criminal Procedure, 1973, no police officer below the rank of Deputy Superintendent of Police shall investigate an offence under the IT Act.

The power to intercept communications is granted to the Controller of Certifying Authorities in India under section 69 IT Act. If the Controller is satisfied that it is necessary or expedient to do so in the interest of (i) the sovereignty or integrity of India, (ii) the security of the state, (iii) friendly relations with foreign states, (iv) public order, or (v) preventing incitement to the commission of any cognizable offence, then, for reasons that must be recorded in writing, the Controller can direct any agency of the government to intercept any information transmitted through any computer resource (section 69 para. 1).

Moreover, the subscriber or any person in charge of the computer resource must, when called upon by any agency which has received an order from the Controller under this section, extend all facilities and technical assistance to decrypt the information. Further, the section states that if the subscriber or any person fails to assist the agency referred to under this section, he shall be punished with imprisonment for a term of up to seven years (section 69 paras. 2 and 3).

Section 76 IT Act provides for the power of confiscation. Section 76 lays down the conditions under which any computer, computer system, floppies, compact disks, tape drives, or any other accessories related thereto that have been used to contravene any provision of the IT Act or any rules, orders or regulations made thereunder can be confiscated. It states that the above-described articles can be confiscated if it is established to the satisfaction of the court adjudicating the confiscation that the person in whose possession, power, or control any such article is found, has committed one of the violations described above. If it is determined that the possessor is not responsible for the offense, the court may, instead of ordering confiscation, make such other order authorized by this Act against the offender as it may think fit.

The Indian cyberlaw provides extensive powers to high-ranking police officials for the investigation of cybercrimes in India. Section 80 IT Act has possibly been the most discussed provision of this law. It has attracted a great deal of attention and generated immense debate. The debate on this provision was held on the Parliamentary floor at the time of the passing of the IT Bill and in various academic forums. This debate centers on the controversial power given to police officers, whose rank is Deputy Superintendent of Police (hereafter: DSP) or higher, to enter and search any public place and arrest without warrant any person who is reasonably suspected of having committed a cybercrime in India. Technically speaking, the DSP can search anywhere in India, but not abroad.

The Explanation to section 80(1) says that the term ‘public place’ includes any public conveyance such as a bus, train, aircraft, any hotel, any shop, or any other place intended for use by or accessible to the public. The definition of ‘public place’ in the explanation to section 80(1) is very wide and is likely to include numerous things within its ambit. For example, a hotel has been considered as a public place. It has not been specified which part of the hotel is a public place and thus, by implication, every portion of the hotel including the rooms booked by clients would come within the definition of public place. In addition, the legislature has used the words ‘any other place intended for use by, or accessible to the public’. This is a very wide definition of the term ‘public place’ and would include almost any place that is accessible to the public including offices, banks, chambers, hospitals and many others.

As per section 80, any police officer whose rank is DSP or higher, or any other authorized officer of the appropriate – central or state – government may enter any public place and search and arrest without warrant any person who is reasonably suspected of:

1. having committed any offence under the IT Act, or
2. committing any offence under the IT Act, or
3. being about to commit any offence under the IT Act.

This is an exceptional power.

Section 80(1) thus gives a DSP two distinct types of discretion. The first is the discretion to enter any public place and search and arrest any person without a warrant. The second is that a DSP can search and arrest without warrant anyone whom he reasonably suspects of having committed, of committing, or of being about to commit any offence under the IT Act. The new law has laid down no standards for exercising the discretion under section 80, and it is silent on the parameters for determining how the DSP should arrive at a reasonable suspicion about the person concerned. Many view the authority granted by section 80(1) as a serious violation of individual liberty and privacy.

Section 80(3) IT Act further states that the provisions of the Code of Criminal Procedure, 1973 shall apply in relation to any entry, search, or arrest subject to the provisions of section 80 IT Act. Thus, the legislature has given primacy to the power of the police under section 80(1) IT Act. It is further stated in section 81 IT Act that the provisions of the IT Act shall have effect, notwithstanding anything inconsistent therewith contained in any other law currently in force; this includes the Code of Criminal Procedure, 1973 (hereafter: CCP). Under the CCP, there is a definite procedure prescribed for entry, search, and arrest; the powers of entry, search, and arrest without warrant under section 80 IT Act, however, conflict with these, and therefore override the conflicting provisions of the CCP.

Nevertheless, provisions of the CCP that are not in conflict with the scheme envisaged by section 80 IT Act, shall apply in relation to any entry, search, or arrest made under section 80 IT Act. Thus, this means that though the DSP or any other officer of such rank can enter the public place and search and arrest, without warrant, any person found therein; he has to be joined, however, by two independent, respectable persons from the locality in order to ensure that the mandatory requirements of section 100 CCP are fulfilled.

It is also important to note that while the Code of Criminal Procedure gives the power of entry, search, and arrest to an investigating officer, that power can only be exercised after the investigating officer has followed the prescribed process. However, there are no such specified processes, restrictions, or parameters binding the DSP for exercising discretion under section 80(1). Also, the DSP is not mandated to record reasons in writing, prior to the exercise of such powers.

As far as network searches or infiltration into on-line porn networks are concerned, there is no information available in the public domain as to how often and to what extent these steps are taken. At the time of writing, no case of this kind has been reported in the public domain and, as such, there is a complete absence of case law in this regard in India.

10.3 Cybercrime Jurisdiction

10.3.1 Legal provisions

In India, there are also certain provisions that have a bearing on the issue of jurisdiction for cybercrimes and cyber-investigations. Section 3 of the Indian Penal Code, 1860 provides for the punishment of offences committed beyond India, but which, by law, may be tried within India.

> '*3. Punishment of offences committed beyond but which by law may be tried within India* – Any person liable by any Indian law to be tried for an offence committed beyond India shall be dealt with according to the provisions of this Code for any act committed beyond India in the same manner as if such act had been committed within India.'

Section 4 of the Indian Penal Code provides for an extension of the provisions of the Code to extraterritorial offences:

> 'The provisions of this Code apply also to any offence committed by –
> (1) any citizen of India in any place without and beyond India;
> (2) any person on any ship or aircraft registered in India wherever it may be.
>
> *Explanation* – In this section the word 'offence' includes every act committed outside India which, if committed in India, would be punishable under this Code.'

Clearly, cybercrime brings along with it numerous issues concerning jurisdiction. The Indian legislators were possibly aware of the potential challenges that the tricky subject of jurisdiction would pose. That is the reason why they have adopted two distinct provisions relating to jurisdiction, in sections 1(2) and 75 IT Act.

Normally, the applicability of laws within India can be broadly divided into the following major categories: laws applicable to all states of India barring Jammu & Kashmir; laws applicable only to Jammu & Kashmir; and laws applicable to the entire country. Jammu & Kashmir has been granted a special status under the Constitution of India, and special laws are applicable to that state. Keeping in mind the universal nature of the impact of computers and the Internet, the legislature has decided that the IT Act shall be applicable to the whole of India including Jammu & Kashmir. However, the law has gone much further.

Section 1 IT Act deals with the issue of applicability of this new law.

> '(1) This Act may be called the Information Technology Act, 2000.
>
> (2) It shall extend to the whole of India and, save as otherwise provided in this Act, it applies also to any offence or contravention thereunder committed outside India by any person.'

This means that the law applies to any violation or contravention of the provisions of the IT Act committed by any person anywhere in the world. The provision confers jurisdiction over those who violate the IT Act while outside the territorial boundaries of India. This worldwide scope is attributable, no doubt, to the fact that, as many have pointed out, cyberspace knows no territorial boundaries; the Internet is a network of computers, joined together by telephone lines throughout the world.

It is difficult to say which portion of cyberspace is within India or which is outside India, as boundaries cease to have any meaning. Today, people, in order to fulfill their criminal motives, are using cyberspace and computers with impunity. This provision enables Indian law-enforcement agencies to pursue cybercriminals who are outside the territorial boundaries of India and who violate the provisions of the IT Act.

The point made by some, i.e., that a law assuming extraterritorial jurisdiction is not enforceable in the real world, has some merit. It is contrary to the principles of international law to assume jurisdiction over citizens of another country, and so, it is likely to lead to a conflict of jurisdiction concerning different courts situated in different national jurisdictions. Also, it is important to note that there are differences between national legislations, laws, legal processes, and procedures.

Further compounding the problem is the issue that a particular act in one national jurisdiction can be legal and not barred by law but, at the same time, it is illegal and barred by the law prevailing in another national jurisdiction. Another ground of criticism has been that section 1 does not lay down the parameters of how such a provision would be enforceable in practical terms across transnational boundaries and jurisdictions. Governments can use the extradition process to bring cybercriminals to their territory for prosecution, if there is a valid extradition treaty in place between the relevant countries. But the route stipulated in section 1 IT Act is likely to throw up a complex arena of difficulties in actual day-to-day implementation.

The existing international law pertaining to the sovereignty of a nation also details that a sovereign nation can make laws affecting people who reside within its territorial boundaries. However, the birth of the Internet has seen geography become history, and transactions taking place over networks are transnational in nature, thereby complicating the entire issue of jurisdiction.

Section 75 IT Act deals with the issue of the applicability of the Indian Cyberlaw for an offence or contravention committed outside of India:

> '(1) Subject to the provisions of sub-section (2), the provisions of this Act shall apply also to any offence or contravention committed outside India by any person irrespective of his nationality.
>
> (2) For the purposes of sub-section (1), this Act shall apply to an offence or contravention committed outside India by any person if the act or conduct constituting the offence or contravention involves a computer, computer system or computer network located in India.'

Section 75 thus makes the provisions of the IT Act applicable to any offence committed outside India by any person, irrespective of his nationality. This enables the law to assume jurisdiction over cybercriminals outside the territorial boundaries of India. The caveat to section 75(1) is explained in section 75(2); in other words, section 75(1) is subject to the provisions of section 75(2). The caveat provided by section 75(2) is that the IT Act shall apply to any offence or contravention committed outside India by any person if and only if the act or conduct constituting the offence or contravention involves a computer, computer system, or computer network located in India.

Section 75(2) of the Indian IT Act uses the phrase 'involving a computer, computer system or computer network located in India'. The word 'involving' is an all-embracing term which leaves no exceptions. Thus, regardless of whether the involvement of a computer, computer system, or computer network is intentional or unintentional, deliberate, accidental or otherwise, all such scenarios would be covered within the ambit of the word 'involving'.

Therefore, the physical location of the computer, computer system, or computer network within the territorial boundaries of India is a condition precedent to the applicability of this Act to any offence or contravention committed outside India by any person irrespective of his nationality. Section 75 thus takes a somewhat saner view of the issue of extraterritorial jurisdiction than section 1(2) IT Act.

It has been argued in India that the necessity of having the present provision is because of the emergence and growth of cyberspace, which does not have any boundaries. As the Internet is making geography history, it is imperative that nations enact laws that have an all-pervasive applicability and impact. Further, such an approach facilitates nations to catch cybercriminals who are located physically outside territorial boundaries. On the other hand, the provision is liable to be criticized inasmuch as no country can assume jurisdiction over the citizens of another nation, merely on the ground that that citizen has violated the national laws of that nation. The move has been criticized as being contrary to the established principles of international law.[6]

---

[6] Pavan Duggal, *Cyberlaw. The Indian Perspective* (Delhi, Saakshar Law Publications, 2004).

10.3.2 **Jurisprudence**

The Indian approach given in section 1(2) as modified by section 75 IT Act has created confusion in the actual implementation of the law. This becomes all the more evident from the emerging principles from various judgments relating to jurisdiction over the Internet. From the beginning of the Internet, the issue of jurisdiction has continued to challenge legal minds, societies, and nations in the context of the peculiarly inherent character of the Internet.

Different principles were being evolved in different national jurisdictions in this regard. In the traditional notions of jurisdiction, the courts assumed jurisdiction on the basis of the place where the cause of action has arisen. Due to the peculiarity of cyberspace, the well-established principles of jurisdiction no longer provide clarity. The courts, while acknowledging some of the challenges which the Internet poses for the law of jurisdiction, have tried resolving these issues with the application of well-established judicial principles.

In the beginning, the courts of different countries, including India, began making mere access to the Internet a sufficient ground for assuming jurisdiction over Internet-related transactions. However, there has been a kaleidoscopic shift in the principles of assumption of jurisdiction in the areas relating to cyberspace.

Considering the entire issue of cybercrime jurisdiction from the Indian perspective, there is, by far, no established principle. However, case law relating to civil-law jurisdiction has been developed. Such jurisprudence is indeed relevant and can be helpful in the evolution of cybercrime case law over a period of time. As such, it will be relevant to examine the said civil-law jurisdiction jurisprudence in India at this stage.

Section 19 of the Code of Civil Procedure, 1908 is a provision that clarifies the position under Indian law in the case of multiple jurisdictions. Section 19 provides that

> 'where a suit for compensation for wrong done to the person or to moveable property, if the wrong was done within the local limits of the jurisdiction of one court and defendant resides, or carries on business, or personally works for gain, within the local limits of jurisdiction of another court, the suit may be instituted at the option of the plaintiff in either of the said courts.'

The same principle has safely been applied to the Internet within India. However, in case of disputes arising in two different countries, the problems are complex, to say the least. Section 1(2) and section 75 IT Act provide for extraterritorial jurisdiction of the Indian courts, which, however, seems unlikely to be implemented. The courts in India at present have been sporadic in following the trend of asserting jurisdiction on the basis of active accessibility of a web site.[7] So far, in various cases

[7] *SAP Systems* v. *Davinder Pal Singh Bhatia*, Delhi High Court, unpublished.

related to Internet domain names, the Delhi High Court has assumed jurisdiction merely on the basis of accessibility of web sites in India.

In the Indian context, in the beginning, the Internet-related disputes that emerged were domain-name disputes. Many of these disputes arose prior to the coming into effect of the domain-name Uniform Dispute Resolution Policy of the Internet Corporation for Assigned Names and Numbers (ICANN). Consequently, various civil suits for injunctions and declarations were filed under the existing trademark law. In a majority of these initial cases, the courts in India, including the Delhi High Court, assumed jurisdiction over Internet domain-name disputes merely on the ground of access to the Internet. In a majority of these cases, most of which are *sub judice* at the time of writing, the courts assumed territorial jurisdiction over the disputes on the ground that the Internet could be accessed from the territories within the territorial boundaries of the concerned court.

In the judgment rendered in the famous Yahoo! France case, *Yahoo!, Inc.* v. *La Ligue Contre Le Racisme et L'Antisemitisme*,[8] the judicial thinking on jurisdiction was further refined. This US judgment has had far-reaching significance and consequences on the entire subject of jurisdiction. Until it issued, the courts anywhere in the world could assume, and were assuming, jurisdiction over Internet transactions and web sites that were located outside the country.

This decision underlines the principle that even if a foreign court delivers a judgment or direction against a legal entity of a particular country, say country A, then that judgment or direction would not be applicable automatically to country A's legal entities or citizens. This is completely contrary to the earlier French Court's decision on the same matter, where the French court assumed jurisdiction over Yahoo! (a U.S. company, based in the United States and amenable to U.S. laws) and held them liable for anti-Semitic material.[9] The author personally believes that the U.S. decision is the more pragmatic approach and is liable to be the forerunner of the evolution of jurisprudence on this subject. This is all the more evident from the current Internet governance debate that is going on, at the time of writing, where countries across the world are moving towards the exercise of their sovereign rights in the context of the Internet. The decision or direction of a foreign court will need to be scrutinized by country A's courts, keeping in mind the touchstone and basic principles enshrined in its Constitution and in its local laws, before it can be enforceable in country A.

It is evident that the courts are looking at the totality of the circumstances when determining whether to exercise jurisdiction over individuals involved in Internet-related activities.

It is still to be seen how the Indian approach on jurisdiction will emerge with the coming of the IT Act and with its provisions on extraterritorial jurisdiction. It is

---

8 *Yahoo!, Inc.* v. *La Ligue Contre Le Racisme et L'Antisemitisme,* US District Court – N.D. California 2001, <http://pub.bna.com/eclr/21275.htm>.

9 <http://www.politechbot.com/p-02390.html>.

likely that the Indian courts are likely to adopt the principle of law enunciated in the Yahoo! case in the United States, as that is in sync with the assertion of the sovereignty of the state, which has been upheld by the courts of India on numerous occasions.[10]

The likelihood of this outcome is further supported by various events that have taken place in India. In mid-2001, the Government of India's Ministry of External Affairs web site was hacked. The year 2001 also saw the hacking of the web sites of the All India Institute of Medical Sciences, the Atomic Energy Research Board, and many other governmental and semi-governmental web sites. All these hacking attacks emerged from computers and entities located outside India. However, in none of the cases was jurisdiction under sections 1(2) and 75(1) IT Act invoked, either for purposes of the registration of criminal cases under section 66 IT Act or for claiming damages under section 43 IT Act. Even the case that was registered by the law-enforcement agencies in the matter relating to the hacking of the web site of the Central Board of Direct Taxes has not seen much progress.

10.4 Evidentiary Issues

As regards electronic evidence and its admissibility in India, the law has provided for some special provisions. The evidentiary status of electronic data in India is governed by the provisions of section 65B of the amended Indian Evidence Act, 1872 as amended by the IT Act.

The relevant provisions are sections 65A and 65B of the Indian Evidence Act. These provisions provide for the admissibility and mode of proving electronic evidence as well as printouts of the same. Section 65 of the amended Indian Evidence Act prescribes the manner in which electronic evidence may be produced and proved in a court of law in India. However, the law does not stipulate what kind of electronic evidence can be permitted as admissible evidence. Thus, in the event of electronic data obtained in the course of extraterritorial investigations in another country of a cybercrime matter that has occurred in India, especially if that country and India have different opinions about the lawfulness of such extraterritorial investigations, the important question to determine in such a case would be as to the legality of the said collected electronic evidence in India. The relevant and competent forum to determine this would be a court of law within India.

The Indian courts have adopted innovative, pragmatic, and proactive strategies in terms of permitting the use of gathering evidence across nations by means of videoconferencing. In various cases, Indian courts have permitted and have indeed recorded evidence by way of videoconferencing, tendered by witnesses physically located in different territorial areas outside the boundaries of India. Such evidence

[10] *Mohammed Afzal* v. *State* (Parliament House Attack case), Supreme Court 2005.

has been made legal and valid in Indian law and Indian court procedure by various laws, including the IT Act and the Indian Evidence Act.

However, if it can be shown that the data so obtained could not have been obtained in a legal manner or that it was obtained outside the parameters of or in violation of existing laws, then the court of law in India is likely to be inclined not to take the said obtained data into consideration. However, at the time of writing, in India, there is no judicial precedent to this effect.

10.5 Analysis and Opinion

The Indian approach to deal with cyber-investigation jurisdiction is clearly not very well-developed at the time of writing. Currently, the Indian law-enforcement agencies are in the process of evolving and crystallizing their practices and procedures relating to cyber-investigations.

When one examines the provisions of the Indian Information Technology Act, 2000, one realizes that, although on paper, technically the law has granted extraterritorial jurisdiction in relation to cybercrime cases, yet in reality it has not really been applicable beyond the territorial boundaries of India. There is now a growing realization that the Indian cyberlaw, despite its paper-tiger extraterritorial jurisdiction provisions, pragmatically and practically speaking, cannot be made applicable to jurisdictions outside the territorial boundaries of India. This is because such provisions directly conflict with the exercise of sovereignty by foreign governments within their national boundaries.

This is also exemplified by the famous case relating to the hacking of the web site of the Central Board of Direct Taxes in 2002. The Central Board of Direct Taxes is a statutory body in India whose web site was hacked by allegedly Pakistani hackers. This was not a new instance. The previous Kargil war in 1999 had seen numerous Indian governmental web sites being repeatedly hacked and brought down by Pakistani hackers. While in previous cases, the government did not register cases of hacking, in the case of the web site hacking of the Central Board of Direct Taxes, the police did register. However, despite more than three years after the registration of this case, no effective breakthrough has been achieved nor any progress made in this case. The reason behind this non-action has been that the allegedly Pakistani hackers are located outside the territorial boundaries of India. India has no legitimate right to arrest such people outside its territorial boundaries. To complicate matters further, the neighboring country does not recognize such people as hackers and instead refers to them as patriots. Therefore in this scenario, it becomes an increasingly futile exercise to register any cybercrime case, wherein the perpetrator of the cybercrime is physically located outside the territorial boundaries of India. In this dilemma, India as a nation is not alone and shares the same boat with other nations facing similar challenges.

There is a complete lack of case law on this issue of cybercrime jurisdiction in India. Apart from that, India, being a large country, is also likely to see interstate jurisdiction issues relating to the registration, investigation, and prosecution of different cybercrime cases in different states of India.

Until such time as the Indian law in this regard is amended and as universally accepted international best practices and principles evolve, it would be prudent for the Indian law-enforcement agencies to detect, investigate, and prosecute cybercrimes within the ambit of existing principles of law as are enshrined in sections 1 and 75 IT Act. Section 81 IT Act declares the law to be a special law and states that the provisions of this law shall prevail over anything inconsistent contained therewith in any other law currently in force in India. As such, the manner of crime investigation and prosecution as embodied in the normal criminal law in India would indeed continue to the extent that they do not conflict with the provisions of the IT Act. However, the provisions of sections 1 and 75 IT Act as discussed above shall continue to be the guiding principles concerning cybercrime jurisdiction in India until the government of India comes up with some new legal provisions in this regard.

The good news is that India is on the cutting edge of development. At the time of writing, the government of India is already in the process of amending its cyberlaw, in particular the Information Technology Act, 2000. It is expected that the said amendments may also throw some light on the tricky issues concerning jurisdiction. However, the proposed amendments are not yet final. It will indeed be interesting to watch the developments in this space and their impact on the evolution of cybercrime jurisdiction jurisprudence in India.

10.6 Conclusion

Seen from a holistic perspective, India promises to be an action spot that is likely to develop rapidly various principles relating to cybercrime jurisdiction. This is not just because of the tremendous use of information technology and the Internet within India. It is also courtesy of the huge spurt in business-process outsourcing or knowledge-process outsourcing industries in India. In the context of Asia Pacific, India is more likely to be the probable candidate to emerge with practical and pragmatic guidelines and solutions for tackling various tricky issues concerning cybercrime jurisdiction within India.

To conclude, it is valuable to state that in India, although it has some provisions in its law books relating to cybercrime jurisdiction, the said provisions have not yet been tested in judicial waters. Further, actual practical day-to-day realities of sovereignty and jurisdictions of different countries have inhibited the use of extraterritorial jurisdiction provided to the Indian law-enforcement agencies for tackling cybercrime cases. But considering that India is rapidly developing its own ingenious methodologies for dealing with complicated outsourcing legal issues, disputes, and cybercrime cases, it will be interesting to see the rapid developments of jurisprudence unfurl in this direction. All eyes will now be on India as to how it proceeds to deal with complicated issues, both in the form of proposed amendments to the Indian Information Technology Act, 2000, and in terms of developing pragmatic, yet effective, remedies, guidelines, and procedures as also adopting workable principles relating to cybercrime jurisdiction in India.

Bibliography

Central Bureau of Investigation, <http://www.cbi.nic.in>.

Pavan Duggal, *Cyberlaw. The Indian Perspective* (Delhi, Saakshar Law Publications, 2004).

Pavan Duggal, *Law of Business Process Outsourcing* (Delhi, Saakshar Law Publications, 2004).

Pavan Duggal, *Cyberlaw in India- An Analysis* (Delhi, Saakshar Law Publications, 2000).

Pavan Duggal, 'Brief Cases', in *The Economic Times*, 2000-2005.

Ministry of Information Technology of India, <http://www.mit.gov.in>.

Mumbai Cybercrime Bureau Station, <http://www.ccicmumbai.com>.

Chapter 11
CYBERCRIME AND JURISDICTION IN ITALY

Giovanni Ziccardi*

11.1 Substantive Cybercrime Law

11.1.1 The Constitution of 1948

The Italian Constitution, drawn up in 1948,[1] is the most important normative document in Italy that includes several specific provisions, contained in many articles, related to data-protection issues, the secrecy of private correspondence, warrants that must be granted during search and seizure, and civil-rights protection regarding any aspect of citizens' social lives.

These articles of the Constitution, of course, do not directly refer to the 'electronic world' – in 1948 the technological era was just beginning – but most of the principles explained in these articles can be extended. The Italian Courts, during the last twenty years, have done so several times with respect to cyberspace issues.

One of the most important articles of the Constitution – an article that Italian courts usually extend to cyberspace and to illegal-access issues – is Article 14. The text of this article is very plain: it states that a) the personal domicile is inviolable, and that b) inspections and searches may not be carried out except in cases, and in certain ways, laid down by law, in conformity with guarantees prescribed for safeguarding personal freedom.

We will see later on in this chapter that the notion of 'domicile', according to the Italian law, is very broad and is, at the same time, a place that is 'physical' and 'virtual'. The Italian Criminal Code (*Codice Penale*) regulates trespassing a virtual 'dwelling' (for example, the computer owned by a user, or an authentication device) in the same manner as trespassing physical doors and windows to get into a 'real' dwelling. The basic idea, in court interpretations during these years, is strictly

* Prof. Dr Giovanni Ziccardi is Professor of Legal Informatics and Advanced Legal Informatics at the Faculty of Law, University of Milan, Italy. Many thanks to Dr Nadina Foggetti for her co-operation during the draft of this chapter (especially the jurisdiction part).

[1] On 2 June 1946, after the public voted for a Republic in the referendum concerning the (future) form of the state, the Italian Constituent Assembly was elected. On 11 December 1947, the new Italian Constitution was passed, and it entered into force on 1 January 1948.

B-J. Koops and S.W. Brenner (Eds), Cybercrime and Jurisdiction

connected to the existence of a 'virtual' or 'electronic' domicile alongside the 'real' one.

The same principles apply to the contents of Article 15 of the Italian Constitution, which states that the liberty and secrecy of correspondence and of *every form* of communication are inviolable, and that limitations thereupon may only be enforced by a decision, for which sufficient grounds must be given, of the judicial authorities with the guarantees laid down by law.[2]

The notion 'every form of communication' in the Constitution is very broad and effective, and extends this high level of constitutional protection not only to the traditional physical – or 'snail' – mail, but also to 'virtual correspondence'. This includes not only, obvious though it may be, e-mail, but also non-public mailing lists and other forms of private transmission of data between individuals.

These two articles of the Italian Constitution have been the first to be applied in cases where the legislative framework did not have specific technological or cyberspace-related legal provisions. This legislative framework, however, was to change a great deal in the 1990s.[3]

11.1.2 **The first real informatic provisions**

The legislative framework related to computer crimes and cyber-investigations in Italy changed significantly during the years 1992 and 1993. The two most important legislative reforms in fact date from more than ten years ago. The first, Legislative Decree (*Decreto Legislativo*) No. 518 of 29 December 1992, modified the existing Italian Copyright Act (Law No. 633 of 1941). The second, Act (*Legge*) No. 547 of 23 December 1993, 'Replacements and introduction of new articles on computer crimes into the Criminal Code and into the Criminal Procedure Code' (*Modificazioni ed integrazioni delle norme del codice penale e del codice di procedura penale in tema di criminalità informatica*), was enacted to modify the Italian Criminal Code and the Criminal Procedure Code (*Codice Procedura Penale*) and to introduce new provisions related to software piracy, computer crimes, and cyber-investigatons.[4]

11.1.3 **Copyright law**

The 1992 Decree No. 518 addressed copyright in the information age and software piracy. It became the heart of the Italian legislation protecting intellectual property

---

[2] For a concise but clear description in English of the legal framework of privacy in Italy, see Privacy International, 'Italian Republic', in *Privacy & Human Rights 2003*, Washington, D.C./London, available at <http://www.privacyinternational.org/survey/phr2003/countries/italy.htm>.

[3] See G. Livraghi, 'Internet freedom, privacy and culture in Italy (and the activity of NGO's)', 1 *Ciberspazio e Diritto* (2000) No. 1, pp. 21-30.

[4] See G. Pica, *Diritto penale delle tecnologie informatiche* [Criminal Law of the Information Technologies] (Turin, Giappichelli 1999).

and copyright. It was enacted to implement in Italy the European Community Directive 91/250 that provides software with the same protection as literary authorship. As two scholars, Monti and Livraghi, have written, this law defines the duplication of software for a 'lucrative purpose' as a criminal offense punished with a term of imprisonment from one to three years. The Decree was intended to repress the sale of illegal software copies in Italy, 'but it was interpreted in such a way as to criminalize even private and non-commercial exchanges.'[5]

The Copyright Act was subsequently modified and updated through several legislative reforms, during the years 2000, 2003, and 2005. These modifications concerned the punishment of 'new' forms of conduct, especially file-sharing, peer-to-peer systems, and circumvention of technological protection measures and digital rights management (DRM) systems.[6] These provisions essentially protect, in the current legislative framework, the integrity of copyrighted software, establishing penalties against selling pirated software and evading taxes on software.

11.1.4 The Italian Computer Crimes Act of 1993

The 1993 Act No. 547, in contrast to the copyright Decree that targeted copyright law, focused completely on criminal issues, updating the Italian Criminal Code (CC) and the Criminal Procedure Code (CPC) to punish also 'non-traditional' or 'virtual' conduct related to computer crimes.

This Act added several articles to the Italian Criminal Code, thus becoming the heart of the Italian computer-crime discipline. It is very complex, too broad and vague in some parts. It contains twelve points concerning many computer-related criminal activities, including illegal access to information systems, voluntary damage to information systems, trafficking of passwords and access codes, the creation and diffusion of viruses and worms,[7] and the creation of false electronic documents. It also includes a definition of 'computer crime': a computer crime, for the purposes of the Italian legislative system, is 'an offense committed by using computer technologies, from a personal one to portable telephone devices created on the basis of microchips.'

In combination with the copyright law, this Act provides, in Italy, government organizations, firms, military institutions, banks, companies, and private citizens

---

[5] For more information about this legislative evolution, see A. Monti, 'The network society as seen from Italy', paper presented at the Conference for Freedom and Privacy (CFP) 2000 in Toronto (6 April 2000), available at <http://www.cfp.org>.

[6] See Art. 71-*sexies*, Art. 102-*quater* of the Italian Copyright Act (Law No. 633 of 1941), derived from Art. 6 of the EC Directive 2001/29/EC concerning the obligation as to technological measures (the Member States shall provide adequate legal protection against the circumvention of any effective technological measures) and Art. 171-*ter* of the same Law.

[7] See Y. Amoroso Fernández, 'Virus informatici: aspetti legali' [Informatics Viruses: Legal Aspects], *Informatica e diritto* (1999) p. 217; G. Ziccardi, 'I virus informatici: aspetti tecnici e giuridici' [The Informatics Viruses: Technical and Legal Aspects], *Ciberspazio e diritto* (2001) Nos. 3-4, p. 347.

with protection from unauthorized access to computer networks, illegal use of protected data bases, unlawful copying of chip topographies, and unauthorized use of codes of credit and phone cards, passwords, or banking accounts.

The Italian Computer Crimes Act is divided into several parts, each one concerning different conduct and provisions. The first part, more specifically the first four articles, deals with the possession, alteration, or destruction of data or computer systems. These provisions are shaped on the basis of 'physical' counterparts, in this case the typical damage that can be encountered in the physical world (for example, someone who voluntarily damages someone else's car), extending these to information-technology objects – in this case, information systems and the data that are managed by those systems. The result of this extension is that someone who damages the data and computer systems of someone else is now also punishable.

The second part of the Act deals with unauthorized or pirated access to systems and with the interception of communications. Also in this case, the Italian legislator moves from the 'physical point of view' (the domicile, such as a house, and physical correspondence, for instance, a letter) to punish the trespassing of virtual property, i.e., the access to a system against the will of the owner, or the illegal interception or possession of private correspondence, either 'static', like an e-mail message, or 'dynamic', such as information flows and private chat conversations.

The third part of Act No. 547 of 1993 concerns forging an electronic transmission, spreading computer viruses, illegally possessing devices to intercept or disrupt communications, and disclosing confidential information. All these provisions carry penalties of up to six years' imprisonment.[8]

The first time these new norms were enforced was in 1994, when the Italian Finance Police started a massive operation, 'Hardware I', that was the first Italian operation concerning computer crimes and copyright violations.[9] It was a nationwide operation, and the results were the shutdown of hundreds of bulletin boards (BBSs) connected to the Fidonet network, alongside many seizures of hardware, software, blue boxes,[10] and other electronic devices.[11] It was the first time, in Italy, that the target of prosecutors and the police were the so-called 'telecom pirates': the

---

[8] For a brief description, in English, of the Italian computer crimes legal frameworks see, *inter alia*, Michael W. Kim, *How countries handle computer crimes* (1997), available at <http://www.swiss.ai.mit.edu/6.805/student-papers/fall97-papers/kim-crime.html>.

[9] See S. Chiccarelli and A. Monti, *Spaghetti Hacker. Storie, tecniche e aspetti giuridici dell'hacking in Italia* [Spaghetti Hackers. Stories, Techniques, and Legal Aspects of Hacking in Italy] (Milan, Apogeo 1997).

[10] 'An early phreaking tool, the blue box is an electronic device that simulates a telephone operator's dialing console. (…) The most typical use of a blue box was to get free telephone calls. Blue boxes no longer work in most western nations, as the switching system is now digital and no longer uses inband signaling.' See <http://en.wikipedia.org/wiki/Blue_box>.

[11] See C. Gubitosa, *Italian crackdown. BBS amatoriali, volontari telematici, censure e sequestri nell'Italia degli anni '90* [Italian Crackdown. BBS Lovers, Telematics Volunteers, Censorship, and Seizures in 1990s Italy] (Milan, Apogeo 1999).

main accusation made against the BBS users was that they downloaded, copied, and transmitted pirated software and that they trafficked data and passwords.

Comparable to the first wave of cybercrime legislation, the years 2000-2005 saw a second wave of legislative reforms, addressing new computer crimes, illegal content, child-pornography material, and the security of the e-commerce environment. For example, in 1998, the Italian Act concerning Child Pornography and the Internet, Act No. 269 of 3 August 1998, was enacted. Several projects have started to modify the original text, including a Bill approved by the Council of Ministers on 7 November 2003, and a self-regulatory initiative, the Codice di Autoregolamentazione 'Internet e minori' (Self-Regulation Code 'Internet and Minors'), is sponsored by many institutions, including the Italian Ministry for Innovation and Technologies. Other examples in this second wave are laws on copyright and related computer crimes,[12] laws concerning terrorism and wiretapping,[13] and a law concerning electronic commerce.[14]

I shall conclude this section by describing some of the most relevant cybercrimes under the Computer Crimes Act of 1993.

Illegal access to a computer system

The conduct which amounts to illegal access to a computer system is clearly defined in the text of Article 615-*ter* CC, carrying a penalty of one to three years' imprisonment for 'anyone who enters without authorization a computer or telecommunication systems protected by security measures, or who remains in the system against the expressed or implied will of the one who has the rights to exclude him.'

As, among others, the scholars Pica and Foggetti have noted in several of their studies,[15] the content of Article 615-*ter* and the other offenses introduced by Act No. 547 of 1993 was drafted using the offense of trespassing (violation of domicile) as defined in Article 614 CC as a model. As noted above, the Act tends to identify new forms of unlawful conduct as different kinds of aggression against traditional legal rights, but it does not consider computer crimes as a new and independent category that needs to be defined on the basis of new legal rights to be protected.[16] The Explanatory Report to Act No. 547 of 1993 clearly shows the legislator's intention to protect in the definition of illegal access 'an extension of the sphere pertaining to each individual, which is safeguarded by Article 14 of the Constitution as well as by Articles 614 and 615 of the Criminal Code.'[17]

---

[12] Act of 18 August 2000, No. 248; Legislative Decree of 9 April 2003, No. 68; Act of 21 May 2004, No. 128; and Act of 31 March 2005, No. 43.

[13] Decree of 18 October 2001, No. 374, and Decree of 27 July 2005, No. 144.

[14] Legislative Decree of 9 April 2003, No. 70.

[15] See N. Foggetti, 'Legal analysis of a case of cross-border cyber crime', IV Upgrade, European Journal for the Informatics Professional (2003) No. 6, p. 43, available at <http://www.upgrade-cepis.org; Pica> (1999) op. cit. n. 4.

[16] See Foggetti, loc. cit. n. 15, p. 43.

[17] Ibid.

Concerning the nature of the security measures that are an element of the criminal provision, Foggetti notes that prevailing case law considers that, while being a constituent element of the concept of illegal access to a computer system as defined in Article 615-*ter* CC, these measures need only show the will of the owner of a specific system to be protected – they do not have to be really efficacious in a technical sense. In other words, such measures are not considered so much in terms of how suitable they are to keep out any intruders, but rather as a way of declaring the 'right to exclude others' (*ius excludendi alios*), in parallel with the legislation that governs the physical domicile (Art. 614 CC).[18]

The same law includes a series of aggravating circumstances that affect the prosecution of the offense, allowing the maximum penalty to be raised to five years, for example, when the system is serving the public interest, or when the intruder is the system administrator of the network.

Illicit possession of access codes

Another very important provision is Article 615-*quater* CC, which defines illicit possession of access codes to information and telematic systems as an offense. This article carries a penalty of up to one year's imprisonment and a fine of up to around 5,000 Euro for 'whoever, in order to obtain a profit for himself or for another or to cause damage to others, illegally acquires, reproduces, propagates, transmits, or delivers codes, keywords, or other means for access to a computer or telecommunication system protected by security measures, or provides information or instructions fit to the above purpose.'[19] It is interesting that for this offense, no actual damage or disruption to the system has to be caused.

11.1.5 The Data Protection Acts of 1996 and 2003

In 1996, a law concerning the protection of personal data was enacted, the Italian Data Protection Act.[20] This Law, No. 675 of 1996, implemented the European Community Data Protection Directive. It was completely modified in 2003 with a brand new 'Italian Privacy Code', enacted through Legislative Decree No. 196 of 2003. This Code protects the privacy and integrity of personal data and penalizes the illegal processing of this kind of data. It is enforced by the Italian Data Protection Authority ('Garante').

From a cybercrime perspective, an interesting provision in the Italian privacy law is the obligation to adopt suitable and preventive security measures aimed at

[18] Ibid. Cf., Corte di cassazione, 6 December 2000 No. 12732.

[19] See Foggetti, loc. cit. n. 15, p. 43.

[20] See J. Monducci, 'La circolazione dei dati personali in Internet' [The Dissemination of Personal Data on the Internet], 1 *Ciberspazio e Diritto* (2000) No. 1, pp. 31-40.

preventing the loss or destruction of personal data and unauthorized access to personal data.[21]

11.2 Procedural Cybercrime Law

11.2.1 Network wiretapping

Wiretapping is regulated by Articles 266 to 271 of the Italian Criminal Procedure Code (hereafter: CPC). It can only be authorized in the case of legal proceedings, and government interceptions of telephone and all other forms of communications must be approved by a court order. They are granted for crimes punishable by life imprisonment or imprisonment for more than five years, for crimes against the administration punishable by no less than five years' imprisonment, for crimes involving the trafficking of drugs, arms, explosives, and contraband, and for insults, threats, abuses, and harassment carried out over the telephone. The government interception powers have their counterpart in the Computer Crimes Act, which contains a provision that penalizes the interception of electronic data flows.[22]

The procedural articles are also used for the interception of communication between two modems, especially through Article 266-*bis* CPC that provides for network wiretapping. Before the Computer Crimes Act of 1993, only telephone interception was allowed and only in cases of serious crimes (such as arms or drugs trafficking or usury) as well as only with the authorized instruments of the inquiring authorities. Some scholars noted that the new legislation introduced a general and undefined concept of network wiretapping that can be used for any suspected crime or violation that uses information or network technologies, and that the interception can be carried out by any means including privately-owned equipment, creating a practically unlimited and unrestricted right of interception.[23]

11.2.2 Search, seizure, and network searches

The procedures that can be used by the police to investigate a computer or a network are the same as the Criminal Procedure Code provides for searching persons or places. These are called instruments of evidence (*mezzi di prova*) and are laid down in Articles 244 through 271 CPC. In particular, there are four instruments used by the police to search for evidence on a computer or a network: inspection

---

[21] See G. Corasaniti, *Esperienza giuridica e sicurezza informatica* [Legal Experience and Informatics Security] (Milan, Giuffrè, 2003); P. Perri and S. Zanero, 'Lessons learned from the Italian law on privacy', 20 *The Computer Law and Security Report* (2004) Nos. 4-5.

[22] For a brief description of these issues in English, see Privacy International, loc. cit. n. 2.

[23] A. Monti, 'Diritto delle tecnologie dell'informazione e protezione dei diritti civili' [Information Technology Law and Protection of Civil Rights], 1 *Ciberspazio e Diritto* (2000) No. 1, pp. 41-51.

(*ispezione*), search (*perquisizione*), seizure (*sequestro*), and tapping (*intercettazione*). All these four instruments can be used to search persons, places, computers, networks, and communications for evidence.

If the investigation of, for example, a network would cross the Italian border, there are various options, depending on the state towards which the investigative activity must be performed. Like with ordinary crimes, in the case of a computer crime, the general rules for assistance through Interpol or, if the state is in the EU, for Europol can be applicable; and for countries that have ratified the Council of Europe Convention on Cybercrime (Budapest, 23 November 2001) – not necessarily members of the Council of Europe –, legal assistance will be possible through the provisions of that convention. For investigation activities within the EU, moreover, the EU Convention on Mutual Legal Assistance can be used for computer crimes as well, together with the general procedures of extradition and the European arrest warrant.

11.2.3 **Data retention**

In 2004, a law concerning data retention was enacted, Law No. 45 of 26 February 2004, which is very important from a cyber-investigation point of view. It was partially reformed by the Law of 31 July 2004, No. 155, issued to prevent terrorism activities. It contains the obligation to retain log files concerning telephonic conversations for a period of 24 months, plus a further 24 months to prevent or verify crimes. During the first 24 months, data are stored by the provider and can be accessed after a court order; during the second 24-month period, data can only be accessed if there is a crime related to terrorism, organized crime, or damage to information systems. This law can not be used for electronic (telematic) data flows, but only for telephone communication systems and telephone data.

11.3 JURISDICTION: THE APPLICABILITY OF ITALIAN CRIMINAL LAW

11.3.1 **The *Locus Commissi Delicti* Issue**

Obviously, the thing that distinguishes cybercrime from other criminal activities is basically the cross-border nature of unlawful conduct over the Internet. It is not always feasible to identify the *locus commissi delicti* (the place where the offense was committed) when the offender makes use of informatic and telematic means to commit the offense, as the same single criminal act often involves many different activities that are carried out via several intermediate systems or stepping-stones.[24] The attacker may, in fact, violate several computer systems with just one act of illegal access and carry out several illegal operations on computers that are inter-

[24] See Foggetti, loc. cit. n. 15, p. 46.

connected but physically located in different territories, sometimes in different countries. In other cases, the place where the initial violation occurs may be the same as the place where the attacker is located, but the person harmed by the offense may be somewhere else.

11.3.2 The obligatory nature of Italian criminal law

The first problem is to determine whether or not Italian law can be applied to a particular event. Article 3 of the Italian Criminal Code, entitled 'Obligatory nature of the criminal law' (*Obbligatorietà della legge penale*), defines the principle that the penal law is imperative, except for the temporal and spatial limits stated by national law. According to Article 3 CC, 'Italian criminal law applies to all citizens or foreigners within the territory of the state, save for those exceptions provided for by national public law or international law.' Article 3 paragraph 2 adds: 'Italian criminal law also applies to all citizens or foreigners who are abroad, but limited to those cases provided for by that same law or by international law.'

The obligatory nature, as Foggetti states, is also expressed in the position of the article itself within the system of the Criminal Code, as it, in fact, comes before the norms referring to the territorial application of criminal law and the principle of *ignorantia legis non excusat* (ignorance of the law is no excuse), and coming after the principles of legality and the norms referring to *ratione temporis* (time limitations governing the applicability of criminal law).

Article 3 determines the non-derogable nature of the application of Italian criminal law based on personal (*ratione personae*) jurisdiction, whereby it is applicable to all persons – whether Italian citizens or foreigners, whether in the national territory or abroad –, the only limitations being the principle of legality and the norms laid down by international law.[25]

11.3.3 The principle of territoriality

The principle of territoriality is dealt with in Article 6 paragraph 1 CC, which defines criminal law as being applicable within the whole territory of the Italian state. It is therefore essential to define where the offense was committed. Article 6 paragraph 2 provides that the 'offense is considered to have been committed within the territory of the state when the action or omission giving rise to the offense is carried out fully or partially there, or if the consequence of the action or omission was suffered there.'

The Italian Criminal Code, therefore, aims to expand the jurisdiction of Italian criminal law by establishing a criterion of ubiquity, with the origin or the result occurring in Italy. This raises the question of how to define the 'slightest part' of a criminal act that can cause the offense to be considered as having been committed

[25] Ibid., p. 46.

in Italy. The resulting problem of interpretation has found no unanimous solution at a doctrinal level and also creates divergences in case law.[26]

Among legal scholars, there has been much debate about the minimum significance of an activity committed within Italian territory in order for Italian law to be applicable. One interpretation holds that acts committed within the national territory should constitute a punishable attempt and not be limited to a mere preparatory act, or even that the offense should be considered as having been committed in Italy even though only a 'fragment' of the offense, or even a mere preparatory act, was committed in Italy. This doctrine holds that a criminal attempt can be considered to have been committed in Italy even though the preparatory acts may not have been committed in Italian territory, provided that the unlawful act could potentially have been committed within the Italian territory.

Conversely, according to another criterion based on a literal interpretation of the norm, the offense should be considered as coming under Italian jurisdiction only when a part of it, whether completed or attempted, has been committed in Italian territory, provided that the 'part' was an essential component of the offense. Such a decision must be taken after the event (*ex post*) and in relation to the specifics of the case, and not merely before the event (*ex ante*) and abstractly. Prevailing case law seems to accept this latter interpretation.[27]

With regard to the minimum requirements to consider an offense as attempted, for the purposes of applying Italian jurisdiction in compliance with Article 6 paragraph 2, prevailing case law consider that 'the part of the act committed in Italy does not in itself have to be actionable but it is enough that the part of the act which was committed in Italy, in conjunction with subsequent unlawful actions committed abroad, could be considered as an attempted or completed offense.' This interpretation would seem to accept the theory of the 'potential commission of the deed'. However, the same ruling[28] continues with a restrictive interpretation requiring that 'an attempted criminal act carried out in Italy must have some corresponding objective impact on the outside world.'

11.3.4 **Applicability of the principle of territoriality**

The criterion of ubiquity is particularly useful to apply to offenses committed over the Internet. The main doctrine on the subject considers that Italian jurisdiction should apply when the data involved in the offense, although they may have been put on the Internet outside Italy, pass through servers located in Italy, or when the storage and copying of the data has taken place in Italy.[29]

---

[26] Idem, p. 44.

[27] Idem, p. 45.

[28] Corte di cassazione, Sezione I, 20 March 1963, *Rivista italiana di diritto e procedura penale* 1965, p. 118 et seq.; Corte di cassazione, Sezione IV, 22 February 1993, *Giustizia penale* 1993, II, n. 517, p. 629.

[29] See Foggetti, loc. cit. n. 15, p. 46.

The principle of ubiquity is specifically applicable in cases of defamation over the Internet. Italian case law states that, on the basis of that principle, an Italian judge can try such an offense, either if it has been committed in national territory or if the *iter criminis* (crime route) was initiated abroad but has been completed, resulting in a crime, in Italy.[30]

11.3.5 **Applicability of the principle of defense**

For the applicability of Italian criminal law, as an alternative to the principle of territoriality, our judicial system provides for the application of the 'principle' of defense, through which the criminal law can be applied not on the basis of where the offense was committed or of the nationality of the offender, but rather on the basis of who the victim of the offense was.

Thus, according to this principle, Italian criminal law is applicable if the offense was committed against the Italian state or against an Italian citizen, regardless of where it was committed. Article 10 CC states that a foreigner who 'commits, in a foreign territory, against the Italian state or against an Italian citizen, an offense for which Italian law specifies life imprisonment or a custodial sentence of no less than a year, will be punished under that law.' This article is a corollary of Article 3 CC, by which Italian law is universally obligatory, unless it is limited by conflicting national or international laws.

Whether an unlawful conduct committed by a foreigner in a foreign territory can be punished under Italian law will also, however, depend on some other conditions: the offender must be present in Italian territory and there must be either a petition from the Italian Ministry of Justice or a lawsuit or complaint by the offended party (Art. 10 para. 1 CC).

Another possibility is provided by Article 10 paragraph 2 CC. If an offense harms the European Community, a foreign state, or a foreigner, the perpetrator can be prosecuted according to Italian criminal law if (and only if) (1) he or she is in Italian territory; 2) the crime carries a penalty of imprisonment for life or not below three years, and (3) if extradition was not granted or was not accepted by the state's government where the crime was committed or the government of the perpetrator's state.

11.4 A Typical Case: an Attack from 'Outside'

The scholar Foggetti describes, in several studies, in relation to the problem of applicable law, a typical cross-border cybercrime case that actually occurred, although it has not yet been tried in court.[31]

[30] Ibid., p. 48. One of the most important decisions here is Corte di cassazione, 29 April 1980, *Cass. Pen. Mass. Ann.* 1981, p. 1558.

[31] Ibid., p. 46.

The case concerns a Swiss hacker who violated a public-interest information system in Switzerland, affecting and damaging Italian users connected to the compromised system. The system attacked was of 'public interest', since thousands of users from all over the world were connected to it, and because experiments were conducted and analyzed using the hardware and software resources located in Geneva. The hacker made use of a local vulnerability of the system, and he upgraded his privileges from 'normal user' to 'root user'.

He went on to install a rootkit, which made the attack a Trojan-like attack, and very complex software, including a 'sniffer', in order to copy the passwords keyed in on-line, and he installed other programs with backdoors that could later be used to get back into the system without having to trespass and break it again. The rootkit also contained some tools to hide any trace of the attack, by altering the system commands that enable the intrusion to be verified, thereby canceling the activity logs.

The attack was launched from Geneva, but the copied passwords belonged to Italian users who were connected to the violated system. The hacker thus committed the crime in Switzerland, compromising the integrity of a computer system there, but he 'cracked' the passwords of user subscribers who connected to the system from Italy. Even though the passwords were keyed in by Italian users, from computers located on Italian territory, the 'minimum requirement' needed for Italian law to apply was *not* fulfilled: the deed of 'copying the passwords' was done wholly in Geneva, and also the rootkit was installed in the Geneva machines. In this case, the territoriality principle cannot be applied in order to determine whether the offense is punishable under Italian law.

Moreover, the principle of defense, explained in the above-mentioned Article 10 CC, was not applicable, since the Italian users had not filed a lawsuit or complaint against the hacker. Likewise, none of the conditions of Article 10 paragraph 2 were fulfilled. Therefore, the case was not punishable under Italian law, and the Swiss law was fully applied.

This would have been different if the rootkit had been installed on an Italian machine, located on Italian territory. In that case, the violation of an Italian system would have constituted the final link in the attacker's criminal project, and Italian criminal law could have been applied, not by virtue of the principle of the nationality of the offended party, but based on the criterion of ubiquity as set out in Article 6 paragraph 2 CC. The attack would then have implied the 'minimum necessary requirement' to allow the entire illegal conduct to be tried under Italian law.

11.5 Conclusion

As we have seen, the Italian legislator has preferred to use the categories of old crimes to discipline computer crimes, and this is probably the main reason for some interpretative problems that are often faced by the Supreme Court.

The criteria for cybercrime jurisdiction are the same as those used in general criminal law, notably the territoriality principle, or the *locus commissi delicti* principle, and the principle of defense. For this reason, one could talk of an adaptation of old principles to new technologies. These principles can be used, with some limitations, to fight cybercrime.

It is very important, given the nature of cybercrime, to regulate investigative activities beyond state borders. The Convention on Cybercrime is a perfect example of an attempt to do this, but the slowness of ratification shows how difficult it is for many states to accept a limit to their sovereignty.

Bibliography

Y. Amoroso Fernández, 'Virus informatici: aspetti legali' [Informatics Viruses: Legal Aspects], *Informatica e diritto* (1999) p. 217.

S. Chiccarelli and A. Monti, *Spaghetti Hacker. Storie, tecniche e aspetti giuridici dell'hacking in Italia* [Spaghetti Hackers. Stories, Techniques, and Legal Aspects of Hacking in Italy] (Milan, Apogeo 1997).

N. Foggetti, 'Legal analysis of a case of cross-border cyber crime', IV *Upgrade, the European Journal for the Informatics Professional* (2003) No. 6, p. 43, available at <http://www.upgrade-cepis.org>.

C. Gubitosa, *Italian crackdown. BBS amatoriali, volontari telematici, censure e sequestri nell'Italia degli anni '90* [Italian Crackdown. BBS Lovers, Telematics Volunteers, Censorship and Seizures in 1990s Italy] (Milan, Apogeo 1999).

G. Livraghi, 'Internet freedom, privacy and culture in Italy (and the activity of NGO's)', 1 *Ciberspazio e Diritto* (2000) No. 1, pp. 21-30.

A. Monti, 'The network society as seen from Italy', paper presented at the Conference for Freedom and Privacy (CFP) 2000 in Toronto (6 April 2000), available at <http://www.cfp.org>.

A. Monti, 'Diritto delle tecnologie dell'informazione e protezione dei diritti civili' [Information Technology Law and Protection of Civil Rights], 1 *Ciberspazio e Diritto* (2000) No. 1, pp. 41-51.

C. Parodi, 'Profili penali dei virus informatici' [Criminal Profiles of the Informatics Viruses], *Diritto penale e processo* (2000) No. 5, p. 632.

G. Pica, *Diritto penale delle tecnologie informatiche* [Criminal Law of Information Technologies] (Turin, Giappichelli 1999).

G. Ziccardi, 'La libertà di espressione in Internet al vaglio della Corte Suprema degli Stati Uniti' [Freedom of Expression on the Internet under the Scrutiny of the U.S. Supreme Court], *Quaderni Costituzionali* (1998) No. 1, pp. 123-134.

G. Ziccardi, 'I virus informatici: aspetti tecnici e giuridici' [Informatics Viruses: Technical and Legal Aspects], *Ciberspazio e diritto* (2001) Nos. 3-4, p. 347.

G. Ziccardi, *Crittografia e Diritto* [Cryptography and Law] (Turin, Giappichelli, 2003).

Chapter 12
CYBERCRIME AND JURISDICTION IN JAPAN

Pauline C. Reich*

12.1 Introduction[1]

In order to discuss Japanese cybercrime issues, it is necessary to put the study of cybercrime and the various forms of legislation adopted and pending in Japan into context. Basically, cybercrime and cyberlaw research is not well-developed in Japan. The country has a few cyberlaw and security organizations, such as JP-CERT,[2] and some isolated cyberlaw academics, but the government's approach to cybercrime and Internet security issues is fragmented. Also, there is a lack of coordination in the enactment of new and amended laws to take into account the use of computers, networks, and the Internet in Japan. According to one of the pioneers in the cyberlaw field in Japan,

> 'there are many difficulties with respect to legislation and law enforcement in the area of cybercrime. There is a lack of law or a delay in drafting legislation to address the information society. On the other hand, there are some incorrect judgments rendered by courts mainly due to misunderstanding. These have been caused by mainly judges' misunderstanding or ignorance of computer technology.'[3]

Nevertheless, something can be said about cybercrime in Japan. According to the National Police Agency of Japan, Cybercrime falls into three categories: violation of the Unauthorized Computer Access Law, crimes against computers or data, and

* Prof. Pauline C. Reich is Professor at Waseda University School of Law and Director of the Asia-Pacific Cybercrime and Security Institute, Waseda University, Tokyo, Japan.

[1] The author wishes to thank Dr Koichiro Hayashi, Vice President, Institute of Information Security, Yokohama, Japan and Tetsuya Ishii, Associate Professor of Criminal Law, Faculty of Law and Economics, Chiba University, for reviewing previous drafts of this chapter. This chapter is written in honor of my professor of Japanese Comparative Law, B.J. George, Jr., a recipient of the Order of the Rising Sun from the Emperor of Japan.

[2] See <http://www.jpcert.or.jp/english/>.

[3] T. Natsui, 'Cybercrime Legislation and Cases in Japan: Update', in Pauline C. Reich, ed., *Cybercrime and Security* (Dobbs Ferry, New York, Oceana Publications, 1998-present) (loose-leaf series) (2005).

B-J. Koops and S.W. Brenner (Eds), Cybercrime and Jurisdiction

'Internet Crime'.[4] The Agency notes that the 'number of arrests [for] violation of the Unauthorized Computer Access Law is increasing every year.'[5] Major crimes include child prostitution and child pornography in relation to 'Internet dating service sites', fraud, distribution of obscene materials, and violations of copyright, e.g., when using Internet-based auction sites, and defamation and threats when using Bulletin Board Systems (BBS).[6]

The National Police Agency has released the following statistics on the number of arrests for cybercrime during the period 2000-2003.[7]

Table 12.1. – *Cybercrime Statistics for Japan*

	2000	**2001**	**2002**	**2003**
Unauthorized computer access	67	67	105	145
Crimes against computer or data	44	63	30	55
computer fraud	33	48	18	34
illegal production or destruction of electro-magnetic data	9	11	8	12
obstruction of business by destroying computers	2	4	4	9
Internet crime	802	1,209	1,471	1,649
child prostitution	8	117	268	269
child pornography	113	128	140	102
Fraud	306	485	514	521
distribution of obscene materials	154	103	109	113
violation of juvenile protection ordinance	2	10	70	120
Intimidation	17	40	33	38
infringement of copyright	80	86	66	87
Defamation	30	42	27	46
Others	92	198	244	353
Total	*913*	*1,339*	*1,606*	*1,849*

As the statistics demonstrate, the National Police Agency reports that arrests for cybercrime were up 115 per cent in 2003 over the number of arrests in 2000. The Agency also reported major increases in the incidence of computer fraud and other types of cybercrime. Perhaps surprisingly, the Japanese police did not identify the

[4] National Police Agency, *Arrests and Consultations of Cybercrime in 2003*, <http://www.npa.go.jp/cyber/english/statics/2003.htm>. For more on this, see, e.g., Takato Natsui, *Cybercrimes in Japan: Recent Cases, Legislations, Problems and Perspectives* (2003), <http://www.netsafe.org.nz/Doc_Library/netsafepapers_takatonatsui_japan.pdf>.

[5] See National Police Agency, loc. cit. n. 4.

[6] The author wishes to thank Mr. Takashi Garcia Sato, former Superintendent, Assistant Director, Cybercrime Division, Japanese National Police Agency for his help in providing the data used in this section.

[7] National Police Agency, loc. cit. n. 4.

country's first loss from phishing, a type of on-line fraud, until the end of 2004.[8] Numerous examples of cases are described by the National Police Agency web site;[9] for instance, the case of someone who collected passwords through a key-stroke logger in an Internet café and used these to transfer about US$ 140,000 to a bank account in a fictitious name; he was arrested for unauthorized computer access, computer fraud, and theft. It is, however, noteworthy that all cases described are national in character and that cross-border cases are not reported.[10]

12.2 Cybercrime Legislation

12.2.1 **Substantive law**

According to Professor Natsui,

> 'many criminal activities relate to computer systems and computer data, and many scholars believe that such activities should be construed to be cybercrimes (…). Due to the fact that such laws have been enacted on an *ad hoc* basis and in different manners, some laws have been enacted as new laws but others have been effectuated as amendments of existing law. In fact, there is no uniform government policy concerning Cyberlaw legislation in Japan (…). On the other hand, while some people think of such legislation as a new type of law, others think of such legislation in accordance with traditional legal dogma, which is often conservative. As a result, many conflicts have occurred both in interpretation and in law enforcement practices relating to such laws.'[11]

Most Japanese cybercrime cases are prosecuted under the provisions of the Penal Code of Japan (Law No. 45 of 1907, amended in 1987) and the Unauthorized Computer Access Law (Law No. 128 of 1999). In fact, most of the cybercrimes defined in the Council of Europe Cybercrime Convention (*ETS* 185) are also punishable under the Penal Code, except that illegal access is not covered by existing Japanese laws.[12]

As is the case with other Japanese laws, the Penal Code includes few definition clauses. The only provision defining computer crime in any of the laws appears in Article 7*bis* of the Penal Code:[13]

---

[8] Ibid.

[9] Ibid.

[10] Research conducted by the author of this chapter indicates that there has been hacking of Japanese government web sites; there were allegations that the hacking has come from North Korea or China, but this has not been substantiated.

[11] Natsui (2005), loc. cit. n. 3, p. 4.

[12] Ibid.

[13] Ibid. As Natsui explains, there is disagreement as to whether this definition encompasses computer programs. See Natsui (2003), loc. cit. n. 4.

> 'The term "electromagnetic record" used in this Code shall mean the record made by any electronic methods, magnetic method or other methods unrecognizable with human perception and provided for the use of data processing in a computer system.'

In the absence of definitions, there are still provisions in various Japanese laws prohibiting cybercrime activities.[14] Article 161*bis* of the Penal Code, for example, prohibits any illegal production of electromagnetic records. It essentially outlaws computer-facilitated forgery. The basic penalty is imprisonment for not more than five years or a fine of not more than 500,000 yen;[15] the penalty rises to imprisonment for up to ten years or a fine of up to one million yen when the offense is 'committed against an electro-magnetic record which should be prepared by a public office or public officer.'

A related provision, Article 163*bis*, criminalizes someone who 'with the intent to bring about [the] improper economic administration of affairs of another person, unlawfully produces an electro-magnetic record which is for the use of the administration of such affairs and composes credit card or other payment cards for cost or charge.' The penalty for this offense is imprisonment for up to ten years or a fine of up to one million yen.[16]

Article 234*bis* of the Penal Code prohibits the use of a computer system to interfere, in any manner, with a business transaction. This makes it a crime to obstruct another person's business by 'impeding the operation' of a computer that is being utilized by that business for a legitimate business purpose, or by 'allowing such a computer to operate in a way which contradicts such a purpose by damaging such computer or an electro-magnetic record for it or by providing such a computer with inappropriate information or command or by any other means.'

Article 246*bis* of the Penal Code criminalizes the use of computer technology to commit fraud, that is, to produce 'a false electro-magnetic record which represents an acquisition, loss or alteration of property rights,' to provide 'a computer used for the administration of another person's business with false information or commands,' or to put 'such false electro-magnetic record in use for another person's business' and thereby acquire 'illicit profit' or cause 'another person to acquire such profit'. The basic penalty for violating this provision is imprisonment for up to five years. Article 250 of the Penal Code makes it a crime to attempt to commit fraud in violation of Article 246.

---

[14] An overview of cybercrime provisions can be found in the 2003 APEC Cybercrime Survey of Japan, <http://www.mastel.or.id/Cybercrime/Country%20Surveys/JapanSurvey.htm>. The relevant provisions in the Japanese Penal Code can also be found at <http://www.isc.meiji.ac.jp/~sumwel_h/Arc-Laws/Penal%20Code%20Japan.htm>; a provisional translation of the Unauthorized Computer Access Law is available at <http://www.npa.go.jp/cyber/english/legislation/ucalaw.html>. The description in this section is based on these sources.

[15] 100,000 yen is approximately US$ 900 [editors' note].

[16] Several related articles define other offenses involving the misuse of electromagnetic records. See Arts. 163*ter*, 163*quater*, and 163*quint* Penal Code.

Articles 258 and 259 of the Penal Code prohibit the destruction of certain types of electromagnetic records. Article 258 criminalizes the destruction of 'any documents or electromagnetic record which ought to be used at a State office', while Article 259 makes it a crime to destroy 'any documents or electromagnetic record relating to' the property of others. The first offense is punishable by imprisonment for at least three months and up to five years, the second offense by imprisonment for up to five years.

The Unauthorized Computer Access Law (Law No. 128 of 1999)[17] has as its purpose, 'by prohibiting acts of unauthorized computer access (...) to prevent computer-related crimes that are committed through telecommunication lines and to maintain the telecommunications-related order that is realized by access control functions' (Art. 1). It punishes only a specific type of unauthorized access to a computer system: remote access obtained 'via a telecommunication line' by someone who has no right to access that computer system. It does not cover any unauthorized access, use, copying, or transfer of computer data, e.g., in stand-alone computers not connected to a network (Art. 3(2)).[18] Unauthorized access is punishable by imprisonment for up to a year or a fine of up to 500,000 yen (Art. 8(1)). Article 4 of the Unauthorized Computer Access law makes it a crime to facilitate unauthorized access to a computer system: no one shall provide an identification code 'relating to an access control function to a person other than the access administrator for that access control function or the authorized user for that identification code.' This is punishable by a fine of up to 300,000 yen (Art. 9).

Finally, three special laws are also relevant. First, on-line child pornography is covered by the 1999 Child Pornography and Prostitution Law. Before the passage of that law, child pornography was not prohibited in Japan, something that was heavily criticized from outside Japan.[19] The Penal Code did have an 'obscene object' provision, but this was only of limited use in relation to child pornography. According to the National Police Agency, after the passage of the 1999 law, the transmission by the Internet of child pornography has diminished.

The second is the Second-hand Dealers Law, aimed primarily at Internet-based auction dealers. It requires dealers to submit documents to local Public Safety Commissions (the local police) when they want to start Internet auctions that deal with second-hand goods. The dealers must report to the police when the auctioned goods

[17] For an analysis of the goals and structure of this law, see Natsui (2003), loc. cit. n. 4, pp. 10-13. For the text of the law, see <http://www.npa.go.jp/cyber/english/legislation/ucalaw.html>.

[18] See also Natsui (2003), loc. cit. n. 4: 'This law can prohibit only a specific type of unauthorized access, that is any remote access without any right to a computer system which has been connected with another computer system.'

[19] The example of child pornography shows the prevalence of cultural differences in relation to criminal law. In this respect, it is worth noting that issues that are not a problem or not significant in other countries are a major problem in Japan, e.g., the formation of on-line suicide pact groups.

are possibly stolen goods. The police can issue a 'stop order' when such goods have a strong likelihood of having been stolen.

The third is the Law on the Control of Dating Services on the Internet, which came into effect in September 2003. It prohibits invitations to engage in sexual intercourse or to participate in a paid dating service with children (under 18) or using a paid dating service over the Internet to or from children. Dating-service providers are required to take measures to prevent children from using dating services over the Internet, in view of the damage to children caused by crimes committed via such dating services.[20]

12.2.2 **Procedural law**

Investigation powers are regulated in the Criminal Procedure Code (CPC). A search is usually conducted on the basis of Article 218 CPC. Searches in cases of cybercrime are not specifically addressed. Search warrants have been applied to electronic searches; however, there has been an issue about how they apply to digital images.

There is no provision concerning the delivery of computer data in the current Criminal Procedure Code. Nevertheless, the police can obtain a hard drive with the co-operation of the server manager. The Government is trying to amend the Criminal Procedure Code (see below), so that a commercial server owner can be ordered to submit a copy of digital data to the police or a court. No Japanese court has yet ordered delivery, but an ISP has voluntarily delivered data to prevent a court from stopping its commercial activity.

There is a Wiretapping Law in Japan[21] that permits communication interception for the purposes of a criminal investigation. There are severe restrictions on the use of the law. It can be used in cases of serious drug trafficking, firearms and human trafficking only. It has been in force for four years but, so far, has only been applied to drug trafficking. It is thus very different from interception laws in most other countries.

With respect to the evidentiary use of digital data, Articles 321, 322, and 323 CPC provide exceptions to the hearsay rule. The exceptions are very broad: if evidence falls within these provisions, the court can admit those items as evidence in

---

[20] See, e.g., National Police Agency, loc. cit. n. 4. See also 'Diet passes bill banning paid sex with minors', *The Daily Yomiuri*, 19 May 1999, p. 1: the new legislation was to 'punish anyone who produces, sells or distributes sexually explicit videotapes and photos involving minors, for example, through the Internet.' It applies 'not only to offenses committed within the nation, but also to those committed overseas'.

[21] Law No. 128 of 1999, Law on Interception of Communication for the Purpose of Criminal Investigation. This law can be applied to cases of communication by computer. See, e.g., 'Japan's Communications Interception Act: Unconstitutional Invasion of Privacy or Necessary Tool?', 35 *Vanderbilt Journal of Transnational Law* (2002) p. 893, and 'Japan's Wiretap Law in Comparison with Major Countries' Systems' (13 August 1999), <http//:www.usc.edu/isd/archives/dsjp/summaries/1999/August/Sm990816.htm>.

court, thus allowing much more indirect evidence than, for instance, in the United States.

Enforcement of the cybercrime laws is quite complicated, as many agencies of the government are responsible for the following: for preventing criminal behavior related to the law (Ministry of Justice), for developing regulations relating to access control (Ministry of Telecommunications), and for enforcing all regulations relating to the information industry and the telecommunications industry (Ministry of Telecommunications and the Ministry of Economy, Trade and Industry).

In addition, the National Information Security Center of the Cabinet Secretariat and the National Police Agency have roles to play in, respectively, 1) developing policy and co-ordinating the ministries' activities, and 2) conducting investigations, cross-border formal and informal co-operation, and enforcement of the laws via arrests.

12.2.3 Japan and the Cybercrime Convention

Japan signed the Council of Europe's Convention on Cybercrime on 23 November 2001, when the convention was opened for signature in Budapest.[22] Like many of the countries that have signed the convention, Japan has yet to ratify it. It cannot ratify the Convention until its legal system allows Japanese officials to implement the various requirements contained in the Convention on Cybercrime. Legislation has been introduced which would bring Japanese law to the level required to implement the convention.[23]

A first proposal was to be submitted to the Legislative Council, an advisory panel to the Minister of Justice, on 24 March 2003. Ministry officials expected at that time that a bill would be introduced at the extraordinary session of the Diet (the Parliament) in the autumn of 2003, and had hoped to be able to ratify the Cybercrime Convention at the same session; however, the bill was abrogated. According to one expert, this was due to the dissolution of the Diet – but the main reason seems to have been that 'the conspiracy clause was thought by representatives to have serious problems'. The Ministry reportedly made minimal amendments, by dropping

[22] See Council of Europe, Convention on Cybercrime (CETS 185), Chart of Signatures and Ratifications, <http://conventions.coe.int/Treaty/Commun/ChercheSig.asp?NT=185&CM=8&DF=10/31/04&CL=ENG>.

[23] See, e.g., Takashi Garcia Sato, 'Countermeasures against Cybercrime in Japan (progress of laws)', presentation at APEC-Tel Cybercrime Capacity Building meeting, Hanoi, Vietnam (25-27 August 2004), and the Japan Times Editorial, 'Clarifying the Cyber-crime Fight', *The Japan Times* (26 August 2004), <http://search.japantimes.co.jp/print/opinion/ed2004/ed20040826a1.htm>: 'To implement the treaty, Japan must first improve related domestic legislation. At present, computer-related crime is covered individually by different laws, including the Code of Criminal Procedure and the International Criminal Investigation Cooperation Law. The means of investigation available under current laws are limited, making it difficult to deal effectively with all types of crime that exploit computer systems.'

the expansion of e-mail monitoring for additional crimes and by excluding restrictions on child pornography in animated form or through the use of composite pictures.[24]

Subsequently, a 'Bill Amending Some Parts of the Criminal Law to Combat Internationalization and Organization of Crimes and the Promotion of Information Technology' was submitted to the Upper House on 20 February 2004 by the Cabinet Office. The bill 'does not change the basic structure of international co-operation to combat crime, but adds a few peripheral procedures'.[25] This Bill, which is now pending, comes down to the following:

> 'Broadly, the government's revision package now before the Lower House of the Diet has two aims: defining cyber-crime as a new category of crime, and introducing new methods of investigation.
>
> First, the list of new crimes includes creating or distributing computer viruses, as well as acts that cause damage to computers or computer data by attacking computer systems. Attempts at such 'business obstruction' would become punishable under the law. Moreover, the crime of distributing obscene material would be widened in scope. For example, those who distributed obscene images and CDs by recording them via hard disks, other electromagnetic devices, the Internet or other means of telecommunications would be punished. (…)
>
> Second, the package would make it possible to gather evidence by new methods. For instance, courts would be able to seize data by copying it from recording mediums that are connected to computers by electric circuits. Police also would be able to obtain data, under court warrants, by ordering those in custody of the data to present copies. Here again, there is criticism that such measures may violate the confidentiality or privacy of communications, such as by revealing exchanges of personal e-mails that have nothing to do with crime. Providers, meanwhile, are said to be worried that their costs of doing business may increase and that their cooperation with investigative authorities could engender suspicion among users.'[26]

This and other bills that have been introduced to amend the Japanese Penal Code and Criminal Procedure Code have been delayed due to the priority of addressing financial-reform issues that are under consideration in the Diet. Thus, until Japan adopts the requisite legislation, its ratification of the Cybercrime Convention will be further delayed.

---

[24] Cf., 'Stiffer E-Data Rules Eyed', *Asahi News Service* (17 March 2003).

[25] Information received from Dr Koichiro Hayashi, Vice President, Institute of Information Security, Yokohama, Japan, 25 July 2005. See, e.g., Transcript of Statement by Prosecutor General Kunihiro Matsuo of Japan, Eleventh United Nations Congress on Crime Prevention and Criminal Justice (2005), <http://www.un.org/webcast/crime2005/statements/23japan_eng.pdf>. For the Japanese-language version see <http://www.shugiin.go.jp/itdb_gian.nsf/html/gian/keika/ID942D2.htm>.

[26] *Japan Times* Editorial (2004), loc. cit. n. 23.

In a position paper issued in April 2005 to the Eleventh United Nations Congress on Crime Prevention and Criminal Justice, the Japan Federation of Bar Associations (JFBA) raised concerns about such issues as privacy and human rights with respect to initiatives to combat computer-related crime. It recommended:

> 'When taking actions to prevent and control computer-related crime, governments should ensure the guarantee of human rights such as those provided by Articles 12 and 19 of the Universal Declaration of Human Rights, and the secrecy and communications and freedom of expression provided by Articles 17 and 19 of the International Covenant on Civil and Political Rights, and to endeavor to find a rational balance with crime prevention and control while taking into consideration the need for careful attention to protecting individual freedoms and personal information as stated in UNGA Resolution 55/63.'[27]

The JFBA position paper notes problems in the Cybercrime Convention, e.g.,

> 'the Cybercrime Convention (...) speaks for the law-enforcement agencies (...) while giving short shrift to privacy and other civil liberties and including no consideration for the Internet and computer industries.
>
> Cybercrime Convention provisions (...) give law-enforcement agencies the authority to preserve the data stored in computer systems, the traffic data and content data maintained and possessed by service providers, and to obtain the subscriber information possessed by providers, and to broadly monitor traffic data and content data in real time for the purpose of investigations. These provisions give law-enforcement agencies broader and stronger authority for computer crime investigations than for the usual criminal investigations.
>
> [There is concern] that law-enforcement agencies would interfere in communication conducted through networks and violate its privacy, and also violate the freedom to send and receive information and ideas. Although it is recognized that computer-related crime threatens international society, (...) it is unacceptable to grant law-enforcement agencies such powerful authority for that purpose, thereby creating a situation in which civil liberties are broadly violated. We therefore have serious doubts about using the Cybercrime Convention as it stands, as the standard for controlling computer crime. Governments should note the great significance of the fact that since its signing in 2001 until the present day, the Cybercrime Convention has yet to be ratified by a single major developed country.'[28]

---

[27] Japan Federation of Bar Associations, *Position Paper from the Japan Federation of Bar Associations to the Eleventh United Nations Congress on Crime Prevention and Criminal Justice* (April 2005), <http://www.nichibenren.or.jp/en/activities/statements/data/2005_27.pdf>.

[28] Ibid., at pp. 10-11. See also Satoshi Takagi, 'Government urged to watch its step in cyberspace', *Mainichi Shimbun* (1 September 2000), p. 1.

On the other hand, there are also people who appear to support amending Japanese law and ratifying the Convention on Cybercrime.[29]

12.3 Jurisdiction in Cybercrime Cases

12.3.1 Jurisdictional provisions

The Penal Code of Japan applies to (i) crimes committed within Japan, (ii) certain crimes committed outside Japan, and (iii) crimes committed outside Japan by Japanese nationals.[30] The main basis for jurisdiction is territoriality:

> 'Article 1 – Crimes within Japan
>
> 1. The Code shall apply to every person who commits a crime within the territory of Japan.
>
> 2. The provision of the preceding paragraph shall also apply to a person who commits a crime on board a Japanese vessel or a Japanese aircraft outside the territory of Japan.'

This covers crimes committed in whole or in part in Japan.[31]

Article 2 of the Penal Code deals with jurisdiction over crimes committed outside Japan. It states that the Code applies to every person who commits any of a selection of crimes outside the territory of Japan, including not only crimes like insurrection, but also forgery of official documents (Arts. 154-158) and the cybercrimes of 161*bis* (for public forgery) and 163*bis* to 163*quint.*

Article 3 of the Penal Code establishes jurisdiction over certain crimes when they are committed outside the territory of Japan by Japanese nationals. It applies to, for example, forgery of private documents (Arts. 159-161 and 161*bis*), defamation (Art. 230), theft (Arts. 235-236) , fraud (Arts. 246-250), and embezzlement (Art. 253).

---

29 See, e.g., *Japan Times* Editorial (2004), loc. cit. n. 23.

30 See Arts. 1 to 4*bis* of the Penal Code, translation available at <http://www2.kobe-u.ac.jp/~nmika/doc1.html>. The quotations in this section are from this translation.

31 See also Shigemitsu Dando, 'Basic Concepts in and Temporal and Territorial Limits on the Applicability of the Penal Law of Japan', translated by B.J. George, Jr., 9 *New York Law School Journal of International and Comparative Law* (1988) p. 237, at p. 256. Cf., OECD, *Japan – Review of Implementation of the Convention and 1997 Recommendation* (21 May 2002), <http://www.oecd.org/dataoecd/15/21/2387870.pdf>: 'This is understood to cover the case where a bribe is offered, promised or given in Japan (including the case where the act of offering, etc., is done from Japan through remittance, telephone, facsimile, etc.); as well as the case where the bribe is offered, promised or given abroad where an act of complicity takes place in Japan (including the case where the complicity is extended overseas).'

Article 3*bis* deals with jurisdiction over crimes involving physical injury or assault committed outside Japan by foreigners against Japanese nationals, and Article 4 covers jurisdiction for certain crimes that public officials of Japan commit outside Japan. Article 4*bis* states that the Penal Code also applies to those who commit crimes for which, 'according to treaties, Japan has an obligation to punish even when they are committed outside Japan'.

Japan can claim jurisdiction even if someone has been tried elsewhere: 'Even if a person has been adjudicated a criminal in another country, there is no bar to the entry of a Japanese criminal adjudication imposing punishment based on the same acts. If the criminal penalties imposed on an offender by a foreign court have been enforced completely or in part, however, the enforcement of the punishment assessed by the Japanese court must be either reduced or remitted.'[32]

12.3.2 Case law on cross-border cybercrime

There have been few verdicts on cross-border or even domestic cybercrime cases in Japan. In one famous case with cross-border features, dating back to 1999, a Japanese national placed pornographic images on a U.S. server and was prosecuted and convicted in Japan.[33] The case resulted in a ruling by the Osaka District Court.

The defendant Japanese national had sent obscene images to a U.S. server from November 1996 to February 1997. The law in effect at the time banning the public display of indecent drawings and pictures did not apply to offenses committed overseas. Moreover, lawyers for the defendant claimed that the act of sending the image constituted only the preparation of data, not the display of images.

The Japanese judge ruled, however, that the Japanese national's acts constituted a public display of obscene materials and that Japanese law was applicable in this case, because the images were sent from Japan and an unlimited number of domestic users were able to access the site, even though it was operated from the United States. The judge ruled that, although the defendant had sent the images to a server in the United States, which stored the data, the site was intended for Japanese users because it was in Japanese. 'In this case, sending the data from Japan played an important role and it is possible to apply domestic criminal law', said the presiding judge.

Another aspect of the case involved a prosecution for assisting in the public display of obscene materials by selling software over the Internet that the defendant had created to remove the digital images that usually cover the genitals in porno-

[32] Dando, loc. cit. n. 31, p. 262.

[33] See Taro Yamato, 'Osaka court takes up issue of online obscenity', *The Daily Yomiuri* (2 September 1997), p. 8; Taro Yamato, 'Mosaic-busting software lands programmer in jail', *The Daily Yomiuri* (22 April 1997), p. 9; 'Man arrested in computer porn case', *The Daily Yomiuri* (12 April 1997), p. 2; Hiroshi Ikematsu, 'Domestic law applied to Net porn', *The Daily Yomiuri* (30 March 1999), p. 10, *Hanrei Times* (1 September 2000); 'Court sentences maker of porn-mosaic remover', *Mainichi Daily News* (31 March 2000), p. 18.

graphic images in movies, magazines, etc., shown in Japan. He was prosecuted for linking his web page to a pornographic web site where genitalia had been concealed by the 'mosaic' and for promising that the use of his software would provide clients with an unhindered view. Consequently, the defendant had assisted in the public display of obscenity by providing links to the pornographic site and providing the means to view the images clearly. This was the first case ever in Japan where hyperlinks were used to convict someone for assisting in the commission of a crime. The defendant was sentenced to one year imprisonment, which was suspended for three years.

The trial also marked the first full-scale legal discussion in Japan on the definition of on-line obscenity; the appeal in this case to the Supreme Court of Japan primarily involved the definition of what constitutes a 'public display' of obscene material according to Article 175 of the Criminal Code. The cross-border aspects of the case were not an issue as such in the appeal.[34]

In another 1999 case, a Tokyo man was arrested for selling pornographic images of children over the Internet. The defendant was arrested for sales of obscene images after he allegedly used a U.S.-based ISP to sell CD-ROMS featuring the images. Although Japanese law forbids the authorities from prosecuting those who use overseas providers to post obscene Internet images, the defendant was arrested because he had allegedly sold the images to people in Japan.[35]

12.3.3 Cyber-investigation and international co-operation

In the case of a cross-border cybercrime, investigation largely depends on mutual international legal assistance. The basic Japanese legislation in effect in this area are the Law for International Assistance in Investigation (Law No. 69 of 1980) and the Law for Judicial Assistance to Foreign Courts (Law No. 3 of 1905, as amended by Law No. 7 of 1912 and Law No. 17 of 1938).[36]

In 2004, the Treaty between Japan and the United States on Mutual Legal Assistance in Criminal Matters was approved by the Diet, and related domestic laws involving international criminal-investigation assistance laws were amended. This is Japan's first bilateral treaty on international criminal investigation assistance, which is aimed at facilitating efficient and effective assistance. In addition, Japan has already begun to prepare legislation to conclude other treaties on international

---

[34] According to a Japanese criminal law expert, the 'territorial principle means that all or part of the criminal activity is carried out in Japan or a result of criminal activity which occurs in Japan. There are no problems regarding the principle in normal cross-border cases because offenders manipulate or use a computer in Japan for their offenses to upload data into servers outside Japan.'

[35] 'Cops use loophole to bust online porn seller', *Mainichi Daily News* (19 June 1999), p. 12.

[36] Jeffrey G. Bullwinkel, 'International Cooperation in Combating Cyber-Crime in Asia: Existing Mechanisms and New Approaches', in Roderick Broadhurst and Peter Grabosky, eds., *Cybercrime: the Challenge in Asia* (Hong Kong University Press, 2005).

mutual legal assistance, such as the United Nations Convention against Transnational Organized Crime and the Cybercrime Convention (see section 12.2.3).

If the Japanese government wants to prosecute a Japanese national who is overseas, it can request a foreign government to extradite the national. However, Japan only has extradition treaties with the United States and the Republic of Korea.

The National Police Agency works closely with overseas law-enforcement agencies to prevent and investigate transnational crimes and to arrest fugitives abroad through diplomatic channels, the International Criminal Police Organization (ICPO-Interpol), and other means. Japan's National Police Agency functions as Japan's National Central Bureau for ICPO-Interpol.

International assistance presents various problems, however. For example, when a person in the United States tries to access a Japanese computer without permission and to deface it, prosecution is difficult. The problem is the short time during which the log file is preserved. Preservation only lasts a few days or perhaps a month, whereas a request to a foreign law-enforcement agency takes too long – and there is no obligation to preserve the evidence. China requires an ISP to keep a log file for 60 days, but there is currently no such obligation in Japan. The amendment to the Criminal Procedure Law recently pending in the Diet (see section 12.2.3) does, however, contain provisions concerning a preservation order.[37]

Another issue is how Japan handles evidence collected abroad. Japanese courts seem to handle standards of evidence only from a Japanese perspective:

> 'If the United States violates human rights in the collection of evidence, there is no relation to the value of proof in Japan. Japanese law enforcement tries to avoid procedure (...). In Japan, there is a strong opinion that violation of foreign procedure is irrelevant in a Japanese court. Admission of such evidence in a Japanese court depends on Japanese Criminal Procedure Law only.'[38]

There are three conditions for admissibility:

1. the person who made the statement is dead or in a foreign country and cannot appear in court;
2. the statement or evidence is indispensable to judge the criminality of specific conduct;
3. the statement was made under reliable conditions.

These exceptions are very broad compared to, for example, U.S. criminal-procedure rules.[39]

---

37 Interview with Takashi Garcia Sato, National Police Agency, Tokyo.

38 Ibid.

39 Ibid.

Altogether, it seems that the Japanese cybercrime laws enacted to date may fall short, in that they do not adequately address all issues of cross-border cyber-investigation. In the words of Takashi Garcia Sato, formerly of the National Police Agency, the laws are 'good compared to what we had before, but weak to combat cyber-criminals.'[40]

12.4 Conclusion

The nature of the Internet is global. Computers linked throughout the world may be affected by cybercrime, and cybercrimes can be conducted across borders with few obstacles based on either technological or legal means. Since the nature of the medium is cross-border, legal jurisdiction must become cross-border as well. Extraterritorial jurisdiction appears in some areas of law, e.g., U.S. antitrust and anti-discrimination laws or Swedish child-prostitution law. It is clear that national laws must be amended or created to keep up with the use of technology such as the Internet, computers, third-generation mobile phones, wireless access, etc. In addition, the cross-border nature of these media needs to be incorporated legislatively, not merely in informal co-operation among law-enforcement agencies in different countries, but through formal, global legal measures.

International agreement on cybercrime jurisdiction and co-operation is not self-evident. Activities involving computers, networks and the Internet that are criminal in Japan may not be designated as criminal in other jurisdictions – and vice versa. In fact, there is no consistent definition of what is a cybercrime from jurisdiction to jurisdiction worldwide, making cross-border jurisdiction a problem. Another problem is that due to limited training and education opportunities, the second largest economy in the world may not have adequate numbers of police and other professionals trained in such areas as computer forensics, cybercrime, and Internet security.

Moreover, concerns such as those raised by the Japan Federation of Bar Associations and other organizations worldwide, to the effect that the Cybercrime Convention requirements are too broad and result in a loss of privacy and human rights, are legitimate. These concerns must be considered carefully before adopting domestic or universal legislation.

Bibliography

Jeffrey G. Bullwinkel, 'International Cooperation in Combating Cyber-Crime in Asia: Existing Mechanisms and New Approaches', in Roderick Broadhurst and Peter Grabosky, eds., *Cybercrime: the Challenge in Asia* (Hong Kong University Press, 2005).

[40] Ibid.

Takashi Garcia Sato, 'Countermeasures against Cybercrime in Japan (progress of laws)', presentation at APEC-Tel Cybercrime Capacity Building meeting, Hanoi, Vietnam (25-27 August 2004).

Japan Federation of Bar Associations, *Position Paper from the Japan Federation of Bar Associations to the Eleventh United Nations Congress on Crime Prevention and Criminal Justice* (April 2005), <http://www.nichibenren.or.jp/en/activities/statements/data/2005_27.pdf>.

National Police Agency, *Arrests and Consultations of Cybercrime in 2003*, <http://www.npa.go.jp/cyber/english/statics/2003.htm>.

Takato Natsui, 'Cybercrime Legislation and Cases in Japan: Update', in Pauline C. Reich, ed., *Cybercrime and Security* (Dobbs Ferry, New York, Oceana Publications, 1998-present) (loose-leaf series) (2005).

Takato Natsui, *Cybercrimes in Japan: Recent Cases, Legislations, Problems and Perspectives* (2003), <http://www.netsafe.org.nz/Doc_Library/netsafepapers_takatonatsui_japan.pdf>.

Chapter 13
CYBERCRIME AND JURISDICTION IN THE REPUBLIC OF KOREA

Jeong-Hoon Lee*

13.1 INTRODUCTION[1]

Escaping from the traditional concept of the place where something occurs, the Internet has given birth to cyberspace, which forms a new sphere of action, transcending the sovereign power of an individual country as a physically inseparable sphere and requiring a fundamental modification of sovereignty, i.e., law enforcement or jurisdiction based on the concept of the place where something occurs.[2] Particularly in crimes using the Internet, or cybercrimes, the fact that the offense occurs through the Internet raises conflicts between criminal jurisdictions according to whether such an offense is committed by the country's citizens or foreigners, or whether the offense occurred domestically or overseas.

Many countries have various cybercrime laws, and include specific provisions about the territorial scope of application of such laws, but the actual application of each country's laws is not straightforward with respect to their relationship to those of other countries. Each and every country may have different rules and different punishments for a certain cybercrime and may adopt dissimilar principles concerning jurisdiction. In the current situation, where an offender commits a crime via many countries through an Internet service provided by a foreign service provider in order to avoid his or her own country's laws, whether or not the country's criminal law may be applicable, will vary according to the country's assessment of whether the service provider is located domestically or in a foreign jurisdiction, and whether the offender is that country's citizen or a foreigner.

Although we might consider an international standard for cybercrime, it seems to be a remote possibility that there can be such a new international order, and we

* Prof. Dr Jeong-Hoon Lee, Ph.D. in Law, is Professor at the College of Law, ChungAng University.

[1] Many thanks to Mr. Sohn Jin, PhD candidate Sungkyunkwan University, for translating this work into English.

[2] Hyewook Won, *Study on evidence and jurisdiction over Internet crime* (Korea Institute of Criminology 2001), p. 91.

B-J. Koops and S.W. Brenner (Eds), Cybercrime and Jurisdiction

can only attempt to reach a concerted order for particular matters relying on the laws of all countries.[3] In this sense, criminal jurisdiction can be confirmed on the basis of all related countries' traditional theories of jurisdiction or resolved through international mutual legal assistance in criminal matters.

In this chapter, I will review the trend in legislation in relation to cybercrime in the Republic of Korea[4] (hereafter: Korea) and the interpretation and theories of laws concerning traditional criminal jurisdiction as well as introducing specific measures to facilitate international mutual assistance in cybercrime investigations.

13.2 Substantive Cybercrime Legislation

Currently, Korea provides for the punishment on cybercrimes in the Criminal Act concerning traditional crimes committed by means of a computer, and in various other laws. The most relevant of these are the Act on the Promotion of Information and Communications Network Utilization and Information Protection, etc. (hereafter: Information and Communications Network Act) and the Information and Communications Infrastructure Protection Act, which are special additions to the Criminal Act. Besides, the following laws are also relevant: the Framework Act on Electronic Commerce and Digital Signature Act concerning E-commerce, the Act on the Punishment of Sexual Crimes and the Protection of the Victims Thereof, concerning cyber-sexual harassment, the Act on the Protection of Juveniles' Sex, etc., concerning child pornography, the Copyright Act or Computer Program Protection Act concerning on-line copyright infringement, the Sound Records, Video Products, and Game Software Act, and the Act on Special Cases Concerning Regulation and Punishment of Speculative Acts, etc., concerning on-line games. Among these laws, I will now briefly consider the Criminal Act and the Information and Communications Network Act, which function as the basic laws against cybercrime.

13.2.1 **The Criminal Act**

Although very much deserving punishment, computer crimes were not punishable under the Criminal Act before 1995. Korea amended and supplemented the Criminal Act in 1995 to add provisions against computer crimes. The amendment includes additions entitled the False Preparation or Alteration of Public Electromagnetic Records (Art. 227-2, Art. 232-2), Fraud by Means of Computers (Art. 347-2), Interference with Business by Computer Destruction, etc. (Art. 314.2), and Destruction of Electromagnetic Records (Art. 141.1, Art. 366.1).

---

[3] Daeho Hyun, *Legislation Research on information protection on the Internet* (Korea Legislation Research Institute 2000), p. 108.

[4] Also known as South Korea [editors' note].

Manipulating electromagnetic records
Electromagnetic records used in computers have evidentiary functions for demonstrating socially relevant facts together with or instead of documents, a function that is to be protected. However, documents referred to in the Criminal Act require continuity, evidentiality, and surety as conceptual elements. Thus, it was difficult to include electromagnetic records containing electromagnetically recorded data into the concept of a document in that they lacked readability and visibility, two elements of continuity, and there was no such thing as the author's name in them for, more often than not, multiple users were involved in preparing them. Therefore, legislative action was required. In correspondence to the division of public and private documents and for the punishment of forgery, alteration and misuse of these documents, the Criminal Act now divides electromagnetic records into public and private electromagnetic records and punishes false preparation, alteration and the unlawful use thereof (Art. 227-2, Art. 232-2).

Computer fraud
As various matters such as management, settlement, or movement of funds and modifications of property rights in various fields, including banking, are increasingly dealt with automatically without manual interference by computers using electromagnetic records, and as the use of electromagnetic records demonstrating property rights (check cards, phone cards, subway tickets, etc.) are increasing, so also the act of deceptively obtaining property interests by misusing such means are increasing. Since these acts are not involved with deception against a person or the transfer of possession of property, such acts cannot be properly countered with the traditional concepts of fraud or theft. The terms 'deception, mistake, disposition' are generally used to refer to fraud by persons, but may not apply to fraud by computers. Therefore, the Article 'Fraud by Means of Computers' (Art. 347-2) was created in order to make such fraudulent acts punishable, understanding them as a form of fraud. This covers 'making any data processed after inputting false information or an improper order, or inputting or altering the data without any authority,' taking into account the fact that the essence of such acts is similar to fraud.

Computer interference with business
As the business processing of financial institutions or administrative offices as well as personal affairs became rapidly automated, expanded and complicated with the proliferation of computers, most activities previously dealt with by human beings came to be done by computers. Consequently, interfering with a computer system by destruction or other illegal methods has the same effect as interference with business. Since fraudulent means or threat of force – the methods of interference with business – are premised to be acts by persons, the drafters of the Criminal Act amendments have inserted a separate offense for violations through computers in Article 314.2.

Destruction of electromagnetic records

Electromagnetic records are worth protecting since they perform a social evidentiary function by recording and preserving information instead of requiring the use of documents, but it is not easy to assume that the records on special media including electromagnetic records are documents and that the data recorded are independent property. Because 'property' under the Criminal Act includes tangible property and controllable energy, the data may neither be classified as tangible property nor as controllable energy. Since electromagnetic records with data, however, might be deemed independent property, it was debated whether or not invalidating the data recorded on such recording media fell under destruction and damage. The Criminal Act amendment drafters inserted a ground for punishing the destruction of and damage to electromagnetic records by stipulating 'the records on special media including electromagnetic records' as the target of the offense of destruction and damage (Art. 141.1, Art. 366.1), thus eliminating the ground for continuing the debate on interpretation.

13.2.2 **The Information and Communications Network Act**

Functioning as a basic measure to cope with cybercrime, the Criminal Act 1995 with its provisions against computer crimes was not without shortcomings in dealing with the new types of crimes occurring in cyberspace or on the Internet. For instance, the Criminal Act before 1995 could not respond to so-called cyberpornography with its limited concept of pornography, and could not respond to data infringement of or through the use of an information network even though it criminalized the destruction of 'electromagnetic records'. Besides, the lack of provisions concerning hacking or viruses further revealed its limitations. Under such circumstances, to protect the information networks *per se* and the data transmitted over such networks, Korea has enacted the Act on the Promotion of Information and Communications Network Utilization and Information Protection, etc., which is pretty much exhaustive in listing cybercrimes, thereby making itself a basic act on cybercrime. Below is a brief introduction to the provisions concerning each kind of cybercrime.

Hacking

Article 48.2 of the Information and Communications Network Act provides that '[a]ny person shall be prohibited from infiltrating information and communications networks without any justifiable access right or beyond his permitted access right.' Article 63.1.1 makes such an act punishable by imprisonment with prison labor for not more than three years or by a fine not exceeding 30 million won.[5] Article 63.2 proscribes an attempt to commit such an act. This provision is to prevent 'hacking',

[5] One million won is approximately US$ 1,000 (1 USD = 1,026 KRW, as of September 2005) [editors' note].

which enables an unauthorized person to infiltrate another person's computer system without permission.

Besides, Article 49 provides that '[a]ny person shall be prohibited from damaging the information of other persons or from infringing, stealing or leaking the secrets of other persons, which are processed, stored or transmitted by an information and communications network.' Article 62.6 makes the acts in Article 49 punishable by imprisonment with prison labor for not more than five years or by a fine not exceeding 50 million won. This provision is to cope with infringements of confidential information by hacking or modifications or the removal of data by hacking. Moreover, if anyone obtains a property interest through hacking, this is punishable as fraud by means of a computer under the Criminal Act.

Viruses

Disseminating viruses in order to interfere with another person's business by computers is punishable by the Criminal Act as interference with business by computer destruction, etc., being interpreted as the offense of business interference. Thus, in order to punish the act of interfering with information networks other than business networks, the Information and Communications Network Act proscribes virus crimes.

Article 48.2 of the Information and Communications Network Act provides: 'Any person shall be prohibited from transmitting or distributing any program [hereafter: "malicious program"] that may damage and destroy an information and communications system, alter and forge the data or programs, etc., or hinder the operation thereof without any justifiable reasons.' Article 48.3 states: 'Any person shall be prohibited from sending a large volume of signals or data for the purpose of hindering the stable operation of an information and communications network or from causing problems in information and communications networks using the method of causing unfair instructions to be processed'; this deals with the transmission or dissemination of viruses, and it also includes distributed denial-of-service attacks (DDoS). Articles 62.4 and 62.5 make such acts punishable. However, the Act does not criminalize the act of *making* viruses; this is being considered for inclusion in future legislation.

On the other hand, this kind of trespass against the information network infrastructure of the country or the society is criminalized by Articles 12 and 28 of the Information and Communications Infrastructure Protection Act.

Cyber-pornography

Article 65.1.2 provides: 'A person who has distributed, sold, rented, or openly displayed lascivious codes, letters, sounds, images, or films through an information and communications network' may be punishable by imprisonment with prison labor for not more than one year or by a fine not exceeding 10 million won. This criminalizes so-called 'cyber-pornography'. The Criminal Act cannot punish cyber-pornography because this is intangible data, unlike 'tangibles' such as documents, drawings, or films. Therefore, it is the Information and Communications Network Act that has to deal with cyber-pornography.

Cyber-stalking

Article 65.1.3 punishes '[a] person who has repeatedly sent words, sounds, letters, images, or films inciting fear and discomfort to any other person through an information and communications network,' which is understood as criminalizing so-called 'cyber-stalking'. Although it is difficult to find any concordant theory in the concept and the scope of the criminalization of cyber-stalking in Korea, this article is considered to be the main weapon against sexual harassment using information networks, together with Article 14 of the Act on the Punishment of Sexual Crimes and the Protection of the Victims Thereof.[6]

Cyber-defamation

Generally speaking, openly libeling or defaming another person's reputation is punishable under the Criminal Act as defamation. However, the Internet is characterized as having as much dissemination as newspapers or broadcasting, thereby requiring more stringent control than the other types of defamation. While Article 309 of the Criminal Act proscribes defamation by publications, which means aggravated defamation by means of media with a high degree of dissemination, the Article does not cover defamation through the use of the Internet, which is therefore only simple defamation. Therefore, Article 61 of the Information and Communications Network Act regulates defamation by the Internet, providing that

> '[a]ny person who has defamed any other person by alleging openly facts through an information and communications network with the purpose of slandering him shall be punished by imprisonment with or without prison labor for not more than three years or by a fine not exceeding 20 million won. Any person who has defamed any other person by alleging openly false facts through an information and communications network with the purpose of slandering him shall be punished by imprisonment with prison labor for not more than seven years or the suspension of qualifications[7] for not more than ten years, or by a fine not exceeding 50 million won'.

13.3 Criminal Jurisdiction over Cybercrime

13.3.1 **Principles of criminal jurisdiction**

In prosecuting crimes with little limitation as to place like cybercrimes, what is most important is which country has criminal jurisdiction thereover. No uniform

[6] Art. 14 (Lewd Act using Communication Media): 'Any person who makes any words, sounds, writings, drawings, pictures, images or things, which may cause any sense of sexual shame or aversion, and which arrive at the other party through a telephone, mail, computer, or other communication media, with the intention of provoking or satisfying his or another person's sexual appetite, shall be punished by imprisonment for not more than one year, or a fine not exceeding three million won.'

[7] These concern professional qualifications, such as qualifications for becoming a public official or the director of a legal person, and suffrage and eligibility qualifications, see Art. 43 Criminal Act.

principle exists for international criminal jurisdiction in the form of a convention or international law, thereby allowing each country to decide whether it has jurisdiction over a particular case in accordance with its domestic laws.

Included in the principles for the application of domestic laws in Korea are the territoriality principle, the personality principle, the protection principle, and the universality principle.

The territoriality principle

The Criminal Act of Korea applies to both Korean nationals and aliens who commit crimes in the territory of the Republic of Korea (Art. 2 of the Criminal Act). As such, it is called the territoriality principle when used to determine the applicability of the Criminal Act pursuant to the territory. This principle is the most important and basic one in determining jurisdiction.[8]

However, the Criminal Act also applies to aliens who commit crimes on board a Korean vessel or Korean aircraft outside the territory of the Republic of Korea (Art. 4 of the Criminal Act), which is called the 'flag-state doctrine'. It expands the concept of territory to such vessels or aircraft. The flag-state doctrine provides a broader interpretation to the territoriality principle.

According to the territoriality principle, it is never easy to determine criminal jurisdiction over cybercrimes, which are characteristically transnational, since the place where the crime occurs, where the consequence occurs, and where the criminal lives may well be in different countries.

The personality principle

The Criminal Act of Korea applies to all Korean nationals who commit crimes outside the territory of the Republic of Korea (Art. 3 of the Criminal Act). As such, it is called the personality principle when used to determine the applicability of the Criminal Act pursuant to the nationality of offenders. Accordingly, the Korean Criminal Act can be applied to any offenders with Korean nationality, even if they are overseas, whether or not such an offense is criminalized at the place of occurrence.

The protection principle

The protection principle means that the Korean Criminal Act applies to aliens who commit any crimes outside the territory of the Republic of Korea against certain legal interests that Korea decides to protect.

Article 5 of the Criminal Act applies to aliens who commit, outside the territory of the Republic of Korea, crimes against important Korean legal interests, including, for example, crimes concerning insurrection, foreign aggression, or relating to currency.

Article 5 of the Criminal Act is thus applicable to certain types of crimes. Article 6 of the Criminal Act, however, expands its applicability to general crimes. This

[8] Won, op. cit. n. 2, at p. 92.

article is interpreted to apply the Criminal Act to foreigners who commit crimes in general, other than those specified in Article 5 above, against the Republic of Korea or her nationals.

However, whereas Article 5 makes the Criminal Act absolutely applicable to the crimes listed, Article 6 is only applicable under certain conditions. Even if aliens commit crimes against the Republic of Korea or her nationals, the proviso of Article 6 of the Criminal Act means that it is not applicable: (1) when such acts do not constitute a crime under the Act in effect at the place of the acts, (2) when the prosecution thereof is discharged, or (3) when only the execution of the punishment is remitted.

The universality principle

The universality principle is a principle under which a country in which the criminal resides has jurisdiction over his or her crime against the universal interest, the importance of which each and every country acknowledges without regard to the place of the crime or the nationality of the criminal or victim. The 'universal interest' here means the interest protected by general principles of the criminal law of each country, international conventions or international laws. There is a need to punish, for example, aircraft hijacking, counterfeiting by international criminal organizations, illicit-substance distribution, etc., for which mutual assistance is required even though such crimes do not affect on Korea's interests.

Having been recently approved by multi-participant conventions, the universality principle is based on the concept of universality prevailing over the territoriality and the personality principles in order to prevent violence against certain universal interests and to ensure the punishment of crimes that violate common interests throughout the world.

No provisions are found in the Korean Criminal Act concerning the universality principle. However, through the medium of Article 6.1 of the Constitution, which states that treaties have the same effect as the domestic laws of the Republic of Korea, the universality principle is addressed. Therefore, if there is a treaty regarding cybercrime and Korea ratifies it, Korea may exercise its jurisdiction over cybercriminals located in Korea.

13.3.2 **Application of the principles of criminal jurisdiction**

For criminal jurisdiction over cyberspace, the above principles need to be considered. However, due to the transnational nature of cyberspace, the principles have to be modified or supplemented in part. This problem may be solved by the interpretation of individual principles, but ultimately it should be adopted into Korean laws when Korea concludes treaties for international mutual assistance. This chapter will now describe how the individual principles of criminal jurisdiction may apply to actual cybercrime.

Perspective of the personality principle
If Korean nationals commit cybercrimes in or outside the territory of the Republic of Korea, no problem arises in applying Korean criminal law. So long as an act is punishable under the Criminal Act of Korea, the law will apply to a Korean criminal residing abroad whether or not such an act is a crime in the place where he or she resides. If, for example, a national of Korea residing abroad disseminates obscene videoclips to Korea through an Internet service in that foreign country, he or she shall be punished under the Criminal Act of Korea even though the foreign country has not criminalized such an act.[9] Also, when a national of Korea residing abroad commits a cybercrime, it is irrelevant whether the victim of the offense was a Korean national or not.

Perspective of the territoriality principle
The territoriality principle, as mentioned above, is the first principle of criminal jurisdiction. To apply this principle, we need to be more specific about the concept of the place of the offense. The 'place of the offense' means where the criminal act is implemented. However, this concept may be expanded to a place where the consequence occurred if the consequence is an element of a result crime[10], or to a place where the consequence was expected to occur in light of the criminal plan of the actor in the case of a criminal attempt, or to a place where an accomplice's aiding and abetting occurred. This is to avoid a deficiency in implementing punishment authority.[11]

From the perspective of the territoriality principle, any illegal acts in cyberspace that occur in the territory of the Republic of Korea shall be subject to Korean criminal law without regard to the nationality of the offender. For example, in the case where a person having residence or domicile in Korea commits a crime utilizing a Korean Internet service, no problem arises in applying the Criminal Act of Korea pursuant to the territoriality principle. Also, if someone who is not Korean and who lives in another country commits a crime by utilizing the Korean Internet service, he or she would be punished under the Korean Criminal Act, because the place of the offense is in Korea where the result of the act through the Internet service occurred.

What is the case when the crime is committed through foreign networks? If a Korean national commits a cybercrime utilizing foreign networks, it is not a problem of territoriality, since the personality principle applies. However, if a non-Korean person residing outside the country utilizes a foreign Internet service in that country to commit an offense against nationals of that country or of another coun-

[9] Bo-Hack Suh, 'The Criminal Responsibility for Distributing Information on the Internet', 12 *Korean Criminological Review* (2001), p. 37.

[10] A result crime can be described as a crime with 'actual harm' (e.g., murder, robbery, etc.), as opposed to 'danger' crimes (e.g., endangering someone's life, regardless of whether someone is actually killed or not) [editors' note].

[11] Dongwon Shin, *Criminal Law (General Principle)* (Bubmunsa 2001), p. 45.

try, the problem arises as to which criminal law of which country will apply. In other words, there may be a jurisdictional conflict, because the place of the offender's residence and the place of the consequence differ. The problem is further complicated if the offender used an Internet service provided by a service provider in a third country, since in that case, all three countries may have partial jurisdiction. Another problem arising in this case is whether or not to criminalize access by nationals to harmful information disseminated by a person residing outside the country through an Internet service in that other country.

No cases on this have been found at present. However, in a case in which a person residing outside Korea uses an Internet service of a foreign country to infiltrate into Korean networks, or when he or she interferes with Korean networks by disseminating viruses, and the consequences of the crime occur in Korea, Korea's Criminal Act can be applied pursuant to the territoriality principle.[12]

On the other hand, in a case in which aliens store obscene materials on an Internet server located in Korea accessible to Korean users, it is debatable whether Korea's criminal law (in this case, the Distribution of Obscene Materials under the Information and Communications Network Act) applies. If we consider the place of the crime to be constituted by the place where the server is located, no difficulty arises in applying Korea's Criminal Law. In such cases, looking at the place or origin of the crime is more relevant than looking at the place of the results. This is because with 'risk' or 'danger' crimes,[13] the Distribution of Obscene Materials does not require any consequences to be punishable, so the place of the consequences has no meaning in determining jurisdiction.

However, this means that if a person residing outside Korea commits a 'danger' crime under the Criminal Act of Korea through a server located *outside* Korea, the conclusion is that the Criminal Act of Korea shall not apply,[14] thereby requiring another principle to supplement the deficiency of punishment. Here, the protection principle or the universality principle come into view.

Perspective of the protection principle

In a case where Korean nationals access harmful information disseminated by a person residing outside the country through an Internet service in that country, the problem is whether the Korean law-enforcement authorities may use the Criminal Act of Korea to shut down the web site, even though such an act is not criminalized in that country because of the right of freedom of expression there.

To begin with, let us review this problem from the viewpoint of the protection principle described in Article 5 and Article 6 of the Criminal Act of Korea. Article 5 says that Korea's Criminal Act shall apply to aliens who commit crimes concerning

---

[12] Heeyoung Park, 'Scope of Territorial Application of Criminal Law on the Internet', 26 *Internet Law* (2004), pp. 54-59 at p. 59.

[13] See n. 10.

[14] Ibid., at p. 54.

insurrection, foreign aggression, the national flag, currency, securities and documents, etc., outside the territory of the Republic of Korea. Accordingly, those aliens instigating an act or propagating an idea that disturbs the Korean constitutional order through a foreign web site, as well as those aliens forging Korean electronic money or documents, shall be subject to the Criminal Act of Korea.

With respect to other crimes, particularly the dissemination of harmful information over the Internet, Article 5 does not apply and we should look at Article 6. For acts disseminating obscene materials through the Internet that are not criminalized by a foreign country, the Criminal Act of Korea does not apply even from the perspective of the protection principle. This is because Article 6 rules out the application of the Criminal Act where the acts do not constitute a crime under the criminal law of the place of the acts.

For acts that are criminalized by a foreign country, we shall now discuss whether Article 6 of the Criminal Act will make them punishable. At present, one may find a consensus of opinion that the 'crimes, other than those specified in the preceding Article, against the Republic of Korea or its nationals' in Article 6 mean violence against the interests protected by Korea. In other words, the Criminal Act will apply to any violence against whatever interests are protected by it. If so, the Criminal Act of Korea may be applied to the on-line dissemination of obscene materials harmful to sound sexual morals, and no problem arises in applying the Criminal Act of Korea if an alien posts obscene materials onto an Internet service in Korea. However, if we persist in applying the protection principle that all aliens should keep in mind Korean laws or even the laws of the world when posting information in cyberspace, then eventually each and every country will enlarge the application of criminal jurisdiction by exclusively taking into account the protection of its nationals.[15]

Therefore, in applying the protection principle under Article 6, one should consider whether the alien has any purpose or intent to violate any legal interest protected by his or her own country, and at the same time whether the site is served in Korean or if the server is located in Korea. If the server is located in Korea, the act of posting obscene materials shall be properly punished through the territoriality principle by seeing the location of the server as the place of the act.[16] If the site is in Korean, even though the server is located outside Korea, the intention to violate the legal interests protected by Korean laws is deemed to be present, thereby justifying punishment pursuant to the protection principle.

However, 'important legal interests' protected by Korean laws do not include all cybercrimes defined by Korean law. For these cases not covered by the protection principle, applicability is still possible based on the territoriality principle if the crime relates to Korean networks or servers in which the result of a cybercrime occurred.

---

[15] Won, op. cit. n. 2, at p. 103.

[16] Suh, op. cit. n. 9, at p. 37.

Perspective of the universality principle
If aliens disseminate obscene materials by means of a service in a foreign country, the simple possibility that nationals of Korea may have access to it will not justify the application of the Criminal Act pursuant to the protection principle. Although Korea has yet to adopt the universality principle, this problem shall be understood as affecting the whole world.

For the present, the Supreme Court has held that domestic laws may apply through the medium of Article 6.1 of the Constitution, which states that treaties have the same effect as the domestic laws of the Republic of Korea.[17] For example, if a Chinese who resides in the United States disseminates child pornography by means of a Japanese ISP or attacks servers in Europe through a Korean network, the Korean Criminal Act could be applied on the basis of international treaties on child pornography or cyberterrorism.

Convention on Cybercrime
In applying the universality principle to cybercrime, the major international treaty that may become the threshold of domestic laws is the Council of Europe Convention on Cybercrime of 2001. This convention was signed by the G7 and most countries in Europe, and it is indeed recognized as a global norm. The Convention contains typologies of cybercrimes, investigation powers, and provisions on jurisdiction and mutual assistance.

Korea has yet to sign the Convention on Cybercrime. It seems that Korea needs to sign the Convention in the near future with the necessary premises settled. When signing, Korea's Criminal Act and Criminal Procedure Act, etc., may apply to cybercrimes committed by aliens outside Korea based on the universality principle in relation to the Convention.[18]

13.4 Evidence and International Mutual Assistance Concerning Cybercrime

Although broader damage is incurred compared to damage in traditional crimes, few cybercrimes are detected and even less evidence is obtained. To combat cybercrimes effectively now that computers and networks become increasingly indispensable, we need to seek efficient investigatory techniques and to solve procedural problems relating to the admissibility of evidence for cybercrimes.

---

[17] Supreme Court 84 Do 39, decision of 22 May 1984.

[18] For more detail, see Jeonghoon Lee, 'The Measures of Criminal Law preparing for the Convention on Cybercrime', 7 *ChungAng Law Review* (2005) No. 1, pp. 209-236.

13.4.1 **Investigation of evidence**

The search for evidence of a cybercrime involves, first, securing and analyzing evidence of damage and logging data, and then arresting the suspect(s) and searching and seizing evidence or evidentiary materials. This process is similar to that used for traditional crimes, but it differs when it comes to the specific investigation of evidence.

The investigation of evidence for a cybercrime begins with securing evidence of damage. For example, if damage is incurred through a web page, evidence must be collected without shutting down the computer when it is in operation. The evidence is secured by printing what is on the screen of the web site at issue, including all clues to identify the contents of the web page and to track down the suspect. If the crime is carried out by a bulletin board, the IP address which the suspect used to access it and the location of the system in which the data are stored should be secured.

Once the evidence of damage is secured, the suspect's logging information should be secured. The storing methods for logging information vary according to the service used in cyberspace, but by securing the service incurring the damage and its log, clues to track the suspect may be obtained. For instance, e-mails, web or shell services such as telnet use different directories for storing relevant files, so one must secure the evidence from the system operator.

Evidence may be provided by the system operator solely with respect to Internet services in Korea. In order to ask an Internet service provider outside Korea to provide evidence of a transnational cybercrime, international mutual assistance in investigations between relevant countries is a prerequisite.[19]

13.4.2 **Search and seizure**

For the search and seizure of electromagnetic records stored in a computer, the investigatory organization of cybercrime, just like other crimes, should first obtain warrants under the legal conditions in force. Therefore, in response to the Constitution, the suspicion, the scope and the place of the search, the target of the seizure, etc., must be specified by the search and seizure warrant for electromagnetic records.

It is not straightforward to limit the scope of search and seizure to specific target computers. Further, it is questionable whether it is possible to seize electromagnetic records, which are intangible data. In a case in which the evidence has a factual relationship to the crime and such evidence could prove the crime, the evidence of seized electromagnetic records may, however, not be ruled inadmissible. Therefore, the evidence for the suspicion specified shall include direct evidence as well as indirect evidence or circumstantial evidence.

[19] Won, op. cit. n. 2, at pp. 53-54.

On the other hand, in a case in which the data stored in a computer supplied for business are subject to seizure, the copying of the data may be included in the permissible scope of seizure in order to minimize the disadvantage to the person who is subject to seizure even though no specific provision exists, since such a computer may process a huge amount of data and exchange a large amount of information in real time.[20]

13.4.3 **Admissibility of evidence**

Electromagnetic records seized by a warrant are not visualized and made readable until printed. The admissibility of the records thus printed, if submitted as evidence, may be questioned. If the conditions of storage, the mechanical correctness of the printing computer, the reliability of the program used, the correctness of the printer, the expertise of the person who printed or who provides witness or expert testimony, etc., are all considered reliable, then electromagnetic records may be deemed authentic and admissible.

Regarding the identity of the electromagnetic records and the printed document, the person who printed out the electromagnetic records by means of a certain program should have to testify to the authenticity of the printed document at the trial. In addition, to the extent that the electromagnetic record is deemed identical to the printed document, the latter should be deemed original.[21]

On the other hand, if the document that is made visible and readable by printing the electromagnetic records is used as evidence of a crime, this document may be deemed as statement evidence made by extracting a human idea through an electronic method, i.e., hearsay evidence without cross-examination. Therefore, the rule of hearsay evidence under Article 311 of the Criminal Procedure and the provisions that follow shall be applied in determining the admissibility of such documents.

13.4.4 **International mutual assistance**

In 1991, Korea enacted the Act on International Judicial Mutual Assistance in Criminal Matters to provide for the scope of, the procedure for, etc., mutual assistance made at the request of, or made in request to, any foreign country in connection with any investigation or trial of a criminal case. Although providing no heed to cybercrimes, this may provide a basic guideline for mutual assistance in relation to cybercrimes. However, given the characteristics of cybercrimes, the procedure for mutual assistance is currently a little too complicated, so that it may impede prompt and systematic investigation.

For instance, according to the Act on International Judicial Mutual Assistance in Criminal Matters, the acceptance of a request for mutual assistance, and the send-

[20] Won, op. cit. n. 2, at pp. 120-121.

[21] Jeonghoon Lee, 'Document and Electronic Record in Criminal Act', 5 *Korean Journal of Comparative Criminal Law* (2003) No. 2, pp. 349-352.

ing of materials of mutual assistance to the requesting country shall be made by the Minister of Foreign Affairs, and any request for mutual assistance shall be made in writing specifying a summary of the case and the objectives and contents of the request (Art. 12). The request in writing must be supplemented by fax or e-mail to respond to the necessity for prompt assistance given the characteristics of cybercrimes.

In addition, the Act on International Judicial Mutual Assistance in Criminal Matters provides that mutual assistance may not be required in a case where the crime at issue does not constitute a crime under the law of the Republic of Korea (Art. 6). However, given the transnational nature of cybercrimes, any request for mutual assistance in investigation should be granted to the greatest extent possible, even if they are not punishable in Korea. The reason for this is that if Korea refuses the assistance because it is against the general principles of Korean law or criminal-justice policy, the requesting country will fail to collect indispensable evidence so that the prosecution of the offense may be delayed or denied. Therefore, it is desirable to refuse assistance in only as few cases as possible, in order to enhance international co-operation.[22]

A related issue is that, in investigating cybercrimes, not only search and seizure of the data stored in the target computer, but also the right to access the computer and collect the data through the network may be required, and without such a right given to the other country, no substantial investigation is possible. Thus, it is appropriate to impose an obligation of mutual assistance by allowing a real-time network search, so that each country may collect such data complying with its national laws.

13.5 Conclusion

It is not easy to determine criminal jurisdiction over cybercrimes, which are characteristically transnational. However, the principles of criminal jurisdiction in Korea can be applied to cybercrimes. If Korean nationals commit cybercrimes in or outside the territory of the Republic of Korea (the personality principle), and if Korean nationals or aliens commit crimes in its territory, no problem arises in applying Korean criminal law (the territoriality principle). Based on the protection principle, the Korean Criminal Act applies to aliens instigating an act or propagating an idea that disturbs the Korean constitutional order through a foreign web site, as well as those aliens who forge Korean electronic money or documents. Although there is no provision on the universality principle in Korean criminal law, the Korean Criminal Act could be applied on the basis of international treaties on child pornography or cyber-terrorism. In order to be able to apply the universality principle to cybercrimes, Korea has to sign the Convention on Cybercrime. Then, Korea's Crimi-

[22] Wan Choung, *International Cooperation for Cybercrime Prevention* (Korea Institute of Criminology 2004), p. 98.

nal Act and Criminal Procedure Act, etc., may also apply to cybercrimes committed by aliens outside Korea.

Bibliography

WAN CHOUNG, *International Cooperation for Cybercrime Prevention* (Korea Institute of Criminology 2004).

DAEHO HYUN, *Legislation Research on information protection on the Internet* (Korea Legislation Research Institute 2000).

JEONGHOON LEE, 'Document and Electronic Record in Criminal Act', 5 *Korean Journal of Comparative Criminal Law* (2003) No. 2, pp. 349-352.

JEONGHOON LEE, 'The Measures of Criminal Law preparing for the Convention on Cybercrime', 7 *ChungAng Law Review* (2005) No. 1, pp. 209-236.

HEEYOUNG PARK, 'Scope of Territorial Application of Criminal Law on the Internet', 26 *Internet Law* (2004), pp. 54-59.

DONGWON SHIN, *Criminal Law (General Principle)* (Bubmunsa 2001).

BO-HACK SUH, 'The Criminal Responsibility for Distributing Information on the Internet', 12 *Korean Criminological Review* (2001).

HYEWOOK WON, *Study on evidence and jurisdiction over Internet crime* (Korea Institute of Criminology 2001).

Chapter 14
CYBERCRIME AND JURISDICTION IN NEW ZEALAND

Noel Cox*

14.1 Introduction

There are comparatively few specific legislative provisions in New Zealand relating to cybercrimes. The general approach has been to amend general criminal provisions where necessary to address specific problems presented by cybercrimes, but not to treat these as being inherently different to crimes committed through more traditional media.

Just as the legislative provisions do not generally treat cybercrimes as *sui generis*, so there is not a generic enforcement agency charged with the detection of cybercrime and the prosecution of cybercriminals. For similar reasons there are few specific provisions with respect to cybercrime jurisdiction. There also remains a reluctance to assert an extraterritorial jurisdiction over cybercrime *per se*, though there are aspects of this in recent legislation covering terrorist-related offences.

The New Zealand Police[1] (the sole uniformed police agency in the country), the Department of Internal Affairs[2] (which has, *inter alia*, general responsibility for the censorship and classification of books and films) and the New Zealand Customs Service[3] (which is responsible for the enforcement of importation controls) are the three principal agencies responsible for electronic crime detection and investigation in New Zealand. In very general terms, Internal Affairs focuses on action against Internet offending, the Police deal with physical offending and Customs with importation offences. Nearly a dozen other government agencies also deal with some aspects of computer-related offences. In most instances they enforce a combination of general criminal laws, and the comparatively few specific electronic or cyber-laws.

This chapter will explore some aspects of national cybercrime law in New Zealand, looking at both substantive law and the broader question of jurisdiction.

* Noel Cox is Associate Professor of Law at Auckland University of Technology, New Zealand.

1 Police Act 1958 (NZ).

2 Films, Videos and Publications Classification Act 1993 (NZ).

3 Customs and Excise Act 1996 (NZ).

B-J. Koops and S.W. Brenner (Eds), Cybercrime and Jurisdiction

14.2 National Cybercrime Legislation

14.2.1 **Brief history**

Until 2002 there was, in New Zealand, comparatively little legislative response to the advent of cyberspace and even of computers in general. The general criminal provisions were utilized in those instances where offences occurred in cyberspace or were committed through the use of computers. While this approach is not always entirely adequate, this was initially satisfactory given the relatively small number of reported cybercrime. The real level of crime may however have been significantly higher, due to an ignorance that offences (such as identity theft) were occurring, or a lack of appreciation that computer-based crimes were distinct from crimes committed through traditional means (if indeed they are), or quantitatively or qualitatively significant.

Article 2 of the 2001 Council of Europe's Convention on Cybercrime[4] required signatory governments to enact such provisions as may be necessary to establish as criminal offences under their domestic laws, when committed intentionally, the access to the whole or any part of a computer system without right. Although New Zealand was not a signatory to this Council of Europe initiative, the Budapest convention is the first international agreement on the control of cybercrime; it has so far been signed by 42 countries,[5] and its influence could not be ignored. The principal New Zealand response – which was also influenced by recent cases highlighting difficulties with the pre-existing law – was to amend parts of the Crimes Act 1961, the primary legislative enactment providing procedures and penalties for serious crimes.

14.2.2 **Provisions on various cybercrimes**

Hacking and related offences

Unauthorized access to computer systems, or 'hacking', is restricted by the Telecommunications Act 1987 and more recently by amendments to the Crimes Act 1961. It is an offence to listen, record or disclose private communications between two or more people without authority. 'Private communications' are however confined to oral communications.

The case of *R* v. *Williamson*[6] had highlighted the legislative and common-law deficiencies with respect to electronic theft which led to the 2003 amendments to the Crimes Act 1961. There is still no specific crime for identity-related fraud or

---

[4] Council of Europe, Convention on Cybercrime (CETS 185) (23 November 2001), <http://conventions.coe.int/Treaty/en/Treaties/Html/185.htm>.

[5] As per 31 July 2005. See Council of Europe, Convention on Cybercrime, Chart of Signatures and Ratifications, <http://conventions.coe.int/Treaty/Commun/ChercheSig.asp?NT=185&CM=8&DF=31/07/2005&CL=ENG>.

[6] [1999] 1 NZLR 403.

theft. This particular type of offence is, however, covered by a number of provisions in the Crimes Act 1961.

The four new crimes, part of the Crimes Act since 2003, are concerned primarily with hacking. They include:

1. Accessing a computer system for a dishonest purpose;[7]
2. Damaging or interfering with a computer system;[8]
3. Making, selling, or distributing or possessing software for committing a crime;[9]
4. Accessing a computer system without authorization.[10]

Accessing a computer system for a dishonest purpose (i.e., obtaining advantage or benefit or causing loss to another person) is subject to a maximum penalty of seven years' imprisonment,[11] or a maximum of five years' imprisonment for accessing with this intent, even if the attempt is not successful.[12]

Damaging or interfering with a computer system is subject to a maximum of ten years' imprisonment where damage or interference is likely to be life threatening, and to a maximum of seven years otherwise. The statute provides that damaging or interfering is defined as where the offender:

> 'damages, deletes adds to, modifies, or otherwise interferes with or impairs any data or software in any computer system; or causes any of the above, or causes any computer system to fail or deny service to authorised users.'

Making, selling, or distributing or possessing software for committing crime has a maximum penalty of two years' imprisonment. Making, selling or distributing applies to software which would enable another person to access a computer system without authorization with the sole or principal purpose to commit a crime, or if they hold it out as being useful to commit a crime (regardless of any other legitimate use). Possession of software is only a crime when the software would enable the user to access a computer system without authorization, and the user intends to use that software to commit a crime.

Accessing a computer system without authorization has a maximum penalty of two years' imprisonment, and applies to anyone who intentionally accesses a computer system, directly or indirectly, knowing that they are not authorized to access that computer system, or when they are reckless as to whether or not they are authorized. This crime does not apply to people who are authorized to access a computer system if they access that system for a purpose other than the one for which that

[7] S. 249.
[8] S. 250.
[9] S. 251.
[10] S. 252.
[11] S. 249(1).
[12] S. 249(2).

person was given access. Law-enforcement agencies, the Security Intelligence Service (SIS), and the Government Communications Security Bureau (GCSB) are also exempt from this section when they possess appropriate warrants.

The existing ban on listening devices has been extended to include any interception device. The definition of an interception device is 'any electronic, mechanical, electromagnetic, optical or electro-optical instrument, apparatus, equipment, or other device that is used or is capable of being used to intercept a private communication.'[13] Offenders are now liable to imprisonment for a term not exceeding two years if they intentionally intercept any private communication by means of an interception device. They are also liable for up to two years' imprisonment for disclosure of the communication, or even disclosing the existence of it.

Computer fraud and identity theft

The case of *R* v. *Music*[14] illustrates the general legal position in New Zealand with respect to computer fraud. Misic downloaded onto his computer from the Internet a programme which enabled him to arrange to make telephone calls overseas without being charged for them. He then operated a system whereby he and friends of his made a large number of overseas calls without paying a fee. He was charged under section 229A of the Crimes Act 1961 with obtaining documents with intent to defraud and with using documents with intent to defraud, namely the computer programme and the computer disk onto which the programme was loaded. After conviction, the accused appealed on the ground that neither the programme nor the disk was a 'document' for the purposes of section 229A, to which no statutory definition of 'document' applied.

The court held that a computer programme and the computer disk were documents for the purposes of section 229A. A document was a thing which provided evidence or information or served as a record.[15] The fact that the offence was committed through the use of a computer and the Internet did not present significant legal difficulties for the court, which simply applied the pre-existing common law to the new circumstances.

Another of the leading cases illustrating the legal situation prior to the enactment of the 2003 amendments to the Crimes Act 1961 is *R* v. *Garrett (No. 2)*.[16] Andrew Garrett was prosecuted for identity-theft crimes, through the use of a Trojan horse programme, Back Orifice, attached to a game called Potato. He was charged under section 298 Crimes Act 1961 and was subject to a potential maximum five

[13] Crimes Act 1961 (NZ), s. 216A(1), definition of 'interception device'. Exceptions from this definition are made for hearing aids and other devices exempted by the Governor-General. See also *R* v. *Stephens* [1997] 3 NZLR 716; (1997) 15 CRNZ 308 (CA), discussing the meaning of 'intercept' and 'monitor' in s. 216A.

[14] [2001] 3 NZLR 1 (CA).

[15] See paras. 31 and 33 of the judgment. *Snow* v. *Hawthorn* [1969] NZLR 776 was approved, and *Grant* v. *Southwestern and County Properties Ltd* [1975] Ch 185; [1974] 2 All ER 465 was adopted.

[16] [2001] DCR 912 (Judge Harvey).

years' imprisonment. Garrett distributed the game by e-mail, knowing that when the recipient opened the e-mail it would infect his or her computer with the Back Orifice programme. During the trial there were legal arguments over whether sending a programme like this could amount to willful damage of the software of the recipient's computer.

The court held, on the basis of authority in *Misic*, that a computer programme is a document. The login information and passwords were obtained through the computer programme that was stored on the hard drive of Garrett's computer and therefore constituted a document. Garrett then took the document and reproduced it on his own computer. There was also evidence that the purpose for obtaining the login and password was to obtain a privilege, benefit or advantage, and thus constituted illegally using a document for pecuniary advantage. This again was an example of courts applying essentially pre-computer provisions in a new environment.

Identity-theft provisions of the Crimes Act 1961 may be summarized including the following – accessing a computer system for a dishonest purpose (s. 249), creating and distributing software for a criminal purpose (s. 251), hacking (s. 252), fraud (s. 229A) and identity theft (s. 298). These are generally pre-computer provisions, or derived from pre-computer provisions.

Objectionable material

Besides provisions with respect to hacking and fraud, there are also specific provisions relating to objectionable material. The Films, Videos and Publications Classifications Act 1993 defines what material is classified as 'age-restricted' and what material is 'objectionable'. 'Possess' is also defined in section 131 of the Act. This particular section has presented some difficulties with respect to Internet pornography which is viewed on a computer but not specifically saved to the hard drive or a disk. There have also been some difficulties with the definition of 'objectionable'.

The offences under the Films, Videos, and Publications Classification Act 1993 which are most regularly committed are those relating to possession. Not only will offenders be liable for publishing objectionable material, but they will also be liable for possessing it within their electronic systems, in particular, within the hard drive of a computer stored on files, or sent and received as e-mail.[17]

Moreover, the Act does not apply to broadcasts on media such as television, radio or the Internet because the definition of publication does not include broadcasts, and in particular, live broadcasts cannot be covered by the Act since no recording of them exists until after transmission.[18]

---

[17] In *Goodin* v. *Department of Internal Affairs* [2003] NZAR 434, the Court found that the definition of 'publication' in the Films, Videos, and Publications Classification Act 1993 (NZ) encompassed computer disks (including hard drives), folders and files stored on computer disks, and images stored in such folders or files.

[18] Films, Videos, and Publications Classification Act 1993 (NZ), s. 2, definition of 'publication'. 'Exhibit' in relation to a sound recording, means to play that sound recording: s. 2, definition of 'ex-

Internet gambling

Internet gambling is also regulated, though only incidentally to the regulation of traditional gambling. The Department of Internal Affairs licenses gambling under the Gaming and Lotteries Act 1977. Under current law is it theoretically possible for an Internet gambling site to be granted a license, though none has ever been granted. However, proposed changes to the law would prohibit Internet gambling sites in New Zealand, other than the official betting agency (the 'TAB') established under the Racing Act 2003.

There are currently no legal Internet gambling sites based on New Zealand, other than the TAB. There are special rules for the TAB itself that allow it to take Internet bets, but 'cyber-casinos' *per se* are prohibited.

14.2.3 **Investigation powers**

In 1979, provisions were enacted criminalizing the unauthorized use of interception devices to intercept private communications.[19] However these provisions do not apply where the person intercepting the communication is a party to it, or does so pursuant to a statutory authority to intercept the communication.[20] It is also lawful for the Police to use an interception device to intercept a private communication where there is an emergency and there are reasonable grounds for believing that the person making the communication is threatening the life of or threatening serious harm to another.[21]

The interception of communications is governed by the Government Communications Security Bureau Act 2003. This allows the interception of communications pursuant to an interception warrant,[22] but not of domestic communications.[23] The New Zealand Security Intelligence Service Act 1969 provides for the issuance of domestic interception warrants.[24]

The interception of private communications by an interception device operated by a person engaged in providing an Internet or other communication service to the

---

hibit'. Ordinary criminal provisions might cover live broadcasts, where, for example, indecent or obscene language was used, although these provisions would apply to the speaker and not to the broadcaster.

[19] Crimes Act 1961 (NZ), s. 216B, inserted by s. 2 of the Crimes Amendment Act 1979 (NZ).

[20] Crimes Act 1961 (NZ), s. 216B(2), as amended by the Crimes Amendment Act (No 2) 1997 (NZ), s. 4. The Acts authorizing interception are the Crimes Act 1961 (NZ), Part XIA (ss. 312A-312Q), Telecommunications (Residual Provisions) Act 1987 (NZ), Part I (ss. 2-20) or the Telecommunications Act 2001 (NZ), New Zealand Security Intelligence Service Act 1969 (NZ), Government Communications Security Bureau Act 2003 (NZ), Misuse of Drugs Amendment Act 1978 (NZ), and the International Terrorism (Emergency Powers) Act 1987 (NZ).

[21] Crimes Act 1961 (NZ), s. 216B(3)(a) and (b). The use of the device must be authorized by a commissioned officer.

[22] S. 15.

[23] S. 14.

[24] S. 4.

public is permitted if the interception is carried out by an employee of the person providing that Internet or other communication service to the public in the course of that person's duties. It is lawful for the interception to be carried out if it is necessary for the purpose of maintaining the Internet or other communication service.[25]

Section 198 of the Summary Proceedings Act 1957[26] gives power to a police constable to require a person who owns or works a particular computer to provide assistance in obtaining information from the computer. This raises important questions with respect to the New Zealand Bill of Rights Act 1990. In particular the computer provision raises the prospect of individuals being compelled to assist a constable to obtain information from a computer, although in so doing they may be incriminating themselves. This could be in breach of sections 25(c) and (d) of the New Zealand Bill of Rights Act 1990, which are the right to be presumed innocent until proved guilty according to law, and the right of everyone charged with an offence not to be compelled to be a witness or to confess guilt.

Everyone also has the right to be secure against unreasonable search or seizure, whether of the person, property, correspondence, or otherwise.[27] A search or seizure authorized by a valid statutory enactment will not contravene the Bill of Rights unless it is carried out in an unreasonable manner,[28] or the statutory provision which permits it is exercised unreasonably.[29] The general power to search a personal computer or laptop is based on provisions of the Summary Proceedings Act 1957, and on specific provisions with respect to indecent publications.[30]

On written application, a District Court Judge, Justice, Community Magistrate, or Registrar (who is not also a constable) may issue a search warrant in the prescribed form if satisfied of certain matters.[31] He or she must be satisfied that reasonable grounds exist for believing that, in any building, aircraft, ship, carriage, vehicle, box, receptacle, premises, or place, there is any of the following. First, anything upon or in respect of which any offence punishable by imprisonment has

[25] Crimes Act 1961 (NZ), s. 216B(5) as inserted by the Crimes Amendment Act 2003 (NZ), s. 10.

[26] As amended by s. 3 Summary Proceedings Amendment Act 2003 (NZ).

[27] New Zealand Bill of Rights Act 1990 (NZ), s. 21. The specific statutory reference to 'person, property, or correspondence or otherwise' suggests a wider definition of search and seizure than was the situation at common law. This interpretation has been confirmed by decisions dealing with s. 21 of the New Zealand Bill of Rights Act 1990 (NZ). It has been held that a 'search' is an examination of a person and a 'seizure' is a taking of what is discovered: *R* v. *Jefferies* [1994] 1 NZLR 290, 300; (1993) 10 CRNZ 202, 214 per Richardson J (CA).

[28] *R* v. *Davis* (1993) 10 CRNZ 327 (CA), and see *R* v. *A* [1994] 1 NZLR 429 (CA).

[29] *R* v. *Laugalis* (1993) 10 CRNZ 350 (CA) and *R* v. *Ririnui* [1994] 2 NZLR 439; (1993) 11 CRNZ 435 (CA).

[30] Films, Videos and Publications Classifications Act 1993 (NZ).

[31] Summary Proceedings Act 1957 (NZ), s. 198(1), as amended by the Summary Proceedings Amendment Act (No 2) 1998 (NZ), s. 50(a). The prescribed form is Form 50 in the First Schedule to the Summary Proceedings Regulations 1958 (RPT 1980/84) (NZ). See *R* v. *Sanders* [1994] 3 NZLR 450 (CA).

been or is suspected of having been committed. Second, any thing which there is reasonable ground to believe will be evidence as to the commission of any such offence. Third, any thing which there is reasonable ground to believe is intended to be used for the purposes of committing any such offence.[32] This procedure may be used to authorize the search of a computer.

In addition, but in a more limited context, the Films, Videos and Publications Classifications Act 1993 confers a power upon inspectors of publications to search for indecent material which are on public display,[33] and for the issue of search warrants to search for and seize indecent publications elsewhere.[34] While the former might conceivably be able to discover some computer-based pornography, for instance, the latter power is more likely to be relevant to searching computers for illicit material of one sort or another.

It is not clear whether enforcement agencies have a power to conduct remote searches of computer systems. The parliamentary Select Committee which considered the Crimes Amendment Bill (No. 6), which was enacted as the Crimes Amendment Act 2003, declined to exclude this power as had been requested by the Privacy Commissioner,[35] saying the purpose of the Bill was to preserve existing powers, and they did not feel it gave law-enforcement agencies additional powers. But the Bill, and the (then) un-amended Crimes Act 1961, did not expressly authorize the remote searching of computers.

Another controversial issue was whether the SIS and GCSB would be able to use keyword searching and filtering, which is regarded as more invasive than other forms of monitoring due to its indiscriminate nature. The Select Committee examining the 2003 Bill also considered that the requirements for explicit warrants were adequate to deal with this, though others disagreed.

14.3 Jurisdiction for Cybercrimes

14.3.1 **Provisions in law**

The standard provisions with respect to cybercrime jurisdiction are those contained in section 7 of the Crimes Act 1961 (as currently enacted):

> 'any act or omission forming part of any offence, or any event necessary to the completion of any offence occurs within New Zealand (…) whether the person charged with the offence was in New Zealand or not at the time of the act, omission, or event.'[36]

---

[32] Summary Proceedings Act 1957 (NZ), s. 198(1).
[33] Films, Videos and Publications Classifications Act 1993 (NZ), s. 106.
[34] Ibid., s. 109.
[35] A statutory officer appointed under the Privacy Act 1993 (NZ).
[36] S. 7.

This confines general jurisdiction to events in New Zealand, though the perpetrators need not have been in New Zealand. Jurisdiction is wider with respect to certain specific offences:

> 'Even if the acts or omissions alleged to constitute the offence occurred wholly outside New Zealand, proceedings may be brought for any offence against this Act committed in the course of carrying out a terrorist act (as defined in section 5(1) of the Terrorism Suppression Act 2002) or an offence against [several specific sections][37] –
> (a) if the person to be charged –
>   (i) is a New Zealand citizen; or
>   (ii) is ordinarily resident in New Zealand; or
>   (iii) has been found in New Zealand and has not been extradited; or
>   (iv) is a body corporate, or a corporation sole, incorporated under the law of New Zealand; or
>
> (b) if any of the acts or omissions is alleged to have occurred [on board a New Zealand-related ship or aircraft]; or
>
> (c) if a person in respect of whom the offence is alleged to have been committed
>   (i) is a New Zealand citizen; or
>   (ii) is ordinarily resident in New Zealand; or
>
> (d) in the case of an offence against section 98A, if the group of people in which the person to be charged is alleged to have participated are alleged to have as their objective or one of their objectives the obtaining of material benefits by the commission in New Zealand of offences or conduct referred to in paragraph (a) or paragraph (b) of section 98A(2).'

These provisions contain some additional grounds for extending jurisdiction, but a strong link to New Zealand is still required – usually a New Zealand citizen or resident as the actor, or an occurrence on a New Zealand ship or aircraft. This is a relatively traditional approach.

The Terrorism Suppression Amendment Act 2003 made some changes to this. In addition to the provision of offences involving the use and movement of unmarked plastic explosives, and the physical protection of nuclear material – and the other

[37] These offences are: s. 98A of the Crimes Act 1961 (NZ) (participation in organised criminal group), s. 98C (smuggling migrants), s. 98D (trafficking in people by means of coercion or deception), s. 100 (judicial corruption), s. 101 (bribery of judicial officer), s. 102 (corruption and bribery of Minister of Crown), s. 103 (corruption and bribery of Minister of Parliament), s. 104 (corruption and bribery of law-enforcement officer), s. 105(2) (corruption and bribery of official), s. 116 (conspiring to defeat justice), s. 117 (corrupting juries and witnesses), and s. 257A (money laundering), s. 298A (causing disease and sickness in animals), s. 298B (contaminating food, crops, water and other products). Nothing in s. A(1)-(3) of the Crimes Act 1961 (NZ) limits or affects the application of s. 7 to the occurrence in New Zealand of an act or omission forming part of an offence or an event necessary to the completion of an offence: s. 7A(4), as inserted by the Crimes Amendment Act 2002 (NZ), s. 4.

specific offences – the Amendment Act 2003 provides for extraterritorial jurisdiction, extradition, and mutual-assistance requirements in respect of those offences. This is provided for by amendments to section 7 of the Crimes Act 1961. Section 7A lists certain provisions under which prosecution may occur although the acts took place overseas. Previously these have related largely to corruption. The amendment greatly extended the extraterritorial application of the Crimes Act, for it will allow proceedings to be brought for any offence against the Crimes Act committed in the course of carrying out a terrorist act anywhere in the world, provided there is some connection with New Zealand.

New Zealand courts have jurisdiction over offences in the Terrorism Suppression Act 2002 which occur wholly outside New Zealand if committed by New Zealanders, or against New Zealand property, against New Zealand facilities or citizens, or 'in an attempt to compel the Government of New Zealand to do or abstain from doing any act',[38] or by individuals present in New Zealand and not extradited. The New Zealand courts have jurisdiction if the acts occurred in New Zealand, by the Terrorism Suppression Act 2002, in compliance with the terrorism conventions New Zealand undertook to implement.[39] Under these conventions, other Member States also have jurisdiction over acts in New Zealand.

New Zealand law thus asserts extraterritorial jurisdiction in four distinct areas: for crimes on ships and aircraft beyond New Zealand; for crimes committed by people serving New Zealand overseas who are protected by diplomatic immunity; in respect of certain offences with transnational aspects[40] – now including terrorism; and for crimes committed by a New Zealand citizen, corporation, or resident, or by someone found in New Zealand who has not been extradited. There is no general provision for Internet jurisdiction, the Internet being regarded as essentially similar to other telecommunications media.

Section 18 of the Terrorism Suppression Act 2002 was also amended to provide that the principal offences (bombing, financing, or nuclear materials offences) also apply to acts outside New Zealand if the alleged offender is in New Zealand and not extradited. Some, if not all, of these offences may be committed through computer-based communications and data-processing systems.

---

[38] Ss. 16(a) and 17(d).

[39] The International Convention for the Suppression of Terrorist Bombings (New York, 15 December 1997; No. 37517, UN Doc. A/RES/52/164, Terrorism Suppression Act 2002, Schedule 1); The International Convention for the Suppression of the Financing of Terrorism (New York, 15 December 1997; No. 38349, UNGA Resolution A/RES/54/109; Terrorism Suppression Act 2002 (NZ), Schedule 2); as well as the United Nations Security Council (Anti-Terrorism) Resolution 1373 (2001), adopted on 28 September 2001, Reproduced in the Terrorism Suppression Act 2002 (NZ), Schedule 4.

[40] Crimes Act 1961 (NZ), ss. 8, 8A, and s. 7A (as inserted by the Crimes Amendment Act 2002 (NZ), s. 4). Jurisdiction over offences committed by those serving New Zealand overseas was added by the Foreign Affairs and Overseas Service Act 1983 (NZ) and applies to any offences punishable by one year's imprisonment or more, whether or not the act or omission is an offence in the place where it is committed.

Where a person does, or omits to do, anything, and is subject to the extraterritorial jurisdiction of New Zealand Courts, that person may be charged with a crime in New Zealand if the act or omission would be a crime if committed in New Zealand.[41] The person will have a defence if the act or omission occurred in the country of which he or she is a citizen or national and it can be shown that that act or omission did not constitute an offence under the law of the country at that time.[42]

There are also other specific extraterritorial provisions which may be relevant to computer crime. Section 144A of the Crimes Act 1961 gives New Zealand Courts jurisdiction in relation to any offences committed outside New Zealand, in that it provides that it is an offence for a New Zealand citizen to do any act to any child under the age of 16 years outside New Zealand, if that act would, if done in New Zealand, constitute an offence. Though in a somewhat different context, this might be utilized to give the courts jurisdiction in certain types of cybercrimes.

In general, although New Zealand may have jurisdiction over cybercrimes, it will rarely prosecute unless the offenders are physically located in New Zealand. In some cases this is due to the limited resources of the investigatory agencies. Terrorist offences may prove to be an exception, but no instance of such a crime have yet been prosecuted.

14.3.2 **Case law**

There is no New Zealand authority which considers the issue of jurisdiction in a case of international computer misuse. Where a person situated overseas commits an offence involving a computer in New Zealand, or where access is gained by a hacker in New Zealand, the Law Commission considered it likely that New Zealand courts would assume jurisdiction.[43] There is some case law to support this conclusion.

In *Solicitor-General* v. *Reid*,[44] where the respondent had sworn a false affidavit in New Zealand for use in proceedings in the Hong Kong Court of Appeal in return for $1m, Paterson J expressly approved the Canadian decision in *Libman* v. *R*,[45] where it was held by the Supreme Court of Canada that the test was whether there was a 'real and substantial link' between the offence and the country asserting jurisdiction to try the offence. Paterson J stated that had he been required to determine the issue, he would have held that New Zealand courts had jurisdiction to hear the case. He also held that there was nothing contrary to international comity in such an assumption of jurisdiction.

---

[41] Crimes Act 1961 (NZ), s. 8(2).

[42] S. 8(2).

[43] New Zealand Law Commission, *Computer Misuse*, Report 54 (Wellington, New Zealand Law Commission 1999), at para. 86.

[44] [1997] 3 NZLR 617 (HC).

[45] (1985) 21 CCC (3d) 206 (SCC).

It might also be expected that New Zealand courts would follow the approach taken in *R* v. *Governor of Brixton Prison, ex parte Levin*,[46] where the Court of Appeal of England and Wales held that 'in the case of a virtually instantaneous instruction intended to take effect where the computer is situated it seems to us artificial to regard the insertion of an instruction onto the disk as having been done only at the remote place where the keyboard is situated.' This is consistent with *Solicitor-General* v. *Reid*.[47] It is likely that the New Zealand courts will assume jurisdiction when a person situated overseas commits an offence involving a computer in New Zealand, or when the hacker is situated in New Zealand.

The New Zealand Law Commission[48] stated that in its view, section 7 of the Crimes Act 1961 was inadequate to deal with computer misuse. It was anticipated that there would be situations where the effects of computer misuse would be felt in New Zealand, even though neither the hacker nor the computer were situated in this country. The Law Commission gives the example of a hacker in New York, the computer in California, and the owner of the computer system in New Zealand.[49] In such a situation section 7 would not give jurisdiction, unless it was a terrorism-linked offence.

It might be impossible to successfully argue, in terms of section 7 of the Crimes Act 1961, that 'any act or omission forming part of [the] offence, or any event necessary to the completion of [the] offence' had occurred within New Zealand. The words 'necessary to completion of the offence' in this context have been held to relate to the completion of the legal ingredients, not the offender's purpose[50] – unless it was terrorism.

In many cases it would be impossible to determine where the hacker was at the time the computer misuse activities took place.[51] However, the 2003 amendments to the Crimes Act 1961 extended jurisdiction to events occurring wholly outside New Zealand where the offence was committed in the course of carrying out a terrorist act, and several other specific offences.

---

[46] [1997] QB 65, 82 (CA).

[47] [1997] 3 NZLR 617 (HC).

[48] New Zealand Law Commission, op. cit. n. 43, at para. 86.

[49] Ibid., at para. 86n.

[50] See *Collector of Customs* v. *Kozanic* (1983) 1 CRNZ 135.

[51] New Zealand Law Commission, op. cit. n. 43, at para. 25 gives the example of the *Ihug* case (1998) where the computer was based in California and was owned by a New Zealand company and some 4,500 web sites were erased.

14.4 Policy Considerations

14.4.1 Claiming jurisdiction for cybercrimes

Historically, there has been a legislative presumption against the extraterritorial application of public-law statutes, as a matter of statutory interpretation.[52] This is based on an historical concern not to infringe on the sovereignty of other states (or provinces) by purporting to regulate conduct that occurs wholly within the boundaries of another jurisdiction.[53] Customary international law however permits a nation to apply its law to extraterritorial behavior with substantial local effect,[54] as well as the extraterritorial conduct of its citizens or domiciliaries.[55] Until very recently, New Zealand law reflected this narrow exemption. Even where an assertion is not aggressive there can be overlapping claims to jurisdiction.

In *Libman*,[56] the Supreme Court of Canada ruled that 'it is sufficient that there be a "real and substantial link"' between the proscribed conduct and the jurisdiction seeking to apply and enforce its law. Clearly, the 'real and substantial link' test for the proper assertion of prescriptive jurisdiction will often result in more than one, and perhaps many, jurisdictions being capable of properly asserting authority over conduct that has effects in more than one jurisdiction. It is this fact that suggests the need for clearer prescriptive jurisdictional rules,[57] especially for consumer laws. In *Dow Jones & Company Inc* v. *Gutnick*,[58] the High Court of Australia found that certain categories of laws did have extraterritorial effect, and certain laws in New Zealand, such as the Consumer Guarantees Act 1993, have been held to have extraterritorial effect. Competing claims to jurisdiction do not necessarily mean that all cases will be prosecuted, however.

The difficulty facing national jurisdictions is one of enforcement, which has led to other forms of regulation, including (but not limited to) trans-national, international, institutional, sectoral and private.[59] There are an increasing number of ex-

---

[52] Though there are important exceptions, including in the consumer law field. For example, the Fair Trading Act 1986 (NZ) states, in s. 3, that '[t]his Act extends to the engaging in conduct outside New Zealand by any person resident or carrying on business in New Zealand to the extent that such conduct relates to the supply of goods or services, or the granting of interests in land, within New Zealand.'

[53] R. Tassé and M. Faille, 'Online Consumer Protection in Canada: The Problem of Regulatory Jurisdiction', 2 *Internet and E-Commerce Law in Canada* (2000/01) p. 41. See also *Buchanan* v. *Rucker* (1808) 9 East 192; 103 ER 546, 547: 'Can the Island of Tobago pass a law to bind the rights of the whole world?.'

[54] The case of the 'SS Lotus', 1927 PCIJ (ser. A) No 10, 18-25. Cf., section 5.6.1 of this book.

[55] *Blackmer* v. *US*, 284 US 421, 436 (1932); *US* v. *Rech*, 780 F2d 1541, 1543 n 2 (11th cir, 1986).

[56] *R* v. *Libman* [1985] 2 SCR 178.

[57] Tassé and Faille, loc. cit. n. 53.

[58] (2002) 194 ALR 433 (HCA).

[59] See, for example, L. Lessig, *Code and other laws of cyberspace* (New York, Basic Books 1999); C. Marsden, *Regulating the Global Information Society* (London, Routledge 2000).

amples of private control or self-regulatory control, sometimes involving codes. Unfortunately these disparate approaches exasperate the already marked divisions. Nor are there signs that international co-operation will be practical outside narrow legal fields such as copyright and cybercrime,[60] even if it is effective there.

Hacking, or the unauthorized access to computer systems, is one aspect of cybercrime which might legitimately be within the jurisdiction of all states – especially if the hacking is malicious, but even when not. As Paterson J observed in *Solicitor-General* v. *Reid*,[61]

> 'There was a real and substantial link between the offence under (…) the Crimes Act and New Zealand. International comity suggests that New Zealand should have jurisdiction as it is contrary to good international relations to stand by and allow events to occur in New Zealand which [causes] harm (...) in another country.'[62]

Hacking is not confined to a single geographical location; by its very nature, it involves the invasion of computer systems physically remote from the offender. For this reason alone, and because of the damage which may occur through damage to systems or data, or through the release of information, jurisdictional considerations ought not to be allowed to inhibit the successful detection, prosecution and conviction of offenders.

If this is true of hacking, it is doubly so for the creation, release and dissemination of computer viruses. With the growth of Internet and e-mail communications across the world it is possible for a virus, whether benign or malignant, to spread extremely rapidly. It is especially dangerous because the degree of security customarily found in computer systems varies markedly around the world. While the traditional early sources of computer viruses included New Zealand, more recently, the sources of virus infections have spread to countries with even less well-developed legal responses to cybercrime. For this reason, and since damage may occur anywhere a virus can reach (which is effectively global reach), criminal jurisdiction should be asserted as widely as possible.

Similar arguments apply with respect to the control of on-line illegal content. Harmful content may be accessed anywhere in the world, and the originator of the content may not even be locatable, since the material may pass from web site to web site by copying or file-sharing, or from e-mail user to e-mail user in the manner of a chain letter, or as 'spam'.

---

[60] See the Copyright Treaty of the World Intellectual Property Organisation, adopted in Geneva on December 20, 1996, and the Council of Europe's Convention on Cybercrime, Budapest, November 23, 2001 (CETS 185).

[61] [1997] 3 NZLR 617, 630, 632.

[62] *Solicitor-General* v. *Reid* [1997] 3 NZLR 617, 630, 632 per Paterson J, *Treacy* v. *Director of Public Prosecutions* [1971] AC 537; [1971] 1 All ER 110 per Lord Diplock at 561-562/121-122 and *Libman* v. *The Queen* [1985] 2 SCR 178; (1985) 21 CCC (3d) 206 followed.

However, the regulation of content also involves consideration of culture-specific values. It may be relatively easy to identify a web site or e-mail that offends against a specific domestic law, but the process involved in searching for these offences may amount to a form of censorship. Indeed, though it is quite possible to censor the content of the Internet, it is possible that its continuing expansion will render this option increasingly difficult. But it remains vital that some claims to jurisdiction are made. The U.S. position is that even if a foreign court passes a judgment or direction against a legal entity of a particular country, say country A, then that judgment or direction would not be applicable automatically to country A's legal entity or citizen.[63] In the numerous international judgments since the advent of the Internet, some courts have simply applied traditional jurisdictional rules,[64] while others have tried to devise new tests to accommodate the peculiarity of the medium.[65] This has caused uncertainty and difficulties for courts, and sometimes possibly led to illegal content being published and spread more than it would have been if jurisdictional claims had been clearer.

The general rule governing criminal jurisdiction in New Zealand is that nothing done or omitted outside New Zealand can be tried in New Zealand as an offence, unless statutes specifically provide otherwise.[66] However, New Zealand law asserts extraterritorial jurisdiction in respect of certain offences with transnational aspects.[67] Proceedings under these specified offences may also be brought if a person in respect of whom the offences alleged to have been committed is a New Zealand citizen, or is ordinarily resident in New Zealand.[68] Proceedings may also be brought for an offence against section 98A of the Crimes Act 1961 (participation in an organized criminal gang), if the group of people in which the person to be charged is alleged to have participated are alleged to have as an objective the obtaining of material benefits by the commission in New Zealand of offences or conduct referred to in section 98A(2)(a) or (b). Both of these provisions may apply to cybercrimes. These are applied to terrorism and certain specific crimes, especially organized crime and corruption, but have no general application.

---

[63] *Yahoo! Inc* v. *La Ligue contre Le Racisme et L'Antisemitisme*, 145 F Supp 2d 1168; 169 F Supp 2d 1181 (2001); A. Manolopoulos, 'Raising 'Cyber-Borders': The Interaction Between Law and Technology', 11 *International Journal of Law and Information Technology* (2003) p. 40.

[64] Such as *Bensusan Restaurant Corp.* v. *King*, 40 USPQ (2d) 1519 (SDNY), confirmed by United States Court of Appeals (2d cir) 10 September 1997.

[65] See O. Renault, 'Jurisdiction and the Internet: Are the traditional rules enough?', paper prepared by the Uniform Law Conference of Canada (1998), available at <http://www.law.ualberta.ca/alri/ulc/current/ejurisd.htm>.

[66] S. 6 Crimes Act 1961 (NZ). This enacts the common law principle that statutes are not to be construed as giving extraterritorial jurisdiction unless there are clear words to that effect, as to which see *Macleod* v. *Attorney-General for New South Wales* [1891] AC 455 (PC). The general rule that 'all crime is local' was repeated by the Court of Appeal in *R* v. *Sanders* [1984] 1 NZLR 636; (1984) 1 CRNZ 194 (CA).

[67] See *supra*, section 14.3.1 and n. 40.

[68] Crimes Act 1961 (NZ), s. 7A(1)(c)(i) and (ii), as inserted by the Crimes Amendment Act 2002 (NZ), s. 4.

The assertion of extraterritorial jurisdiction may be justified as based on a state's responsibility for the actions of its people, wherever situated. A general assertion of jurisdiction would be seen to be contrary to the notion of the sanctity of state sovereignty. But, as we have seen, this self-imposed limitation has been weakened with respect to terrorism offences.

14.4.2 Dealing with cyber-investigation jurisdiction

This problem of jurisdiction is not unique to New Zealand, or the Asia Pacific region, or elsewhere – though countries such as New Zealand are particularly vulnerable as they are small and geographically remote from major trading partners, and therefore major potential users of the Internet.

Law-enforcement co-operation with foreign counterparts is critically important to U.S. efforts (in particular) to address the challenges of cross-border Internet fraud. The same technology that Internet frauds use is proving invaluable to international law enforcers whose job is to track down fraudsters and stop their activities. This is achieved by identifying non-complying web sites, and informing them that they are acting illegally. Only as a last resort is legal action undertaken. The U.S. Federal Trade Commission (FTC) also plays an active role in public policy discussions on international consumer-protection principles for the global economy.[69] New Zealand has also relied heavily on international co-operation.

New Zealand and other countries cannot investigate crimes without reliance on international co-operation. Cybercrime generally (though not invariably) occurs across jurisdictional boundaries – or at least is often oblivious to jurisdictions. This situation requires a balanced approach of 'co-regulation', or what has been called 'a new paradigm for governance that recognizes the complexity of networks, builds constructive relationships among the various participants (including governments, systems operators, information providers, and citizens), and promotes incentives for the attainment of various public policy objectives in the private sector.'[70]

Proper enforcement of such applicable criminal laws as exist requires effective investigatory powers. These powers need to be grounded in technology-neutral legislation, which will not become outmoded as computer technology advances. For example, police require authority to conduct network searches, just as they require authority to conduct physical searches. It is unsatisfactory that the current legislative provisions in New Zealand are not clear – except perhaps with respect to the rather more specific powers conferred upon the Police with respect to investigating terrorist activities. If evidence of criminal offending were to be gathered through

[69] J. Bernstein, Director, Bureau of Consumer Protection, U.S. Federal Trade Commission, 'Fighting Internet Fraud: A Global Effort', *Economic Perspectives, An Electronic Journal of the United States Department of State*, 5 (May 2000), available at <http://usinfo.state.gov/journals/ites/0500/ijee/ftc2.htm>.

[70] J.R. Reidenberg, 'Governing Networks and Rule-Making in Cyberspace', in B. Kahin and C. Nesson, eds., *Borders in Cyberspace* (Cambridge, MIT Press 1997), pp. 84-105

police searches of computer networks, it is not even certain that this evidence would be usable in a prosecution.

While the power to authorize the interception of telecommunications is vital for the preservation of national security, it is also a useful, indeed invaluable, tool for the detection of crime, including cybercrime. However, unlike authorizing the searching of computers where suspicion of offending has arisen, there is a danger that a too-wide right to intercept telecommunications might be used rather as a 'fishing net', in the hope of discovering something of interest. The consequence for the great majority of users of telecommunications is that their privacy is infringed – generally without their knowledge, and always without their consent. The investigatory powers of interception need careful control, therefore, especially where this information may be passed on to other countries, or where the interception is at the behest of another country.

There is much greater justification for allowing the infiltrating of on-line child-pornography networks. Although there are difficulties of definition and degrees of offending, this sort of material is generally relatively readily identified as offensive. It also is very frequently international in scope, with vice-rings creating, swapping and collecting material from multiple sources. It is often this very internationality which renders the detection and prosecution of offenders difficult. There have already been many examples of international police operations aimed at disrupting these large-scale offenders, which have often been very effective, for a time. However, the scale of the problem is such that it cannot be tackled by any single country or small groups of countries, and would be more effectively dealt with as simply another form of offence for the national authorities to deal with. This requires the existence and exercise of jurisdiction in all countries where the Internet operates – for it is not reliant on the existence of Internet Service Providers.

14.4.3 **Positive and negative jurisdiction conflicts**

Given that most cybercrimes are agreed to be criminal offending and worthy of punishment, but that criminal law is domestic and not international in nature, one of the biggest dangers is that some instances of this offending escape prosecution because of a failure to prosecute, or the failure of a prosecution due to jurisdictional or evidentiary difficulties. Extradition of offenders from one country to another is not practical except in a few instances – and even this requires that the offence is criminal in both countries.[71] In the absence of an international police agency empowered to investigate and prosecute before domestic or international courts, the best solution may well be a gradual process of consolidating and standardizing laws, both criminal and procedural. This would not only reduce the chances of a failure in prosecution, but would also assist those countries that have less well-developed technology laws.

---

[71] This is the rule, though there are exceptions.

Another potential danger however is a conflict of jurisdictions, where multiple countries claim jurisdiction over an offence. This not only raises the danger of protracted trials and litigation, but also offers the possibility of over-criminalizing activities and creating situations where double jeopardy may arise. Even the existence of multiple individual claims does not guarantee that a single prosecution will occur. Again, gradual standardization would help to reduce these possibilities.

As an initial step, co-operative agreements between policing agencies should be utilized. Much can be done without the necessity of legislation enactments, for there is a considerable degree of investigative discretion in most countries, and many investigative powers which are common. This may proceed as bilateral and multilateral agreements, but ideally should include international conventions. Conventions such as the Budapest Convention on Cybercrime would be strengthened and their effectiveness greatly enhanced if appropriate administrative and investigative procedures and processes existed.

14.5 Conclusion

New Zealand has still not fully addressed the jurisdictional issues that cybercrime raise. There is no single assertion of jurisdiction. Even if this were made, it is doubtful that jurisdiction would be sought or exercised in practice. New Zealand, largely for reasons of limited resources, does not take an especially pro-active role. While it co-operates with the law-enforcement agencies of other countries, its own ability to combat cybercrime is reduced by lingering uncertainty regarding the nature of the electronic media – concerns only partly allayed by recent legislative changes.

Pragmatism and a lingering belief in the notion of state sovereignty have prevented a wide assertion of extraterritorial jurisdiction over cybercrime. The former is in recognition of the limited practical scope for discovering, prosecuting and punishing offences committed overseas. The latter is perhaps due to a strong sense of individualism, a less well-developed sense of national comity, and continued support for the post-Westphalian notion of jurisdictional sovereignty.

If all states were to have jurisdiction over cybercrimes – and were to exercise that – and domestic laws were made consistent with one another, there could be a gradual move towards the development of an international customary law. This could reconcile both the concept of state sovereignty and the need to ensure that cybercrimes are prosecuted efficiently and properly.

Bibliography

J. Bernstein, 'Fighting Internet Fraud: A Global Effort', *Economic Perspectives, An Electronic Journal of the United States Department of State* (May 2000), <http://usinfo.state.gov/journals/ites/0500/ijee/ftc2.htm>.

D. Harvey, *Internet.law.nz: selected issues* (Wellington, LexisNexis, 2003).

A. Manolopoulos, 'Raising 'Cyber-Borders': The Interaction Between Law and Technology', 11 *International Journal of Law and Information Technology* (2003) p. 40.

P. Myburgh and E. Schoeman, 'Jurisdiction in trans-national cases', *New Zealand Law Journal* (2004) p. 403.

New Zealand Law Commission, *Computer Misuse*, Report 54 (Wellington, New Zealand Law Commission 1999).

O. Renault, 'Jurisdiction and the Internet: Are the traditional rules enough?', paper prepared by the Uniform Law Conference of Canada (1998), available at <http://www.law.ualberta.ca/alri/ulc/current/ejurisd.htm>.

J.R. Reidenberg, 'Governing Networks and Rule-Making in Cyberspace', in B. Kahin and C. Nesson, eds., *Borders in Cyberspace* (Cambridge, MIT Press 1997).

T. Smith, 'Fighting on the ocean blue: New Zealand's extra-territorial jurisdiction and maritime protest', 32 *Victoria University of Wellington Law Review* (2001) p. 499.

R. Tassé and M. Faille, 'Online Consumer Protection in Canada: The Problem of Regulatory Jurisdiction', 2 *Internet and E-Commerce Law in Canada* (2000/01).

Chapter 15
CYBERCRIME AND JURISDICTION IN UNITED KINGDOM

Ian Walden*

15.1 Introduction

The range of criminal activities involving computers can be broadly distinguished into three categories, as adopted under the Council of Europe Cybercrime Convention (hereafter: Convention).[1] First, computer-related cybercrime, such as fraud and theft, where computers are simply the tools for the crime, manipulating data to commit traditional criminal activities. Second, content-based cybercrimes, such as child pornography, where computer and communications technologies facilitate the distribution of illegal data. The third category of cybercrime are those activities where the intention is to compromise the integrity, availability and confidentiality of the computers and systems connected to the Internet and the data being processed on them, such as hacking and the distribution of viruses.

Computer crime often inevitably has a transnational aspect to it that can give rise to complex jurisdictional issues; involving persons present and acts being carried out in a number of different countries. Even where the perpetrator and the accused are located in the same jurisdiction, relevant evidence may reside on a server located in another jurisdiction, such as a Hotmail account. As with most aspects of Internet-based activities, traditional legal concepts and principles are sometime challenged by the nature of the environment. As a consequence, legislators and the judiciary have had to address issues of cybercrime jurisdiction at a number of levels. This chapter examines issues of material and procedural jurisdiction under English criminal law applicable to cybercrime activities.[2]

* Dr Ian Walden is Reader in Information and Communications Law and Head of the Institute of Computer and Communications Law in the Centre for Commercial Law Studies, Queen Mary, University of London. He is also solicitor and consultant to the law firm Baker & McKenzie.

[1] Council of Europe, Convention on Cybercrime, Budapest, November 23, 2001 (CETS 185) (hereafter: CCC).

[2] Note that Scotland and Northern Ireland are separate criminal jurisdictions from England and Wales. In Scotland, substantive criminal law, such as fraud, is based primarily on common law, i.e., past decisions from the courts, rather than statute, while criminal procedure is codified. Many statutory offences are shared with England and Wales, through UK-wide legislation, such as the Computer Misuse Act 1990. For the purposes of this chapter, references to the United Kingdom and England are used synonymously.

B-J. Koops and S.W. Brenner (Eds), Cybercrime and Jurisdiction

15.2 Material Jurisdiction

The general principle of international criminal law is that a crime committed within a State's territory may be tried there, although the territoriality of criminal law does not coincide with territorial sovereignty.[3] Under English common law, the general principle for determining jurisdiction has recently been stated by the courts to be where 'the last act took place in England or a substantial part of the crime was committed here'.[4] Previously, the general principle was drawn more narrowly, as being where the *actus reus* is completed,[5] also referred to as 'result crimes' or the 'terminatory theory'. The 'last act' rule echoes the civil law principle *lex loci delicti commissi*, whereby torts are governed by the law of the place where the act was committed.

However, an act may be initiated in one jurisdiction and completed or terminated, i.e., the effect or harm felt, in another jurisdiction. While with physical crimes the initiatory and terminatory elements of a crime are generally concurrent, such as murder (unless the person fires the gun from another state!), where criminal activity is information-based, a jurisdictional distinction between the initiation and termination of an act becomes the norm. The courts had previously recognized this, Lord Diplock stating for example that 'there is no reason in principle why the terminatory theory should have the effect of excluding the initiatory theory as an alternative ground of jurisdiction.'[6] However, the terminatory theory proved remarkably resilient until an expansive approach was adopted by the Court of Appeal in *Smith (Wallace Duncan)*.

An example of the issues that arise in a cybercrime environment are illustrated in the Citibank fraud.[7] In 1994, Citibank suffered a significant breach of security in its cash management system, resulting in funds being transferred from customer accounts into the accounts of the perpetrator and his accomplices.[8] The eventual sum involved was $12 million, although the vast majority, $11.6 million, was transferred subsequent to the discovery of the breach as part of the efforts to locate the perpetrators. After significant international co-operation between law-enforcement agencies, an individual was identified. Vladimir Levin was eventually arrested in England and, after appeals, was subsequently extradited to the United States.

---

[3] A. Cassese, *International Criminal Law* (Oxford, Oxford University Press 2003), p. 277.

[4] *Smith (Wallace Duncan) (No.4)* [2004] QB 1418, at 57.

[5] *Manning* (1998) 2 Cr App R. 461.

[6] *Treacy* [1971] AC 537.

[7] *R* v. *Governor of Brixton Prison and another, ex parte Levin* (1996) 4 All ER 350. The decision was appealed unsuccessfully to the House of Lords (1997) 3 All ER 289.

[8] The system, called the 'Financial Institutions Citibank Cash Manager' (FICCM), provided large institutional customers with dial-in access from any geographic location to the on-line service, based on a system in Parsipenny, New Jersey. Once accessed, customers could carry out a range of financial transactions, including the execution of credit transfers between accounts.

One jurisdictional issue in *Levin* revolved around the question of *where* the offences were held to have taken place. Defendant's counsel claimed that the criminal act occurred in St. Petersburg at the moment when Levin pressed particular keys on the keyboard instigating fraudulent Citibank transfers, and therefore Russian law applied. Counsel for the extradition applicant claimed that the place where the changes to the data occurred, the Citibank computer in Parsipenny (U.S.), constituted the place where the offence took place. The judge decided in favor of the applicant on the basis that the real-time nature of the communication link between Levin and the Citibank computer meant that Levin's keystrokes were actually occurring on the Citibank computer.[9]

Such an approach might suggest that a message-based system of communication, such as e-mail, operating on a 'store-and-forward' basis, might produce a different result if an interval in the course of committing the act could be shown to exist. In *ex parte Osman*,[10] for example, the court held that the sending of a telex constituted the act of appropriation and, therefore, the place from where the telex was sent was where the offence was committed.[11] With the decision in *Smith (Wallace Duncan)* and other subsequent statutory developments, such an issue would likely no longer arise. However, the nature of computer and communications technologies can create legal uncertainty about where an act occurs, which is likely to be a common ground for challenge by defendants.

One consequence of the common jurisdictional dissonance between initiation and termination in an Internet environment is that English criminal law has had to be amended to extend the territorial reach of certain offences. In addition, the general concern about the growth and societal impact of computer crime has also led governments to apply extraterritorial principles to cybercrime.

15.2.1 **Statutory rules**

In terms of ensuring legal certainty, common-law principles of criminal jurisdiction have been made concrete or supplanted through express jurisdictional provisions in substantive legislation. Such rules generally claim jurisdiction if one of the elements of the offence occurs within the state's territory.

The primary statute governing computer integrity offences, such as hacking and viruses, is the Computer Misuse Act 1990. The Act was initially a private members bill rather than a governmental initiative, although the government eventually supported its passage onto the statute books. The need for a specific legislative instrument to criminalize activities such as hacking had become widely accepted during the 1980s, spurred on particularly by the House of Lords decision in *Gold and Schifreen*.[12]

[9] *R* v. *Governor of Brixton Prison and another, ex parte Levin* (1996) 4 All ER 350, at p. 363a.
[10] *Governor of Pentonville Prison, ex parte Osman* [1989] 3 All ER 701.
[11] Ibid., at 295e-f.
[12] *R* v. *Gold, Schifreen* [1988] 2 All ER 186.

In *Gold*, the defendants gained unauthorized access to BT's Prestel service and discovered the password codes of various private e-mail accounts, including the Duke of Edinburgh's! The defendants were prosecuted under the Forgery and Counterfeiting Act 1981 for creating a 'false instrument', by entering customer authorization codes to access the system. The Act defines an 'instrument' seemingly broadly to include 'any disc, tape, sound track or other device on or in which information is recorded or stored by mechanical, electronic or other means'.[13] In addition, the meaning of 'induce' expressly avoids the need for a real person, as required in respect of 'deception' for fraud:

> 'references to inducing somebody to accept a false instrument as genuine (...) include references to inducing a machine to respond.'[14]

However, the House of Lords held that the electronic signals that comprised the identification codes could not be considered tangible in the sense that a disk or tape were. It also held that the signals were present in the system for such a fleeting moment, that they could not be considered to have been 'recorded or stored'.[15] The Court of Appeal was also highly critical of the application of the Act to such a set of circumstances:

> 'The Procrustean attempt to force these facts into the language of an Act not designed to fit them produced difficulties for both judge and jury which we would not wish to see repeated.'[16]

Such explicit recognition by the judiciary of the need to draft new legislation, rather than try to extend traditional terminology to fit computer technology, lent significant pressure to the calls for reform of the criminal law.

The Computer Misuse Act 1990 created three substantive computer integrity offences: unauthorized access to computer material (section 1); unauthorized access with intent to commit or facilitate commission of further offences (section 2),[17] and unauthorized modification of computer material (section 3). The Act has had a problematic history,[18] and the fact that it was adopted prior to rapid expansion of the Internet has raised concerns about its effectiveness against new forms of criminal activity such as 'denial-of-service' attacks. As a consequence, in July 2003,

---

[13] S. 8(1)(d).

[14] S. 10(3).

[15] Lord Brandon, *R* v. *Gold, Schifreen* [1988] 2 All ER 186, at 192c.

[16] [1987] 3 W.L.R. 803, at 809H. Such sentiment was echoed by Lord Brandon in the House of Lords: [1988] 2 All ER 186, at 192d.

[17] The further offence must be one for which the sentence is fixed by law, e.g., life imprisonment for murder, or where imprisonment may be for a term of five years or more for a first-time offender at 21 years of age or over.

[18] I. Walden, 'Computer Crime', in Reed and Angel, eds., *Computer Law*, 5th edn. (Oxford, Oxford University Press 2003) pp. 295-329.

the UK government declared its intention to reform the Computer Misuse Act 1990.[19]

Under the Act, the offences may be committed by any person, British citizenship being immaterial to a person's guilt.[20] Jurisdiction in transnational activities is asserted through the concept of a 'significant link' being present in the 'home country', i.e., England and Wales, Scotland or Northern Ireland.[21] Where an unauthorized access offence has been committed, the following are considered a 'significant link':

> '(a) that the accused was in the home country concerned at the time when he did the act which caused the computer to perform the function; or
> (b) that any computer containing any program or data to which the accused secured or intended to secure unauthorised access by doing that act was in the home country concerned at the time.'[22]

Where a section 2 offence is involved, the Act addresses two potential scenarios. First, the need for a 'significant link' is dispensed with in respect of the unauthorized element of the action, as long as the further offence is triable under English law.[23] If the further offence is extraterritorial in nature, then an offence may be committed which requires no connection with England and Wales at all.[24] Second, in the alternate, if a 'significant link' does exist, and what was intended to be committed would involve the commission of an offence under the law of the country where the act was intended to take place, whether under the laws of England and Wales or elsewhere, then the domestic courts can still seize jurisdiction.[25]

In the case of an unauthorized modification, under section 3, the 'significant link' is either the presence of the accused or the fact that the modification occurred in the UK.[26]

Where computer-related offences have been committed, such as fraud or forgery, the Criminal Justice Act 1993, Part I, provides for jurisdiction on the basis of a 'relevant event' occurring in England and Wales (s. 2(3)). A 'relevant event' means:

> 'any act or omission or other event (including any result of one or more acts or omissions) proof of which is required for conviction of the offence.'[27]

[19] Caroline Flint MP, Parliamentary Under-Secretary, Home Officer Minister in speech made at a EURIM meeting, 14 July 2003.

[20] S. 9.

[21] S. 4(6).

[22] S. 5(2). Ss. 6 and 7 address the territorial scope for the inchoate offences, i.e., conspiracy, attempt or incitement.

[23] S. 4(3).

[24] M. Hirst, *Jurisdiction and the Ambit of the Criminal Law* (Oxford, Oxford University Press 2003), p. 194.

[25] Ss. 4(4) and 8(1).

[26] S. 5(3).

[27] S. 2(1). These provisions only came into force on 1 June 1999. They were recommended in Law Commission Report No. 180, *Jurisdiction over Offences of Fraud and Dishonesty with a Foreign Element*, Cm. 318 (1989), although the phrase was first proposed in a Law Commission Working Paper, *Territorial and Extraterritorial Extent of the Criminal* Law, No. 29, 1970.

This would include, for example, an e-mail message sent as part of a conspiracy. A court can seize jurisdiction if any 'relevant event' occurs in England and Wales even though all other such events may have occurred abroad.

The Criminal Justice Act 1993 also provides for rules to determine the location of certain 'relevant events'. In relation to the obtaining of property, the act occurs in England and Wales if it is either dispatched from or received at a place in the jurisdiction. In the case of a conspiracy to commit fraud, a communication of 'any information, instruction, request, demand or other matter' is a 'relevant event', and it takes place in England and Wales if the message is sent or received here.[28] As such, while the United Kingdom does not have an offence comparable to wire fraud in the United States,[29] a similar result could be achieved to that held recently by the Supreme Court in *Pasquantino*,[30] where the accused were prosecuted in the United States for wire fraud in the course of a broader criminal act of smuggling to evade Canadian revenue laws. While in *Pasquantino* two distinct offences were involved, the UK authorities would only be concerned with one offence, of which only the communication element need touch English jurisdiction.

In terms of content-related offences, the issue of jurisdiction has been raised in respect of the 'publication' of material prohibited under the Obscene Publications Act 1959. The Act criminalizes the publication of *any* material which tends to 'deprave and corrupt' those persons likely to read or view it (s. 1(1)); pornographic images of children are generally subject to prosecution under separate legislative provisions.[31]

Section 1(3) of the 1959 Act defines 'publication' in the following terms:

> '(a) distributes, circulates, sells, lets on hire, gives, or lends it, or who offers it for sale or for letting on hire; or
> (b) in the case of an article containing or embodying matter to be looked at (...) where the matter is data stored electronically, transmits that data.'

In *Waddon* (2000),[32] the court held, in respect of pornographic images made available through a web site, that two distinct acts of publication take place (para. 12). The first occurs when the data is uploaded to a web site, the second when it is subsequently downloaded. The court was satisfied that such an approach was clearly encompassed by section 1(3)(b). Subsequently in *Perrin*,[33] in accepting the *Waddon* position, the court drew further support from the different forms of publications recognized in section 1(3)(a), specifically the reference to 'offers it for sale', which as a passive form of 'publication' has obvious parallels with the establishment of a

---

28 S. 4.
29 18 USC § 1343.
30 73 USLW 4287 (2005).
31 I.e., Protection of Children Act 1978, s. 1, and the Criminal Justice Act 1988, s. 160.
32 [2000] All ER (D) 502.
33 *Perrin* [2002] All ER (D) 359.

web site (para. 18). The defendant was a French citizen and claimed that 'where sites were developed abroad they were legal where they were managed' (para. 4). However, such an approach was ignored by the court, finding guilt on the basis that the publication through downloading occurred in England.

The issues raised in *Waddon* and *Perrin* contain interesting parallels with the *Yahoo!* case in France.[34] In *Yahoo!*, one of the determining factors in attributing liability was the perceived targeting of French citizens. Counsel in both English cases raised the issue of jurisdiction. In *Waddon*, the court declined a request to rule on a situation where material was placed on a web site with no intention for subsequent transmission back to England; although they did opine that it would likely 'depend upon questions of intention and causation in relation to where publication should take place' (para. 11). In *Perrin*, counsel for the defendant suggested that 'a prosecution should only be brought against a publisher where the prosecutor could show that the major steps in relation to publication were taken within the jurisdiction of the court' – a suggestion dismissed by the court.

For computer integrity and computer-related crimes, we can see a statutory trend towards expanding the jurisdictional reach of English criminal law, which English common law, in *Smith (Wallace Duncan)*, has only recently been willing to follow. It is perhaps both inevitable and appropriate that Parliament responds more rapidly to the increasing internationalization of criminal activity than the judiciary. However, by contrast, in *Perrin*, an expansive judicial interpretation of the *actus reus* may be seen as criminalizing unwitting foreign citizens, simply on the basis of the nature of the technological environment in which they operate.

15.2.2 **Extraterritorial criminal law**

While the jurisdictional norm of criminal law is the territoriality principle, there are four broadly recognized principles under which extraterritorial jurisdiction is claimed or exercised in cases of international criminal activity:

- the 'active nationality principle', which is based on the nationality of the perpetrator;
- the 'passive personality principle', which is based on the nationality of the victim;
- the 'universality principle', for crimes broadly recognized as being crimes against humanity, such as genocide or piracy;[35]

---

[34] *League Against Racism and Antisemitism (LICRA), French Union of Jewish Students,* v. *Yahoo! Inc. (USA), Yahoo France*, Tribunal de Grande Instance de Paris, 20 November 2000; EBLR (2001).

[35] On 19 July 2005, a former Afghan warlord became the first person to be prosecuted for offences of torture and hostage-taking, following the House of Lords decision in *Pinochet* [2000] 1 AC 147, which expressly accepted the validity of the 'universality principle' under English law.

- the 'protection principle', to safeguard a jurisdiction's national interest, such as the planning of cyber-terrorism.[36]

The territoriality principle has also expanded over the years, extending the locus of the crime to include acts committed abroad which have an effect in the jurisdiction. This has become known as the 'objective territoriality principle', although it is obviously related to the 'passive personality principle'.[37]

Under English law, the general common-law position is that the courts will not accept jurisdiction if the offence is committed outside England and Wales, even if the accused is a British subject.[38] However, this position has been altered by statutory provision in respect of certain offences, including indecent images of children, a major form of content-related computer crime. The Sexual Offences Act 2003, section 72, provides that:

> '(1) Subject to subsection (2), any act done by a person in a country or territory outside the United Kingdom which –
>
> (a) constituted an offence under the law in force in that country or territory, and
> (b) would constitute a sexual offence to which this section applies if it had been done in England and Wales or in Northern Ireland, constitutes that sexual offence under the law of that part of the United Kingdom.
>
> (2) Proceedings by virtue of this section may be brought only against a person who was on 1st September 1997, or has since become, a British citizen or resident in the United Kingdom.'[39]

This provision is applicable to both the supply and possession of child pornographic photographs and 'pseudo-photographs'.[40] In the event of proceedings, it is presumed that the subsection 1(a) condition is met, although a defendant can submit a notice or require the prosecution to prove such equivalence, where the offence may be described differently in the foreign country.[41]

However, such extraterritorial provisions remain the exception to the rule. At the end of 2004, for example, the government published a proposal to reform fraud law, driven in part by a desire to address problems prosecuting cyber-fraud due to the

---

36 See generally Cassese, op. cit. n. 3, chapter 15.

37 See I. Bantekas, S. Nash and M. Mackarel, *International Criminal Law* (Cavendish 2001) at p. 16 et seq.

38 See *Harden* [1963] 1 QB 8.

39 This re-enacts a provision under the Sex Offenders Act 1997.

40 Under the Protection of Children Act 1978 (PCA), s. 1, and the Criminal Justice Act 1988 (CJA), s. 160, respectively (Sexual Offences Act 2003, Schedule 2, para. 1(d)). A 'pseudo-photograph' is defined as 'an image, whether made by computer-graphics or otherwise howsoever, which appears to be a photograph' (PCA, s. 7(7) and CJA, s. 160(4), inserted by the Criminal Justice and Public Order Act 1994, s. 84).

41 S. 72(4), (5).

existing requirement that a person rather than a machine be deceived.[42] The proposal considers but rejects the suggestion that the active nationality principle should be adopted.[43] It raises four key arguments against such a position. First, the practical difficulties that would arise from the need to gather evidence overseas and the possibility of bringing witnesses from abroad. Second, the potential conflicts with local laws, which may prevent such evidence being garnered, or the accused being extradited. Third, doubts may be raised whether the public interest in served in the prosecution of cases where there is no impact on the UK.[44] Finally, the report asks whether it is appropriate to make UK nationals abroad subject to domestic law as well as local law.

Despite these views, the government will need to reconsider its position in respect of computer crimes, being a signatory to the Cybercrime Convention and being subject to the obligations under the EU Framework Decision on attacks against information systems.[45] Both these instruments contain jurisdictional provisions that include extraterritorial jurisdiction on the basis of the 'active personality' principle.[46] As such, the government will be obliged to adopt appropriate provisions to reflect these obligations of public international law. However, the Crown Prosecution Service (CPS), the public agency tasked with the conduct of most criminal proceedings,[47] would be required to consider the public interest when deciding whether to proceed on the basis of jurisdiction through 'active personality', which may be unlikely given the arguments outlined above.[48]

15.3 Procedural Jurisdiction

This section considers English law rules governing the obtaining of evidence for investigative and prosecutorial purposes, both in terms of the direct use of law-enforcement powers to gather such data available from the territory, as well as mutual legal-assistance procedures to obtain evidence from a foreign jurisdiction. In addition, a cyber-criminal may be located outside English law jurisdiction and commit a criminal act in the English territory, or he may be located in the United Kingdom, but be wanted for a criminal act committed in another territory. In both

---

[42] See Law Commission Consultation Paper No. 155, *Legislating the Criminal Code: Fraud and Deception*, 1999, paras. 8.36-8.58.

[43] *Fraud Law Reform: Government response to the consultation* (November 2004), paras. 57 et seq.

[44] Under English law, prosecutors are required to consider three issues when deciding to proceed with a prosecution: (a) the public interest, (b) evidential sufficiency and (c) jurisdiction.

[45] Council Framework Decision 2005/222/JHA of 24 February 2005 on attacks against information systems, *OJ* L69/67, 16.3.2005.

[46] Ibid., Art. 10(1)(b), and Art. 22(d) CCC.

[47] Established under the Prosecution of Offences Act 1985.

[48] See Crown Prosecution Service, 'Code for Crown Prosecutors' (2004), at section 5.6, available at <http://www.cps.gov.uk/victims_witnesses/code.html>.

situations, the question of extradition arises: can the perpetrator be obtained from or sent to another state for prosecution?

15.3.1 **Investigating cybercrime**

In terms of obtaining evidence, relevant data may be resident or stored on the computer system of the victim, the suspect, or some third party, such as a communication service provider. Alternatively, evidence may be obtained from data in the process of it being transmitted across a network, generally referred to as intercepted data. Specific rules of criminal procedure address law-enforcement access to both stored data and data in transmission, which include jurisdictional elements.

Search and seizure

Generally, powers to enter and search premises, where data stored on the computer system of a suspect may be found, will either be granted by a magistrate,[49] which then confers a general power of seizure,[50] or arise in the course of an arrest, which confers certain powers of search and seizure.[51] In respect of computer integrity offences, the Computer Misuse Act offences under sections 2 and 3 are 'arrestable offences',[52] the section 1 offence of unauthorized access is not arrestable, therefore a special provision is made for a search warrant (with a power of seizure) to be granted by a circuit judge.[53]

In a networked environment, however, what is the geographical scope of such warrants? Under the Police and Criminal Evidence Act 1984, a constable may require 'any information which is stored in any electronic form and is accessible from the premises to be produced in a form in which it can be taken away (…)' (s. 19(4)).[54] On the face of it, this provision would appear to enable law-enforcement officers to obtain information held on remote systems, since information in electronic form will be accessible from a networked computer on the searched premises. Although this provision has no explicit jurisdictional limitation, a limitation exists on the exercise of statutory powers by the police.[55] Distinguishing between territorial and extraterritorial located evidence, investigators are obliged to give mind to the legal-

---

49 Police and Criminal Evidence Act 1984, s. 8.

50 Ibid., s. 19. Powers of seizure under other enactments are extended to include 'computerized information' by s. 20.

51 Ibid., s. 32.

52 Ibid., s. 24, which includes offences where the sentence may include imprisonment for a five-year period.

53 Computer Misuse Act 1990, s. 14.

54 As amended by the Criminal Justice and Police Act 2001, Sch. 2(2), para. 13(2)(a). See also s. 20, which extends this provision to powers of seizure conferred under other enactments, such as the Computer Misuse Act, s. 14.

55 Police Act 1996, s. 30 ('Jurisdiction of constables'): '(1) A member of a police force shall have all the powers and privileges of a constable throughout England and Wales and the adjacent United Kingdom waters.'

ity of any extraterritorial activity, since evidence obtained unlawfully from a foreign state is likely to be excluded by the court, either as an abuse of process[56] or through the exercise of statutory discretion.[57] The unlawful nature of the activity may arise through breach of specific foreign-law provisions, such as unauthorized-access provisions, or may be based on general principles of breach of national sovereignty and the comity of nations implied into the operation of such principles.

Accessing remote data became problematic for law-enforcement agencies during the early 1990s, as a consequence of the Computer Misuse Act 1990. Certain electronic bulletin boards, containing illegal material such as virus code, began placing messages at the point of access to the site stating that 'law enforcement officials are not permitted to enter the system'. Such a warning was considered to be an effective technique in restricting the police from monitoring the use made of such bulletin boards.[58] As a consequence, in 1994, the Computer Misuse Act was amended to prevent law-enforcement agencies committing a section 1 offence of unauthorized access:

> 'nothing designed to indicate a withholding of consent to access to any program or data from persons as enforcement officers shall have effect to make access unauthorised for the purposes of the said section 1(1).
>
> In this section 'enforcement officer' means a constable or other person charged with the duty of investigating offences; and withholding consent from a person 'as' an enforcement officer of any description includes the operation, by the person entitled to control access, or rules whereby enforcement officers of that description are, as such, disqualified from membership of a class or persons who are authorised to have access.'[59]

While this provides protection in a domestic context, law-enforcement officers could still be in breach of similar offences in other jurisdictions. In addition, the scope of this exception should perhaps have been more narrowly drafted so as not to legitimize the use of 'hacking' and related techniques by law-enforcement agencies to circumvent data-security measures utilized on remote systems. Following the July 2005 terrorist attacks in London, the police have called for new powers 'to attack

---

[56] See *R* v. *Loosely (Attorney General's Reference No. 3 of 2000)* [2001] UKHL 53; (2001) 4 All ER 897).

[57] Police and Criminal Evidence Act 1984, s. 78(1): 'In any proceedings the court may refuse to allow evidence on which the prosecution proposes to rely to be given if it appears to the court that, having regard to all the circumstances in which the evidence was obtained, the admission of the evidence would have such an adverse effect on the fairness of the proceedings that the court ought not to admit it.'

[58] See Home Affairs Committee Report No. 126: 'Computer Pornography', p. xii, paras. 31-32, HMSO (February 1994).

[59] The Criminal Justice and Public Order Act 1994, s. 162, amending s. 10 of the Computer Misuse Act 1990.

identified web sites', which is recognized as having significant cross-border implications.[60] Such proactive techniques by investigators will obviously need to be subject to specific procedural controls, akin to interception regimes.

Interception

Interception of the content of a communication is governed in the United Kingdom by the Regulation of Investigatory Powers Act 2000 (RIPA). The RIPA regime is not primarily designed to tackle the activities of those intercepting communications in the furtherance of their criminal activities; rather its purpose is to control the interception practices of law-enforcement agents and the use of intercepted material as evidence. The European Court of Human Rights has at least twice found UK law to be in breach of the Convention in respect of protecting the right of privacy of those who have been subject to state-based interception.[61]

The Act makes it an offence to intercept a communication being transmitted over a public telecommunications system without a warrant issued by the Secretary of State, or over a private telecommunication system without the consent of the system controller.[62] An interception warrant should only be issued by the Secretary of State in the interests of national security; for the prevention or detection of 'serious crime'[63] or to safeguard the 'economic well-being of the United Kingdom'.[64] A fourth ground for the issuance of a warrant arises where the Secretary of State considers that a situation equivalent to circumstances in which he would issue a warrant to prevent or detect serious crime, is required for the purpose of 'giving effect to the provisions of any international mutual assistance agreement'.[65] Therefore, a request from a foreign law-enforcement agency to intercept a suspect's data communications can be authorized.

The Secretary of State has also issued regulations governing non-warrant based interception activities carried out by a foreign communications service provider, authorized in accordance with the laws of the foreign jurisdiction, but which requires the use of telecommunication systems located in the United Kingdom in order to carry out the interception.[66] This was designed to enable the United Kingdom to comply with Article 17 of the Convention on Mutual Assistance in Criminal

---

[60] See ACPO Press Release (55/05), 'Chief Police Officers recommend changes to counter the terrorist threat' (21 July 2005), <available at http://www.acpo.police.uk/asp/news/index.asp>.

[61] I.e., *Malone* v. *United Kingdom* [1984] 7 EHRR 14 and *Halford* v. *United Kingdom*, (1997) IRLR 471.

[62] S. 1.

[63] I.e., '(a) (...) an offence for which a person who has attained the age of twenty-one and has no previous convictions could reasonably be expected to be sentenced to imprisonment for a term of three years or more; (b) that the conduct involves the use of violence, results in substantial financial gain or is conduct by a large number of persons in pursuit of a common purpose' (s. 81(3)).

[64] S. 5(3)(a)-(c).

[65] S. 5(3)(d).

[66] Regulation of Investigatory Powers (Conditions for the Lawful Interception of Persons outside the United Kingdom) Regulations 2004, SI No. 157.

Matters ('Convention 2000'),[67] specifically the use of satellite communication systems, which have a transnational footprint although they are controlled from a single territory.

In terms of UK authorities requiring an intercept to be carried out in a foreign jurisdiction, as provided for under Article 18 of the Convention 2000, a request can be made through a 'judicial authority' in accordance with the Crime (International Co-operation) Act 2003.[68]

However, one unique feature of the UK interception regime is that it does not permit data obtained through an interception being adduced as evidence in legal proceedings.[69] Such data is for intelligence purposes in the course of an investigation, not for use in any subsequent prosecution. The reasoning behind such a provision is to protect from disclosure information about the investigative activities of law-enforcement agencies, which would enter the public domain if intercept evidence was used in court and became subject to challenge by defendant counsel. As a consequence, however, there is a lack of reciprocity in terms of mutual legal assistance. While a request by a foreign agency for an interception of communications for evidential purposes would be refused by the UK authorities,[70] such a request may be made by UK agencies, as foreign intercept evidence may be admissible in the United Kingdom if the evidence would be admissible in the foreign court, and it would not reveal anything about the activities of UK law enforcement.[71]

One key policy driver behind the adoption of RIPA was the need to update the regime to address the complexities of lawful interception in a liberalized communications market, where a vast range of different networks and service providers are present. However, while such rules have clarified domestic interception, cybercriminals will often route their transmissions via multiple jurisdictions, using numerous service providers, to obstruct the process of investigation, a process referred to as 'communications laundering'. In such circumstances, the complexities of lawful interception, coupled with an absence of harmonized rules, continue to mean a lack of clarity, legal certainty and transparency.

15.3.2 **Moving evidence**

Evidence residing abroad may be obtained through a range of mechanisms. In the age of the Internet, it may be publicly accessible from a web site.[72] Alternatively,

---

[67] *OJ* C197, 12.7.2000, p. 1.

[68] Part 1, chapter 2, s. 7.

[69] S. 17. However, it may be retained for certain 'authorized purposes' (s. 15(4)), e.g., 'it is necessary to ensure that a person conducting a criminal prosecution has the information he needs to determine what is required of him by his duty to secure the fairness of the prosecution,' and may be subsequently disclosed to the prosecutor or trial judge (s. 18(7)).

[70] See Home Office, *Mutual Legal Assistance Guidelines: Obtaining assistance in the UK and Overseas*, 2nd edn. (December 2004), p. 7, available at <http://www.homeoffice.gov.uk/docs4/HO_MLA_Webguidelines2nd.pdf>.

[71] See *R* v. *P & others* (2001) 2 All ER 58.

[72] E.g., telephone account holder details. See Art. 32 CCC.

an investigating authority may use a search warrant to obtain material from a foreign jurisdiction. A third route would be to ask the potential witness to travel to the United Kingdom to make a witness statement. However, the investigation and prosecution of cross-border computer crimes will often require mutual assistance between national law-enforcement agencies and prosecuting authorities. In *Levin*, for example, assistance was required not only from the St. Petersburg police, but also from the local telephone company. Obtaining such assistance in a timely and efficient manner will often be critical to the success of a cybercrime investigation. Historically, however, mutual legal assistance (MLA) procedures have been notoriously slow and bureaucratic, and therefore most mutual assistance occurs through informal co-operation and liaison between authorities.[73]

Among European Union Member States, mutual legal assistance is primarily governed by the European Convention on Mutual Assistance in Criminal Matters (1959), which has subsequently been supplemented on a number of occasions, most recently by the Convention 2000.[74] Parts of the Convention 2000 has been incorporated into English law through the Crime (International Co-operation) Act 2003, which repeals and replaces parts of the Criminal Justice (International Co-operation) Act 1990. In addition, the Eurojust[75] initiative is designed to facilitate the exchange of information between authorities and cross-border co-operation in the investigation and prosecution of serious and organized crime.

The 2003 Act details mechanisms for the mutual provision of evidence, either obtaining evidence from abroad for use in the United Kingdom or assisting overseas authorities to obtain evidence from the United Kingdom. In the former situation, a judge, on the application of a prosecuting authority, may issue requests for evidence from abroad.[76] Such a request, historically known as a 'letter rogatory' or 'commission rogatoire', will only be made where it appears that an offence has been committed and that proceedings have been instituted or an investigation is underway.[77] The request may be sent to a court in the relevant jurisdiction, to an authority designated in the jurisdiction for receipt of such requests, or, in cases of urgency, to the International Criminal Police Organisation (INTERPOL).[78] The evidence, once received, should then only be used for the purpose specified in the request, known as the 'speciality principle':

---

[73] See Crown Prosecution Service Guidance, *Evidence And Information From Abroad: Informal Enquiries & Letters Of Request*, available at <http://www.cps.gov.uk/legal/section2/chapter_e.html#_Toc44563266>.

[74] An Explanatory Report has been published in *OJ* C379, 29.12.2000, p. 7. Between Commonwealth countries, MLA is governed by the 'Scheme Relating to Mutual Assistance in Criminal Matters' (the 'Harare Scheme'). With the United States, the United Kingdom signed a bilateral 'Treaty on Mutual Legal Assistance in Criminal Matters' in 1994 (TS 014/1997, Cm 3546).

[75] Council Decision of 28 February 2002, setting up Eurojust with a view to reinforcing the fight against serious crime (2002/187/JHA), *OJ* L63/1, 6.3.2002.

[76] Chapter 2, ss. 7-12.

[77] S. 7(1).

[78] S. 8.

> 'Evidence obtained by virtue of a letter of request shall not without the consent of such an authority (...) be used for any purpose other than that specified in the letter: and when any document or other article obtained pursuant to a letter of request is no longer required for that purpose (or for any other purpose for which such consent has been obtained), it shall be returned to such an authority unless that authority indicates that the document or article need not be returned.'[79]

Requests for UK-based evidence by overseas authorities must be sent to the Secretary of State at the Home Office, referred to as the 'territorial authority'.[80] The Secretary of State may then nominate a court to receive the requested evidence. As well as achieving the disclosure of particular evidence, the MLA procedure also provides for the obtaining of evidence. The Secretary of State may direct that a warrant be applied for from the courts in order that a search can be undertaken and evidence seized. Law-enforcement agencies may also obtain a warrant to intercept communications, as discussed above. However, such coercive powers may only be exercised where the conduct constitutes an offence in both the requesting country and under the laws of England and Wales, the so-called 'double criminality' principle, as also required in extradition proceedings.

In terms of informal mechanisms for obtaining evidence from abroad, as the CPS note, such assistance is 'dependant in many cases on their own domestic laws, how good the relations are generally between the country and the United Kingdom and, frankly, the attitude and opinions of the people on the ground to whom the request is made'![81] While informal requests are the norm, often in the course of preparing a formal request, they are less frequent in cybercrime cases, where the evidence required often involves either the seizure of equipment (e.g., a server) or disclosure of information by a foreign communication service provider, both of which generally require the use of coercive powers, only available through the formal mechanisms referred to above. However, in this scenario, an alternative informal approach may also exist where the perpetrator's activities constitute an offence under foreign law as well as under UK law. As such, the foreign authorities can choose to investigate without formal request even though they have no real intention to pursue a domestic prosecution. Such an approach can be viewed as a version of the 'double criminality' principle, where the act is in actuality, rather than in theory, an offence in both jurisdictions.[82]

---

79 S. 3(7). This principle is also generally present in extradition treaties, requiring the requesting state only to prosecute the accused for the crimes detailed in the extradition request.

80 Ss. 13 and 28(9). In practice, this is the UK Central Authority for Mutual Legal Assistance (UKCA) located in the Home Office.

81 See Crown Prosecution Service Guidance, op. cit. n. 73.

82 Such an approach has been adopted in the United States, according to a statement made by Michael Sussman, Senior Counsel, U.S. Department of Justice, Criminal Division, Computer Crime and Intellectual Property Section, at an Academy of European Law conference in Trier, Germany (20 February 2003).

Although there are no special conditions governing the admissibility of computer-derived material under English rules of evidence, prosecutors will often be challenged to prove the reliability of any such evidence presented. Auditable procedures will need to be adhered to, often supported by independent expert witnesses, to show the probative value of any evidence generated.[83] Where such evidence has been generated abroad, compliance with such procedures, and evidence of such compliance, is much more complex and vulnerable to defence claims of errors, technical malfunction, prejudicial interference or fabrication, especially where the evidence was obtained through informal means; it is therefore more likely to be subject to an application to exclude.[84]

15.3.3 **Moving people**

It is clear that when a UK-based computer system is 'hacked', the perpetrator may be located anywhere in the world. Therefore, if a prosecution is to be mounted, the accused has to be brought to the United Kingdom. The formal procedure under which persons are transferred between states for prosecution is known as 'extradition'. Either bilateral or multilateral treaties or agreements between states generally govern extradition.[85] In the absence of such a treaty, the state where the perpetrator resides is not required under any rule of public international law to surrender the person. In such situations, informal mechanisms may be used to bring the perpetrator to justice. In the case of *Levin*, for example, the accused was enticed to leave Russia, with whom the United States did not have an extradition treaty, to travel to America. As soon as he landed in a country with which the United States did have an extradition arrangement, i.e., the United Kingdom, he was arrested.[86]

In an action for extradition, the applicant is generally required to show that the actions of the accused constitute a criminal offence exceeding a minimum level of seriousness in both jurisdictions, i.e., the country from which the accused is to be extradited and the country to which the extradition will be made. Here, again, the 'double criminality' principle applies. In *Levin*, the defendant was accused of committing wire and bank fraud in the United States. No direct equivalent exists in English law, and therefore Levin was charged with 66 related offences, including sections 2 and 3 of the Computer Misuse Act. Currently, the section 1 unauthorized-access offence only attracts a maximum penalty of six months, which means

---

[83] See generally the *Good Practice Guide for Computer Based Evidence*, published by the Association of Chief Police Officers, available at <http://www.nhtcu.org/media/documents/publications/ACPO_Guide_for_computer-based_electronic_evidece.pdf>.

[84] See nn. 56 and 57 and accompanying text.

[85] E.g., Agreement on extradition between the European Union and the United States of America, *OJ* L181, 19.7.2003, p. 27.

[86] See also *Yarimaka* v. *Governor of HM Prison Brixton*; *Zezev* v. *Government of the United States of America* [2002] EWHC 589 (Admin).

that it is not an extraditable offence.[87] However, this is one area expected to be reformed when the Act is reviewed.[88]

Under the Extradition Act 1989, an extradition offence had to be punishable by a minimum 12-months imprisonment in both states.[89] The Cybercrime Convention also provides that the offences it details should be extraditable, provided that they are punishable under the laws of both parties 'by deprivation of liberty for a maximum period of at least one year, or by a more severe penalty.'[90] It also provides that the Convention itself may be the legal basis for extradition in the absence of a treaty between the relevant states.[91]

However, the 1989 Act was repealed and replaced by the Extradition Act 2003, under which 'double criminality' is no longer required for offences listed in Schedule 2 (as specified in the European Arrest Warrant Scheme) in relation to Category 1 territories, which are part of the European Arrest Warrant Scheme.[92] Extradition is a complex and often lengthy process, involving, at least in common-law jurisdictions, both judicial and executive decision-taking. In *Levin*, for example, the defendant was arrested in March 1995 and yet the judicial process was not completed until June 1997. Therefore, in order to simplify the process, the EU Member States have established the concept of a 'European Arrest Warrant'.[93] The Council Decision abolishes the formal extradition procedure in favor of a simplified process in which a warrant issued by a Member State court will be granted mutual recognition by other Member States and will result in the arrest and surrender of the requested person. The surrender may be conditional upon the acts detailed in the warrant being an offence in the executing state.[94] However, in respect of certain offences, including 'computer related crime',[95] which are punishable in the issuing Member State by a custodial sentence of a maximum of at least three years (e.g., Computer Misuse Act 1990, sections 2 and 3) will be subject to automatic execution of the warrant, i.e., surrender, without consideration of dual criminality. Extradition under such circumstances will also be available even though some element of the conduct occurred in the United Kingdom.[96]

---

[87] S. 1(3).

[88] See *Revision of the Computer Misuse Act*, Report of an Inquiry by the All Party Parliamentary Internet Group (June 2004), at paras. 95 et seq.

[89] S. 2(1). See also *R* v. *Bow Street Magistrates' Court, ex parte Allison* [1998] 3 WLR 1156, where the court held that ss. 2 and 3 of the Computer Misuse Act 1990 were extradition crimes (confirmed by the House of Lords, at 625G).

[90] Art. 24(1).

[91] Art. 24(4).

[92] Designated by the Secretary of State under s. 1(1), which could include non-EU states.

[93] Council Framework Decision (2002/584/JHA) of 13 June 2002 on the European arrest warrant and the surrender procedures between Member States, *OJ* L190, 18.7.2002, p. 1.

[94] Ibid., at Art. 2(4).

[95] Extradition Act 2003, Schedule 2, at 11.

[96] See *Office of the King's Prosecutor, Brussels* v. *Cando Armas* [2004] EWHC 2019.

As with the obtaining of evidence, while there are formal procedures governing extradition, there are also informal elements involved prior to, or alternate to, extradition. In a situation of cross-border hacking, for example, the perpetrator will often have committed offences in more than one country. As such, a decision may need to be made by the national authority where the perpetrator is located (e.g., the CPS), whether to commence a domestic prosecution or comply with a request for extradition. Where extradition is available, a process of negotiation should take place between the relevant states about the most appropriate forum to prosecute.

While the rules discussed in section 2 above, indicate *whether* English law is applicable, they do not assist us in determining *which* jurisdiction is the most appropriate in a multi-jurisdictional context, nor the process by which that decision is reached. However, a number of questions concerning process need to be considered.[97] First, at what point should the decision be made: when the investigation starts, during its course, or at completion? Second, which agencies should be involved in the negotiation: the police, the prosecution, or the judiciary?[98] Third, what criteria are applicable, e.g., where the majority of the harm was suffered or where evidence resides? In June 2005, extradition proceedings were commenced against Gary McKinnon, who is accused of hacking into U.S. military and NASA computers in 2001 and 2002.[99] This is the first time a UK national has been subject to such proceedings, and it is likely to be robustly challenged. One issue that will need to be addressed is how the decision to extradite was negotiated, between the CPS and their U.S. counterparts, since both had a jurisdictional claim. The courts may be asked to judicially review both the procedure and substance of the negotiation, in the broader context of the Human Rights Act 1998.[100]

As noted at the outset of this chapter, cybercrime inevitably and increasingly involves parallel and competing jurisdictions, as indeed do civil claims in an Internet environment.[101] As such, determinations of which jurisdiction should prosecute will involve a much more difficult decision-making process than the initial question of whether an offence has been committed. There are currently no national or internationally agreed criteria for making such determinations, which raises concerns for individual defendants, law-enforcement authorities and governments.

---

[97] These issues are based on comments made by Bill Wheeldon, CPS, in an interview with the author (6 July 2005).

[98] Under the Prosecution of Offences Act 1985, s. 3(2)(eb), the CPS have a duty to give 'advice on any matters relating to extradition proceedings or proposed extradition proceedings.'

[99] See the Indictment filed by the U.S. Department of Justice in November 2002, available at <http://news.findlaw.com/hdocs/docs/cyberlaw/usmck1102vaind.pdf>.

[100] This Act directly incorporated the European Convention on Human Rights into English law.

[101] In the defamation context, for example, see *Lewis Lennox* v. *Don King* [2004] EWCA Civ 1329 (CA).

15.4 Concluding Remarks

A very high proportion of cybercrime will involve an international element, compared with more traditional crimes. The international dimension may arise in respect of whether an offence has been committed or not, or it may form an element of the forensic process, the obtaining of evidence. In terms of substantive rules, the concern of policy makers and legislators about cybercrime has been reflected in moves to extend the reach of relevant offences beyond traditional jurisdictional principles. Although criminal procedures may have improved in respect of the obtaining of evidence in a transnational context, significant issues continue to exist in the usage of such evidence in the course of a prosecution, as well as in the location of any subsequent criminal proceedings.

Bibliography

I. Bantekas, S. Nash and M. Mackarel, *International Criminal Law* (Cavendish 2001).

A. Cassese, *International Criminal Law* (Oxford, Oxford University Press 2003).

M. Hirst, *Jurisdiction and the Ambit of the Criminal Law* (Oxford, Oxford University Press 2003).

Home Office, *Mutual Legal Assistance Guidelines: Obtaining assistance in the UK and Overseas*, 2nd edn. (December 2004), <http://www.homeoffice.gov.uk/docs4/HO_MLA_Webguidelines2nd.pdf>.

J. Knowles, *Blackstone's Guide to The Extradition Act 2003* (Oxford, Oxford University Press 2004).

I. Walden, 'Computer Crime', in Reed and Angel, eds., *Computer Law*, 5th edn. (Oxford, Oxford University Press 2003) pp. 295-329.

M. Wasik, *Crime and the Computer* (Oxford, Clarendon Press 1991).

Chapter 16
CYBERCRIME AND JURISDICTION IN THE UNITED STATES

Jessica R. Herrera-Flanigan*

16.1 Introduction

In the 1980s, a 'new' type of criminal started to appear on law-enforcement's radar screen. This criminal, often male and technologically-savvy, discovered that computers and networks allowed him to gain power, information, and wealth. Sometimes he acted alone, at other times he organized into groups with names such as the 414s (named after the Milwaukee, Wisconsin area code), Legion of Doom, and the Chaos Computer Club.[1] These individuals used their skills and knowledge of technology to, among other things, break into others' networks, steal proprietary information, or fraudulently obtain telecommunications services at no charge.

These individuals and groups challenged the United States legal system and made it necessary for the U.S. Congress and state governments to enact new laws to combat the cybercriminal. This chapter examines the substantive and procedural laws that the United States enacted on a federal level to combat crimes involving the use of technology and computers. In addition, it looks at the challenges that law enforcement has encountered in investigating and prosecuting computer-enabling crimes that cross international borders.

* Jessica R. Herrera-Flanigan is a former Senior Counsel with the Computer Crime & Intellectual Property Section of the United States Department of Justice and currently serves as the Democratic Staff Director of the Committee on Homeland Security in the U.S. House of Representatives. Kandis Gibson and Gloria Eldridge provided assistance and insight in the development of this chapter. The views expressed in this publication are entirely those of the author and do not necessarily reflect the views of the U.S. government, the U.S. House of Representatives, the Committee on Homeland Security, or any Congressional Member.

[1] See, e.g., *A Brief History of Hacking*, available at <http://tlc.discovery.com/convergence/hackers/articles/history.html>.

B-J. Koops and S.W. Brenner (Eds), Cybercrime and Jurisdiction

16.2 Cybercrime Substantive Laws

16.2.1 Computer Fraud and Abuse Act of 1986

Prior to 1984, the United States did not have laws that specifically prohibited network crimes, including hacking, malicious code dissemination, and denial-of-service attacks. The closest applicable laws were the wire and mail fraud statutes. For example, in the first known federal prosecution for computer hacking, *U.S.* v. *Seidlitz*,[2] the government convicted the owner of a computer company who stole confidential software by hacking into his previous employer of wire fraud, because that individual had made two of the fifty access calls across state lines. While the wire and mail fraud provisions were useful, many law-enforcement officials made it clear to the U.S. Congress that they did not provide the best remedies for the forms of criminal activity occurring over new technologies.[3]

Congress responded to the law-enforcement community's cry for help by including provisions to address the unauthorized access and use of computer networks in the Comprehensive Crime Control Act of 1984 by providing 'law enforcement community, those who own and operate computers, as well as those who may be tempted to commit crimes by unauthorized access to them (…) a clearer statement of proscribed activity.'[4]

In 1986, Congress solidified its commitment to combating network crimes by enacting the Computer Fraud and Abuse Act (CFAA), which amended 18 USC 1030. The statute provided the means by which to protect the *confidentiality*, *integrity*, and *availability* ('CIA') of computers and networks. Protection of the 'CIA' has remained the focus of the statute, even through extensive amendments in 1990, 1994, 1996, and, most recently, in the 2001 USA Patriot Act.

In the CFAA, Congress addressed federalism issues by balancing the federal government's interest in computer crime and state interests to punish such offenses. It did so by limiting federal jurisdiction to those cases in which there is a compelling federal interest (i.e., national security or where there is an interstate nexus or effect on interstate commerce).[5] Congress made additional changes to the CFAA over the next fifteen years, so that today it includes seven types of criminal activity. See 18 USCA § 1030. The following outlines the various offenses found in the CFAA (all sections of 18 USC):

---

[2] 589 F.2d 152 (4th Cir. 1978).

[3] See John C. Keeney, Deputy Assistant Attorney General, Criminal Division, U.S. Department of Justice, Statement Before The Subcommittee on the Judiciary, U.S. House of Representatives (18 November 1983), citing two 'computer crime' cases involving prosecutions under the wire fraud statute; H.R. Rep. No. 894, 98th Cong., 2nd Sess. 1984, 1984 USCCAN 3689.

[4] H.R. Rep. No. 894, 98th Cong., 2nd Sess. 1984, 1984 USCCAN 3689.

[5] S. Rep. No. 432, 99th Cong., 2nd Sess. 1986, 1986 USCCAN 2479.

- § 1030(a)(1): obtaining national-security information;
- § 1030(a)(2): compromising the confidentiality of a computer;
- § 1030(a)(3): trespassing in a government computer;
- § 1030(a)(4): accessing a computer to defraud and obtain something of value;
- § 1030(a)(5): damaging a computer;
- § 1030(a)(6): trafficking in passwords;
- § 1030(a)(7): threatening to damage a computer.

Attempts to commit these crimes are also covered by the Act (18 USC § 1030(b)). Authorized 'hacking' is explicitly excluded from the section (18 USC § 1030(f)). In addition, § 1030(g) allows any person who suffers damage or loss from a violation of the CFAA to bring a civil action against the violator for compensatory damages and injunctive relief, with some limitation.

To understand how the CFAA covers various types of network crimes, it is important to master several definitions found in the statute. For the most part, the CFAA covers 'protected computers', which are defined as all government and financial institution computers and any other computers that are used in 'interstate or foreign commerce or communication of the United States' (18 USC § 1030(e)(2)(B)). Consequently, virtually all computers that are plugged into the Internet are protected by the CFAA. In addition, the inclusion of computers used in 'foreign commerce or communication of the United States' in the CFAA makes it possible for domestic law-enforcement agencies to pursue international cases as domestic offenses, as discussed later in this chapter. Thus, the CFAA potentially could cover hackers from the United States who attack foreign computers as well as foreigners who route communications through the United States to attack computers in other countries.

16.2.2 **Other relevant laws**

In addition to the provisions contained in the CFAA, there are other federal laws that might be applicable in cybercrime cases. For example, the 'Wiretap Act,' found in 18 USC 2510 et seq., can be used against computer hackers who break into systems and monitor others' computers. Under 18 USC § 2511, it is illegal to intentionally endeavor to intercept any wire, oral, or *electronic* communications. The latter includes communications that travel over the Internet. If a hacker breaks into a system and intercepts in 'real-time' any communications or uses a sniffer or keystroking device once he has broken in, he potentially has violated the Wiretap Act and could face up to five years in prison and/or a $250,000 fine.

The Electronic Communications Privacy Act (18 USC § 2701 et seq.) is also applicable to computer-intrusion attempts. ECPA, as it is known, makes it illegal to intentionally access without authorization or in access of authorization a facility through which an electronic communication service is provided and thereby gain access, alter, or prevent others from accessing communications that might be stored on that system.

The federal wire fraud statute, codified at 18 USC § 1343, may also be used to prosecute computer intrusions or, for that matter, most network crimes. Often referred to as the 'workhouse of federal prosecutors', the provision is used to prosecute fraud carried out through interstate electronic communications. It essentially prohibits using the wires in 'furtherance of a scheme or artifice to defraud, or for obtaining money or property by means of a false or fraudulent pretenses.' Today's Internet operates in such a fashion that all communications over it are carried in whole or part by a 'wire' within the meaning of the wire fraud statute. This may change in the coming years as technology advances and more communications become wireless.

An example of how a computer crime can be charged under the wire fraud statute is *United States* v. *Scheier*,[6] in which the defendants were successfully convicted under the wire fraud statute for accessing American Airlines' computer reservation system. While on the system, the defendants replaced the names of real passengers with a non-existent person that they enrolled in American's frequent-flyer program. Not all computer crime cases, however, have been successfully prosecuted under section 1343.[7]

If a hacker attacks U.S. military computers or systems, he might be in violation of 18 USC 1362, which makes it a crime to interfere with U.S. military computers or systems. While this statute is not used that often, it is relevant to computer hacking attempts.

The theft and trafficking of passwords and other access devices to computer networks is an increasing phenomenon that law enforcement is attempting to combat. In 1984, in the same bill that contained the Computer Fraud and Abuse Act, Congress added section 1029, entitled 'fraud and related activity in connection with access devices' to Title 18. Section 1029 was enacted to address the increasing amount of credit and debit card fraud that our country saw in the early 1980s.[8] Section 1029, however, is more than just a 'credit-card fraud' statute and is often used in the prosecution of computer crimes. For example, the infamous hacker Kevin Mitnick was charged and pled guilty to violating 18 USC § 1029(a)(3) for his possession of unauthorized-access devices with the intent to defraud.[9]

Identity theft is generally covered by 18 USC § 1028: 'Fraud and related activity in connection with identification documents and information.' This section prohib-

---

[6] 908 F.2d 645, 646 (10th Cir. 1990), *cert. denied*, 498 US 1069 (1991).

[7] See *U.S.* v. *Czubinski,* 106 F.3d 1069, 1072-74 (1st Cir. 1997).

[8] See H.R. Rep. No. 894, 98th Cong., 2nd Sess. 1984, 1984 USCCAN 3689.

[9] See *U.S.* v. *Mitnick,* 145 F.3d 1342 (9th Cir.), *cert. denied*, 525 US 917 (1998); see also *United States* v. *Brewer*, 835 F.2d 550 (5th Cir.1987): a hacker who called into a telephone company's toll-free phone number and guessed possible access-code combinations until he found valid codes that gave him free long-distance service violated 18 USC § 1029(a)(1). *United States* v. *Brewer* also addressed what constituted 'counterfeit' for purposes of s. 1029. The Fifth Circuit determined that Brewer's guessing of valid codes still met the s. 1029 definition of 'counterfeit' because they were 'forged'. The court stated that the defendant had 'fabricated codes that just happened to be identical to the [company's] codes.'

its false identification documents with intent to defraud. Section 1028(a)(7) is relevant to network crimes because of the definition given to 'means of identification'. The term includes any name or number that may be used to identify a specific individual, including 'unique electronic identification number, address, or routing code (...) or telecommunication identifying information or access device (as defined in section 1029(2)).'

Thus, 'means of identification' is intended to capture all the technologically feasible varieties of individual identification information that can be compromised and criminally transferred or used. The definition is intended to incorporate other means of identification that may be developed in the future but are not currently available.[10] The legislative history also makes clear that each means of identification in any one identification or fake identification document can not be treated as separate offenses under (a)(7).

This definition would include spoofed e-mail or IP addresses, passwords, or any other information that may be used for user authentication if the other elements are present. Subsection (a)(7) requires as a predicate an intent to violate any federal law or a violation that is a felony under state law. Note that there is no requirement that the violation amount to a felony under federal law. Consequently, in cases where hackers have usurped a means of identification to commit a felony under state law (e.g., state hacking or privacy laws) or have violated *any* federal law, a charge may be brought under 18 USC § 1028(a)(7).

16.3 Cybercrime Procedural Laws

The Electronic Communications Privacy Act (ECPA), 18 USC §§ 2701-2712, governs how the federal government accesses stored account information from Internet service providers. During an investigation, ECPA allows law-enforcement agencies to obtain stored e-mail, account records, or subscriber information from a service provider.

As noted by the U.S. Department of Justice's manual *Searching and Seizing Computers and Obtaining Electronic Evidence at Criminal Investigations,* law-enforcement agencies 'must apply (...) various classifications devised by ECPA's drafters to the facts of each case to figure out the proper procedure for obtaining the information sought.'[11] U.S. law enforcement must review the facts of each case to determine which procedural process to use to obtain evidence.

First, they must determine what type of provider they are dealing with. They must then determine what type of information they are looking for and where it

---

[10] S. Rep. 105-274, 1998 WL 429672.

[11] U.S. Department of Justice, *Searching and Seizing Computers and Obtaining Electronic Evidence at Criminal Investigations* (July 2002), available at <http://www.cybercrime.gov/s&smanual2002.htm#_IIIA>.

may be located. Next, they must consider whether they need to require the provider to disclose or whether the provider can lawfully disclose voluntarily.[12] The three types of processes that can be used to compel disclosure of information are a search warrant, a court order obtained in accordance with 18 USC 2703(d), or a subpoena. Table 16.1 is a chart provided by the U.S. Department of Justice showing how different types of information may be obtained under U.S. law.[13]

In addition to ECPA, there are several other surveillance tools found in U.S. law available to law-enforcement officials investigating cybercrimes. The U.S. wiretap statute, found at 18 USC §§ 2510-2522, which is often referred to as 'Title III', provides law-enforcement officials the ability to intercept and examine communications in real-time. Title III allows law enforcement to 'wiretap a suspect's phone,

Table 16.1. – *U.S. Department of Justice's 'Quick Reference Guide'. References to Specific Sections are all within ECPA and 18 USC.*

	Voluntary Disclosure Allowed?		**Mechanisms to Compel Disclosure**	
Kind of Information	*Public Provider*	*Non-Public Provider*	*Public Provider*	*Non-Public Provider*
Basic subscriber, session, and billing information	Not to government, unless § 2702(c) exception applies [§ 2702(a)(3)]	Yes [§ 2702(a)(3)]	Subpoena; 2703(d) order; or search warrant [§ 2703(c)(2)]	Subpoena; 2703(d) order; or search warrant [§ 2703(c)(2)]
Other transactional and account records	Not to government, unless § 2702(c) exception applies [§ 2702(a)(3)]	Yes [§ 2702(a)(3)]	2703(d) order or search warrant [§ 2703(c)(I)]	2703(d) order or search warrant [§ 2703(c)(I)]
Accessed communications (opened e-mail and voice mail) left with provider and other stored files	No, unless § 2702(b) exception applies [§ 2702(a)(2)]	Yes [§ 2702(a)(2)]	Subpoena with notice; 2703(d) order with notice; or search warrant [§ 2703(b)]	Subpoena; ECPA does not apply [§ 2711(2)]
Unretrieved communication, including e-mail and voice mail (in electronic storage more than 180 days)	No, unless § 2702(b) exception applies [§ 2702(a)(I)]	Yes [§ 2702(a)(I)]	Subpoena with notice; 2703(d) order with notice; or search warrant [§ 2703(alb)]	Subpoena with notice; 2703(d) order with notice; or search warrant [§ 2703(alb)]
Unretrieved communication, including e-mail and voice mail (in electronic storage 180 days or less)	No, unless § 2702(b) exception applies [§ 2702(a)(I)]	Yes [§ 2702(a)(I)]	Search warrant [§ 2703(a)]	Search warrant [§ 2703(a)]

[12] Ibid.
[13] Idem.

"keystroke" a hacker breaking into a computer system, or accept the fruits of wire-tapping by a private citizen who has discovered evidence of a crime.'[14]

If a law-enforcement agency only wishes to obtain non-content information in real-time, it would apply for a court order under the pen/trap statute (18 USC § 3122(b)(2)). The standard for obtaining such information is that the information be relevant to an ongoing criminal investigation. This provision allows for the interception of addressing information; a pen register records outgoing information while a trap-and-trace device records incoming information.

16.4 United States Determination of Jurisdiction

This section specifically deals with U.S. *federal* jurisdiction over cybercrimes and focuses on the CFAA, as the primary vehicle for prosecuting cybercrimes in federal courts. In the CFAA, the U.S. Congress addressed federalism issues by balancing the federal government's interest in computer crime and state interests to punish such offenses. It did so by limiting federal jurisdiction to those cases in which there is a compelling federal interest (i.e., an impact on national security or where there is an interstate nexus or an effect on interstate commerce).[15] Congress did not intend to confer federal jurisdiction over all possible scenarios by which someone may obtain information via a computer. It only intended to make criminal those that clearly had a federal nexus.

Individual states within the United States still have the ability to prosecute many types of cybercrimes.[16] Unfortunately, many states have faced jurisdictional hurdles in their attempts to combat Internet crime. First, states often faces issues with trying to enforce legal process against entities located outside their states. Next, many state courts have taken very different approaches on whether a state can exert long-arm jurisdiction over an Internet site that can be accessed in an individual state. In an effort to overcome many potential jurisdictional limitations created by the international nature of the Internet, many states reformed their jurisdictional provisions so that they were no longer limited to requiring all or part of a crime to occur within a state or 'causing' harm to someone in a state through extraterritorial activities to the state.[17] This chapter does not specifically address U.S. state jurisdictional issues and, instead, focuses on federal national jurisdictional issues.

As the CFAA has evolved over the years, there has been great concern over the United States' jurisdiction over international computer-crime cases. As early as the National Information Infrastructure Protection Act of 1996 (NIIA), Congress at-

---

[14] Idem.

[15] S. Rep. No. 432, 99th Cong., 2nd Sess. 1986, 1986 USCCAN 2479

[16] Susan W. Brenner, 'State Cybercrime Legislation in the United States of America: A Survey', 7 *Rich. J.L. & Tech.* (Winter 2001) p. 28, <http://www.richmond.edu/jolt/v7i3/article2.html>.

[17] Ibid. See also Susan W. Brenner and Bert-Jaap Koops, 'Approaches to Cybercrime Jurisdiction', 4 *Journal of High Technology Law* (2004) p. 1, for examples of state jurisdiction provisions.

tempted to include computers used in 'foreign' communications within the purview of CFAA. In NIAA, the definition of 'federal interest computer' was changed to confer jurisdiction on international computer-crime cases. 'Federal interest computer', as defined by 18 USC § 1030(e)(2), was changed to 'protected computer' and included a computer 'which is used in interstate or foreign commerce'. Previously, the definition of federal interest computer referred to computers that involved multiple states. It did not explicitly refer to international communications. As U.S. laws are generally construed to be domestic in nature,[18] a change was necessary to provide a specific grant of extraterritorial jurisdiction.

An additional change was made in the U.S.A. Patriot Act, enacted in the months following the 11 September 2001 terrorist attacks on the United States. There was concern that the definition of protected computer did not specifically include computers outside the United States. The changes made in 1996 were deemed not sufficient for ensuring that the United States could pursue hackers from within the country that targeted foreign computers. Likewise, law-enforcement officials determined that they might not be able to assist other countries in their cybercrime-fighting efforts in those instances where a computer in the United States was merely a 'pass-through' for criminal activity originating and ending in foreign nations.

In order to remedy this ambiguity, Congress changed the CFAA's definition of 'protected computer' to include a computer

> 'which is used in interstate or foreign commerce or communication, including a computer located outside the United States that is used in a manner that affects interstate or foreign commerce or communication of the United States (…).'[19]

This change was, in part, to allow the United States to assist international law-enforcement officials in their investigations. The United States also hoped that this change would serve as an incentive to other nations to change their laws similarly to allow the United States to purse cases that 'originate' in other nations but adversely affect U.S. persons.[20]

16.5 United States Determination of Venue, Once Jurisdiction is Established

In U.S. law, both jurisdiction and venue issues must be considered when bringing cases to court. This section briefly discusses potential venue issues for cybercrimes. Once jurisdiction – the authority of a court to exercise judicial power – is estab-

[18] *E.E.O.C.* v. *Arabian American Oil Co.*, 499 US 244 (1991).

[19] 18 USC § 1030(e)(2)(B).

[20] U.S. Department of Justice, *Field Guidance on New Authorities That Relate to Computer Crime and Electronic Evidence Enacted in the USA Patriot Act of 2001* (2001), available at <http://www.usdoj.gov/criminal/cybercrime/PatriotAct.htm>.

lished, venue is then determined. Venue refers to the district in which a particular case may be brought.

Prosecution of CFAA offenses generally may be brought in the district in which the defendant is located or in the district in which the affected computer is located. There may also be the possibility, under CFAA's 'damaging the computer' provision (18 USC § 1030), to bring charges in the district in which the victim is located. It is unsettled whether charges of CFAA violations may be brought in the district of a pass-through computer.

Determining proper venue for a computer-crime prosecution is not always straightforward, as network crimes typically implicate more than one district. The U.S. Federal Rules of Criminal Procedure specify that '[e]except as otherwise permitted by statute or by these rules,' the prosecution of a case 'shall be had in a district in which the offense was committed'.[21] This rule codifies two provisions of the U.S. Constitution. Article III, Section 2, Clause iii requires that the trial of all crimes 'shall be held in the State where the said Crimes shall have been committed', except when the crime took place in no state. The Constitution's sixth Amendment guarantees the defendant in a criminal prosecution the right to trial 'by an impartial jury of the State and district wherein the crime shall have been committed.'

Even under these rules, prosecutors may have a choice of several different venues in a cybercrime if multiple districts are implicated by a specific offense.[22] If a cybercrime is continuing (e.g., a hacker weaving through various computers in various jurisdictions), the U.S. Code allows for the prosecution in any district where the offense took place (18 USC § 3237(a)). It is well-established in U.S. jurisprudence that the accused does not have to be physically present in a district for him or her to be charged with a crime in that district.[23]

U.S. case law has determined that the act of accessing a U.S. computer from a foreign computer meets jurisdictional and venue requirements.[24] Likewise, the site of receipt for illegal materials or information can also meet the necessary venue requirements.[25]

16.6 Jurisdictional Issues with Cybercrime Investigations

As noted earlier, the United States amended its basic substantive cybercrime law, the CFAA, in 2001 to ensure that U.S. law-enforcement officials had the ability to

---

[21] See Federal Rules of Criminal Procedure, Rule 18.

[22] 'Where a crime consists of distinct parts which have different localities the whole may be tried where any part can be proved to have been done.' *United States* v. *Lombardo*, 241 US 73, 77 (1916).

[23] *Travis* v. *United States*, 364 US 631 (1961).

[24] *See United States* v. *Ivanov*, 175 F. Supp. 2d 367, 371 (D. Conn. 2001), where the defendant in Russia accessed computers in the U.S. state of Connecticut, the accessing took place in Connecticut.

[25] See *United States* v. *Thomas*, 74 F.3d 701 (6th Cir. 1996): the operator of an electronic bulletin board distributing obscene materials may be prosecuted in any district where materials were received, regardless of whether the operator knew the recipients' locations.

pursue international cybercriminals and to assist foreign nations in their investigations. That said, the United States law regarding searching, seizing, or obtaining evidence located outside the United States is ambiguous and unsettled.[26]

16.6.1 Ivanov-Gorshkov, McKinnon, and Zezev cases

There are three significant incidents that serve to define the U.S. approach to international cybercrime jurisdiction. The first involved Alexey V. Ivanov and Vasiliy Gorshkov of Russia in 2001, the second Gary McKinnon of London, United Kingdom in 2002, and the third, in 2003, Oleg Zezev of Kazakhstan.

The Ivanov-Gorshkov case made headlines and raised concerns among some about the U.S. procedures for pursuing cybercriminals.[27] Ivanov and Gorshkov were Russian nationals who flew to Seattle, Washington in the United States in hopes of obtaining jobs with a network security company named Invita. What the two did not know, however, was that the company did not exist and was created by the Federal Bureau of Investigation (FBI) as part of a sting operation.

Once the two arrived in the United States, they were asked by undercover FBI agents to demonstrate their hacking skills on a computer that recorded their keystrokes. The two men were arrested shortly after this demonstration, in which they had typed multiple account numbers and passwords to show the agents the data that they had stored on their computers in Russia. After arresting the men, the FBI agents downloaded evidence from the Russian computers to assure that the information was not lost or destroyed by associates of the men in Russia. This last action was done before the agents were able to obtain a search warrant for a court.

Gorshkov challenged the case against him, arguing that the FBI had violated the Fourth Amendment of the U.S. Constitution, which protects against unreasonable search and seizures. He also argued that the search violated Russian law. A U.S. court found for the U.S. government, determining that Gorshkov's Fourth Amendment rights were not violated, as it does not apply to extraterritorial searches against non-citizens.[28] Even if the Fourth Amendment had applied, the agents' actions were justified because of exigent circumstances.[29] As a result of the case, Gorshkov was sentenced to serve 36 months in prison,[30] while Ivanov was sentenced to 48 months in prison, followed by three years of supervised release.[31]

---

[26] See, e.g., *United States v. Verdugo-Urquidez,* 494 US 259 (1990), considering the extent to which the Fourth Amendment applies to searches outside of the United States.

[27] See, e.g., Brenner and Koops, loc. cit. n. 17, at section III(F).

[28] *U.S.* v. *Gorshkov*, 2001 WL 1024026 at *1 (W.D.W.A. 23 May 2001).

[29] Ibid.

[30] U.S. Department of Justice Press Release 'Russian Computer Hacker Sentenced To Three Years In Prison' (2002), <http://www.cybercrime.gov/gorshkovSent.htm>.

[31] U.S. Department Of Justice Press Release, 'Russian Man Sentenced For Hacking Into Computers In The United States' (2003), <http://www.cybercrime.gov/ivanovSent.htm>.

Gorshkov also included in his defense a charge that the FBI's actions violated Russian law.[32] The U.S. Court found that Russian law was not violated and, regardless, it was irrelevant to the matter in the United States. In response, Russia's counterintelligence branch filed charges against an FBI agent for both luring Ivanov and Gorshkov to the United States and illegally downloading information from Russian computers.[33] The Interfax news agency claimed that one source said: 'if the Russian hackers are sentenced on the basis of information obtained by the Americans through hacking, that will imply the future ability of U.S. secret services to use illegal methods in the collection of information in Russia and other countries.'[34] In part, Russia claimed that it filed charges against the FBI to assure that traditional law-enforcement jurisdictional boundaries remained intact.[35] This international incident demonstrates the uncertainty that exists on an international level about the ability of countries to reach into the sovereign territories of other nations while conducting criminal investigations. It is possible that the United States would have acted in a manner similar to Russia's, if another nation had conducted investigations within the nation's borders.

Gary McKinnon was charged and prosecuted for accessing and damaging 92 computers belonging to various federal agencies and businesses between 2001 and 2002. Since many of these computers were located at military and national security sites, the charges included one for damaging a computer used by the military for national defense and security. The United States requested that the United Kingdom extradite McKinnon to the United States. McKinnon appeared before a U.K. magistrate court on 27 July 2005 to fight extradition. He was released on bail and his case was adjourned until 18 October 2005.[36] The outcome of this case could help assess the United States' ability to work with other nations to extradite and prosecute their citizens in U.S. courts for criminal acts originating abroad but affecting U.S. computer systems.

The third case of interest involves Oleg Zezev, who was convicted in 2003 of extortion relating to attempts to hack into the Bloomberg financial news service's computer system. Zezev attempted to extort $200,000 from Michael Bloomberg by telling him that he would disclose confidential information he obtained from his hacks to the public.[37] Bloomberg co-operated with U.S. law-enforcement officials and invited Zezev via e-mail to meet him in London to explain how he broke into

---

[32] Brenner and Koops, loc. cit. n. 17.

[33] Michael Brunker, 'FBI Agent Charged With Hacking: Russia alleges agent broke law by downloading evidence', *MSNBC*, <http://www.msnbc.com/news/563379.asp?0si=-&cp1=1>.

[34] Ibid.

[35] Idem.

[36] Associated Press, 'British Hacker Appears In Court To Fight U.S. Extradition Request', *Information Week* (27 July 2005), <http://informationweek.com/story/showArticle.jhtml?articleID=166402941>.

[37] U.S. Department Of Justice Press Release, 'U.S. Convicts Kazakhstan Hacker of Breaking Into Bloomberg L.P.'s Computers and Attempting Extortion' (2003), <http://www.usdoj.gov/criminal/cybercrime/zezevConvict.htm>.

the Bloomberg system. Zezev traveled to London, where he was met by Bloomberg and some undercover U.K. law-enforcement officials. Zezev was arrested by London officials and extradited to the United States in 2002.[38] He was convicted and sentenced to 51 months in prison.[39] This case is of interest jurisdictionally because the jurisdictional nexus to the case would appear to be in Kazakhstan and the United States. By arranging for the criminal to meet the victim in a third country, the United Kingdom, to complete the crime of extortion, the United Kingdom was able to nab Zezev and send him to the United States for prosecution.

All three of these cases show the complexity of potential jurisdictional issues involving multiple nations, whether those nations serve as a criminal's or victim's home or as a third-party intermediary who can assist in pursuing and capturing cybercriminals. As cybercrime continues to grow globally, the issue of jurisdiction must be fully addressed. The United States' broad approach, so long as it builds in basic privacy protections, may be the most effective method for dealing with criminals who act globally not locally.

16.6.2 Procedures for searching computers internationally and providing assistance

In order to deal with the potential legal and policy problems with international computer searches and seizures, the United States has established specific procedures and safeguards. U.S. investigators and prosecutors must consult and seek approval from the Office of International Affairs (OIA) within the Department of Justice before attempting to obtain information stored on a foreign computer, unless exigent circumstances exist. Even when such circumstances exist, law enforcement is required to contact the appropriate authority immediately to assure that foreign sovereignty and comity issues are addressed.

When receiving assistance from foreign law-enforcement officials, U.S. law enforcement should follow official processes, rather than go through informal contacts. This is necessary to ensure that any evidence gathered will be admissible under the U.S. Federal Rules of Evidence 901(b)(7) and 902(3).

When United States law-enforcement officials are asked by foreign officials to preserve evidence on network servers in the United States, they can do so under 18 USC § 2703(f), which requires service providers to preserve, but not disclose information. This process will allow relevant information to be preserved pending the somewhat tedious process of obtaining the necessary approvals and agreements.

---

[38] Ibid.

[39] U.S. Department Of Justice Press Release, 'Kazakhstan Hacker Sentenced to Four Years Prison for Breaking into Bloomberg Systems and Attempting Extortion' (2003), <http://www.usdoj.gov/criminal/cybercrime/zezevSent.htm>.

16.7 Conclusion

For the most part, the United States had taken a broad approach to construing its jurisdiction in federal cases that have international connections. The changes in the U.S.A. Patriot Act in 2001 assured that the United States have the authority to pursue not only international cases that originate or conclude in the United States, but also those cases where networks or computers in the United States are merely used as pass-throughs.

As the U.S. pursues criminals internationally through extradition or undercover stings, questions will continue to exist regarding the validity of the nation's actions. It is not clear how other nations will view the U.S. approach in the long-run.

Likewise, it is unclear whether other nations will allow the United States to search remotely computers and networks located within their sovereign nations. Interestingly, it is doubtful that the United States would condone or approve of other nation's searching the computers of U.S. citizens located within the boundaries of the United States. If it did condone such behavior – whether explicitly or implicitly – there could be potential violations of the U.S. Constitution, in particular, the 4th (prohibition of unreasonable search and seizures) and 14th (due process) Amendments.

Bibliography

Associated Press, 'British Hacker Appears In Court To Fight U.S. Extradition Request', *InformationWeek* (27 July 2005), <http://informationweek.com/story/showArticle.jhtml?articleID=166402941>.

Susan W. Brenner, 'State Cybercrime Legislation in the United States of America: A Survey', 7 *Rich. J.L. & Tech.* (Winter 2001) p. 28, <http://www.richmond.edu/jolt/v7i3/article2.html>.

Susan W. Brenner and Bert-Jaap Koops, 'Approaches to Cybercrime Jurisdiction', 4 *Journal of High Technology Law.* (2004) p. 1.

U.S. Department of Justice, *Field Guidance on New Authorities That Relate to Computer Crime and Electronic Evidence Enacted in the USA Patriot Act of 2001* (2001), available at <http://www.usdoj.gov/criminal/cybercrime/PatriotAct.htm>.

U.S. Department of Justice, *Searching and Seizing Computers and Obtaining Electronic Evidence at Criminal Investigations* (July 2002), available at <http://www.cybercrime.gov/s&smanual2002.htm#_IIIA>.

Chapter 17
THE NEXT STEP: PRIORITIZING JURISDICTION

Susan W. Brenner*

Cybercrime is, as previous chapters noted, almost inherently transnational. In 2000, the Love Bug virus infected computers in at least twenty countries.[1] Four years later, the Sasser worm 'crippled computers worldwide.'[2] Spammers and other online scammers ignore national borders, sending solicitation e-mails to potential victims in a host of countries.[3]

Cybercriminals operating from a 'secure' jurisdiction can perpetrate these and other offenses on victims in many countries, often with relative impunity. The preceding chapters of this book have analyzed the extent to which specific countries can exercise criminal jurisdiction over a cybercriminal who victimizes their citizens, in their territory, while operating from a remote location. This chapter is concerned with a different issue: prioritizing jurisdiction among various countries.

17.1 Jurisdictional Conflicts

Since cybercrime tends to transcend national borders, it follows that the activities of a particular cybercriminal (or particular group of cybercriminals) are likely to represent the commission of crimes in multiple countries. If, for example, John Doe uses a version of the 419 email scam[4] to defraud victims in countries A, B, and C, he will have committed a crime (fraud) against victims in each of those jurisdictions. As long as each country has penal law in place that criminalizes the use of a

* Prof. Susan W. Brenner is NCR Distinguished Professor of Law & Technology at the University of Dayton School of Law, Dayton, Ohio, United States.

[1] See, e.g., '"Love Bug" Investigation Turns to 2 Computer School Students in Philippines', *CNN* (11 May 2000), <http://archives.cnn.com/2000/ASIANOW/southeast/05/10/ilove.you.02/>.

[2] 'Sasser Creator Avoids Jail Term', *BBC News* (8 July 2005), <http://news.bbc.co.uk/1/hi/technology/4659329.stm>.

[3] See, e.g., *IC3 2004 Internet Fraud – Crime Report* (2005), <http://www1.ifccfbi.gov/strategy/2004_IC3Report.pdf>.

[4] See, e.g., U.S. Secret Service, *Public Awareness Advisory Regarding '4-1-9' or 'Advance Fee Fraud' Schemes*, <http://www.secretservice.gov/alert419.shtml>.

B-J. Koops and S.W. Brenner (Eds), Cybercrime and Jurisdiction

computer and e-mail to perpetrate fraud[5] and procedural law that authorizes the exercise of criminal jurisdiction, John Doe can be prosecuted by country A, country B, *and* country C. If we assume, as seems reasonable, that all three countries want to prosecute Doe, this creates a positive jurisdictional conflict, i.e., a situation in which more than one country claims jurisdiction over a perpetrator based on the same general course of conduct.[6]

We will assume that John Doe's activities constituted a continuing course of criminal conduct that can be parsed into discrete offenses committed against individual victims in each of the three countries. In this sense, therefore, countries A, B, and C are not each seeking to prosecute Doe for the 'same' crime; each is seeking to prosecute him for specific crimes that were committed against its citizens as part of an ongoing course of on-line criminal activity.

We will also assume, for the purposes of analysis, that there are no substantive obstacles to John Doe's being prosecuted by all three countries, in whatever order. The principles of double jeopardy and *ne bis in idem* both prohibit the 'sanctioning of a person more than once for a single unlawful course of conduct based on the breach of a law that protects the same legal interest.'[7] But since both prohibitions are 'primarily, if not exclusively,' concerned with barring multiple prosecutions for the same offense by the same sovereign, they have little, if any, applicability to a scenario such as that outlined above, in which three different sovereigns seek to prosecute Doe, each for crimes against different victims.[8] And the drafters of the Convention on Cybercrime[9] left the option of sequential prosecution open, 'arguing that it is more a matter to be regulated by extradition treaties than by the convention itself.'[10]

The need to resolve conflicting jurisdictional claims over a cybercriminal will certainly arise, given the transnational nature of most cybercrime. Indeed, one source maintains that '[o]verlapping jurisdiction will be the rule rather than the exception.'[11]

---

5 See, e.g., Susan W. Brenner and Joseph J. Schwerha IV, 'Transnational Evidence Gathering And Local Prosecution Of International Cybercrime', 20 *John Marshall Journal of Computer and Information Law* (2002) p. 347.

6 See, e.g., Susan W. Brenner and Bert-Jaap Koops, 'Approaches to Cybercrime Jurisdiction', 4 *Journal of High Technology Law* (2004) p. 1.

7 Andre Fiebig, 'Modernization of European Competition Law As A Form of Convergence', 19 *Temple International and Comparative Law Journal* (2005) p. 63 at p. 77. See, e.g., Nuno Garoupa and Fernando Gomez-Pomar, 'Punish Once or Punish Twice: A Theory o the Use of Criminal Sanctions in Addition to Regulatory Penalties', 6 *American Law and Economic Review* (2004) p. 410 at p. 414.

8 See, e.g., Albin Eser, 'For Universal Jurisdiction: Against Fletcher's Antagonism', 39 *Tulsa Law Review* (2004) p. 955 at pp. 963-964.

9 Council of Europe, Convention on Cybercrime (CETS 185) (23 November 2001), <http://conventions.coe.int/Treaty/en/Treaties/Html/185.htm>.

10 As quoted in Brenner and Koops, loc. cit. n. 6.

11 Andreas Fischer-Lescano and Gunther Teubner, 'Reply to Andreas L. Paulus: Consensus As Fiction Of Global Law', 25 *Michigan Journal of International Law* (2004) p. 1059 at p. 1061.

17.2 Prioritizing Jurisdictional Claims: Lack of Guidance

This brings us to the 'next step'. Once we decide that all three countries have jurisdiction to prosecute John Doe, how do we prioritize their respective claims? That is, how should we go about deciding which country should be given the first opportunity to prosecute Doe, which should be given the next opportunity, and which should have the last opportunity to prosecute him? (It is reasonable to refer to giving countries the 'opportunity' to prosecute Doe because the second and third countries might conclude that the outcome in the initial prosecution satisfies their need for justice and so decline to prosecute him.)

Traditional legal sources provide very little guidance on these issues, presumably because transnational crime was, until recently, unusual.[12] And what would seem to be the most likely source of guidance – the Council of Europe's Convention on Cybercrime (hereafter: CCC) – really does not address these issues.[13] Article 22 paragraph 5 CCC merely says that '[w]hen more than one Party claims jurisdiction over an alleged offence established in accordance with this Convention, the Parties involved shall, where appropriate, consult with a view to determining the most appropriate jurisdiction for prosecution.' The Explanatory Report accompanying the Convention explains the obligation imposed by paragraph 5 as follows:

> 'to avoid duplication of effort (...) or to otherwise facilitate the efficiency or fairness of the proceedings, the affected Parties are to consult (...) to determine the proper venue for prosecution (...) . [T]he obligation to consult is not absolute, but is to take place 'where appropriate.' Thus, (...) if one of the Parties knows that consultation is not necessary (e.g., it has received confirmation that the other Party is not planning to take action), (…) it may (...) decline consultation.'[14]

The Council of Europe's provision on prioritizing jurisdiction is similar to that found in other international instruments. The United Nations Convention Against Transnational Organized Crime, for example, declares that '[i]f a State Party exercising its jurisdiction under (...) this article has (...) learned, that one or more other States Parties are conducting an investigation, prosecution or judicial proceeding in respect of the same conduct, the competent authorities of those States Parties shall, as appropriate, consult one another with a view to coordinating their actions'.[15]

---

[12] See generally Patricia L. Bellia, 'Chasing Bits Across Borders', *University of Chicago Legal Forum* (2001) p. 35 at p. 55.

[13] See, e.g., Ellen S. Podgor, 'Cybercrime: National, Transnational or International?', 50 *Wayne Law Review* (2004) p. 97 at p. 108: the Convention 'provides no guidance to countries who seek to resolve which jurisdiction is the most appropriate for prosecution.'

[14] Convention on Cybercrime, *Explanatory Report*, <http://conventions.coe.int/Treaty/en/Reports/Html/185.htm>, Art. 22, para. 239.

[15] United Nations Convention Against Transnational Organized Crime, Art. 15 para. 5 (2001), <http://www.unodc.org/pdf/crime/a_res_55/res5525e.pdf>.

The observations one scholar made about the United Nations Convention seem also to apply to the Convention on Cybercrime:

> 'one of the objects of the Convention against Transnational Organized Crime is to make sure that there are no safe havens. Potential [for] this (...) lie[s] in the (...) clashes of jurisdiction where two or more States may act concurrently (...). Since general international law has not established a priority system among various jurisdictional theories, the solution is negotiation, especially on the basis of where the strongest case may be mounted. The danger of the 'risks of concurrent jurisdiction' was downplayed at an early stage of the drafting, when it was 'pointed out (...) that (...) conflicts of jurisdiction were rather rare and were invariably resolved at the practical level by an eventual determination of which jurisdiction would be ultimately exercised on the basis of the chances for successful prosecution and adjudication of the particular case.'[16]

Since neither the Convention on Cybercrime nor more traditional sources offer guidance on this issue, this chapter will suggest factors countries should consider in resolving a positive jurisdictional conflict such as that outlined above. The factors have been derived from practical processes that have been used to resolve such conflicts in the past, from standards that have been articulated for use in resolving other types of jurisdictional conflicts, and from certain distinctive aspects of cybercrime. In articulating these factors, the author has assumed that the conduct at issue is a crime in all three jurisdictions.[17]

17.3 Factors in Prioritizing Jurisdictional Claims

The factors outlined below are not intended to be a mandatory set of conditions, each of which must be satisfied to establish jurisdictional priorities. The author does not propose that the prioritization of cybercrime jurisdiction in a specific case should be predicated upon the extent to which the respective countries claiming jurisdiction can satisfy *all* of these factors. The author proposes, instead, that these factors serve as elements that structure the assessment of whether it is 'reasonable' to assign first prosecution priority to country A, B, or C in a particular instance.[18]

The factors set out below are not necessarily to be given equal weight. Some may militate more heavily in favor of giving a country priority than others, in a

---

[16] Roger S. Clark, 'The United Nations Convention against Transnational Organized Crime', 50 *Wayne Law Review* (2004) p. 161 at p. 181, quoting the Report of the Meeting of the Inter-Sessional Open-Ended Intergovernmental Group of Experts on the Elaboration of a Possible Comprehensive International Convention against Organized Transnational Crime (Warsaw, 2-6 February 1998), UN ESCOR, 7th Session, at 10, UN Doc. E/CN. 15/1998/5 (1998)).

[17] Cf., Restatement (Second) of Foreign Relations Law of the United States (1965), § 40, on resolving conflicts of jurisdiction when national laws impose inconsistent obligations.

[18] See, e.g., Restatement (Third) of Foreign Relations Law of the United States (1987), § 403 Comment a: 'The principle that an exercise of jurisdiction' must be 'reasonable' is 'established in United States law, and has emerged as a principle of international law as well.'

specific case and/or in general. Although it might be reassuring to have a hierarchical, ranked system of factors for use in this analysis, the fact-sensitive nature of the analysis makes this inadvisable. In this, the author agrees with the architects of a much more ambitious effort – the Princeton Principles on Universal Jurisdiction.[19] The drafters of that document initially considered ranking the factors they identified for use in prioritizing conflicting jurisdictional claims, but ultimately decided against doing so. They noted, however, that while the factors they identified were not ranked, some would 'often be especially weighty' in prioritizing jurisdictional claims.[20]

Finally, the factors examined below are not intended to be exhaustive, i.e., are not intended to be the exclusive list of factors that should be considered in resolving positive jurisdictional conflicts.[21] Other factors that are relevant in particular instances should also be considered in resolving positive jurisdictional conflicts in cybercrime cases. This is an approach that has been used in resolving other jurisdictional issues.[22]

17.3.1 Place of commission of the crime

In deriving these factors, the author assumed that John Doe, the hypothetical cybercriminal whom various countries (A, B, and C) wish to prosecute, committed one or more cybercrimes in each of these countries. This essentially nullifies a factor that has heretofore been of significance in resolving jurisdictional conflicts, i.e., 'the place of commission of the crime'.[23]

In 2004, for example, U.S. officials in North Dakota and Minnesota were negotiating over which jurisdiction would try the man charged with abducting and murdering college student Dru Sjodin.[24] North Dakota's claim was based on the fact that it was 'the place of commission of the crime', in that her abduction and murder occurred in that state.[25] Minnesota based its claim on the facts that Sjodin was a permanent resident of Minnesota, as was the alleged perpetrator, and that her body was found in that state.[26]

---

[19] Princeton Project on Universal Jurisdiction, *The Princeton Principles on Universal Jurisdiction* (2001), <http://www.princeton.edu/~lapa/unive_jur.pdf> (hereafter: Princeton Principles), Principle 8, Commentary at 53.

[20] Ibid.

[21] Idem, at n. 29.

[22] Ibid. See, e.g., Restatement (Third) of the Foreign Relations Law of the United States (1987), § 403, listing factors to be considered in determining whether exercise of jurisdiction to prescribe is reasonable.

[23] See Princeton Principles, op. cit. n. 19, Principle 8 subpara. (b).

[24] See, e.g., Dave Kolpack, Midland, Aberdeen American News (20 April 2004), 2004 WLNR 4662109.

[25] Ibid.

[26] Idem.

The place of commission of the crime is important in resolving jurisdictional conflicts that arise with regard to real-world[27] crimes because they are, for the most part, zero-sum crimes – crimes the commission of which occurs in a single jurisdiction.[28] The physical constraints real-world criminals operate under make it difficult for them to commit multiple offenses in multiple jurisdictions within a short period of time.[29] Positive jurisdictional conflicts in the real world consequently tend to be concerned with a single offense or a single course of conduct that represents the commission of multiple, albeit related offenses.[30]

This is not true for the virtual world: as noted earlier, since cybercrime is automated crime, a perpetrator can very easily commit multiple offenses, almost simultaneously, in many different countries.[31] In the scenario given above, John Doe perpetrated distinct fraud offenses against victims who were physically located in, and were citizens of, countries A, B, and C, respectively. Each of the countries vying to prosecute Doe can therefore legitimately claim to be the 'place of the commission of the crime[s]' (against its citizens) because Doe did, in fact, commit cybercrimes 'in' country A, 'in' country B, and 'in' country C.

The analysis outlined above applies when jurisdictional conflicts arise from an offender's committing discrete, free-standing offenses in multiple jurisdictions. Jurisdictional conflicts can also arise from a different scenario: the situation in which a cybercriminal located in country A commits a cybercrime against a citizen of country B. Here, the difficulty arises not from the cybercriminal's committing discrete offenses in multiple countries, but from the need to ascertain what, precisely, is the 'place of commission of the crime'. In the real world, there is usually only one 'place of commission of the crime', because real-world offenses generally require physical proximity between perpetrator and victim.[32] As noted above, this is not true for cybercrimes; computer technology makes it possible for the commission of a single cybercrime to span two or more jurisdictions.[33] Jurisdictional statutes address this by authorizing prosecution whenever an element of the offense is

---

[27] 'Real-world' is use to denote crimes the commission of which occurs in physical space, as opposed to cyberspace. Here, 'real' is used not as the antonym of 'unreal', but instead as a term denoting actual, physical existence. See, e.g., Webster's Revised Unabridged Dictionary (1913), <http://machaut.uchicago.edu/cgi-bin/WEBSTER.sh?WORD=real>.

[28] See, e.g., Susan W. Brenner, 'Toward A Criminal Law for Cyberspace: Distributed Security', 10 *Boston University Journal of Science and Technology Law* (2004) p. 1.

[29] Ibid.

[30] See, e.g., S.S. Lotus (*France* v. *Turkey*), 1927 PCIJ (ser. A) No. 9, at 30-32 (7 September 1927): conflict between France and Turkey over prosecuting a ship's officer for negligence in allowing two ships to collide. The case is discussed in John Eisinger, 'Script Kiddies Beware: The Long Arm of U.S. Jurisdiction to Prescribe', 59 *Washington & Lee Law Review* (2002) p. 1507 at pp. 1516-1518. Cf., section 5.6.1 of this book.

[31] For more on this, see ibid.

[32] See, e.g., Brenner, loc. cit. n. 28.

[33] Ibid.

committed in a jurisdiction.[34] The 'place of commission of the crime' therefore ceases to be the zero-sum concept it is for real-world crimes.

Because 'the place of commission of the crime' is not a zero-sum phenomenon for cybercrime, this factor is unlikely to be particularly helpful in resolving positive jurisdictional conflicts. In the scenarios we have outlined, for example, it results in a wash: multiple countries are the 'place of commission of crimes' perpetrated by Doe.

17.3.2 **Custody of the perpetrator**

The most obvious, and perhaps most logical, factor to be considered in resolving conflicts of jurisdiction such as those outlined above is that a particular country (country A, say) has physical custody of the alleged perpetrator.[35] A person's presence within a jurisdiction is the most basic, and most ancient, rationale supporting jurisdiction to adjudicate the individual's liability for criminal activity.[36] As the Restatement (Second) of Conflict of Laws explains, '[p]hysical presence in the state was the traditional basis of judicial jurisdiction at common law. It is immaterial that the individual is only temporarily in the state. His presence in the state, even for an instant, gives the state judicial jurisdiction over him.'[37]

As one author has noted, an alleged offender's presence in the territory of an aspiring forum state is a consideration that was used to resolve positive jurisdictional conflicts that arose in an analogous context: high-seas piracy.[38] Like cybercrime, high-seas piracy was a variety of criminal activity that transcended, and eluded, national boundaries and national officials.[39] It seems states developed a very pragmatic approach to resolving positive jurisdictional conflicts with regard to trying high-seas pirates for their offenses.

> 'States may try pirates only after apprehending them, hence only when the pirates are (...) under their physical control: this is a typical application of the well-known maxim ubi te invenero, ibi te judicabo.[40] One of the reasons most likely motivating this legal regulation is that, at a time when piracy was rife and all states of the world were there-

[34] See Brenner and Koops, loc. cit. n. 6. See also, e.g., Ohio Revised Code § 2901.11(1)(A)(1), claiming jurisdiction to prosecute if 'any element' of an offense 'takes place in this state'.

[35] See, e.g., Restatement (Second) of Conflict of Laws (1971), § 28. See generally Art. 22 paras. 1(d) and 3 CCC.

[36] See, e.g., Restatement (Third) of Foreign Relations Law of the United States (1987), § 421(2)(a).

[37] Restatement (Second) of Conflict of Laws (1971), § 28(a).

[38] See Antonio Cassese, 'When May Senior State Officials Be Tried for International Crimes? Some Comments on the Congo v. Belgium Case', 13 *European Journal of International Law* (2002) p. 853 at pp. 857-858.

[39] See, e.g., Marc D. Goodman and Susan W. Brenner, 'The Emerging Consensus on Criminal Conduct in Cyberspace', *UCLA Journal of Law & Technology* (2002), p. 3, available at <http://www.lawtechjournal.com/articles/2002/03_020625_goodmanbrenner.php>.

[40] The maxim can be translated as 'where I will find you, there I will try you' [author's note].

> fore eager to capture persons engaging in this crime, potentially innumerable 'positive conflicts of jurisdiction' were settled in this way (...). [I]f all states had been entitled to claim jurisdiction over pirates wherever they were, very many positive conflicts would have ensued. Instead, granting jurisdiction to the state apprehending the pirates neatly resolved the matter.'[41]

Custody should play a rather more complex role in establishing jurisdictional priority with regard to cybercrimes than it does for real-world crimes. As noted earlier (section 17.3.1), competing claims to jurisdiction over real-world crimes tend to be predicated on the commission of a single offense or a single course of conduct that constitutes the commission of multiple offenses.[42] In this context, the issue to be resolved is which of several competing countries will be allowed to bring the individual to justice for the commission of that offense or course of conduct; here, the jurisdictional conflicts all focus on the same criminal activity. This means, in effect, that none of the competing countries actually 'loses' if it is not given the first opportunity to prosecute the perpetrator; he will still be brought to justice for his role in the underlying criminal transaction. And that may well resolve the matter; the other countries that were competing to prosecute him may decide, once he has been convicted and sanctioned, that this is sufficient, that there is no reason for them to pursue sequential prosecutions. This is no doubt why simple 'custody' so neatly resolved the positive jurisdictional conflicts that historically arose out of high-seas piracy; prosecution by *a* jurisdiction resolved the issue by bringing the accused pirate(s) to justice, exacting retribution and incapacitating them from re-offending, for whatever period of time.

In the cybercrime context, the jurisdictional conflicts focus on a perpetrator's committing discrete criminal offenses against unrelated victims in each of the countries vying for the opportunity to prosecute him. Instead of the scenario outlined above, in which each country asserts a claim to prosecute based on the same criminal transaction, which presumably occurred in the territory of one and only one country, in the cybercrime context, each country asserts a claim to prosecute that is based upon a severable criminal transaction unique to that country. The transaction is the victimization of the country's citizens, usually while they were physically within its territory, by someone who happens to have also inflicted similar victimization upon citizens of other countries. Because the criminal transactions at issue are factually and legally severable, prosecution of the perpetrator by one of the competing countries may vindicate that country's interest in protecting its citizens, but it does nothing to vindicate the other countries' interest in doing so. Aside from

---

[41] Cassese, loc. cit. n. 38.

[42] In the *Achille Lauro* case, for example, the United States wanted to prosecute the hijackers for the murder of an American citizen, while Italy wanted to prosecute them for hijacking, the murder of the American citizen, kidnapping, and the possession of arms and explosives. See, e.g., John Tagliabue, 'Top Italian Court Upholds Arrest Warrant for Abbas', *New York Times* (31 October 1985); 'Italy Presses Hijack Charges', *Miami Herald* (12 October 1985).

anything else, the remote victimization typical of cybercrime gives jurisdictions a heightened interest in pursuing their own prosecutions of those responsible for victimizing a country's citizens; such prosecutions symbolically attest to the country's commitment, and ability, to pursue justice for its citizens against this emerging and unprecedented threat.

Perhaps an example will illustrate the difference between the two scenarios. Assume, first, that Max Schultz, a German national and a terrorist, hijacks a bus traveling from Barcelona to Cordoba and kills three of the passengers (a U.S. citizen, a citizen of Japan, and a citizen of Ireland) before he is apprehended. Spain wants to prosecute Schultz for hijacking the bus, killing three passengers, jeopardizing the safety of the other passengers, and terrorism. The United States, Japan, and Ireland each want to prosecute him for killing their citizen, so we have a positive jurisdictional conflict.

As this scenario illustrates, custody is often coupled with 'place of the commission of the crime' for real-world offenses. This circumstance commonly arises for physical crimes because one must usually be physically 'in' a country to commit crimes there; the remote commission of crime is a function of technology, and so has not been a typical feature of real-world criminality.[43]

Logically, the fact that Spain has custody of Schultz, coupled with the fact that he committed his crimes 'in' Spain, weighs heavily in favor of giving Spain the first opportunity to prosecute him, even if we ignore the effect of other factors (see sections 17.3.1-2).[44] If Spain were to prosecute, convict and impose a suitable penalty upon Schultz, the other three countries might decide this outcome was sufficient, and not pursue their own prosecutions.

A prosecution by the United States, Japan, and/or Ireland would be factually derivative; such a prosecution would be predicated upon the criminal transaction, and the underlying 'harm' addressed by the Spanish prosecution. These three claimant countries might decide, therefore, that the 'harm' inflicted by Schultz had been adequately addressed by the Spanish prosecution, and elect not to proceed with their own claims. This seems to occur in the United States: while the constitutional prohibition against double jeopardy does not bar sequential prosecution (i) by a state after a federal prosecution and/or (ii) by state A after a prosecution by state B, sequential prosecution is, in fact, the exception.[45] And since the citizen of each of the three countries was 'harmed' while outside their territory, the country's interest in pursuing such a prosecution is further attenuated.

---

[43] See, e.g., Brenner, loc. cit. n. 28.

[44] Since Spain is the 'scene of the crime', it is reasonable to assume that Spanish authorities will have the strongest case against Smith; and it is also reasonable to assume Spain is likely to be the most convenient forum for those who will be called as witnesses in the case. These factors are discussed later in the text.

[45] See, e.g., U.S. Department of Justice, *United States Attorney's Manual*, § 9-2.031, on the policy limiting the instances in which federal authorities will prosecute based on the same act or transaction at issue in a state prosecution.

Now, however, assume that Schultz is a cybercriminal instead of a terrorist. Assume he victimized citizens of Ireland, Japan, Spain, and the United States by conducting an on-line fraud scam, a 419 fraud scheme, from his apartment in San Francisco.[46] Assume that Schultz defrauded 10 victims in Ireland, 15 in Japan, 25 in Spain, and 15 in the United States, and that U.S. officials have him in custody. U.S. authorities want to prosecute Schultz for victimizing U.S. citizens; Ireland, Japan, and Spain each want to prosecute him for victimizing their citizens. In resolving the jurisdictional conflict, how much weight should be given to the fact that the U.S. has Schultz in custody?

One factual circumstance that differentiates this scenario from the first scenario is the relationship between custody and the criminal transaction. Like Schultz-the-terrorist, Schultz-the-cybercriminal committed crimes 'in' the country that has him in custody. Schultz victimized U.S. citizens while physically located in the United States. Unlike Schultz-the-terrorist, Schultz-the-cybercriminal also victimized citizens of three other countries (i) while they were in their own countries and (ii) while he was in the United States. Schultz's being in the United States seems coincident, a matter that is factually and logically irrelevant to the crimes he has committed. The United States has custody of him because he happened to choose that country as the *situs* for his fraud operations. Unlike the Schultz-as-terrorist scenario, there is no inherent factual or logical nexus between Schultz's criminal conduct and his being in the United States; he could as easily have victimized the same individuals, in the same way, if he had operated from Ireland, Japan, Spain, Russia, or any other country.

It therefore seems appropriate, in resolving conflicting jurisdictional claims concerning an alleged cybercriminal, to use a 'custody-plus' standard. If we were to apply this standard to the scenario given above, the U.S. claim to jurisdictional priority over Schultz would be strengthened if it demonstrates that it acquired custody of Schultz as the result, say, of intensive investigatory efforts that resulted in his being apprehended when he might otherwise have escaped official notice. Such an effort reasonably supports the inference that U.S. officials were dedicated to pursuing justice in this case and were, to that end, willing to devote substantial resources to tracking him down and apprehending him. Under a 'custody-plus' standard, this aspect of the U.S. claim to jurisdictional priority would be eroded if it acquired custody of Schultz through inadvertence.[47] This does not mean that U.S. custody of Schultz would play no role in the jurisdictional prioritization analysis; it simply means it would be given less emphasis than if its custody of Schultz were the result of affirmative efforts to locate and secure him.

---

[46] See *supra* n. 4 and accompanying text.

[47] See, e.g., Kim S. Nash, 'What Happens to Computer Criminals in Jail?', *CNN* (23 October 1998), <http://www.cnn.com/TECH/computing/9810/23/jail.idg/>. The United States acquired custody of Citibank hacker Vladimir Levin after he was arrested in Heathrow Airport in London and then extradited to the United States

17.3.3 Harm

The Schultz-as-cybercriminal scenario discussed above suggests another factor that should be considered in resolving positive jurisdictional conflicts: the 'harm' the perpetrator inflicted upon the respective countries seeking to prosecute him. To incorporate 'harm' into the jurisdictional calculus, we need to identify indicators of 'harm' – metrics we can use to assess the relative extent to which each jurisdiction has been injured by the perpetrator's activities.

One obvious measure of 'harm' is the number of victims. In the scenario given above, the 'harm' Schultz-the-cybercriminal inflicted in each jurisdiction is essentially equivalent in terms of the number of victims. We know he defrauded 15 people in the United States, 10 in Ireland, 15 in Japan, and 25 in Spain; if we use the number of victims as our measure of the 'harm' Schultz inflicted in each country, then this indicator is of little assistance in this instance. The use of victim number as an indicator of 'harm' may, though, be more helpful in other instances. Assume, for example, that cybercriminal Doe creates and releases a computer virus that spread unevenly among a number of countries. Assume, further, that the Doe virus inflicts 'harm' (loss of computer files and computer services, and similar injuries) upon (i) 2 million victims in the United States, (ii) 100,000 victims in France, and (iii) 150 victims in Japan. If we use the number of victims as an indicator of 'harm' resulting from Doe's efforts, then 'harm', in this instance, would weigh toward giving the United States first priority, followed by France and then by Japan.

The notion of 'harm' as measured by discrete victimization might be more useful in this analysis if we had an assessment of precisely 'how much' each victim was injured. The most objective indicator of 'how much' a victim was injured is monetary loss. This can encompass not only funds that the cybercriminal defrauded, extorted or stole from the victim; it can also encompass 'any reasonable cost to any victim, including the cost of responding to an offense, conducting a damage assessment, and restoring the data, program, system, or information to its condition prior to the offense, and any revenue lost, cost incurred, or other consequential damages incurred because of interruption of service.'[48] Monetary losses would give us a benchmark for the precise level of injury inflicted on each individual victim; it would also give us an indicator of the collective 'harm' Schultz inflicted in each country. So, let us assume that, in the scenario hypothesized above, the victims (i) in the United States lost a combined sum of $2 million dollars, (ii) in France lost a combined sum of $10 million, and (ii) in Japan lost a combined sum of $3 million. If we use this indicator to assess the collective 'harm' Doe inflicted on each jurisdiction, then 'harm' would weigh toward giving France first priority, followed by Japan and then by the United States.

Using victim numbers and victim monetary losses as indicators of 'harm' is satisfactory for the more routine cybercrimes, e.g., for fraud, extortion, malware,

[48] 18 USC § 1030(e)(11).

and other crimes that target 'civilian' victims, whether individual or corporate. Other types of cybercrime, such as economic espionage, can inflict monetary losses, but they also inflict systemic 'harms'; a successful act of economic espionage, for example, can jeopardize a nation's ability to compete successfully in the international marketplace.[49] Incorporating the 'harm' caused by economic espionage into the jurisdictional prioritization analysis would require articulating some metric that could be used to quantify the 'harm' resulting from the offense.

Much the same will be true for cybercrimes committed for other than economic reasons. This category of cybercrime would encompass attacks on national infrastructures, on medical and educational facilities, and on government computer systems.[50]

Finally, an issue that may (or may not) be relevant to the 'harm' analysis is the extent to which it was foreseeable that the perpetrator's actions would cause 'harm' in a specific country. Under the Model Penal Code's standard of intentionality, which is followed in most American jurisdictions, an offender's culpability depends, in part, upon the extent to which he (i) 'intended' to inflict a 'harm' upon a victim, (ii) was aware that his conduct would inflict the 'harm', or (iii) ignored a 'substantial and unjustifiable risk' that the 'harm' would result from his conduct.[51] Some cybercriminals, such as those who commit economic espionage, specifically intend to inflict 'harm' in the jurisdiction(s) they target. At the very least, these offenders, along with the other cybercriminals who target specific victims, are aware that their conduct will inflict 'harm' upon persons in specific jurisdictions. Other cybercriminals, such as those who create and disseminate viruses and worms, may not specifically intend that their conduct inflict 'harm' in a given jurisdiction; they are aware that their conduct will inflict 'harm' generally, but ignore the consequences it may have for particular countries. An offender's specific intention to inflict 'harm' in a given jurisdiction might be a useful element to incorporate into the calculus we use to resolve positive jurisdictional conflicts; if nothing else, it establishes the foreseeability of his or her being brought to justice by that jurisdiction.

17.3.4 **Nationality**

Nationality – both of the perpetrator and the victim – has traditionally been a factor that has been considered in resolving jurisdictional conflicts.[52] As is explained below, the author does not regard nationality, in either guise, as an important factor in a calculus designed to resolve positive jurisdictional conflicts arising from cybercrime.

---

[49] See, e.g., Susan W. Brenner and Anthony Crescenzi, 'State-Sponsored Crime: The Futility of the Economic Espionage Act', 27 *Houston Journal of International Law* (forthcoming 2006), p. 1.

[50] See, e.g., 18 USC § 1030(a)(5)(B) on non-monetary damage.

[51] See American Law Institute, *Model Penal Code* (1962), § 2.02.

[52] See, e.g., Princeton Principles, op. cit. n. 19, Principle 8 subpara. (b). See generally Art. 22 para. 1(d) CCC.

Victim nationality

We begin with victim nationality, an issue that was not included in the jurisdictional provisions of the Convention on Cybercrime.[53] First, since we are assuming that John Doe, our fictive cybercriminal, committed crimes in each of the countries seeking to prosecute him (A, B, and C), it does not seem that victim nationality is a particularly significant factor in the calculus used to resolve the positive jurisdictional conflicts resulting from their claims. On the one hand, since we know Doe committed cybercrimes 'in' countries A, B, and C, it is reasonable to assume that some, if not all, of the offenses he committed in each country were directed at citizens of that country who were 'in' the country at the time.[54] As with the 'place of commission of the crime' factor discussed earlier, this puts the three claimant countries in a position of equivalence; each has citizens who were victimized by Doe.

If, on the other hand, we assume, somewhat unrealistically, that John Doe (i) committed cybercrimes in each of the three countries but, in so doing, (ii) managed to victimize only persons who were not citizens of that country (but were in the country), we would still conclude that victim nationality is not a significant factor in the jurisdictional priority analysis. We derive this conclusion from the following premise: our analysis incorporates the foundational assumption that Doe, our fictive perpetrator, committed cybercrimes against victims located in each of the countries that seeks to prosecute him.

A fundamental, albeit implicit, principle of criminal law is that each state must maintain a baseline of internal order; this threshold level of order makes it possible for the state, and its individual constituents, to carry out the activities essential to individual and political survival.[55] Criminal law has historically been concerned with internal threats, because it was not physically possible to commit crimes remotely, from another state; as a result, criminal law, and the system that evolved to enforce criminal law, focused on the commission of crimes against citizens of a state. This focus effectively conflated the 'place of commission of the crime' and victim nationality; the goal is to protect those within a state (presumptively citizens) from being preyed upon by others who were also located within that state. Cybercrime makes remote victimization possible and, in so doing, blurs the distinction between maintaining internal order (criminal law and law-enforcement officials) and maintaining external order (military force and international agreements).[56] It should, therefore, be irrelevant to country A that John Doe victimized citizens of country B while they were physically located within the territory of country A; since John Doe's victimization of non-citizens of country A was, in effect, an attack

[53] Cf., chapter 2, sections 2.2 and 2.3 of this book.

[54] The scenario in which, for example, Doe victimizes a citizen of country A while that person is in country B is discussed later in the text.

[55] See, e.g., Brenner, loc. cit. n. 28.

[56] Ibid.

on country A's sovereignty, it should not matter to country A whether the individual targets of the attack were its own citizens or resident aliens.

There is a residual category in which victim nationality can become an issue: John Doe victimizes a citizen of country A while that person is in country B, victimizes a citizen of country C while that person is in country A, and victimizes a citizen of country B while that person is in country C. For real-world crimes, this scenario can generate a compelling desire on the part of national officials to prosecute those who victimized their citizen while he or she was abroad.[57] We do not, however, see this as a significant issue in the context of cybercrimes. For one thing, victimization is empirically more likely to occur while someone is at work or at home in their own country.

Even if someone is victimized on-line while they are physically located in another country, the victimization is likely to occur while they are utilizing computer resources that are physically located in their own country. If I, an American citizen, were, for example, victimized by an on-line fraudster while I was traveling in Spain, the consummation of the fraud would be predicated upon the use of credit card or banking facilities that are physically located in the United States.

Also, while on-line victimization can inflict financial and, perhaps, psychological 'harm,' it does not produce the type of physical harm that gives rise to the compelling desire noted above. When a citizen of country A is killed or severely injured by a criminal in country B, A may seek to prosecute the country B perpetrator because it believes this demonstrates its commitment to protecting its citizens' physical safety even when they are abroad. So far, individual safety has not been jeopardized by cybercrime, which suggests that this commitment is unlikely to play an important role in assertions of cybercrime jurisdiction. This inference is further supported by the complicating factor of remote commission. Assume that John Doe victimizes a citizen of country A while that person is in country B and while Doe is in country X, halfway around the world. Doe's presence in country X is a matter of happenstance; he has no particular connection to it and, indeed, bounced the signals he used in victimizing the citizen of country A through servers located in several other countries (e.g., M, N, and O). It seems highly unlikely that country A would seek to prosecute Doe in this scenario; its citizen suffered no physical injury, and it is exceedingly doubtful that such a prosecution would markedly advance A's citizens' virtual safety when they were traveling abroad.

Perpetrator nationality

We must now consider the nationality of the perpetrator.[58] In the context of real-world crime, nationality is a factor that militates in favor of awarding jurisdictional

[57] See, e.g., the Achille Lauro incident, *supra*, n. 42, on U.S. efforts to extradite and prosecute a terrorist who executed a U.S. citizen on board of a cruise ship.

[58] See, e.g., Art. 22 para. 1(d) CCC. See also Princeton Principles, op. cit. n. 19, Principle 8, subpara. (c).

priority.[59] We will assume this treatment of nationality is a sensible approach for real-world crimes, even though it has been questioned.[60] In the cybercrime context, it seems that perpetrator nationality should operate as an inverse factor; that is, it seems to be a factor that militates against, rather than for, the assertion of jurisdiction.

To understand why this is so, we need only consider the original scenario set out above, in which John Doe commits discrete cybercrimes against respective citizens of countries A, B, and C. We will, for the purposes of this particular analysis, assume Doe is a citizen of country A, which, like the other two countries, seeks to prosecute him. Factually, Doe's citizenship does give him a unique connection to country A, and this, alone, might suggest that country A be given priority over the other two countries. Logically, however, Doe's citizenship should weigh in favor of giving first priority to country B and country C (in whatever order is dictated by a consideration of other factors), and reserving country A for last.

This conclusion is based on the premise that since country A's citizen victimized citizens of B and C, those countries should be given the initial opportunities to exact justice from him. Country A is, in a pragmatic, empirical sense, 'responsible' for what Doe has done; that is, he is a 'product' of country A and, at least in a symbolic sense, country A can be said to have 'allowed' him to prey on citizens of other countries.[61]

As one scholar noted, 'nationality-based criminal jurisdiction reflects the need [for one state] to maintain good relations with other states (...) by deterring conduct by its own nationals that reflects poorly on the state abroad.'[62] Historically, the concern has been with a citizen who commits crimes while in another country and then returns home; the goal has been to ensure that the offender's own country does not shield him from justice by declining to prosecute him or to extradite him.[63] Indeed, the principle of *aut dedere, aut iudicare* ('either to hand over, or to bring to trial'), which was incorporated into the Convention on Cybercrime,[64] was developed to address this possibility.[65]

The 'aut dedere, aut judicare' principle, and the assumption that nationality is a factor that weighs in favor of awarding jurisdictional priority, both assume traditional, real-world crime. That is, they assume a scenario in which John Doe, a citi-

---

[59] See, e.g., Antonio Cassese, 'Is The Bell Tolling For Universality? A Plea For A Sensible Notion Of Universal Jurisdiction', 1 *Journal of International Criminal Justice* (2003) p. 589 at p. 593.

[60] See, e.g., Henry J. Steiner, 'Three Cheers For Universal Jurisdiction – Or Is It Only Two?', 5 *Theoretical Inquiries in Law* (2004) p. 199 at p. 203.

[61] See generally CCC *Explanatory Report*, op. cit. n. 14, on Art. 22, para. 236.

[62] Geoffrey R. Watson, 'The Passive Personality Principle', 28 *Texas International Law Journal* (1993) p. 1 at p. 17.

[63] Ibid.

[64] See Art. 22 para. 3 CCC.

[65] See, e.g., Alex Schmid, 'Terrorism – The Definitional Problem', 36 *Case Western Reserve Journal of International Law* (2004) p. 391 at p. 395.

zen of country A, travels to country C, commits a crime against one of its citizens while he is there, and then returns to A. Both country A and country C want to prosecute Doe; the 'aut dedere' principle gives A the option of handing Doe over to C for prosecution or prosecuting him itself. We will assume, for the purposes of analysis, that A has established jurisdiction over the conduct at issue and can prosecute Doe for the crime he committed in C. We therefore have a positive jurisdictional conflict. Under the traditional analysis,[66] Doe's nationality weighs heavily in favor of giving priority to country A. The generally-articulated rationale for this is the strength of the factual and legal link between Doe and country A.[67] This deference is also implicitly predicated on the proposition noted earlier, i.e., that country A is, in effect, 'responsible' for its citizen's criminality. This proposition has on occasion been made explicit with regard to real-world crime; one notable instance is efforts to combat sex tourism, which encourages 'sending countries' to prosecute their nationals who travel abroad for the purpose of having sex with children.[68]

Efforts to combat sex tourism encourage countries to prosecute their nationals both because of the recognition that the countries are 'responsible' for the crimes of their citizens and because of a concern that the receiving countries, the 'place of commission of the crime', may not seek to prosecute them. We, of course, are dealing with the converse situation: the scenario in which multiple countries are vying to prosecute a cybercriminal who has committed crimes 'in' each country. The second issue noted above, i.e., lack of prosecution by 'the place of commission of the crime', is therefore inapplicable. We are left with the premise that a state should be given first preference to prosecute its citizen for a real-world crime committed abroad because it is 'responsible' for the conduct of its citizens.

To understand why the opposite should be true for cybercrimes, it is helpful to consider an example. Assume our friend John Doe is a citizen of the United States who used a rented office in San Jose, California to commit cybercrimes against citizens of other countries. Assume Doe successfully conducted a 419 fraud scheme[69] for over a year, and that he focused his efforts on citizens of other countries because he believed this would minimize his chances of being investigated and apprehended in the United States. Assume, further, that Doe victimized (i) 100 citizens of England, (ii) 200 citizens of South Korea, and (iii) 50 citizens of Brazil. Each of these countries seeks to prosecute him for victimizing its citizens.[70]

---

[66] See *supra* n. 59 and accompanying text.

[67] See, e.g., Steiner, loc. cit. n. 60.

[68] See, e.g., Karene Jullien, 'The Recent International Efforts To End Commercial Sexual Exploitation Of Children', 31 *Denver Journal of International Law and Policy* (2003) p. 579 at p. 595: 'After the Council of Europe condemned sex tourism and alleged the responsibility of sending countries, it recommended (...) member States(...) establish extraterritorial jurisdiction to allow prosecution of nationals.'

[69] See *supra* n. 4 and accompanying text.

[70] Doe victimized many other individuals, but these are the only countries that seek to prosecute him for his crimes.

Should Doe's nationality weigh in favor of allowing him to be prosecuted in the United States? We will assume, for the purposes of analysis, that (i) Doe *can* be prosecuted in the United States for the crimes he committed against the citizens of these other countries,[71] and (ii) U.S. authorities are *willing* to prosecute him for those crimes (which may not, of course, always hold in a real situation). Why should Doe's nationality weigh in favor of giving the United States priority to prosecute? Since 'the place of commission of the crime' is, in a non-zero-sum sense (see section 17.3.1), England, South Korea, and/or Brazil, respectively, the United States' only claim to priority is Doe's nationality. Aside from that, the United States has no factual or legal connection to the offenses; its only connection with them is that its citizen victimized citizens of other countries, a circumstance which hardly seems to warrant giving the U.S. priority.

A crime is a transgression against a sovereign; it represents a breach of the sovereign's obligation, and ability, to ensure order within its territory. Historically, crime has been an internal matter; countries have been able to maintain the necessary baseline of order by controlling the behavior of those within the territory they control.[72] Cybercrime challenges that ability; countries now have to deal with external threats from cybercriminals such as Doe. His activities are an affront to the sovereignty of England, South Korea, and Brazil; they in no way compromised the sovereignty of the United States. And we can, as noted earlier, conclude that the United States is, in a sense, 'responsible' for Doe's crimes: they did not encourage, facilitate, or otherwise directly contribute to the commission of his crimes, but it did default on its obligation to deter criminality on the part of its own citizens, a default that resulted in 'harm' to citizens of other countries. Logically, therefore, the injured sovereigns should be given priority over the non-injured sovereign, the United States; here, nationality should function as an inverse factor in the jurisdictional priority analysis.

The same conclusion holds if we modify the initial scenario so that Doe also commits crimes against citizens of the United States. The United States is now an injured sovereign, like England, South Korea, and Brazil. But unlike those countries, the United States is, at least to some extent, 'responsible' for Doe's criminality. The host country's defaulting on its obligation to control criminality by its citizens should still function as an inverse factor in the jurisdictional priority analysis; the 'victim' sovereigns should be given preference over the host country.

17.3.5 **Strength of the case against the perpetrator**

A factor that should be very important in resolving positive jurisdictional conflicts is the strength of the case(s) each country can bring against John Doe.[73] This has

---

71 18 USC § 1030(e)(2), on extraterritorial jurisdiction over cybercrimes.

72 See *supra*, nn. 55-56 and accompanying text.

73 See, e.g., Princeton Principles, op. cit. n. 19, Principle 8, subpara. (f).

been a factor that has been considered in the United States, when multiple states seek to prosecute the same individual(s).[74]

The ultimate goal, after all, is to ensure that Doe, and other cybercriminals, are brought to justice; it would, therefore, not be reasonable to give priority to, say, country A that has a weak case against Doe, instead of to country C that has a very strong case against him. In making this determination, it will be appropriate to consider not only the extent to which a particular jurisdiction has investigated and collected evidence tying Doe (or whatever suspect) to the cybercrime(s) it wishes to prosecute; the analysis should also consider whether the defendant(s) may be able to raise objections to the use of this evidence and, perhaps, have it ruled inadmissible.[75] The analysis might also focus on related issues, such as the applicability of the statute of limitations or other defenses which the defendant(s) might raise.

17.3.6 **Punishment**

This brings us to a related factor: the punishment that can be imposed upon conviction. This is a factor prosecutors in the United States often raise when multiple states are seeking to prosecute the same individual(s).[76] The goal here should be to ensure just punishment, not to seek punishment for punishment's sake.

To understand why this can be important, it is useful to consider a variation on the events surrounding the dissemination of the 'Love Bug' virus in 2000. In May of 2000, the Love Bug virus appeared and quickly spread around the world, causing billions of dollars in damage.[77] Because the virus caused damage in the United States, Federal Bureau of Investigation agents investigated and soon pinpointed Manila as the source of the virus.[78] Agents from the Philippines' National Bureau of Investigation, working with FBI agents who had been sent to Manila, identified Onel de Guzman as the person who was likely to have been responsible for creating and disseminating the virus. The agents searched de Guzman's home and discovered evidence linking him to the crime.[79] Unfortunately, however, the Philippines had not, at the time, criminalized any form of cybercrime, including the creation and dissemination of a virus. Since de Guzman could not be prosecuted in the Philippines, he could not be extradited for prosecution in the United States or in any

---

[74] See, e.g., 'Deciding which Jurisdiction Should Prosecute Sniper Case', *Tampa Tribune* (30 October 2002), 2002 WLNR 981106: 'Of paramount importance to prosecutors (...) should be which jurisdiction has the most admissible evidence to tie the suspects to the killings.'

[75] See, e.g., ibid.

[76] Ibid. See also Adam Taylor, 'Anti-Gun Messages Might Resurface', *Ohio News Journal* (2 December 2003), 2003 WLNR 12888988: state and federal prosecutors met to review 'gun cases to decide which office should prosecute them, based on which jurisdiction has the most severe sentence.'

[77] See, e.g., Lynn Burke, 'Love Bug Case Dead in Manila', *Wired News* (21 August 2000), <http://www.wired.com/news/politics/0,1283,38342,00.html>.

[78] See, e.g., CNN, loc. cit. n. 1.

[79] See, e.g., 'Love Bug Suspect Detained', *BBC News* (8 May 2000), <http://news.bbc.co.uk/1/hi/sci/tech/740558.stm>.

other country that had criminalized the creation and dissemination of viruses and that had suffered damage from the Love Bug.[80] Consequently, no positive jurisdictional conflict arose.

Assume, for the purposes of analysis, that the Philippines had previously adopted law criminalizing the creation and dissemination of a computer virus, and that the law had gone into effect months before the Love Bug appeared.[81] Now assume that we have, say, three different countries which want to prosecute de Guzman for disseminating the Love Bug virus: his home country – the Philippines, the United States, and South Korea (which has also criminalized the dissemination of a virus). Each of the countries has citizens who were victims of the Love Bug, so we have victim nationality and 'place of the commission of the crime' satisfied for each. We will assume that each can assemble a strong case, based on admissible evidence and free from procedural or other defenses, against de Guzman. The government of the Philippines 'has' de Guzman, which cuts in their favor (see section 17.3.2); the effect of the Philippines' having custody of the alleged perpetrator is, however, offset by his being a Philippine national (see section 17.3.4).

We now consider the penalties de Guzman would face if he were convicted in each of the three countries. Although the Philippines has, in our hypothetical, criminalized the creation and dissemination of a computer virus, it has made the crime a very minor offense, one that is punishable only by, say, two weeks' imprisonment in a local jail and a fine equivalent to $100. In the United States, disseminating a computer virus is punishable, federally, by up to ten years' imprisonment plus a fine of, say, $250,000.[82] And we will assume, purely for the purposes of this hypothetical, that South Korean law makes the dissemination of a computer virus a felony that is punishable by up to three years in prison and a fine of, say, $5000. Since the Love Bug inflicted millions of dollars in damage on citizens of these three countries, along with citizens of many other countries, it seems that the prosecution should have a certain gravitas, i.e., should result in the imposition of sanctions that might deter a similarly-situated individual from engaging in similar misconduct in the future. If we accept that proposition, then it seems reasonable to consider the punishment that can be imposed, if prosecution is successful; based on that factor, alone, it seems that prosecution would be most appropriate either in the United States or in South Korea.

In the scenario given above, the severity of the punishment that can be imposed acts as a positive factor; that is, the countries that impose the most severe punishments are favored in the assignment of jurisdictional priority. Punishment can also, however, play a negative role in determining the appropriate locus for prosecution. Many countries, for example, will decline to extradite someone accused of murder

---

[80] See, e.g., Burke, loc. cit. n. 77.

[81] In June of 2000, the Philippines adopted cybercrime laws that, among other thing, criminalized the dissemination of computer viruses. See Goodman and Brenner, loc. cit. n. 39.

[82] See 18 USC § 1030.

to the United States unless the United States agrees that the person will not be subject to capital punishment.[83] So far, anyway, it does not appear that any country currently imposes the death penalty on cybercriminals, though a proposal to that effect has been advanced.[84] Regardless of the severity of the specific punishment that can be imposed in a given case, the jurisdictional priority analysis should incorporate an assessment of the extent to which the punishment available in each of the claiming jurisdictions can be considered to be 'too much' punishment, especially for the crime charged.

17.3.7 **Fairness and convenience**

Another factor that should be incorporated in the calculus that is used to resolve a positive jurisdictional conflict involving an alleged cybercriminal is the anticipated fairness and impartiality of a prosecution in a specific country.[85] The analysis might also focus on the extent to which prosecution in a particular country would be convenient (or, conversely, inconvenient) for witnesses and others involved in the proceeding,[86] and on the extent to which any possible inconvenience could be mitigated by allowing witnesses to testify remotely, via video.[87]

17.4 Conclusion

As noted earlier, the factors outlined above are not meant to be mandatory, nor are they intended to be weighted equally in resolving a jurisdictional conflict. The goal of this chapter is to articulate general factors that are appropriately considered in resolving positive jurisdictional conflicts in cybercrime cases. The chapter seeks to provide a structure, a framework, that can be utilized to determine the 'reasonableness' of awarding jurisdictional priority to a particular country or countries.

The various sections above used examples to demonstrate the role specific factors play in this analysis. It may be helpful to conclude with a general example that illustrates how the various factors can work together.

Assume that our friend John Doe, who is a U.S. citizen, is residing in Switzerland when he creates and releases a particularly destructive computer virus, the

---

[83] See, e.g., 'Senate Approves Sen. Chambliss Amendment To Bring Foreign Criminals To Justice', *U.S. Federal News* (20 July 2005).

[84] Steven E. Landsburg, 'Feed the Worms Who Write the Worms to the Worms', *Slate* (26 May 2004), <http://slate.msn.com/id/2101297/>.

[85] See, e.g., Princeton Principles, op. cit. n. 19, Principle 8, subpara. (g).

[86] Ibid., subpara. (h).

[87] See, e.g., Frederick I. Lederer, 'The Potential Use of Courtroom Technology in Major Terrorism Cases', 12 *William & Mary Bill of Rights Journal* 887 (2004). This would require a consideration of whether the country allows witnesses to testify remotely, and whether courtroom facilities are available that could accommodate real-time remote video testimony.

'Katrina virus'. The virus installs itself on hard drives and deletes some files while encrypting others; it eventually locks the user out of his or her computer. The Katrina virus races around the world in twelve hours, infecting millions of computers in 30 countries; the extent of the damage is difficult to quantify with any precision, but the virus is clearly responsible for billions of dollars in lost data and lost time, the losses being differentially apportioned among the victims in all 30 countries.

Assume that four countries – the United States, South Korea, Brazil, and Switzerland, all of which have criminalized virus dissemination – want to prosecute Doe for releasing the Katrina virus. This creates a positive jurisdictional conflict, which we will resolve using the factors articulated above.

We begin with the 'place of commission of the crime' which, as was noted earlier, is not a zero-sum concept for cybercrimes. We can say that Doe's cybercrime was committed, in part, in Switzerland (the acts involved in creating and releasing the virus, plus damage to Swiss citizens) and in each of the other countries where it caused damage. This factor weighs slightly in Switzerland's favor because both the conduct involved in the perpetration of the cybercrime and the resulting 'harm' inflicted on victims occurred there.

The next factor is custody. As was noted earlier, we apply a custody-plus standard in resolving positive jurisdictional conflicts for cybercrimes. Switzerland has custody of Doe, but its custody is essentially inadvertent. We will assume that the virus was traced to Switzerland by investigators operating in other countries; the leads those investigators provided to Swiss authorities led the latter to Doe, whom they arrested. Switzerland's custody of Doe is, therefore, the product of minimal investigative efforts on the part of that country's officials; its possession of the perpetrator is as much a function of chance as of anything else. Like the first factor, custody weighs slightly in Switzerland's favor.

The next factor is 'harm'. Assume that (i) 3.5 million victims in the United States lost an estimated $25 billion to the virus; (ii) 100,000 victims in South Korea lost an estimated $1.6 billion to the virus; (iii) 16,000 victims in Brazil lost an estimated $15 million to the virus; and (iv) 50 victims in Switzerland lost an estimated $50,000 to the virus. We will assume, for simplicity's sake, that the losses were all economic; we do not, in other words, have the infliction of the type of intangible 'harm' (economic espionage, threats to national security) noted above. This factor seems to weigh heavily in favor of the United States; it has the greatest number of victims and the greatest amount of aggregate economic loss, followed, respectively, by South Korea, Brazil, and Switzerland. At this point, therefore, we have two factors weighing slightly in favor of giving Switzerland first priority for prosecution, and one counterbalancing factor weighing heavily in favor of the United States, South Korea, and Brazil.

The fourth factor is nationality. Each of the claimant countries has citizens who were injured by Doe's virus, so victim nationality seems a null factor in this instance. (The respective number of victims in each country is more appropriately considered in assessing 'harm'.) Doe is a U.S. citizen which, as is explained above, operates as an inverse factor, i.e., weighs against giving the United States priority. At this point, if we conclude this factor nullifies the significance of the 'harm' inflicted on U.S. citizens, then the calculus would tend to favor South Korea and Brazil, based on the 'harm' inflicted on the citizens of those two jurisdictions.

The fifth factor is the strength of the case against the perpetrator. Since Doe created the virus in Switzerland, it is reasonable to assume, for the sake of analysis, that important evidence which is not available elsewhere is located in that country.[88] We now have an additional factor weighing in Switzerland's favor; and unlike the other factors, this one would weigh heavily in Switzerland's favor.

The sixth factor is punishment. We will assume that the creation and dissemination of a computer virus is (i) a felony punishable by up to 5 years in prison in the United States, (ii) a felony punishable by up to 2 years in prison in South Korea, (iii) a misdemeanor punishable by up to six months in prison in Brazil, and (iv) a misdemeanor punishable by a fine in Switzerland. In considering this factor, it is appropriate to assess the level of 'harm' Doe inflicted globally, since it is inconceivable that every injured country will prosecute him. The punishment that can be imposed should, therefore, be significant enough to indicate that global legal systems take this type of activity very seriously. Using that benchmark, the sixth factor weighs most heavily in favor, either, of the United States or South Korea; both countries treat virus dissemination as the most serious category of crime (felony) and impose significant periods of incarceration.

The seventh factor set out above combines two issues: (i) the anticipated fairness and impartiality of the proceeding in a given country; and (ii) convenience for those who will be called as witnesses. It seems reasonable to assume that each of the claimant countries would provide Doe with a fair, impartial trial. As to convenience, we will assume that the law in both the United States and South Korea allows the use of remote video testimony in criminal trials, while the law in Brazil and Switzerland does not. This complicates the process of incorporating convenience into the analysis: on the one hand, we have assumed that important evidence is located in Switzerland; we will also assume this includes both physical evidence and witnesses who can testify about Doe's virus creation efforts. These assumptions suggest it would be most convenient to give Switzerland first priority. On the other hand, if we were to do that, victims from other countries would have to travel to Switzerland to testify against Doe; this is an important issue because, as noted above, it is inconceivable that every country injured by Doe's virus will seek to prosecute him. Indeed, it is reasonable to assume that, if we give Switzerland first priority to prosecute Doe, several, if not all, of the other countries seeking to prosecute him may ultimately decline to do so. If we assume that is a possibility, then we may want to weigh the analysis in favor of a country that allows remote witness testimony; this would accommodate both the witnesses in Switzerland and those in other countries.

---

[88] Cf., CNN, loc. cit. n. 1.

As this example should illustrate, resolving positive jurisdictional conflicts cannot be a precise process. The best we can hope to do is to reliably determine which country or countries should 'reasonably' be given priority to prosecute a cybercriminal. If we are to do this, we need to identify the factors that are relevant in making this assessment. In the real world, the process seems to be idiosyncratic, the product of negotiations between two or more claimant countries; this approach may be satisfactory in that context, if only because positive jurisdictional conflicts are rare for traditional crime. Since cybercrime tends to be transnational in nature, we can expect such conflicts to be increasingly common, and increasingly complex, for this type of criminal activity. Identifying the factors that will be used to resolve jurisdictional conflicts in cybercrime cases will expedite the process, and will enhance its perceived fairness.

As was noted earlier, this outline of factors is not intended to be, and assuredly is not, exhaustive. Situational factors may well become important in resolving conflicts that arise as to particular prosecutions; and other general factors may emerge as significant as our experience with cybercrime evolves.

Bibliography

Susan W. Brenner, 'Toward A Criminal Law for Cyberspace: Distributed Security', 10 *Boston University Journal of Science and Technology Law* (2004) p. 1.

Susan W. Brenner and Bert-Jaap Koops, 'Approaches to Cybercrime Jurisdiction', 4 *Journal of High Technology Law* (2004) p. 1.

Susan W. Brenner and Joseph J. Schwerha IV, 'Transnational Evidence Gathering And Local Prosecution Of International Cybercrime', 20 *John Marshall Journal of Computer and Information Law* (2002) p. 347.

Antonio Cassese, 'Is The Bell Tolling For Universality? A Plea For A Sensible Notion Of Universal Jurisdiction', 1 *Journal of International Criminal Justice* (2003) p. 589.

John Eisinger, 'Script Kiddies Beware: The Long Arm of U.S. Jurisdiction to Prescribe', 59 *Washington & Lee Law Review* (2002) p. 1507.

Albin Eser, 'For Universal Jurisdiction: Against Fletcher's Antagonism', 39 *Tulsa Law Review* (2004) p. 955.

Marc D. Goodman and Susan W. Brenner, 'The Emerging Consensus on Criminal Conduct in Cyberspace', *U.C.L.A. Journal of Law & Technology* (2002), p. 3, available at <http://www.lawtechjournal.com/articles/2002/03_020625_goodmanbrenner.php>.

Princeton Project on Universal Jurisdiction, *The Princeton Principles on Universal Jurisdiction* (2001), <http://www.princeton.edu/~lapa/unive_jur.pdf>.

Henry J. Steiner, 'Three Cheers For Universal Jurisdiction – Or Is It Only Two?', 5 *Theoretical Inquiries in Law* (2004) p. 199.

Geoffrey R. Watson, 'The Passive Personality Principle', 28 *Texas International Law Journal* (1993) p. 1.

ABOUT THE EDITORS AND AUTHORS

Brenner, S.W.
e-mail: Susan.Brenner@notes.udayton.edu
Susan W. Brenner is NCR Distinguished Professor of Law & Technology, University of Dayton School of Law, Dayton, Ohio, United States.

Chacon de Albuquerque, R.
e-mail: r_albuquerque@hotmail.com
Roberto Chacon de Albuquerque, Master of Law (University of Brasília) and Ph.D. in Law (University of São Paulo), is a lawyer and Professor of International Law at the Catholic University of Brasília.

Cox, N.
e-mail: noel.cox@aut.ac.nz
Noel Cox is Associate Professor of Law at Auckland University of Technology, New Zealand, and a Barrister. His main research interest is constitutional law (especially domestic and international aspects of statehood and sovereignty, and the constitutional implications of cyberspace law).

Duggal, P.
e-mail: pduggal@vsnl.com, pavanduggal@hotmail.com
Pavan Duggal is an Advocate at the Supreme Court of India, the Founder and President of Cyberlaw Asia, and the President of Cyberlaws.Net <www.cyberlaws.net>.

Grabosky, P.
e-mail: peter.grabosky@anu.edu.au
Peter Grabosky is Professor in the Regulatory Institutions Network at the Australian National University, and a Fellow of the Academy of the Social Sciences in Australia. He was formerly Deputy Director of the Australian Institute of Criminology, President of the Australian and New Zealand Society of Criminology, and Deputy Secretary-General of the International Society of Criminology.

Herrera-Flanigan, J.R.
e-mail: Jesirae@aol.com
Jessica R. Herrera-Flanigan is a former Senior Counsel with the Computer Crime & Intellectual Property Section of the United States Department of Justice and currently serves as the Democratic Staff Director of the Committee on Homeland Security in the U.S. House of Representatives.

HERT, P. DE
e-mail: paul.de.hert@uvt.nl
Paul de Hert is Associate Professor of Law & Technology at the Tilburg Institute for Law, Technology, and Society (TILT), of Tilburg University, the Netherlands, and Professor of International Law at the Free University of Brussels, Belgium. He researches human rights, technology-related issues, and the history of ideas, in particular, privacy law, Internet law dilemmas, the impact of new technologies on legal systems, and the fundamentals of criminal law.

HOSEIN, G.
e-mail: i.hosein@lse.ac.uk
Gus Hosein is a Visiting Fellow at the Department of Information Systems at the London School of Economics, researching technology policy, regulation, and data protection. He is also a Senior Fellow at Privacy International, a London-based non-governmental organization, where he directs the Terrorism and the Open Society programme.

KASPERSEN, H.W.K.
e-mail: H.W.K.Kaspersen@rechten.vu.nl
Henrik W.K. Kaspersen is Director of the Computer/Law Institute of the Vrije Universiteit of Amsterdam. He chaired the Council of Europe drafting committees that developed the Recommendation of 1995, the Cybercrime Convention of 2001, and the First Additional Protocol to the Convention on Racism and Xenophobia of 2003.

KOOPS, B.J.
e-mail: e.j.koops@uvt.nl
Bert-Jaap Koops is Professor in Regulation & Technology at the Tilburg Institute for Law, Technology, and Society (TILT), of Tilburg University, the Netherlands. His main research interests are investigation powers and privacy, computer crime, cryptography, DNA forensics, constitutional rights, and principles of technology regulation.

LEE, J-H.
e-mail: ilsam@cau.ac.kr
Jeong-Hoon Lee, Ph.D. in Law, is Professor at the College of Law, ChungAng University.

LONDOÑO, F.
e-mail: fernando.londono@unife.it
Fernando Londoño, graduate in Law (Universidad de Chile), is a lawyer and Instructor in criminal law at the Universidad de Los Andes, Chile.

REICH, P.C.
e-mail: pcreich@yahoo.com
Pauline C. Reich is Professor at Waseda University School of Law and Director of the Asia-Pacific Cybercrime and Security Institute, Waseda University, Tokyo, Japan.

SIEBER, U.
e-mail: u.sieber@mpicc.de
Ulrich Sieber is Director of the Max Planck Institute for Foreign and International Criminal Law in Freiburg, Germany, scientific director of the Center for Information Technology in Law at the University of Munich, Germany, and an honorary Professor of the Albert Ludwig University of Freiburg, of the Ludwig Maximilian University of Munich, and of the Renmin University of Beijing.

SPANG-HANSSEN, H.
e-mail: hssph@attglobal.net
Henrik Spang-Hanssen is Attorney-at-Law at the Danish Supreme Court and Senior Researcher in Silicon Valley, California. He is a member of the American Bar Association's committee on Cyberspace Law. He was formerly External Deputy District Attorney at a Court of Appeals in Denmark, and he has lectured several courses in Computers & Law at several universities. Research homepage: <www.geocities.com/hssph>.

URBAS, G.
e-mail: UrbasG@law.anu.edu.au
Gregor Urbas is Lecturer in Law at the Australian National University. He teaches in criminal law, evidence, and intellectual property. He is a qualified lawyer in Australia and was formerly a Research Analyst at the Australian Institute of Criminology.

WALDEN, I.N.
email: ian.walden@ccls.edu
Ian Walden is Reader in Information and Communications Law and Head of the Institute of Computer and Communications Law <www.ccls.edu>. He is a consultant to the global law firm Baker & McKenzie and is a Public Interest Board Member of the Internet Watch Foundation <www.iwf.org.uk>.

ZICCARDI, G.
e-mail: g.ziccardi@tin.it
Giovanni Ziccardi is Professor of Legal Informatics and Advanced Legal Informatics at the Faculty of Law, University of Milan, Italy.

ZÚÑIGA, R.
e-mail: rzuniga@minjusticia.cl
Rodrigo Zúñiga, graduate in Law (Universidad de Chile), is a lawyer and Legal Adviser at the *Ministerio de Justicia* (Justice Department) of Chile.

INFORMATION TECHNOLOGY & LAW SERIES

1. E-Government and its Implications for Administrative Law – Regulatory Initiatives in France, Germany, Norway and the United States (The Hague: T·M·C·ASSER PRESS, 2002)
   Editor: J.E.J. Prins / ISBN 90-6704-141-6
2. Digital Anonymity and the Law – Tensions and Dimensions (The Hague: T·M·C·ASSER PRESS, 2003)
   Editors: C. Nicoll, J.E.J. Prins and M.J.M. van Dellen / ISBN 90-6704-156-4
3. Protecting the Virtual Commons – Self-Organizing Open Source and Free Software Communities and Innovative Intellectual Property Regimes (The Hague: T·M·C·ASSER PRESS, 2003)
   Authors: R. van Wendel de Joode, J.A. de Bruijn and M.J.G. van Eeten / ISBN 90-6704-159-9
4. IT Support and the Judiciary – Australia, Singapore, Venezuela, Norway, The Netherlands and Italy (The Hague: T·M·C·ASSER PRESS, 2004)
   Editors: A. Oskamp, A.R. Lodder and M. Apistola / ISBN 90-6704-168-8
5. Electronic Signatures – Authentication Technology from a Legal Perspective (The Hague: T·M·C·ASSER PRESS, 2004)
   Author: M.H.M. Schellekens / ISBN 90-6704-174-2
6. Virtual Arguments – On the Design of Argument Assistants for Lawyers and Other Arguers (The Hague: T·M·C·ASSER PRESS, 2004)
   Author: B. Verheij / ISBN 90-6704-190-4
7. Reasonable Expectations of Privacy? – Eleven Country Reports on Camera Surveillance and Workplace Privacy (The Hague: T·M·C·ASSER PRESS, 2005)
   Editors: S. Nouwt, B.R. de Vries and J.E.J. Prins / ISBN 90-6704-198-X
8. Unravelling the Myth Around Open Source Licences – An Analysis from a Dutch and European Law Perspective (The Hague: T·M·C·ASSER PRESS, 2006)
   Authors: L. Guibault and O. van Daalen / ISBN 90-6704-214-5
9. Starting Points for ICT Regulation – Deconstructing Prevalent Policy One-Liners (The Hague: T·M·C·ASSER PRESS, 2006)
   Editors: B-J. Koops, M. Lips, J.E.J. Prins and M. Schellekens / ISBN 90-6704-216-1
10. Regulating Spam – A European Perspective after the Adoption of the E-Privacy Directive (The Hague: T·M·C·ASSER PRESS, 2006)
    Author: L.F. Asscher / ISBN 90-6704-220-X
11. Cybercrime and Jurisdiction – A Global Survey (The Hague: T·M·C·ASSER PRESS, 2006)
    Editors: B-J. Koops and Susan W. Brenner / ISBN 90-6704-221-8